PRAISE FOR
FOR SPACIOUS SKIES

"A worthy addition to U.S. space flight history: Carpenter's anecdotes about the early days of NASA and his fellow Mercury astronauts are unique . . . vivid and insightful." —*Library Journal*

"Lively. . . . One can get the flavor of the times and a sense of the people responsible for bringing America into the space age." —*Publishers Weekly*

"By many miles the best memoir of Project Mercury. *For Spacious Skies* is a splendid, writerly combination of personal and national journeying, full of thoughtfulness, thrills, and a deep, dignified emotion. For anyone who remembers the first light of the space age—or had the bad luck of being too young to live through it—this is an indispensable book."—Thomas Mallon, author of *Aurora 7* and *Mrs. Paine's Garage*

"Back in the early sixties, when America's fixation with the newly hatched space program was at its peak, Scott Carpenter didn't fit in like the other six astronauts of the so-called Mercury Seven. . . . *For Spacious Skies* is as quirky as its author. . . . Carpenter sees his role in the space program as one small piece of a convoluted puzzle. Well, it may be small, but it's certainly interesting." —*Fort Worth Star-Telegram*

"Scott Carpenter was definitely among the coolest of the early astronauts. . . . Carpenter is clearly too cool to have written a book, but now he's signed one written by one of his daughters, and she's nearly as good a writer as he was a pilot. The book is deeply researched, suspenseful, and full of interesting anecdotes. . . . This is a vivid book and quite moving." —*National Geographic Adventure*

"*For Spacious Skies* is everything a book about the space program should be. . . . Richly detailed, informative, and exciting, at times deeply moving, it examines America's space program in the 1960s from inside as well as one man's path both in and out of it." —January Magazine

"Carpenter has never before told his story, so his account of lifting off in the tiny *Aurora 7* on May 24, 1962, is especially interesting . . . suspenseful, extremely well-written, and a nice historical account of one of the earliest space missions." —*Deseret News* (Salt Lake City, Utah)

SCOTT CARPENTER
AND KRIS STOEVER

FOR
SPACIOUS
SKIES

THE UNCOMMON
JOURNEY OF A
MERCURY ASTRONAUT

NEW AMERICAN LIBRARY

New American Library
Published by New American Library, a division of
Penguin Group (USA) Inc., 375 Hudson Street, New York, New York 10014, U.S.A.
Penguin Books Ltd, 80 Strand, London WC2R 0RL, England
Penguin Books Australia Ltd, 250 Camberwell Road,
Camberwell, Victoria 3124, Australia
Penguin Books Canada Ltd, 10 Alcorn Avenue,
Toronto, Ontario, Canada M4V 3B2
Penguin Books (N.Z.) Ltd, Cnr Rosedale and Airborne Roads,
Albany, Auckland 1310, New Zealand

Penguin Books Ltd, Registered Offices:
80 Strand, London WC2R 0RL, England

Published by New American Library, an imprint of New American Library, a division of Penguin Group
(USA) Inc. This is an authorized reprint of a hardcover edition published by Harcourt, Inc. For information address Harcourt, Inc., 6277 Sea Harbor Drive, Orlando, Florida 32877-6777.

First New American Library Printing, January 2004
10 9 8 7 6 5 4 3 2 1

 REGISTERED TRADEMARK—MARCA REGISTRADA

Library of Congress Cataloging-in-Publication Data

Carpenter, M. Scott (Malcolm Scott), 1925–
    For spacious skies : the uncommon journey of a Mercury astronaut / Scott Carpenter and Kris
Stoever.
      p. cm.
    Originally published: 1st ed. Orlando : Harcourt, c2002.
    Includes index.
    ISBN 0-451-21105-7
    1. Carpenter, M. Scott (Malcolm Scott), 1925– 2. Astronauts—United States—Biography.
3. Project Mercury (U.S.)—History. I. Stoever, Kris. II. Title.

TL 789.85.C37A3 2004
629.45'0092—dc22   2003060818
[B]

Excerpt from "The Cure at Troy: A Version of Sophocles' *Philoctetes*" by Seamus Heaney, copyright © 1990
by Seamus Heaney. Reprinted by permission of Farrar, Straus, and Giroux, LLC. "A Prayer at Bedtime"
and "Sunday Noon," copyright © 1929 by E. B. White. Used by permission of Allene M. White, for the
E. B. White Estate. "Balada de la placeta," from *Libro de poemas*, by Federico García Lorca. Translation by Léa
Calegaris Park. Reprinted by permission of Léa Calegaris Parak. "Welcome Home," copyright © 1954 by
Harold Rome, from *Fanny*. Used by permission of Joshua Rome, for the Harold Rome Estate. "The More
Loving One," copyright © 1957 by W. H. Auden, from *W. H. Auden: The Collected Poems*, by W. H. Auden.
Used by permission of Random House, Inc. "Waiting for Dad" originally published in *The New York Times*.

Set in Spectrum MT
Designed by Linda Lockowitz

IN MEMORY OF

Victor Irwin Noxon
1864–1939

Florence "Toye" Noxon Carpenter
1900–1963

Heroes. Victims. Gods and human beings.
All throwing shapes, every one of them
Convinced he's in the right, all of them glad
To repeat themselves and their every last mistake,
No matter what.

—SOPHOCLES' *Philoctetes*

Contents

PROLOGUE

EARLY ONE SPRING morning in 1962, New York commuters strode purposefully through the concourse of Grand Central Station. The details of the vaulted ceiling, awash with stars and constellations, had been obscured by the passage of time and a cumulative veil of smoke, fumes, and other exhalations, human and mechanical. Few looked up to ponder the ceiling's art. Few paused to admire a group of statues by Jules-Alexis Coutane. In front of an eagle stood the sculptor's Mercury, the fleet news-bearer, flanked by wise Minerva and Hercules the strong. His gods and heroes supported Time, in the form of an enormous clock. Together they were Transportation, the great country's lifeblood. Together they were witnesses to a time when this great terminal connected nearly every city and town in North America.

Commuters did stop that morning, however, to ponder not old gods but new, for suspended on a giant black-and-white television screen over their heads stood CBS newsman Walter Cronkite. There in a strangely familiar landscape of coastal Florida scrub, he was reporting something called "T-minus 11 and holding." Sure enough, behind him, poised for launch, was the country's newest Mercury-Atlas rocket, nearly obscured by distance, morning haze, and smoke from a persistent brush fire. Commuters glanced at their wristwatches, unfolded their newspapers to check the headlines. It was 8:43 A.M., May 24, 1962.

New Yorkers were on Eastern Daylight Time. But down the coast, Floridians maintained Eastern Standard and were preparing for a launch at 7:45. Commuters had plenty of time to watch the launch, now only two minutes away, and make it into the office by nine. Bolted inside the spacecraft at the top of the Atlas rocket, strapped into his contour couch, lay Scott Carpenter, preparing to be the second American to orbit the earth.

Back to Cronkite and T-minus 11 and the "flying flivver" of a Mercury spacecraft. United with households and classrooms across the country, New York commuters shifted automatically into a new national ceremony of countdown, all finding their voices to chant "10, 9, 8, 7, 6…"

The 1960s had begun in jittery fashion despite a new president's powerful inaugural summons for citizens to pay any price, bear any burden, oppose any foe—but with a puny, unpopular space program unable to lob anything much larger than a grapefruit into orbit. Soviet Russia held the secret to monster missiles, launching satellites that even then might be orbiting overhead, invisible to the naked eye, crowding our free and spacious skies. Only months after President John F. Kennedy's inauguration, on April 12, 1961, Americans had awakened to devastating, demoralizing news: The Soviets had scored the ultimate space triumph by launching a man into earth orbit and returning him safely—to cheering millions in Red Square.

It got worse. Three days later, at the Bay of Pigs, the new administration bungled a CIA-led military incursion of Communist-controlled Cuba in a debacle ending in the capture or death of all one thousand volunteers, most of them Cuban-born patriots. As the country's confidence unraveled, newspaper columnists and politicians assailed the inept new administration that couldn't shoot straight, a government that couldn't protect its citizens.

Then, literally flying out of the blue, came seven military pilots to the rescue. Gutsy, practical, and cool, they were husbands and fathers who exuded confidence and professed surprise that anyone could doubt them or their mission. They were Mercury astronauts, and the country loved them. Led by Alan Shepard's suborbital flight on May 5, 1961, just weeks after the Cuban debacle, these seven men trained in a borrowed hangar, their launch schedules compressed and compressed again, each of them ready and eager to be launched into space from Pads 5 or 14, Cape Canaveral, Florida. One by one, Shepard, Grissom, Glenn, Carpenter, Schirra, and Cooper would test their unlikely spacecraft with proud names, *Freedom, Liberty Bell, Friendship, Aurora, Sigma, Faith,* their every effort conducted, studied, and recorded in full public glare with thousands of journalists reporting blood pressure, heart rate, urinary functions—a thousand lenses.

Here in Grand Central, on a Thursday morning, the commuters became a community as everyone stopped to watch for the heart-pounding drama to begin: "...5, 4, 3, 2, Engine Start, 1, Lift-off, and the clock started." It was a perfect countdown. Vapor, flame, and super-heated steam bloomed like gray-white space-age petals around the base of the enormous Mercury-Atlas. Hoots and applause erupted from the crowd, the sound of collective American relief as everyone pushed and helped with their voices: *Go, Go, Go, Go!* Roaring and shuddering through Max Q, the rocket now sped upward and into the outer limits. *Wow. Gee whiz! Damn!* American know-how had done it again! Hand shakes all around and slaps on the back as the rocket pierced the hazy vault of sky, leaving nothing to see but the faintest wisp of contrail.

IT WAS A PERFECT launch. No indefinite holds for weather, no mysterious and unspecified mechanical difficulties. Best of all, no explosions. Just a lovely spring space launch and another national vindication—and confirmation of John Glenn's stupendous achievement, three months before, aboard *Friendship 7.* Astronaut Scott Carpenter would make one complete circumnavigation of the planet in only ninety minutes. The three-orbit flight was scheduled for reentry after lunchtime, Eastern

Daylight Time—about five hours away. In the New York train terminal, most onlookers relaxed and walked to the exits, but some lingered
to watch the live coverage. In a "News Extra," CBS would cover every
minute of the entire five-hour flight, and then some.

FIVE HOURS LATER, Cronkite was down to his shirtsleeves, having doffed
his jacket during Carpenter's third orbit. His normally serene brow
was furrowed with worry as he listened to reports from his producers
being transmitted through an enormous black headset, a sartorial
handicap he sought to soften with an ascot. The crowd at Grand Central had grown larger, watching while Cronkite sipped water from a
glass on his desk. Commercial breaks for Chase and Sanborn coffee,
Fleischmann's corn oil, Philip Morris cigarettes, and Aerowax floor
polish interrupted what had become a cliffhanger.

Sometimes Cronkite just sat there, thinking, a finger pressed to his
lips, while onlookers at Grand Central, alert and pensive, watched him
at his news desk, gazing into the middle distance, worrying about the
fate of the country's latest astronaut. Where was he? Was he alive? Was he
dead? If dead, how had he died? If alive, then where has he landed?

After another commercial break the camera returned to Cronkite,
a study in concern. NASA, the country's young space agency, was
feeding him *zilch*. It occurred to him that he was presiding over a possible astronaut death watch—with no news, little footage, and virtually no fill. There were no shots of the Carpenter family home, then at
Langley Air Force Base behind all the front-gate security precautions of
a cold war Tactical Air Command. Besides, Rene Carpenter and the
four children weren't there but "in seclusion," somewhere along
Florida's Atlantic coast. No one knew where. A reporter and camera-
man were planted outside the Colorado home of Mrs. Florence Carpenter, the astronaut's mother. She declined to come out.

In desperation, Cronkite used some copy supplied by Claude M.
Carpenter, the astronaut's Denver uncle. "It seems our astronaut is descended from nobility," the newsman intoned, with evident misgiving.
According to Uncle Claude, England's King Charles I had knighted a
seventeenth-century ancestor for heroic services as courier and Cava-

lier. Meanwhile, turning in their stony New England graves, were the astronaut's true forebears. Claude meant well, but in truth their real ancestors would just as soon burn their English translations of Scripture as run messages for King Charles I. They were Dissenters, and in 1638 had managed to place an entire ocean between them and the Roman Catholic king.

EACH AMERICAN is a traveler—or was one once—propelled by tumult, hunger, ideals, civil wars, stories, dreams. Some were compelled, and traveled in chains. Some journeyed alone, nursing heartache and loneliness. Others went gladly with families, to be greeted by loved ones at their destinations. All of them—pioneers of their own lives—had something to prove and were prepared, more or less, to make a new home, and in doing so to give up their old ones.

A somber crowd watched in 1962 to see how one American journey, a five-hour spaceflight, might end. In fire and death? In a watery grave? Far better, everyone agreed, in triumph and smiles and dry astronaut feet on a carrier deck. But that is the end of the story. Better here to go back to the beginning: At Grand Central in 1927, a small family made its way through the jostling humanity embarked on journeys across the continent. Only two years old at the time, Scott Carpenter was in the company of his young parents on a trip to Colorado. His parents called him Buddy.

It would be their last journey together as a family.

PART
ONE

EARTH

1

BUDDY

And so he would now study perfumes . . . wondering what there was in frankincense that made one mystical, and in ambergrise that stirred one's passions, and in violets that woke the memory of dead romances.

—OSCAR WILDE

ON A SUMMER DAY in 1927, Dr. M. Scott Carpenter stepped out of a New York taxicab onto the sidewalk outside Grand Central Station. Impatient with his mother's slower and more decorous exit, Carpenter's two-year-old son appeared next, an escape the boy achieved simply by hopping across his mother's lap to sunny freedom outside. "Train! Train!" he shouted, for he was embarking on a wildly anticipated train trip to Colorado.

After motioning to a porter, Carpenter turned to help his wife. The twenty-seven-year-old mother and wife was a pitiable sight. Dressed in a dark-green cotton suit that drooped on her frame, Toye had been unable, the day before, to pack her things and wash the dark and once extravagantly abundant hair that now lay flat and dull against her head. She pressed a handkerchief to her mouth, stopping to muffle a cough before resuming her march to the concourse, willing her every step to the departure gate.

Already worn out from excitement, Buddy looked up at his mother, raising his arms, throwing his head back in childhood's universal and irresistible pose of helplessness—"Up!" he added, in case there were any uncertainty. She only smiled as a paternal arm scooped the boy off his feet. From his perch in the crook of his father's arm, Buddy surveyed the extraordinary vista of New York faces—so much better than the bewildering sea of knees.

Carpenter was fond of explaining how his two-year-old represented an unbroken line of first-born sons going back a dozen generations to Plymouth Colony. The Plymouth Colony part is true enough, and twelve generations about right—if one counts back to William Carpenter, who in 1638 arrived in the New World with wife, Abigail, and sons one, two, and three. Several more sons and daughters would be born to the enterprising couple in Rehoboth, Massachusetts.

Carpenter's dynastic-sounding boast, however, about an unbroken primogenitural descent was sheer fancy (there were but seven firstborn sons). Besides which, the claim rather slights New England's daughters—the Elizabeths, Phoebes, Marys, Renews, and Sarahs, without whom there would be no children, nor generations of any number.

By the war of 1812, after defending New London from the British, a few intrepid Carpenters of generations seven and eight had ventured as far west as the Quinebaug River valley. There in northeastern Connecticut they found stony farmland to clear, to toil over, and to till. More work, more children, more mouths to feed, and more seasonal poverty, until something marvelous was built at Quinebaug Falls—a cotton mill and the beginnings of the industrial revolution. By the 1830s Smith Wilkinson, early patriarch of the American mills, had transplanted an English invention to power-generating waterfalls like the one on the Quinebaug. One of the first young men Wilkinson hired was Lucien Carpenter, mule spinner—representing highly skilled labor at the very apex of factory life. Having nothing to do with mules, mule spinning has everything to do with mass production of fabric, and is more difficult to describe than rocket science. Suffice it to say that the United States was never the same.

By the time of the Centennial (and the collapse of Reconstruction) in 1876, a pretty new state beckoned to the Carpenters. They felt right at home in Denver, for Colorado boasted more rocks than a Connecticut field. Producing yet another scion of Yankee manhood in 1901, Mr. and Mrs. Marion Ernest Carpenter christened their first child Marion Scott. By the age of twenty-seven, the Denver native and Manual High School graduate was beloved son, brother, husband, and father. He was also research chemist, bon vivant, and possessor of a recently concluded, two-year postdoctoral fellowship at Columbia University. His field was the relatively new one of synthetic fragrances. He would enjoy a brilliant career.

Carpenter chose his traveling clothes carefully for the return trip to Denver: tan cotton whipcord trousers, two brown-and-white tattersall-checked shirts with monogrammed pockets—MSC—hand-sewn by his wife, Florence, whom everyone called Toye. They were certainly handsome enough to display, he thought, if he needed to remove his lightweight wool jacket on a warm rail car. Despite the rigors of a long train trip with a robust two-year-old and an ailing wife, Carpenter felt sure he could make a presentable entrance into that apogee of the civilized world, the dining car.

HE WALKED SLOWLY and importantly through the train terminal with his small son, pointing out the architectural features of this glorious New York landmark. Pointing to a group of statues, the father asked Buddy whether he knew about the gods represented there. But back on his feet, Buddy simply yelled, "Train! Train! Train!" and ran to catch up with the porter. Toye, in the early stages of tuberculosis, had meanwhile already begun to flag. Carpenter was conscious of appearances, and in a lapse of affection saw his wife as a stranger might. Perhaps after a summer in Boulder, resting, she would recover her looks.

That year, while he was completing the second year of his postdoctoral fellowship at Columbia, Toye had become increasingly bedridden, unable even to care for their boy. She could not lift him. She could not clean or cook. A recurring fever, then a cough, and in time drenching night sweats sent the couple to St. Luke's Hospital. An X-ray of her lungs told the story. "You see that spot?" the specialist asked her. "That's a bit of tuberculosis." Not to worry overmuch, he assured them. She was only in the early stages, he added, but cautioned: "If you want to live, you must leave New York." Toye wanted to live.

The doctor brightened upon learning the couple hailed from Colorado and quickly recited the catechism for "Lungers"—bed rest and more bed rest, sunshine, dry mountain air, and a diet rich in eggs and cream. She was young and strong, he added, and given the right treatment would soon be back on her feet. He did not lay out the more torturous elements of the T.B. regime: surgical interventions that collapsed affected sections of the lung, excised ribs, and stripped out the brachial nerves that controlled the diaphragm. This was 1927. Antibiotic cures for the infectious disease were a generation off. For now, cures belonged to the realms of magic and luck.

FLORENCE NOXON CARPENTER was not only ill, she was also madly, romantically in love with this handsome man, her husband. Seven years ago he had stood on the steps of the Engineering Building on the Boulder campus of the University of Colorado as she approached, mindful of his appraising male gaze. The nineteen-year-old was hard to ignore, with his lordly bearing, his red mustache, and intense blue eyes. "And where might *you* be going?" he demanded, in an impudent gambit that perfectly suited Toye. "Certainly not into *your* building," came her cheeky reply that perfectly suited Carpenter. The girl could not be flustered. Thus began their campus romance.

They studied together, had lunch together, and from September through June strolled each night together in Chautauqua Park. He called for her at eight o'clock at her parents' home at Seventh Street and Aurora Avenue. When separated by summer vacations and the impossible distance then dividing her Boulder from his Denver, they wrote nightly. By the time they became seniors, Carpenter had pinned her; some rumored they were secretly engaged.

His early, passionate letters to her survived only long enough for Toye's single, hand-to-throat scan. A quick trip to the coal furnace in the basement of her parents' house converted words and paper to ashes. Her letters to Carpenter survive still, revealing a cool, breezy style that captivated their recipient.

After eighty years, Toye's sturdy, off-white stationery has yellowed slightly, the ink faded slightly, but the girl's sentences still leap off the page. Her early letters were "about nothing," the lovers agreed with approval. In time, though, and with motherhood, her insouciance would give way to life-and-death matters. *Leadership, service, scholarship*—Toye had been elected to the Mortar Board, the honorary society for female undergraduates. She would need these qualities and more. From the birth of their son into the decades that followed, she would of necessity become the consummate advocate—her reasoning relentless, her entreaties implacable, her cause just. When not explaining, Toye would report, correct, soothe, calm, console, cajole, intervene, and most of all plead tirelessly on behalf of the child she and her husband produced in 1925 rather by surprise.

WHILE THE SMALL FAMILY made its way through the crowds at Grand Central, their respective parents were making final preparations to receive them in Colorado. Although told of Toye's diagnosis, neither family knew what permanent domestic arrangements the couple had in mind. Was Carpenter staying? Returning to New York? The young couple hadn't said. The parents hadn't asked.

But Carpenter's father, Marion, guessed the worst and was right: "You mean to tell me," he said to his wife, Ruby, "that he's going to *leave* them in Boulder?" The matter was on everyone's mind and it sorely vexed the senior Carpenter—a quiet, silver-haired land-title man. His elder son was a mystery—still in school and still, he suspected, supported by Ruby with money from the cookie jar. "He dresses like the Prince of Wales, for god's sake," he said to her, "and neither of 'em's earned a dime."

He did not often disparage their son in this way, for when he snapped, his wife snapped back. This time, though, Ruby Frye Carpenter held her tongue, and her secret. Over a four-year period, yes, she had indeed supported her elder son with cash from her household account, loans she justified by believing he would prove a success. She felt certain her confidence would be rewarded—and more.

So the Carpenters put their best face on, resolved to meet the family of three at the Denver train station and motor them to Boulder.

THIRTY MILES AWAY, in Boulder, Toye's parents were busy in their large brick house at the corner of Aurora Avenue and Seventh Street, just beyond city limits. Vic Noxon, publisher of the *Boulder County Miner & Farmer,* was supervising the renovation of the front balcony on the second floor. It would become a screened-in sleeping porch, suitable for a convalescent. Here also his wife, the resourceful Clara, was hard at work. Although battling a thyroid condition and other ailments of advancing age, she was painting and papering an adjacent storage room to serve as her grandson's room. Where her son-in-law would stay, Clara, sixty-three years old, did not know. She, too, guessed the worst.

Before producing their nine children in the early Colorado gold town of Idaho Springs—she added "seven living," in that elliptical way mothers have—Clara Rose Batchelder had delivered the U.S. mail on horseback, eagerly applying for the Clear Creek County job after the regular mailmen, tired of being held up at gunpoint, balked at riding the mountainous route. Later, the mother slyly explained to her brood that she felt safe because she knew trail robbers drew the line at pulling a gun on a lady.

Clara was no lady but a Canadian farm girl with little schooling. For twenty years in Boulder she had sustained a thriving milk-and-egg operation with a variety of fowl, a herd of Holsteins, a rhubarb patch, fruit trees, and berry bushes. She, and later her daughters, milked the cows, gathered the eggs, put up fruit, made the pies, and delivered the same to half the families on "the Hill," the neighborhood above the university. With the proceeds, she sent five daughters to be educated at C.U., as Coloradans call their university. There they each pledged Alpha Chi Omega, the top sorority on campus, and there each daughter received an undergraduate degree.

Viewed through Clara's prism of unstinting labor, Carpenter, her fourth daughter's suitor, was no mystery—and no prize either. She was all too aware that her brilliant girl, with her own academic and musical talents, had made this eternal student his clothes, bought (and brought) him food, lent him money. He never seemed to have a job. He pinned her. Over the summers, separated, they wrote a torrent of letters. There was talk, talk, *talk* of getting engaged, and a marriage, and a honeymoon. Carpenter sulked. Toye ran upstairs to cry in her room. She blushed when his letters arrived, read them in private, and consigned them to the basement furnace within an hour of receipt.

These letters were no mystery either, their central aim, as far as Clara could tell, being "a roll in the snow." As they continued pouring into the house, as profuse with ardor as her summer fruit, Clara began presenting them on a platter, garnished with her raspberries. "The Swede wrote you again," she drily announced.

Try as he might, Carpenter had not charmed Clara Noxon. The doyennes of Colorado Springs might cluck over his social graces, on display for them during the summer social season, but the Boulder mother had long since placed him in the trail-robber category. "He's nervous around the animals, if you really want to know," she explained to her husband, Vic, who did not reply.

So in the summer of 1924, a year away from his doctorate, when Carpenter found lodging three short blocks from the Noxon home, Clara arranged for Toye to spend the summer traveling. An edifying train trip east—to Massachusetts and New York—with a chaperone was just the ticket. The mother also arranged long visits on the way there and back with Toye's two sensibly married sisters, Ella in Des Moines and Frances in Deadwood, South Dakota.

Still the lovers wrote what lovers always do: I miss you, I long for you, I am desolate... I loathe you for leaving me—angry letters culminating in Toye's dismissive "Good-bye!" penned in Des Moines. Still, a persistent Carpenter was at Denver's Union Station in August 1924, waiting for the tears and fateful embraces of reunion.

THAT YEAR, CARPENTER was on to something important in the chemistry laboratories of C.U. What was the connection between odor and chemical constitution? What were the secret chemical signatures of menthol, jasmine, and ambergris? Of lavender, rose, and musk? Could these be rendered synthetically? The research was more than an intellectual challenge, for the answers had untold commercial applications. In the sixteenth century, only queens could afford perfumes as precious as ambergris—Elizabeth I scented her gloves with it. But thanks to Carpenter, modern American housewives could spritz their décolletage with the rare if ersatz scent.

As it happens, the United States was poised on the brink of a consumer revolution, with women still struggling with their kitchen-made beauty aids. Hoping for soft hands, they mixed glycerine with rose water; half a lemon held brown spots at bay. Help was on the way, however: in 1925, two days before his secret wedding, on Valentine's Day, to Toye, Carpenter submitted his doctoral thesis, entitled "Condensation Products of Diethyl Ketone," to the National Research Council in New York City. It was the culmination of years of research under the guidance of Professor John B. Eckeley, head of the chemistry department at C.U., and, after Ruby and Toye, his chief booster. The submission was promptly read "with great interest" by the head of the Council's chemical research committee, Columbia's own Marston Taylor Bogert, who wrote immediately: "Your work bears indirectly upon research with which we ourselves have been occupied." He invited Carpenter to apply for the Fritzsche Fellowship, at Columbia University, where he himself headed the chemistry department. "It will be a great pleasure to welcome you and assist you in your attack on this topic."

Amidst the hand-shaking and felicitations, Carpenter and Eckeley laughingly considered a waltz among the test tubes. The letter was read aloud at the Noxon dinner table and sent on by mail to the Denver Carpenters, where Ruby read it to her husband. Puzzled, Marion asked, "So, this is a job?"

Well, no—not exactly employment. But it did provide $1,500 for the 1925–26 academic year. It was also a ticket to the excitement of New York and the lucrative world of industrial research. On April 29, Dr. Bogert confirmed Carpenter's postdoctoral fellowship. Two days later Toye produced their son, Malcolm Scott Carpenter. The happy event took place on May 1, 1925—which is to say, precisely nine months after their reunion at Denver's aptly named Union Station. Toye's involuntary railway sojourn in the summer of 1924 had succeeded in separating the lovers for a season. But all journeys end, and this one concluded, too, with tears giving way to joy, then yearning, and finally consummation, with Toye's chaperone nowhere in sight. In the aftermath, with five Noxon sisters counting on their fingers, acerbic Alice, age twenty, observed only, "He *might* have waited until they reached the car."

LARGE AND COHESIVE FAMILIES, like the Boulder Noxons, have their own subcultural tics, social norms, face-saving gambits, and survival tactics. Which is to say, they lie. And five sisters lying in sororal unison make a new truth, transcending deceit and designed with a clement goal: to protect a wee one to come and the reputations of the grown-ups responsible. The ruse extended to forgery, apparently, for someone supervised the production of an elaborate four-color, gilt-edged, signed church certificate attesting to a June 1924 wedding—held, it claimed, at St. Mark's Church, Denver—between Florence Kelso Noxon and Marion Scott Carpenter. The likeliest culprit and mastermind is Toye's older sister, Frances Noxon Norman, then a newly married twenty-six-year-old schoolteacher in Deadwood.

Finally, his doctorate in hand and a postdoctoral fellowship before him, the new husband and father was off to New York, alone, in July 1925 to claim the first part of his prize—freedom. "New York extends a clenched fist to newcomers," his friend Hal Borland warned him, "but one of our family will meet you at the train station!" Floored by his friend's raft of news, Borland recalled sitting "in a stripped Flivver" the last time he'd seen his fraternity brother. "You in a broad-brimmed hat and behind a red mustache."

The Borlands took Carpenter sightseeing the day after his arrival. The twenty-five-year-old was besotted with the city, besotted with the freedom from his father's disapproving rumblings and the barely suppressed antagonism of his mother-in-law, in whose home he had been forced to encamp during the "awkwardness," when Toye was pregnant. He was free, too, to liberate his wife, when she and the baby arrived, from her provincial ways and surround her with smart, conversant, and above all *modern* people. All of it promised a Real Life.

Borland already had a plan: "We want to go West. You could lease this apartment, convenient to Columbia, furnished with our stuff... two rooms, kitchenette, and bath." The apartment on Sherman Street, in the Inwood section of New York, was a godsend. Carpenter whetted Toye's appetite with a preview of their digs: "Hal and Helen have left everything they could not get into three suitcases and a small trunk...A beautiful bedroom set, a complete baby layout...silver, dishes, to say nothing of hundreds of books and a full larder!"

His excellent adventures continued in Greenwich Village ("called 'the Village,'" he explained to his parents), which just that year Richard Rodgers and Lorenz Hart were celebrating in their first hit musical, *Manhattan*. Then he ratcheted up the travelogue another notch of sophistication. He was "very much disappointed by 'the Village'...but, of course, in New York it is difficult to judge by exterior appearances.... The gayest, liveliest, most lavish places are reached by side or alley entrances and...in the Village a man and woman can live together and no questions asked."

Prohibition was no impediment to good times, as he and a companion found an Italian restaurant with a wine list where one was admitted "only upon recognizance...and the best wines are served in cold-blooded English—no secret signs or passwords necessary." He described the entire meal in a letter to his parents, adding, "We had an excellent sherry and upon leaving I was given a card of admission."

Ruby had been reading the letter aloud to her husband on the side porch in Denver. At this last remark, Marion snorted, "I hope his money lasts 'til Christmas."

Modern! What an intoxicating ring the word possessed for Carpenter. Better than Boulder's high-minded, fusty old *progressive*, it was redolent with a permissive, droll, cold-martini charm. Modern couples, especially modern New Yorkers, he imagined, never stooped to the Victorian hypocrisies. None of the old daytime pieties (and nighttime debaucheries) favored by their parents' generation. *Modern* meant none, in fact, of the old pieties at all. In a modern marriage, Carpenter finally imagined in a kind of swoon, nothing was wrong, really. Modern meant candor, brutal honesty, and acceptance. Above all, it meant being free.

The arrival of wife and child brought reality and change. Toye took over the budget while her husband repaired in obsessive fashion to the laboratory, his immersion in his work total. At dinnertime, still in his lab at Havemeyer Hall, he tapped out a letter to his mother, admitting that "putting work away is one of the hardest things" for him to do.

The grandmothers begged for news of the baby, the first grandchild for both families. Toye obliged in a letter to Ruby, her mother-in-law: "Buddy is getting his first tooth," and his daily schedule had expanded to two daily outings, "10 to 11:30 and 2 to 3." Carpenter noticed his "son and heir possesses keen eyesight. . . . He will spy a piece of lint and in preference to any of his playthings travel to it. . . . To date his expeditions have netted him one hook-and-eye and several threads." The infant's 20-10 vision would later equip him for a career in aviation. For Toye, in the meantime, it meant a career in keeping the floors with meticulous care.

Here in this apartment, for two years, was the whole of their family life. They entertained, took weekly walks to the Hudson River, watched their child grow. A New Year's Eve letter home seems to sum up their joy: "I have never seen such a crowd as there was at Times Square at Midnight," Carpenter wrote. "We were in the thick of it and for once it seemed glorious. We were fully 15 minutes passing the Astor Hotel. The din was terrific . . . everyone carried horns or rattlers. I shall never forget the sights and sounds."

That spring, Carpenter attended a game at Yankee Stadium. It was April 24, 1926, and "Babe Ruth knocked what is considered to have been one of his longest homers. . . . I never saw such a wallop. His bat, a young war club, flashed out quicker than thought and the next instant the ball was nearly over the bleachers." Toye, who was tired, was not with him that day. They were worried about her health.

In their second year in New York, after Columbia arranged another, more remunerative fellowship for the young research chemist, the letters to Colorado trickled off. Husband and wife struggled to keep their household going. Somehow Toye had contracted tuberculosis. The airborne bacterium was everywhere, with everyone at all times exposed. In the 1920s one in ten Americans was susceptible. Toye was that one. She and her husband began making sad and difficult plans for her to return to Colorado.

As they prepared to leave, the couple sought to put the best possible face on their predicament. Instead of sidewalks and a two-room apartment, Buddy would have a rambling, three-story Boulder home to explore and sunny, open spaces in which to run. He would be in the arms of adoring grandparents, aunts, and uncles. Toye would receive proper rest and care. On her feet by Thanksgiving, she would surely, they planned, be back at her husband's side by spring. Carpenter would return to New York. T.B., they decided, might kill their dream of being together, but it would not extinguish their long-shared dream of his brilliant career.

In vindication of this plan, Carpenter had been offered his first job. A breadwinner at last, he was offered a salaried position to begin in the summer of 1927. He began looking for a bigger apartment and surprised Toye with a new Singer sewing machine. For himself, he splurged on a typewriter. Meanwhile, she did her best to bolster her husband's sometimes flagging confidence, though to little avail. The morning of their departure from Grand Central, Carpenter considered himself in the mirror darkly. Twenty-seven years old, with eight years of grueling, continuous schooling, he took the blame for his wife's sickness. Despite sprightly letters home, he knew the reality. Pennies hoarded at Toye's insistence, meals missed. He was still in debt to his mother.

His mood darkened as he packed his son's playthings in a box to be mailed to Colorado. A trip to run errands, among them mailing the bulky box, was rendered a daylong ordeal with the triumphant arrival, that June day, of America's new hero, Charles A. Lindbergh, Jr., for whom all superlatives failed: first, bravest, blondest, most handsome, most historic, most eligible, most transatlantic—most bankable. On June 13, 1927, while the research chemist struggled on the subway with a toddler and box, four and a half million screaming, cheering New

Yorkers were celebrating the aviator's arrival with a tumultuous ticker-tape parade. Unbidden, a failure-tinged memory stirred: Carpenter recalled Lindbergh barnstorming in Boulder and with five of Toye's dollars in hand taking *his* pretty girl into the skies while he watched helplessly, pennilessly, from the ground.

WHILE NEW YORKERS mobbed the subways because of that "knucklehead from Minnesota," he thought bitterly of his once-vaunted promise, his reams of academic parchment, enough to paper the privy at Palmer Lake. He could barely afford postage for his son's few possessions home. Buddy stood trustingly between his feet as the subway car lurched and swayed downtown, while New York awarded Lindbergh, the Lone Eagle and indifferent student, the city's Medal of Honor. How strange to think that another June, thirty-five years in the future, Carpenter would reconcile himself to knucklehead pilots. In 1962 he would watch as Buddy stood, flanked by former presidents, to be awarded the great city's same Medal of Honor.

2

A Frozen Sea

Once I shot a sparrow dead
(Hit him in the head).
Give me again the tears I shed.

—E. B. White

On the second floor of the big house in Boulder, Buddy's bedroom had five doors and a window that faced east—across the High Plains. Through the bars of his crib he could touch the wallpaper his mother had chosen, decorated with peace pipes, flintlocks, powder horns, and tomahawks. Strewn across a dusty brown background, they hovered in space from ceiling to baseboard. One of his doors adjoined his mother's sleeping porch. At night the voices of mother and young son traveled through the half-dark until he fell asleep. Toye's bedside lamp stayed on late, lighting the papers or mending work she had on her knees. Grandma Noxon came and went quietly, and Buddy heard their soft conversations and sighs. "Oh, dear," his mother said and then coughed again and again and again.

Through another door lay Grandma's bedroom. Still another led to the Aunt Alice's. A fourth door led to a small porch. Behind the fifth door was his closet. He would sleep in this room until he was fifteen years old and a freshman at Boulder High School. When he was four years old, a World War I army cot replaced his crib.

AS HIS FATHER, Dr. M. Scott Carpenter, prepared to return to New York and his waiting job, the mood in the Noxon house was sad. Conversations, however, sounded optimistic notes. The couple had agreed he would not stay. He would work for a paycheck in New York, which would in turn pay the bills in Colorado. Forced to forgo the dream of being together, they were unmoveable on the other—his brilliant career, which would secure their future.

On Monday, August 8, 1927, Toye tucked a note into the bag she packed for her husband: "Let's put our hearts to sleep for the winter." He would read it, she knew, while unpacking at their apartment. "We will bid them dream of the past and future—for there is no present." The next day she wrote again, less bravely, "I have lived an age since you kissed me goodbye." Then she wept.

At age two Buddy was old enough to recognize his mother's distress, as Toye related a week later:

> He insists he is 'dada's boy' today. He said 'pie' for 'up high' and 'feet down' to me when he wanted the bed to be smooth for his blocks....He puts my slippers on me when I get up, sits a few minutes in my chair with me, brings my papers, announces all my meals as they come up the stairs, calling them *suppah* or *dinnah,* which ever the case may be.

In letter after letter, she wrote to her husband that Buddy "takes such good care of me." The work of nursing the invalid—part of it at least—had fallen on the shoulders of a two-year-old.

The success of the couple's gamble rested largely on the job offer extended to Carpenter in June, before they left New York. But by August the position had evaporated. He was not hired. There were no paychecks. The news hit Toye like "a thunderbolt out of the not very blue." Though allowing that she was "very disappointed," she wrote him:

I do hope you won't worry on our account....I still have my
train ticket to sell. Please, please, don't get downhearted. Let me
know by air mail when you get something, will you? for it takes
five days for a letter to come....I love you and Buddy loves
you, and you love us, and we aren't starving yet by a long shot.

CARPENTER WOULD CONFRONT this long stretch of joblessness alone.
Fruitless job interviews through fall and winter left him discouraged,
then depressed and angry, and finally nearly paralyzed with a mortifying sense of failure. In the end he was left with a deep wound that
never seemed to heal. Writing him twice a week, Toye made it her
habit to send cheerful news. Buddy was two and a half and "runs to
me when the moon is up," she wrote that fall, "announcing 'Moon
awake!'" He was a bright child, alert to family inflections: "He called to
Mama the other night from his bed," she wrote, "and when Mama said
she wasn't coming any more, he said, 'Oh, I see.'"

The night sky is a spectacular sight on the Front Range, and Toye
wrote that she had "the prettiest little star....It almost never fails me
because it is so constant." Arcturus was her star, and its constancy a
virtue she thought wise to praise. Six weeks into her rest cure, in October 1927, the doctor permitted her to sit up for an hour and a half,
later increased to three hours of vertical life, and finally to taking one
meal downstairs. By January, she was out of bed every day for a half-
block walk. Dr. Gilbert expressed "joy," she reported, upon learning
she had regained nearly all the thirty pounds she had lost in New
York.

In New York, Carpenter could not be buoyed by Toye's bright letters. Worried inquiries from his wife and his mother finally prompted
an outburst: He'd interviewed at "seventy-four different firms" and
was now going "without breakfast." "Going without *breakfast*!" his
wife admonished. "Your health is too important for that."

Ruby Carpenter noticed the self-pity and wrote, "Keep cheerful—
Toye does. She surely is a good sport. I know she must get awfully
lonesome up there." In what would be a recurring and nasty reflex,
Carpenter wrote his wife a cruel letter. After describing his own "mis-

erable" Thanksgiving, he savaged her appearance in the first photos she sent him. She turned the other cheek:

November 27, 1927

> My dear Cottie Boy,
> Your last letter wasn't nice at all, at all. After saying those mean
> things, you continue in a sarcastic tone about my pictures. Now
> all you have to do with pictures of me that you don't like or
> want is return them, or throw them away. The enclosed seem
> to be a little better....

Meanwhile, her own trial by elements went on: The sleeping porch was a "cold, cold place" that winter. Ruby Carpenter was appalled at the temperatures, and after her first visit to Boulder had soon made her daughter-in-law a thick wool "comfort." On cold nights, Toye lay under a foot-high stack of blankets, handmade comforters, and other bed coverings. During the day her room was heated with a potbellied coal-fired stove, which Buddy learned to replenish on his own. At night there was no heat at all. "Last night was about the worst yet....It was 18 below in town, and of course it is colder up here."

Carpenter once asked for fuller accounts of his son's vocabulary, his "temperamental development," his daily schedule, his diet. Toye complied. "As yet he doesn't talk very plain, but what he says is rather cute: *aforning* for 'this morning' and *fweetheart* for 'sweetheart,'" adding:

> He says everything in good, long sentences with a very large
> vocabulary, but he doesn't say them very distinctly. He is the
> greatest little explainer. I realize he gets that honestly from
> our constant explaining to him why he should or should not
> do certain things....He rattles on at great length about reasons
> for his doing things he knows we would rather he didn't do.

It was Carpenter's only question about their son that winter. He reverted, when he wrote at all, to forlorn-sounding reminiscences, as though his life were over. Worse were his envious accounts of the good fortune his friends and acquaintances were enjoying. Toye told her husband to buck up:

January 3, 1928

Dear old Disconsolate,

You write to me so seldom that I really should avoid any
unfavorable comments on what you put in your letters, but
this one . . . just broke my heart to read it, for you seemed so
bitter toward the world. Please don't get that way. Everything
has gone against us—the small as well as the big things, I know,
but let's not forget what few blessings we have. Jane may have a
squirrel coat, but she hasn't a little boy, and Frank may have
had better luck . . . but I know he has no one whose soul thrills
at the sight of his picture, as mine does at yours. Christmas may
have been desperately lonely, but it is past. . . .

As February approached, Carpenter needed money. "For God's
sake what do you do all day?" Toye asked, "You need to rustle up a
job." But then she told him not to "worry about the board and doctor's bills" and sent him sixty dollars—carefully saved from her
sewing and mending income. With the money she enclosed valentines
she and their son had made. She did not write that the T.B. had spread
to her left lung or that the "fashionable" cold she had half-reported
the month before had in fact been a month-long siege of the flu.

Nearing the age of three, Buddy had like most sensible children
begun to balk at the word *death* in his bedtime prayers, as his mother
explained: At "If I should die," it was always "Not 'if I should die.' I
don't want to die!" And at "Make Buddy well," it was always: "But I all
well." They worked out a new prayer:

> Now I lay me down to sleep.
> I pray the Lord my soul to keep.
> And of the family still awake,
> the very best of care to take,
> to bless us all in every way
> and guide our steps through every day.

Carpenter had moved to 202 Riverside Drive, with views that winter of an ice-choked Hudson. While his young son struggled, back in

Boulder, to reword his bedtime prayer—one without death—Carpenter found another. Struggling with his personal desolation, he happened on a newly published poem, "A Prayer at Bedtime," by kindred spirit, E. B. White.[1] It seemed to wholly capture his misery. "This is a prayer before I sleep," it began, borrowing the old cadence of "a lay-me-down and a soul-to-keep." The poet then confessed a childhood sin—"Once I hit a sparrow dead"—and prayed, "Give me again the tears I shed." Carpenter prayed, too, for weeping would have been a great mercy. But remorse and innocence were for children. He was a modern man now, in a cold world. Like the poet, who found himself on "a ship in a frozen sea," Carpenter had finally "glimpsed a thing that was really me."

The couple were, by springtime, deeply in debt to their parents. Carpenter had made no payments on the room and board Clara Noxon charged. Toye urged him to keep "every cent," while she borrowed stamp money from Alice, her younger sister. Clara paid her medical bills. But then, in May, a job! The professional triumph was handled in traditional small-town fashion, with a story trumpeted in the local paper:

> Marion Scott Carpenter and Chester L. Read, classmates at the University of Colorado in 1922, are meeting with great success in the chemical world....Dr. Carpenter has become an outstanding authority in essential oils—the medicinal oils of vegetables—and of perfumes.

Carpenter had "recently received a fine contract with Givaudan-Delawanna, Inc., the largest producer of perfumes in this country." Here indeed was a *big* deal, for Givaudan was an august firm dating back to the reign of Louis XVI. Carpenter was soon hard at work at Givaudan's labs in Delawanna, New Jersey. Clippings were sent throughout the ranks of friends and family.

"GOD DAMN EVERYTHING!" Toye wrote, a week after Buddy's third birthday, on May 1. "It seems that a few hours of relief from despair is the limit. You get the much desired job, and a little happiness is in sight, so I had to have difficulties to make sure that everything wouldn't be well with us." Toye did not write that she might die from her difficulties.

Carpenter was in the meantime making up for a dreary winter. Bursting forth like a butterfly from a cocoon, the gladsome virtual bachelor flitted through the New York summer of 1928. He met an entrancing dancer, Cora Quick, whose indifferent husband remained in Omaha that summer while she trained under a renowned Russian émigré. All summer Carpenter and Cora danced and dallied. They traveled to Chicago by train, and her love notes joined his great cache of correspondence: "I can never tell you," she wrote Carpenter at the end of the summer, "what you have meant to me. Your companionship was more to me than I dreamed anyone's could be."

Carpenter meanwhile pleaded poverty to family members anxious for him to return to Colorado. He ignored Toye's increasingly irksome, one-note letters of "I love you, Buddy misses you." Reminders about their debts were more difficult to sidestep. They owed Clara four hundred dollars. "Please tell me what you plan to do about it," was Toye's hammer inside the velvet glove. August passed without one letter from him.

Toye knew she was losing her two-front war for her health and for her husband. Abandoning for the first time her cheerful code, she gave vent in an angry letter—to which Carpenter penned an immediate, mollifying reply that soothed her hurt feelings. Still, she restated her central grievance: "I would have been much less overwrought had you taken the time from Cora (not from your own rest) to write to me. You ignored that part of my complaint....your letters...are the only things I have which bring me any real pleasure. I love you such a God-awful lot." Then an oblique request: "I wish you would tell me what emotions are bewildering you. I won't lose my head again, and perhaps I could help you"—willed ignorance that her husband did not address. By the end of the summer, in a lapse of judgment, Carpenter wrote his mother, thinking she might enjoy an account of his good times: "Never have the days passed in such a perfect whirl as they have the last three months." Then rhapsodic descriptions of Cora.

An unamused Ruby replied. In tribute to her stern influence came Carpenter's lightning-quick response: "Now stop your worrying about Toye and me, little Mother. Nothing is going to come between us except death.... Girls like Toye are made to order on rare occasions. Don't think I don't know it and intend to profit by it. I sha'n't ever lose her. So there. Now grin."

Little mother. Ruby's eyes narrowed. The white-haired woman was descended from the formidable Landis clan—her cousin Kenesaw Mountain Landis had recently breathed rectitude back into baseball after the Chicago "Black Sox" scandal. She might fail to do the same with her son. But she could try.

BUDDY, MEANWHILE, tired of his parents' separation. He was fully three years old and his father had been absent half his life. Worse than the confusion about the man himself was the flat disappointment, for his father had not returned that summer, as his mother had promised. Undeterred, at least in her letters, Toye wrote in September how "brown" Buddy was from his "sun baths" and how "very strong in the arms" he was. She wrote her husband bold reminders that they had a son—a theatrical son, it appears, whose solitary front-yard performances were held for at least his own enjoyment. "His latest pastime," she wrote her husband, "is standing in the front yard calling at the top of his voice, 'When are you coming home, Daddy?' 'Is Santa Claus going to bring you, Daddy?'" From her perch on the sleeping porch, Toye heard every soliloquy, many of which her son sang—in tune. What folly had she arranged? She had taught a boy to adore his father but was powerless to arrange the reverse.

"WHEN I WENT TO BED, I was twenty-six years old," Toye wrote in September 1928, "and now I am twenty-eight. Isn't that alarming?" It was her birthday. Her days proceeding at a glacial pace, Toye contemplated her husband hurtling headlong through his own days and nights half a continent away. She continued to cling to a treasured image of him as a "fine man" and to hope that "right thinking" would bring them together again. But even she saw, or sensed, the worst: "You were very casual about my return to you," she wrote that fall. "I shall act accordingly."

As Christmas approached, Toye implored her husband to visit, this time with a cynical twist: "Before receiving your regrets, I want to further my invitation for Xmas. You simply must come for Buddy's sake. He would be the happiest child in Boulder if I told him definitely that you were coming, and he does grow so fast that he will be a man before long." Buddy was, in fact, starting to ask, "Is that my daddy?" every time he saw a particular professor at the university. There was a resemblance in "everything but coloring," Toye agreed, but still it was "rather strange that he should always notice that one man." Odder still that a boy could not distinguish stranger from father.

Christmas 1928 came and went without Carpenter's return. Buddy would be four years old that spring. Unmoved by his mother's reading of *The Little Red Hen,* he was captivated by bloodthirsty tales about brave boys, magic beans, and slain ogres. "Fi, Four, Fump," Buddy chanted and stomped throughout the house, "I fell the blood of a Englishmun." Engines constituted another new enthusiasm. He asked his mother to draw him a "big picture" of one. Toye was preparing her lonely four-year-old to enter kindergarten that fall, a year early. He needed the companions, she explained:

> Buddy & I play school every morning now & you should see him. He loves it. He puts an apple and perhaps a cookie in his little lunch box & at "moon" eats it. At the opening of school he marches in—responds to my greeting with "Good morning, dear teacher." We sing "Jingle Bells" and "Rock a bye Baby"... and then I ask questions like "How many of you know your phone number?" or "Who can tell me 'Little Boy Blue'?"
>
> He raises his hand and when called upon as "Scott" stands up at his chair & recites. He has learned to stand fairly still & keep his hands at his side. Formerly he would recite his poems running around, climbing, or twisting his suit into knots. Then sometimes we have painting lessons or writing lessons. He loves

it. He is learning to talk so plainly that he doesn't say funny
things any more. But one thing he does say is funny. Instead of
saying "All aboard" when he starts his train, he says "All the
boards!"

Now he has come in from outdoors & is demanding school
so I must submit, I can't write when he is around....

Buddy's birthday on May 1 came and went without acknowledgment
from his father. Toye did not explicitly reproach her husband; to do so
would have been crude. Shame and guilt were her sole remaining
weapons, which she employed with care:

May 3, 1929

My dear old Cottie Boy,
Well, your son is now 4 years old. Isn't that alarming? You and I
will be getting grey hairs before long, we all are getting so old.
Your mother & father, Claude...were up for the afternoon on
Wednesday, May 1st, and we had a nice visit. Your mother made
the cake and gave him a sunsuit, your dad gave him a ring
toss....

The postman has passed me up again....Experience has
taught me...first that your letters are always late when I am
sick in bed; second that it does no good to scold you to write to
me or to beg you to. I think tho this time that you must be sick.
For goodness sake, take care of your self. Buddy is consoling
himself by going through all his old letters from you.

Carpenter was not sick but in love, with someone new. Her name
was Heddy. With Heddy he was happy again, for she was happy with
him. It was, in truth, far better than the unrelenting disappointment—the opprobrium of failure—he associated with Toye. Heddy
was a schoolteacher on Long Island. They had met in May. They went
to speakeasies and saw Broadway shows. Occasionally, he was able
to sneak her into his apartment for blissful overnight visits. They

whispered conversations, over coffee, in the morning. She tiptoed in the hope the landlord downstairs would hear only one set of footsteps. Carpenter stopped reading Toye's letters. Then he stopped writing.

On June 12, 1929, almost six weeks after his fourth birthday, Buddy held a pen while his mother transcribed a thank-you letter for some belated gifts. Seven legible lines—Toye's—stood sensibly amid a sea of Buddy's linear scribbling.

> Dear old Daddy, When are you coming to see me?
> I had a good time on my birthday.
> Thank you for my presents.
> When you come please bring me some perfume. I like to put it
> on me and my handkies.
> I liked the pictures of you and Uncle Frank.
> How do you like my box of stationery?
> Goodbye, Buddy

Toye may have been willing ignorance about her husband, but she was not naive: "Moonlit nights must be having their way with you," she wrote in June. By midsummer, arch equanimity had given way to fury. "The ever-lengthening intervals between your letters fan my resentment at your neglect to ever-lengthening periods of white heat— which are rather destructive."

Carpenter had meanwhile in some moral vacuum resolved to seize the day. He would be happy at all costs. He would divorce his wife—yes, he would—and marry Heddy. Toward this end he hastily arranged a trip to Colorado. Whatever he had resolved in New York was undone, however, by the spectacle awaiting him in Colorado: his parents' anger, the silent censure of Vic and Clara Noxon, and Toye's piteous situation, her tenacity, and her mortifying faith—in him of all men.

Buddy appalled him. He was skinny and rude. His neck was dirty. His manner was entirely unacceptable. To a man unaccustomed to small children, the boy was also a forceful adversary. Unaccustomed to open dislike, especially from a man he expected to love him, Buddy argued and talked back. He'd been waiting for Santa Claus. Instead he met a mean man who jerked him by his shirt collar.

For ten days Carpenter commanded a desolate family battlefield. Well-dressed and cool, he declined to discuss his debts with Clara Noxon. He informed his wife about Heddy and excoriated their four-year-old—an unpleasant, argumentative boy who didn't even like him. He returned to New York in mid-August, leaving Toye shaken.

17 August 1929, Saturday night

Cottie Boy,

Two years is a long, long time, and ten days a moment indeed
for me when…I had not only to repair the damages to your
faith that those two years of discontent had made but also to
give to you a philosophy which could guide you safely through
another long year back to me.…

Do you remember writing to me, "As I have come to
realize, we live for ourselves and must seek our own happiness
when and where we can find it.…" You must think straighter
than that. No one ever finds happiness for themselves.…But
some have been able to get at least contentment and peace, and
they have never done it by seeking it for themselves alone.

Buddy *did* miss you when you left. He kept repeating—
"Poor old Daddy. He's gone away." Friday morning, when he
came into our room, he looked all around, even in the closet, &
said "Where's Daddy?" just as he remembered the answer to his
own question. He washes his neck vigorously, too, and is being
taught not to argue. I really was disappointed in his actions
while you were here. He could have been so much more
loveable.…

As Toye's world contracted and faltered, Buddy's expanded mightily. Later in August he dictated this letter to his father on his academic, and other, prowess:

August 23, 1929

How do you do? I go to kindergarten. They teach me good things like letting the girls get in the car first. When I get enough things from school why I'm going to send them to you. I like kindergarten awful lot. I have a swing put up now. It has a turning bar and a seesaw on it. It cost mother an awful lot. I'm going to have two teeth filled.... I'll write to big strong daddy while I'm at Grandma Carpenter's.

Why don't you write to me? Do you remember when we saw the chicken hawk up in Palmer Lake? When it takes a long time to get there, why it's "Long Distance." We go *up* a hill to get to Palmer Lake so it is "up to Palmer Lake" and when we go *down,* why it's down. Elma sent me a little cornet and a tractor with a wagon 'tached to it. I saw a man downtown with a suit on like daddy's. Grandma Carpenter is sick. Isn't that too bad? I have a cold but I am drinking soda so I can go to school Monday.

Buddy

P.S. we caught a squirrel in our basement.

Meanwhile, a recent letter from Toye had sent Carpenter into a rage. How dare she dissect his rationalizations, call his logic "muddled and superficial," his moral choices "selfish"! He responded with sarcasm, mocking her words, dismissing the entire exercise. He "couldn't write," he said in disgust.

Carpenter couldn't write, but Toye could. And their correspondence reached a destructive crescendo, as she explained:

September 10, 1929

You can't write to me because you have nothing to say, and I haven't been able to write to you because I have too much. You find it hard to write to me because you either won't or can't give expression through your pen to your emotions and your innermost thoughts; and I find it hard to write to you because I must restrain myself lest I unburden my whole soul to you, and that would be painful in both the reading and the writing.

My last letter was not a "lovely" thing nor a "masterpiece of beautiful thought," nor was it meant as the cheap lecture (the shaking of a finger) which you considered it. What I wrote to you were the Facts, and you will learn them some time—soon, I hope....

Toye threw herself at her husband's mercy for one last time: "I am making a frantic effort not to lose Hope, and now I implore you— can't you help me?—can't you at least be kind?" Then she closed with two unalterable truths—his debt and her love. First, the debt: "I appreciate that you think I am asking too much....Please don't discuss this with me. I mean to have what I have asked for." Then the love: "To have me tell you again that I love you may bore you, but it won't hurt you, as your 'Love to all' hurt me. I do love you, Cottie, in spite of everything. I love you so passionately and so completely that I am afraid for myself."

Carpenter was in a fix. He had left Toye. Now Heddy was leaving him. They couldn't continue as things were, she had announced, with his marriage unresolved. She staged a dramatic departure for South America, aboard the *HMS Orduna,* sailing on October 30, 1929. She would stay there until the "unpleasantness with Toye" was over.

Days after the October 1929 stock market crash, with Heddy bound for the Chilean Andes aboard a steamship, Carpenter wrote his invalid wife requesting a divorce. Clara Noxon was apoplectic at the news, having read the letter Alice retrieved from the floor of the sleeping porch, where it had fallen from Toye's hands. Carpenter's parents had it in hand the following day in Denver, for Vic Jr. had driven it to the Carpenters' Quince Street home. In the driveway Toye's brother handed it wordlessly to Buddy's grandfather.

Marion E. Carpenter was no stranger to mayhem and terror. As a watchful Yankee boy in Reconstruction South Carolina, he had seen just about all a body could witness by way of violence—political, emotional, and otherwise. Although never the fluent, thundering writer his father, the Honorable L. Cass Carpenter, had been, the man managed to state his feelings with sufficient force:

Wed PM, November 6, 1929

Dear Son,

Within the past few days I have read with extreme surprise, sorrow, and regret your letter to Flo...I can conceive no reason for you to write such a letter to any one, and especially to a sick woman, and that woman your wife, whom you vowed to protect and cherish until death parted you. Such a letter would be a staggering blow to a woman in the best of health and how you could lower yourself to write such things is to me almost unbelievable.

...

Are you perfectly willing to give up Buddy and all that you should hold dear in life as your letter indicates you are?...Are you willing to have Buddy go thru life with the stigma that always attaches to the children in such case? If so I must say that your spark of manhood is nearly extinguished.

Do you wish to have the finger of scorn pointed at you by all your uncles, aunts, cousins, and friends? Think carefully before you decide. When a man marries, it is always more or less of a gamble, but because the game does not turn out exactly as you had hoped, don't be a quitter and a squealer.

Mother and I have arrived at the state of life where we had thought our sons were safe from scandal, and neither of us ever dreamed of receiving such a shock from you.

...

Try to patch up this affair, and relieve mother and me of the feeling that our son has proved to be a dud.

Daddy

3

THE UNPLEASANTNESS

Cuck, the hen says, in the heat of the morning.
Cuck and cuck for having laid an egg;
Dreaming on in the heat of the morning—
Mornings to come, and other eggs.

—E. B. WHITE

"CLEAN YOUR PLATE," Grandma Noxon decreed toward the end of each meal. Buddy complied, not because he feared hunger, for food abounded. Nor was he compelled by duty. At stake were simple thrift and logistics. In the Noxon household, circa 1930, the problem of food and waste disposal was addressed with a smelly domestic ecology involving chickens, a septic tank, and an ash pit, all of them in the backyard.

The kitchen, with its backyard adjuncts, was Clara Noxon's realm, and she made the most of it. It began with her White Leghorns, Rhode Island Reds, Plymouth Rocks, Buff Orpingtons, and a few staunch guinea hens. The hens not only recycled leftovers from the family meals into good garden fertilizer, but they also produced nutritious eggs and an aromatic weekly roast or two. Clara dispatched candidates for the table with a deft, one-handed neck-wringing and a hatchet.

Clara's pies were celebrated, her eggs Boulder's best, and the milk from her Holsteins the finest in the county, for she pastured them on a pristine forty-acre tract between Sixth Street and the road up Flagstaff Mountain, a peak due west of Boulder named for the flagstaff at its top, from which an American flag always flew. Family stories—about chickens, the horse-drawn carts, Holsteins, pies, and the scholar-daughters—were told over and over again at Sunday suppers.

Mostly to keep the youngster out from under foot, Clara appointed Buddy, at age four, assistant supervisor of the backyard operation of chickens, garden, and ash pit. For the first, Buddy daily scattered a grain diet of wheat and cracked corn, supplementing it with choice left-overs: stale cinnamon buns, crusted porridge, radish leaves, apple peels, and old lettuce leaves. Into the eternally smoldering mouth of the ash pit, covered with a heavy concrete lid, went paper from the butcher, bones, chicken fat, feathers, unusable fabric scraps, old news-papers, and other household detritus. It was an unpleasant, smelly chore.

Balancing the acrid with the fragrant at Seventh and Aurora were Clara's yellow and red rosebushes, which reigned over the east-facing front yard; petunias filled the large flower boxes on the front steps. In the backyard were flower and vegetable gardens, apple and cherry trees, and chokecherry bushes, their produce and fruit dutifully put up in season. Here Buddy had another detested chore: weeding.

Buddy, in short, needed little encouragement to clean his plate. It was mute, chewing obedience at the table or additional work at the mouth of the ash pit. But truth be told, he preferred even ash-pit duty to egg collection. A setting hen is a grave creature, prone to violence with beak and talon if given more than a day with a new egg or two. What an infinitely more pleasurable job, Buddy found, was the trans-fer of these pale, plundered treasures to the bran-filled barrel Grandma kept in the cool, dark basement.

Because the youngster was alone among busy and preoccupied adults at the big house—Grandma and Grandpa, Aunt Alice, Uncle Vic—Toye arranged for her four-year-old to slip away to the en-trancing new world of kindergarten, on which she reported that fall of 1929:

Buddy has just left for his Kindergarten. He has been going
since last Thursday & and how he loves it. He has to walk along
over to Grant Street, where the teacher picks him up in her car.
Just being able to go that far alone is an adventure each
morning. He is saving all the things he makes to send to you.

   Last night he had your picture again, and without being
asked, he said it didn't look like you except from far away, and
then he would go out into the hall to view it from there. He
said a peculiar thing the other day. He described the thunder as
"going across the sky with lights on it."

Toye herself was approaching the more austere precincts known
only to the chronically ill. But the two families, Noxon and Carpenter,
made sure her son barely noticed. Besides, Buddy was now assistant
superintendent of all the outdoors—an honorary position. Face down
in clover, his nose pressed into fragrant earth, Buddy thought at the
time how he should never again be so happy in his life. As it happened,
he had no idea he was the object of pity. Benign neglect, his world
without parents, seemed a form of paradise—though sometimes a
lonely one.

BUDDY'S TWO GRANDMOTHERS, Clara Noxon and Ruby Carpenter, had
been doing their best, and their duty, for two years. In Boulder, this
meant Clara made two more beds every morning and prepared more
food at each mealtime—kindnesses unnoticed by small boys. To
Buddy, Grandma Noxon was scary-looking, with her goiter and her
curt way. For Clara's part, the restless boy required supervision she
could ill provide, and which he defied in any event. Age and her experience with raising nine closely spaced children (and the loss of two of
them) had left her with a relaxed child-rearing philosophy.

   For her part, Grandma Carpenter was Buddy's champion—a doting, energetic, white-haired angel, all soft hands and pink cheeks.
"Your lordship," she called him, for the maternal vacuum at Seventh
and Aurora was a powerful draw for her. But another vacuum troubled

her even more. Where was her own son in this family drama? His letters, she thought, were self-absorbed reports, devoid of any interest in
his son's life, any curiosity about Toye's illness. He had asked Ruby for
money when he owed her money. Was he supporting his family? She
didn't know. His divorce letter to Toye had rocked the Carpenters
to the core—Marion had written him out of the family. Ruby took a
mother's tack, writing letters, preserving ties, yet hewing to a hard
line. His letter to Toye, she wrote plainly, was "hardly a humane way
to kill any one." She loved her enterprising scholar son, but her code
remained. *Right is right, wrong is wrong.*

Among the right things in Ruby's life was her grandson. And Toye
was generous with the boy's visits to the Carpenters' new home. They
had recently left their old Denver neighborhood near Capitol Hill and
moved into a brick farmhouse, built in 1896, that sat astride five city lots
at the easternmost edge of the city, where Denver was then building its
very first airport, Stapleton Field, a mile north of the Carpenter home.
Soon, a mile *south* of the Carpenters, the U.S. Army would begin con-
structing Lowry Air Field. Denver, in short, was on the map, giving the
good citizens more to talk about than dog fights, bordellos, drunks, and
the weather. They could now discuss *airplanes.* Fittingly, Grandma Carpenter's gift to Buddy that Christmas of 1929 was a toy airplane, a tribute to the boy's keen interest in the aircraft now filling the skies.

Five months later, Buddy had settled on a career: "He is going to be
a pilot and do stunts," Ruby wrote, "and I can be his friend and come
out and watch him." Full of derring-do herself, she added:

> Wasn't it thrilling—Lindy making Los Angeles to N.Y. in such
> a few hours?...Do you suppose I could learn to pilot one?...
> The Army planes are coming here on the 29th—55 of them I
> believe, and there will be big doings. I have invited Buddy
> down....I don't blame any boy for wanting to go in the Air
> Service. I am really wild to go up in a ship. I might be just as
> wild to come down.

And off to the Stapleton air show they went. But Buddy was disappointed and puzzled. "Where are all the *big* airplanes in the air?" he

asked a pilot standing next to a silver flying machine, who patiently explained to boy and grandmother the first rules of distance and perspective: "*This* big airplane," he explained, patting the machine, "only *looks* small up there."

ALTHOUGH THE DIVORCE pervaded their every thought, Ruby and Toye managed to remain close, even loving, at a difficult time—a feat they accomplished by an unspoken agreement not to discuss Carpenter. They had something else in common: Buddy. Far better, they tacitly agreed, to focus on the good. This clement arrangement, however, complicated Ruby's relationship with her son: One of her duties, since 1927, had been to report on Toye's convalescence. How could she manage this family diplomacy without sounding accusatory or unfair toward her son? At first reflexively protective, and only dimly perceiving his agenda, Ruby dutifully gathered and reported the news.

In those long-ago days of a formal family correspondence, which was how intelligence was then relayed, the rules of etiquette were severe and unforgiving. One never began a letter with bad news. Unpleasant topics were broached delicately if at all, usually three or four pages into the usual six-page letter, and were hedged about with euphemisms. One had two weeks, no more, in which to reply to a letter; gifts had to be acknowledged within ten days.

No exceptions were made for five-year-olds. Buddy's early thank-you notes to his father, penned with the help of grown-ups, provided occasions for canny boasts and questions about things masculine. Thanks to Toye, they contained a glaring meta-message: *I am an altogether satisfactory son. You will be an altogether satisfactory father.*

Hello Dear Daddy,
Thank you a million times for the boat and sailor suit. Why don't those short pants button just like the long pants? I like the long pants the best. Daddy... I am the smartest boy in kindergarten. I wish I lived with you. I can do stunts on my turning pole. I can hang by my legs and sit up on it and pull myself up to my chin. Write to me again, I liked my birthday

letter. I am going to have my tonsils taken out after
kindergarten is over. I am afraid to have it done out if I do
something I am afraid to do. I will be brave won't I.

> With love from Buddy

He figured large in the family correspondence not only as a sender
and recipient of letters but also as an exhortatory device. Buddy was
the future. Accordingly, Ruby wrote her son "to live so that Buddy
will be proud of you, for someday he will make you proud, I'm sure."

Toye had responded reluctantly to Carpenter's letter requesting a divorce. Conceding that "we must talk it over," she asked for more time:
"As yet…my physical condition will require you to keep the matter
pretty much in your own hands and to give me plenty of time." She was
implacable, however, on the issue of money: "Tell me when you write
how you plan on settling your debts.…You of course expect to support
both Buddy and me until I am able to do something for myself. The
amount of money I have been asking for I ask for again and I trust you
will be as generous with my request as I am being with yours."

Although tough, Toye was concealing a terror that heartbreak
would kill her sooner than the T.B. could manage. As 1929 became
1930, the twin specters of heartbreak and illness dogged her every
hour. Wouldn't it be easier, she may have thought, simply to die? The
same question haunted her husband. Toye's death was the perfect res-
olution to his present difficulties. But she wouldn't die. Too sick to be
a proper wife, too sick to appear in court (a legal requirement for di-
vorces in 1930), Toye was nevertheless not sick enough to die.

In June 1930 Ruby reported to her querulous son, who had complained about the glacial pace of the divorce proceedings, that Warren
Gilbert, Toye's doctor, had advocated divorce as best from a *medical*
point of view. But Clarence Eynon, the Noxon attorney, opposed one.
A divorced spouse residing out-of-state, he explained, could not be
compelled to send alimony. His client, Mrs. Carpenter, required at
least financial support if she were to have any hope of recovery. "I immediately saw his point," Ruby editorialized, for she had caught a first
ugly glimpse of her son through the gimlet eyes of an attorney.

Reading this dry report, Carpenter realized his mother might no longer be a co-conspirator, nor even an ally. Heddy, writing from the Chilean Andes, was curious about "the unpleasantness." "Tell me, Scottie dear, if Toye is just starting proceedings, how long will it be before the business is finished, and is it going to be very disagreeable for you?"

Thus pressed, he complained to Toye. What did she intend to do? When did she intend to do it? Now the victim, he complained she was "cracking the whip." Toye replied with her usual drumbeat of logic. He had not once inquired about her illness, but, she wrote, "this sickness is of importance to you for two reasons." She spelled it out:

> First,...I can't possibly do anything for you when I am flat on
> my back, and for you to urge me to formulate plans is not only
> absurd but most unkind....In being so unkind, you hinder my
> progress.
>
> Second,...my position is too precarious to permit me the
> luxury of trusting to chance or the generosity of a divorced
> husband. My support is not a question of my comfort but of
> my life....Call this "cracking the whip" if it pleases you, but I
> have an idea my purposes are as honorable as yours.

She could suit Carpenter by getting well enough to walk into a courtroom or by dying outright. By the end of the summer, it appeared she would do the latter. We know only from Ruby's letters of the doctor's alarm, of Toye's hemorrhages, of her tearful confessions—she knew, she told her sisters, she would die. She could not even feed herself or get out of bed. She was physically unable, Ruby explained, to make the legally required court appearance for the divorce Carpenter was demanding. After this grim recitation, she added tartly that she was simply "reporting the facts as I hear them."

Sensing a new hard line, Carpenter attempted a charming letter, complaining of his "feverish" work at the plant and trilling about the change of seasons:

> The melancholy, pensive autumn days are here again. The
> shallow brook trickles faintly, the cadence of the crickets has

slowed, the sunlight is softer, mellower, the distant hills are a
shade more purple. Inexplicably, thought of autumn brings to
my mind the strains of Rubinstein's *Melody in F*—it is to me
the musical essence of that season just as surely as the olfactorial
essence is contained in the odor of burning leaves.

Write soon again, won't you please? Love to you all.

In the High Andes, Heddy was holding out for her marriage proposal. Her many letters during their year apart reveal Carpenter to
have been a generous lover given to bouts of sarcasm, self-pity, and
withering cruelty. He sent her airmail letters ("thanks to Lindbergh,"
wrote a grateful Heddy), a pearl necklace, and crates of hardcover
books. The Depression had not affected his income: Geneva-based Givaudan was awarding salary bonuses.

Heddy's windfall was, alas, Toye's penury. Toye disbelieved her
husband's letters begging financial incapacity, writing:

> The egotism and, above all, the stupidity which make it possible
> for you to write such ridiculous but nonetheless cruel rot to me
> would make it impossible for you to understand my answer.
> This is a request that you reconsider my request that you send
> me $150 a month.
>
> In asking for that I am not prompted by spite, avarice, or
> the desire to be smart. I am asking for what belongs to Buddy
> and to me. Buddy should go to Kindergarten, and if he does, he
> must dress well enough. He should be dressed as well as you are.

It angered Toye to beg for life's basics. Anger prompted her, finally, to
identify the lie at the heart of her husband's defense:

> Such a statement of accounts is as distasteful to me as to you....
> I hope you will not refuse me this time, for otherwise that will
> necessitate my explaining to your mother a number of things
> about you. That, I fear, would be painful all around. You
> haven't meant to do wrong, neither have you meant to do
> right. Perhaps therein is the reason for your making such a mess
> of everything.

Despair filled the house at Seventh and Aurora. Family members trod quietly; Clara was up at night changing her daughter's sweat-soaked nightclothes before they froze on her. She was carried from room to room. As her daughter declined, the stoic grandmother, ailing herself, would now climb the long staircase to change sheets from a night spent coughing blood, carry them down again to scrub out the red clots of tissue, boil the offending linens in a large kettle, and dry them on the outside clothesline, freezing weather or fair. She kept track of Buddy, coaxed him to eat, washed his hands frequently as the doctor had instructed her to do, and at a whistle from the speaking tube installed in the front hall, climbed the stairs again. A tray of food came up by dumbwaiter. Holding her daughter's head upright, Clara encouraged her to swallow just a few spoonfuls of broth.

Carpenter was cornered: abandoned by Heddy, persecuted by a stubborn invalid, and now, finally, to judge from his mother's recent letters, given the maternal cold shoulder. Exasperated, he complained the fall of 1930: "A whole year has passed now and we have got exactly nowhere....I can't stand this static, utterly empty existence much longer....Is there no way to speed things along? Cannot a plaintiff be represented in court by counsel?" And finally, a peevish-sounding threat: "If nothing happens before long I shall try recourse to Cuban courts."

"Cuban courts?" Marion shot his wife a look. "What drivel," he offered before stomping out for a smoke under the grape arbor. Ruby meanwhile steered her steady course. *Right is right, wrong is wrong.* She had also, finally, chosen sides. Not Toye's side nor her son's, but a third one. It was Buddy's.

"Under the conditions," Ruby wrote, she didn't see how he could "well start suit. It would seem rather a heartless thing to do," she added, "filing divorce proceedings, when she is ill and helpless, don't you think?" She urged her son to "come through the ordeal without any pangs of conscience." She sympathized and reasoned:

Try to see how much better off you are than she is. Of course, I know you want a home and companionship, but again let your

conscience be your guide....I do not think Florence has ever
ceased to care for you and has always talked to Buddy about
you as if nothing were wrong between you....

HEDDY, FINALLY, WAS sailing home to Carpenter after nearly eighteen
months away. Her ship, the *Santa Clara,* would arrive in New York the
day after Christmas 1930. Carpenter's feelings were mixed. She had,
after all, abandoned him when he needed her the most, her thank-you
notes hadn't been effusive or grateful enough, and her other letters
were not very well written. In this long-distance romance, he had tried
to take Heddy as she was. But she remained who she was, a plucky,
bright woman he had failed to polish to his satisfaction. It was further-
more an effort that required him to ignore the fact that his wife was
dying in Boulder. In the end, Heddy could not manage the same in-
human task. "To have made Toye utterly miserable," she finally admitted, "is a thing I did not want to be accountable for." The suffering
was too great for a relationship so frail: It faltered and failed three weeks
after her return to the States. Carpenter was "sorry," he wrote in a surviving draft,

> for the many ugly letters I sent you—for the untold
> unkindnesses I visited upon you....I didn't realize I was killing
> your love....One of the keenest of my many regrets is that I
> cannot turn to Toye; the time is past. Even though we were
> both willing, her life and mine are far too short for me to atone
> for my wrongdoing.

Putting aside the matter of atonement, which Carpenter conceded
was not to be had, he nevertheless longed for the connection only
family can provide. A letter from his mother, written on March 23, signaling her retreat from a prodigal son, had him on the next train to
Denver.

A lesser man, or one less desperate or ashamed, might have remained fugitive in New York the rest of his days. Spending the first day
home with his parents, he was made to understand how his "New York

behavior" had shamed his family and precipitated a scandal. He had forced his parents to dissemble—to protect themselves and what had been their good name. He may have been dimly aware that his mother had transferred her allegiance to Buddy and that his father was entirely disengaged. In Boulder his mother-in-law, Clara Noxon, screeched at him as he stood at the front door of the old house at Seventh and Aurora. Only Toye welcomed him with open, forgiving arms.

He found her at the Mesa Vista Sanatorium, at 2121 North Street, where anxious doctors had placed her in January. For Toye, Carpenter's homecoming was bittersweet. He would not stay long. There would be no family life for them, or for Buddy. He would support her financially and he would pay for her medical care, whatever the doctors mandated. The euphoria created by their talking and touching throughout their one long day and night together would have to last her through the long, solitary years of recurring illness. She wrote after he left:

> The joy of having seen you again, of having been in your arms
> again, and most of all knowing that there really is to be an end
> to this existence and that I can go on loving you all I please, is
> so real that I can almost ignore the fact that each moment
> you are being carried farther and farther away from me
> physically....
>
> I love you, Cottie Boy. That's the beginning and the end of
> all the many, many things I would tell you had I the strength to
> write them, so I repeat it to you....my hope has revived and I
> am happy again....

He did admire the qualities in this woman, but not enough, he knew, to undergo life "as a shoe salesman," as he told his in-laws during one notable confrontation. He returned to New York, eventually removing to a small apartment in Nutley, New Jersey, close to the Givaudan plant. He was chastened enough to begin a fresh correspondence with his wife, one that was kinder and more frequent. He mastered the anniversary gesture, sending her yellow jonquils each

Easter and red roses on the birthday of their child. He made an effort to learn about her disease. He would pay for her recovery and support her until such time as they agreed to part.

TOYE WOULD LIVE another thirty-two years. In 1945, as she and Carpenter prepared to divorce when their son turned twenty-one, it was she who comforted her husband, still stricken by the choices that had brought them, finally, to such a sad pass. A sanatorium houses not just patients but also their wrecked lives and broken hearts. Doctors, nurses, and roommates saw everything. "Mona was my roommate... when you first saw me there," Toye wrote Carpenter in 1945. "She passed you on the stairs as you left, and saw you weeping." *"Give me again the tears I shed."* Carpenter's borrowed poem-prayer had finally been answered.

He would marry his longtime companion, Edyth, a kind widow who lived in the apartment on the floor above him. His mother protested the union, for Edyth was a Jew, loosing a senile, anti-Semitic screed of a letter as World War II raged. Thinking his mother still sane, Carpenter wrote a three-page ode to tolerance. Ruby eventually accepted her new daughter-in-law. They exchanged Christmas cards.

Carpenter's correspondence with his grade-school son was largely critical and mean. He often lapsed into ridicule, sometimes returning Buddy's letters, sternly noting their youthful spelling errors and grammatical infractions in the margins. In 1948 he even ridiculed Bud's momentous decision to fly U.S. Navy airplanes. Yet at the moment his astronaut son was poised to fly the nation's second manned orbital mission, in 1962, he wrapped himself in the flag of science and exploration and wrote a letter that sometimes appears in collections of the century's finest. Conceding nothing, the retired research chemist welcomed his son and namesake to share his lofty modern perch.

Regaining some of her strength by the close of World War II, Toye would become the chief medical librarian at Boulder Community Hospital. A walking medical legend there, she counseled and comforted new T.B. patients, her X-rays always at hand for a reverential viewing. Her own painful medical education had made her a stickler for record-keeping. At age forty-five, she took a course in Gregg short-hand and stalked the halls of the hospital with her steno pad, tracking down errant doctors behind in their records.

As the Korean war approached, with her son in flight training at Pensacola, Toye stood by as her daughter-in-law, Rene, gave birth to her first grandchild, yet another Scott. A few years later, she spent a day selecting her granddaughters' first dresses, and lived to see her son ride into space. She succumbed, finally, to bronchial pneumonia at the age of sixty-three. With her son by her side, she woke briefly in the same Boulder hospital to ask, "Are you still there, Bud?" "I'm still here," Bud replied.

4

POCKETKNIVES, PENS, AND OTHER EDGE TOOLS

Give back to me
My old soul,
The one I had as a child,
Ripened by legends,
With its cap of feathers
And its wooden sword.

—FEDERICO GARCÍA LORCA

IN EARLY 1931 when his mother, Toye, entered the Mesa Vista Sanatorium, Buddy acquired an old scout knife while visiting his grandparents in Denver. "He...asked if he could have it," Ruby reported, "and I want to tell you it was a rare treasure—took it to bed with him & it was never out of his hands for a minute."

Buddy did not say it, but in his secret, hidden heart he imagined the treasure, if properly loved, might bring his father home forever. But the man never came home, nor did he once look for his old scout knife. Back home in Boulder, neither the knife nor his grandson escaped Vic Noxon's notice. Approaching age six, the boy was becoming an appealing companion in a household recently reduced to two outnumbered men. The two had already cemented an alliance by the kitchen stove each morning. In that sure sign of male affection, the boy mimicked the old man's posture, hunching his shoulders against the cold of the house, as they waited by the warmth for their oatmeal to cook.

Grandma Noxon, up before sunrise, stoked the fire in the cast-iron wood stove. When her grandson appeared, she commandeered his hands for a scrubbing, an unpleasant ritual, for her hands were as rough and as hard as iron files. Clara's husband since Christmas day 1888, Vic Noxon was born in Idaho Springs, then Colorado Territory, and was sixty-six years old the year Buddy found his first pocketknife.

The house of Buddy's childhood was stalked by ghost-giants. Even Grandma Noxon confessed to a brush with greatness. "I once rode Buffalo Bill's horse," she announced once as Bud headed out the back door for a day of riding. Stopped cold in his tracks, he turned to study her face for signs of a tease, but she was focused on her work. Clara Noxon had, in fact, been an accomplished horsewoman before giving her life over to a husband and children. Buffalo Bill Cody, with his horse, had been a regular guest back in the day. Yet the showman had ultimately fallen in Grandma's esteem—a bad thing to do, Buddy noted. He left his wife, on his many world tours, with no funds at all, Clara explained, forcing the poor Mrs. Cody to "take in laundry."

Grandpa Noxon was six-foot-one—taller than his two sons and his four sons-in-law—slightly stooped through the shoulders and long in the legs. By the time his grandchildren began to arrive, the old man had thinning, steel-gray hair and an expansive brow softened by large, brown, exophthalmic eyes—only slightly tamed by wire-rimmed glasses. He wore a dusty suit, the jacket of which usually hung from the back of a chair. His shoes were memorably lumpy creations. To accommodate the bunions he had developed from a lifetime of walking, his cobbler had carved out swaths of shoe leather, patching the holes with matching bits of softer material.

He was a great walker, claiming it was good for his health, so Bud endeavored to walk with his grandfather whenever he got the chance. After supper they would stroll down to Gregory Creek, which then ran through a culvert under Aurora Avenue. He'd smoke his cigar, and man and boy would watch the creek—not talking much, just considering the water.

In contrast to their contemplative evening strolls, Sunday mornings meant longer, more talkative walks, for they both had Sunday obligations downtown. Grandpa's obligation was to type up the first draft of his editorial for the *Boulder County Miner & Farmer,* the weekly newspaper he owned and published from offices that for years presided over the southeast corner of Fourteenth and Walnut. Buddy's obligation involved maintaining a perfect Sunday School attendance at St. John's Episcopal Church, a gray-stone structure at the corner of Fourteenth and Pine.

So on Sundays, certain he could command a precious half-hour of the old man's undivided attention, Buddy saved up a week of questions, for he had discovered his grandfather knew practically everything. Because Grandpa was an important man, and knowledgeable, the boy tried to be rigorous about what, and how, he questioned his "walking encyclopedia." For many years Buddy thought he himself had coined the term.

Hungry for all manner of things (knowledge, ability, speed, chocolate, and caramel), Buddy sometimes used a purloined offertory coin to buy a Baby Ruth candy bar at Walgreen's. But he always stopped at Grandpa's office for the funnies. They had an ongoing debate about the superheroes of the day—his Tarzan versus Grandpa's Alley Oop. Tarzan could whomp Alley Oop in a flash, Buddy claimed. The editor played devil's advocate and said it would take Alley Oop about one minute to beat up Tarzan if they ever met in the jungle.

The Noxon household was the scene of some notable political meetings, for Grandpa was a Democratic party activist, a Progressive, perennial state convention delegate, and what was then called an internationalist. He read a great many newspapers, which he got on exchange-subscription, and had a number of devoted friends at the University of Colorado: "One of the Professor's of the University has fell in love with Papa," Grandma reported in a family letter, "and is going to give him a big dinner for his birthday—just men—a big affair. Papa has got to buy a new suit. My, you should see the one he wears."

He knew everybody and everything in state politics. He hated government corruption and cronyism, which he said knew no party. He supported Franklin D. Roosevelt (descended, like Grandpa, from the Hudson Valley Dutch) when the Democrat was elected president in

1932, and he argued unfailingly in his editorials that the new president's economic program, called the New Deal, was going to get the country out of the Depression.

Grandma Carpenter in Denver, by way of contrast, was a rip-roaring, Roosevelt-hating, isolationist, conservative-activist Republican. She worked polling stations in her election district, sat on political committees, and was obstreperous about all things political. The tension between Buddy's two family camps—on the one hand Noxon Democrats in Boulder, and on the other Carpenter Republicans in Denver—may explain his lifelong indifference to politics. As a child he learned to negotiate the partisan terrain by telling his Denver grandmother that "Grandpa Noxon is a Democrat, Mother is a socialist" but he was "a Republican like *you*, Grandma." Back on Noxon turf, he assured his mother he was "really a socialist like *you*, Mom."

Boulder County had a number of articulate and solid Democratic editors like Vic Noxon. None was revered like Vic Noxon—perhaps because Coloradans knew he was a living witness. He could recount Colorado's earliest days, when talented first-comers like his parents had built a town out of a gold camp and a state out of a territory. The man had forgotten more about hard-rock mining—its prospecting, assaying, economics, policy, management, engineering, explosives, metallurgy—than most people could learn by trying for a lifetime. Unusual among mine owners (he had inherited most of his holdings), Vic Noxon was pro-union, probably because he knew the hard men who journeyed inside mountains with only explosives and picks. By way of eloquent visual testimony about the worth of their work, on display in a locked case at the *Miner* offices were spectacular geodes and ores—huge, bubbling, fist-sized pieces of gold and silver still locked into their parent rock, attesting to a Colorado as it was when Grandpa Noxon was born—gold and silver still locked in the rock and no one with the key.

After a winter or two in the Rockies, most of the territory's Fifty-niners (so-called after the Colorado gold rush of 1859) had tossed their low-tech gold-panning equipment and returned home to the States. No one in Colorado—not the Forty-niners, nor the Fifty-niners, nor world-roaming professionals from Wales or Cornwall or Slovakia—knew how to liberate the precious minerals from the imprisoning, refractory Rocky Mountains. By dint of experiment, perseverance, investment, and time, however, Coloradans—among them, Vic's father, Dr. A. M. Noxon—had devised new ways to coax metals from the mountains, and to become rich.

So Vic Noxon had had a paradoxical young life: part log-cabin-born, rustic boyhood, part Gilded Age youth, Rocky Mountain style. His parents sent him to Boulder Preparatory School, where he proved an able student, then enrolled him in the new university, where not even his father's suicide, a front-page story, derailed his studies. Vic Noxon graduated with a degree in civil engineering in 1886, along with four other young men—C.U.'s first engineering class. He returned to Idaho Springs, went into the newspaper business, and married his childhood sweetheart, Clara Rose Batchelder.

Although mild-mannered and kind (he was uncommonly patient with his grandson), this son of pioneers could be provoked: During the election year of 1923, Noxon is reported to have punched his rival, L. C. ("Gov.") Paddock, on the sidewalks of Boulder. The editor of the *Daily Camera* had published an editorial Grandpa, apparently, deplored.

THE MAN ALSO deplored a dull knife blade. His own was always very sharp, and a fortnightly ritual kept it that way. Appraising his grandson's new pocketknife with a frown, he sent the boy to fetch his whetstone. His worn, double-sided Carborundum whetstone was kept in the junk drawer in the pantry, Grandpa's cache for found things, fascinating tools, and hard-to-classify objects—one of them a heavy, constantly accreting ball composed of lead wrappers. The metal was too precious to consign to the ash pit, and for fun Bud would drop it on the sidewalk, where it landed with a satisfyingly deep thud in an exercise that wholly justified its existence. Grandpa and Buddy were owners of the junk drawer, the mysterious contents of which, he told Buddy, were of little use to women.

So the two men sat at the kitchen table with their pocketknives. Bud watched his grandfather reassess the blade, place a folded newspaper on the oilcloth, spit copiously on the stone (you could use either oil or spit, Grandpa said, but spit was just as good and a whole lot handier), place it at just the right angle, and begin the sharpening process—an elliptical movement of tilted blade against stone, honing one side of the blade and then the other. He would alternately hone the edge, feel it, hone it, and feel some more until he was satisfied. Buddy watched him feel the stone through the blade, listen to the blade on the stone, observe the color of the spit, watch the edge straight on, and adjust the honing angle in accordance with everything he heard, felt, and saw.

This, Vic taught his grandson, was a black art.

To demonstrate what he had accomplished, Grandpa Noxon would shave a patch of hair off the back of his arm, or hold up a single piece of newspaper, slicing it from its right edge all the way to the bottom: it cut the paper like a razor. Then he handed his knife to the boy so he could feel a well-honed blade for himself. Grandpa watched and helped him, always making sure the boy had his own knife to work with. When he thought he was done, he'd hand it to the expert for inspection. "*Pshaw!*" Grandpa would say, "That knife wouldn't cut hot butter!" They'd laugh, but his message was clear: Buddy had much to learn.

And the old man had much to teach. So much, in fact, that he was in Buddy's imagination an equal among all his heros. He was Deerslayer. He was the last of his tribe. He was Pathfinder and Pioneer. He was all these things. Yet he of the long legs tarried for the boy of short ones. He was everything his grandson ever wanted to be, and while Vic Noxon lived, Buddy Carpenter was the luckiest boy in the entire world.

As BUDDY ENTERED the first grade, at University Hill Elementary School, Toye was still at "the San." After classes he walked two miles to see her before going home, another walk of two miles. His mother would not be home that Christmas or the following. She wrote to her husband about it—sad letters that Bud would not see or read until he was seventy-three years old and took them from their ancient boxes.

Grandpa Noxon taught Buddy to make a willow whistle the spring he was in second grade. They took a walk up by Gregory Creek, where, the old man told him, the sap was rising in the willows—a good time for making whistles. The boy watched his grandfather cut a small branch into a section about ten inches long, with one end cut on a diagonal. An inch from the end with the diagonal cut, he made a notch perpendicular to the long axis of the stick on one side and slanting on the other. That was the beginning of what he called the whistle hole. Down lower on the stick, he used the knife to incise the circumference of bark. With the knife handle, he gently pounded all the tender, springtime skin above that cut and, by twisting and pulling, peeled off the bark.

Magically, the top part of the whistle slipped right off the stick because, as Grandpa had said, "the sap was running." He made an air hole in the top, cut away some of the wood below the whistle hole, and put the bark back. The whistle was finished. To make it warble, he put a small pebble in the whistle hole. With practice, Buddy learned how to make the whistle himself.

Grandpa also showed him how to make a figure-four trap for small animals, a bit of wood-lore going all the way back to Warrensburgh, in the Adirondacks, where his own father had been born, in 1824. That was Leatherstocking territory, birthplace of the Hudson River, with its dense, dark forests rich with rabbits.

Buddy used an old orange crate for the trap enclosure. The lever system he made himself, learning a lot about its intricacies in the process. After he was satisfied with the trap, he placed it in some tall grass by the creek behind the house. It sat there for days. Grandpa had shown the boy how to make a good trap, but not where to put it. Truth be told, the man's experience with rabbit-trapping was limited to the wilderness of the next county over—Clear Creek County circa the 1870s. It was clear to Buddy that Boulder County had some very wily rabbits.

These times with his grandfather shimmer in Bud's memory. He sees his hands, his glasses, hears the old man's voice as he begins some rare task and takes him steadily to its end.

———

NEITHER OF THE TWO FAMILIES, Noxon or Carpenter, was much affected by the Depression that had swept Franklin D. Roosevelt into office. Vic Noxon kept his own newspaper and printing businesses humming along and the Noxons made do. The Carpenters, too, simply tightened their belts and pressed on through the decade. They continued to own a comfortable home, kept a summer cottage in Palmer Lake, drove two cars, and took vacations in California.

Buddy was the Brave Little Dutch Boy in the second-grade school play. Toye was well enough, that spring of 1933, to see him perform in it. He was also a "perfect height," at age eight, to support her during her first walks about the house. She came home late that spring: "I have breakfast & dinner at the table and spend the morning on the porch down-stairs," she wrote in a letter. "Then I come up to my sleeping porch for the remainder of the day and Buddy & I have supper alone together."

Home from the San, Toye was compelled by financial need to find work and by medical fashion to be outdoors, in the sunshine, as much as possible. She settled on an exotic conservationist scheme: raising bobwhite quail and chukar partridges for regional game preserves. And so it happened that the chukar was introduced to the Great Plains.

As these plans came to fruition the summer of 1933, Carpenter returned to Colorado for a visit, an event fraught with family politics. Buddy was to have two entire weeks with his father and his favorite uncle, Claude. Later Toye wrote with approval:

> From his glowing accounts I can understand that you were
> able to give him a lot more individual attention than I had
> expected...and I can see the results. Two weeks out of 52
> don't offer many opportunities to you on which to build
> your friendship with him, and I am happy to see that what
> opportunities were possible were put to such good use. It does
> mean such a lot to him, and to you too, I think.

At Palmer Lake that summer, Buddy learned that acorn fights—and terrifying nighttime stories about monsters called the double-hobgoblin and the black panther—were a ritual for Carpenter men. The acorn fights began with choosing fortified positions and stockpiling ammo from the scrub oaks. The father, of course, always ended up with a much greater supply of acorns. He had big hands and bigger pockets. He was a better shot. He was a bully. It didn't matter who—wife, lover, little kid—when Carpenter got the better of someone, the man never knew when to stop.

On the occasion of their first epic acorn fight, Carpenter pelted his eight-year-old in a lopsided contest that left his son's face and arms scratched and bleeding. Furious, knowing the fight was unfair, the boy determined to wrestle his opponent to the ground. But after tackling his father about the knees, Buddy just slid down the man's legs. Carpenter was wearing his high jodhpur boots, so his son ended up in a puddle around his ankles. "Don't do that, boy," he said, laughing, "You might hurt yourself!" His father's laughter, and his own impotence, was the ultimate boyhood humiliation.

He got over it. At home he had two able allies: Grandpa, who was his soul, and his mother, who after ten minutes of discussion could turn nearly every problem inside out. Although throughout the 1930s Toye had some perilous return bouts of T.B., she was on hand for the most part to supervise her son's upbringing. It was a powerful intervention. While Buddy may have been more aware of his companionable grandfather and a pioneer world of handmade kites, figure-four traps, willow whistles, and sharp pocketknives, it was the mother who perceived her son's love of the outdoors—and of speed and flight. It was she who set the standard for physical bravery and character. It was she who saw Buddy had a new lathe in his basement workshop. A bicycle. A horse. It never occurred to him how or why these things arrived. They were simply part of that big house and part of growing up with Grandpa.

Most interesting, perhaps, is that the mother argued in favor of risk to a cautious father, whose one sport (Buddy noticed) was walking while swinging a walking stick: "The children here do have bicycles," she argued in one such letter. "They can be rented at a stand down by the campus." They were, she continued, "a considerable part of traffic....I don't want him hurt," she insisted, "but in this as in every-thing, it seems to me he has to take his chance and that in doing so he learns to take care of himself."

Finally, when speed became his primary calling, Toye was brave. He had to go as fast as his legs could carry him, she saw, and when his legs supplied insufficient speed, she orchestrated a succession of ever-faster vehicles: a tricycle and a pony, followed by a bicycle, a pair of skis, and a horse named Lady Luck. In his senior year in high school, a 1934 Ford coupe was purchased. And finally airplanes, when World War II meant military service for the able-bodied. Bud was seventeen when he enlisted in the Navy as an aviation cadet. She gave her assent and arranged the consent of her husband. She was his champion in the face of Carpenter's customary opposition. She believed in him.

DURING FOURTH GRADE, a classroom misunderstanding, involving a girl, caused the teacher to ask Bud to stay behind. As the rest of the class filed out to recess, she left the room to supervise their departure. It gave him enough time to lift a window sash. He assessed the drop—only ten or fifteen feet. He quickly hopped on the sill and leapt to safety below. "Wow, Scott!" Ray Joyce said as the truant ran to join his friends on the playground. "What'd the teacher say?" Bud replied, truthfully, that he didn't know.

Mrs. Bogess, fourth-grade teacher, was the principal's wife who at the end of each school year celebrated each of her students in verse—"So clear the track, make way for Anne, she always does the best she can," and, "Raymond Joyce, who speaks right out with a good, strong voice." About Bud she wrote, "Great Scott," who did his work "right on the dot."

> Through open window he did soar,
> Instead of going out the door.

Anything to avoid a confrontation. The boy had enough correction at home—from grandmother, aunt, and mother—to last a long lifetime.

At St. John's, where Bud was confirmed two years later, Father Hubert M. Walters laid his hands on the twelve-year-old's head and sent the young Christian out into the world fortified with a verse fragment from First Corinthians: "Be strong." Of course he'd be strong: He could do fifteen chin-ups. Chin-ups and after-lunch recess, now the crowning athletic event of all sixth-grade existence. It began with a work-up softball game, which in turn began with getting there *first*. The first ones to touch home base after lunch got to pick the best positions—arrive late and you'd end up in the outfield. But everyone went home for lunch. For Bud this meant an uphill bike ride of a mile and, afterward, a downhill race back to the sixth-grade playground. He usually got there ahead of everyone else.

But it cost him, for he lived farther from school than all of his classmates. On the day of a bad bike accident, he was hurtling down Aurora Street, his book case and clarinet case hooked over the handlebars. He woke up hours later on the old horsehair-stuffed daybed in Grandpa's den, with a headache and a wet washcloth on his forehead. Lucky for him, no one took away his bike. Bud figured out what had happened on a later headlong downhill race that replicated the chain of events. His knee hit his dangling clarinet case. His clarinet case jerked the handlebars hard to one side. Not enough, on that occasion, to knock him to the ground, but enough to explain the earlier event.

ALTHOUGH BUD'S FATHER was more abstract than real, proof of his existence came from the many books he sent: *King Arthur and His Knights of the Round Table, Robin Hood,* most of Mark Twain, and nearly everything by Ernest Thompson Seton and Robert Louis Stevenson. When he was older, there was James Fenimore Cooper's Leatherstocking saga: *The Deerslayer, The Last of the Mohicans, The Pathfinder, The Pioneers,* and *The Prairie.* After that intense literary foray, Toye told her son he sounded like an eighteenth-century frontiersmen, with a lot of quaint contractions and verb-first sentences: "Say not, mother, what you fear..." or "What means this hubbub?" and so on. Cooper's adventures and romantic woodscapes were a great influence on the boy and filled his solitary hours.

Dear Dad,

Thank you very much for my Christmas presents. Mother and I are reading *Huckleberry Finn*. We both like it. I like all of my presents.

I am writing this letter with my own pen. I bought it with my allowance. Mother gives me 5¢ every Monday.

When you come out next summer I think I will be up to your pocket. I weigh 60 pounds.

With love,
Buddy

Two Little Savages, arriving on his tenth birthday, sent Bud tearing out of the house one night. First he located the Big Dipper, which is part of the Great Bear constellation, and then identified the tiny Papoose, a fifth-magnitude star also called Alcor. There it was, hugging the back of the Old Squaw (or Mizar, a second-magnitude star). Bud had passed, according to *Two Little Savages,* a "mighty good test of eyes."

May 13, 1935

Dear Dad,

Thank you very much for the nice birthday present. I am already on page 496 in *Two Little Savages*. It is the very nicest book I have ever had. I know I am going to like the others too.

All the pioneer ghost-giants who sprang to life at the dinner table, the mountains behind his house, his many hours of solitary play, the books he read—all this and something in him, unarticulated but deeply felt—created a sense of dislocation. Maybe, Bud thought, he'd been born at the wrong time—a century too late, or too early. He longed for something supremely difficult, great, even heroic to do. He despaired of ever getting a chance to prove himself.

After finishing *Two Little Savages,* Bud became obsessed with archery and its Indian lore and woodcraft. He devoted himself to making his own arrows. "Anyone can make a good arrow," he learned, "but only an artist can make a dozen arrows that all fly the same." He started an archery club at school. In Cub Scouts he was confident enough to teach the scoutmaster a couple of things. Archery, in fact, was the perfect expression for Bud's natural engineering bent, for it combined an exacting craftsmanship (in ballistics no less) with the precise athleticism of the sport itself.

At about this time Grandma Carpenter, with no sense of irony, gave her one grandchild a bantam rooster. He became a treasured pet and cut a dashing figure among the biddies of the Noxon backyard. Therein lay the difficulty. With thrift and food storage at stake (fertilized eggs don't keep well, even under the ideal conditions of a bran-filled barrel in the cool Noxon basement), Grandma had a word with Toye, and Toye had a word with her son, explaining that the rooster had to go. Destroyed at the news, he went immediately downstairs and out the back door to fetch his banty. She would have to say it to the rooster's face. So up he clambered, clutching his feathered pet, up to the very empyrean heights of his mother's hospital bed on the sleeping porch—climbing on a chair to get up there—and implored her again to spare the banty rooster, this final time with an outrageous fiction: "Mom," he said, "we just *can't* get rid of this rooster. He loves me so much he just laid an egg in my hand!"

THE SUMMER OF 1936 was to be Carpenter's first vacation, together with Edyth, in Colorado—and in full view of the families. Bud was eleven years old and had for the past year been anticipating this two-week visit with a kind of crazed ardor. His father, meanwhile, unhappy with Toye's recent financial demands (for Clara had increased room and board), anxious for Edyth to enjoy her first trip to Colorado, and unprepared for two weeks with an eleven-year-old boy ravenous for his attention, allowed his Mr. Hyde to escape once more. He ignored his son for the duration of the visit.

In an October letter crackling with anger, Toye wrote:

So you spoke with him twice? Once when you scolded him for playing in the pool, and once . . . when you scolded him for

resenting Mrs. Scher's criticism? I do not oppose you
disciplining him…, but I do regret…that scolding and teasing
should be the only means of exchange between you.

BUD'S FATHER OVERWHELMED him that Christmas with his first pair of
skis. Bud wrote straightaway in that mixture of boasting and gratitude
he had developed since age five:

January 1, 1937

Dear Dad,
I am starting the New Year right by writing you the long letter
you have been looking for. First of all I want to thank you for
the camera, books, and skies [*sic*] you sent me, which are all
right in front of me. I am reading *Mysterious Island* first. I hope
you read it, for it is very interesting.

It is snowing outside now…so I will probably be able to use
my skies [*sic*] tomorrow.

Mother gave me some skates for Christmas…and I have
learned several tricks: the flying Dutchman, shoot the duck,
and I can skate backwards.

The S's on my card stand for superb, superior, superhuman,
and splendid—at least that's what I think, but the teacher
meant them for satisfactory, the highest grade you can get.
…

With love from us both,
Bud & Mom

The skis and the snow and all those report-card Ss made for a very
merry Christmas. But then Toye contracted the flu and nearly died.
She was carried through the Sanatorium doors in the arms of Father
Walters. Buddy went with them, fearing for the first time that his
mother was finally beyond rescue. Father Walters would return three
times that winter to administer extreme unction to his parishioner
and friend. Bud was summoned, too, permitted to witness the grave
proceedings only through a window.

That same year Bud got his first job at Grandpa's print shop, folding newspapers. The *Boulder County Miner & Farmer* was a weekly, printed every Thursday. Grandpa Noxon paid him thirty-five cents a week. He held other jobs, too. His mother's bobwhites and chukars laid eggs that required precisely timed tending and turning under their incubating lamps in the basement. There were his grandmother's hens, and all those weeding and trash-management jobs—for which he earned a weekly allowance of twenty-five cents. The job at Grandpa's office, however, was an honor. Vic Noxon made the offer in Toye's presence, and it was she who spoke first: "*Bud,* your first job!" It was a big deal, and of course Bud said yes.

He walked down to the *Miner* every Thursday afternoon after his classes. Working alongside Mrs. Johnson, one of Grandpa Noxon's longtime employees, the sixth-grader learned how to take the papers off the Maile press, which delivered newly printed sheets of paper to a big rack that was suspended over a bar laced with lots of little holes; gas came through those holes. Mrs. Johnson lighted the gas, and the paper ran over those gas flames to dry the ink. As soon as the paper got past the gas pipe and onto the rack, the rack flipped 180 degrees, placing the paper on the table. Now the borders moved away from the papers to accept the new paper coming down, and as the rack rotated back to get the next paper, the sides of the tray would squeeze back in and center the papers in a neat pile—a wonder to watch.

Their job, Bud's and Mrs. Johnson's, was to grab the papers and place them on the table to collate and fold. For the folding part of the operation they used beautiful, old ivory folding knives: A full newspaper was folded once down the middle, vertically, then once down the middle, horizontally, and then once again, vertically. Each paper was folded three times.

The shop was a beehive on Thursdays, and Grandpa Noxon was busy with the mailing labels, made from long strips of paper, three inches wide, on which were printed the names and addresses of all the subscribers. He put them upside down on a table covered with dried paste, dipped a big paintbrush in a pot of flour paste, and swabbed the back of the labels—slopping paste over everything in the process. He then carried these labels over to the pile of newly folded newspapers and hand-labeled each one. The same kind of ivory knife was used for this operation—the flat of the blade held the label down, the edge was used to tear it off.

Bud was a "printer's devil," an apprentice—the obvious target of fun. Everyone played jokes on him, such as handing him hot lead slugs fresh from the linotype. He was sent over to the *Daily Camera* to ask "Gov." Paddock for spotted ink, and then, another time, for striped ink. The staffs of the two newspapers had fun at his expense. Once he was sent to fetch a left-handed monkey wrench, reporting to the *Camera* as an innocent and returning wise to the *Miner*.

Another practical joke, about linotype slugs, relied on a mystery. Did Bud know, Bob Estey, the linotype operator, inquired seriously, what caused those tiny holes in the slugs? No, he did not, his eyes widening. "Type lice," Estey declared, a vexation to almost every news operation there was. He then spread the slugs out in some water and told the boy that if he looked "real close," he could actually see the type lice eating holes in the lead. Of course, once Bud's face got down low so he could see, Estey squeezed the slugs together so all the water squirted up in the boy's face. Uproarious laughter issued from all.

One Thursday afternoon instead of going to his job, Bud went straight home from school. When Grandpa Noxon came home for supper, he asked what had happened. Only then did Bud realize it was Thursday and he hadn't gone to work. He had let his grandfather down. Yet the old man insisted that his newspaper folder take his thirty-five-cent wages, pressing the coins into his hand. "No, no! I don't *want* that money," Bud protested. But Grandpa Noxon insisted. It was their labor contract.

CARPENTER AND EDYTH would not visit that summer of 1937, so it was hoped Carpenter would come for a long-planned family reunion at Christmas.

The man sent his regrets.

Bud tried pleading:

December 11, 1937

Dear Dad,

We are all so disappointed that you couldn't come that we think
that if we asked you especially your boss might change his mind.

We three have never been together Cristmas that I
remember anyway especialy on a big occasion like this. You
would meet a lot of people that we know that you haven't
seen before.

Please, Please, come it'll be *awful* dull without you and we
know it costs a lot of money but please come.

With love,

Bud

Carpenter sent telegrams and apologies. Bud submitted a dignified
report about a grand celebration, with twenty-five seated for dinner—even the colored cook from Alpha Chi Omega. He continued to
dabble in photography, his father's hobby—there was all that equipment the man had sent him, after all. But he was through feigning interest in it. He would gain the man's approval. Although the ultimate
how and why of that daunting task would take some figuring, of one
thing he was sure: it would be on his own exceptional terms.

So began Bud's many renegade years, beginning with the acquisition of a BB gun and culminating, episodically, with rare personal
achievement and self-destruction of equal virtuosity: six cars totaled.
Four marriages. Seven children. From all of them, somehow, boy and
man always managed to walk away.

THE ACQUISITION OF a BB gun inevitably translates into unsupervised
target practice. Bud was no exception. Street lights were irresistible targets, for when the BB shattered the glass, the filament flamed up and
gave a wonderful light just before dying. To avoid suspicion, he moved
on to lights on Cascade, south of his house, and ruined many city light
bulbs with his trusty gun. He learned a lot about the range and trajectory of BBs, lobbing them quite a distance, like tiny mortars, some-

times using as a target grazing horses about 125 yards away. Their startled flinches helped him gauge the accuracy of his lob shots.

Sound effects with BBs were good entertainment, too. The galvanized pail in the backyard, filled with water, produced satisfying plinks and plonks when hit. Bud was thus engaged one afternoon when one of his BBs ricocheted and caught a White Leghorn in the throat. Killed her right off. Grandma Noxon came out and picked up the hen and said, "I wonder what happened to this chicken." Bud didn't tell her. Of course, she knew all along, and they ate it for supper that night.

By the age of twelve, Bud had acquired a large number of treasures—large at least for a boy during the Depression. He had a mummy-shaped eiderdown-filled sleeping bag, weapons of all sorts, including a BB gun and a slingshot, and a beanie made from a willow fork, which his grandfather had found for him down by the creek. He had a beautiful bow and some arrows, thanks to the L. E. Stemmler catalogue. But his most life-changing boyhood possession was a seven-eighths Arab mare named Lady Luck. She was the love of Bud's life, and he looks for her to this day in every open field he passes.

THE FORTY-ACRE PASTURE that held Lady was still superintended in 1937 by the legendary Mr. Arthur Hayden, the Cockney-born park ranger who was a guest at the Noxon supper table nearly every Sunday. When Bud began getting interested in camping and the outdoors, the Boer War veteran gave him his army blanket and several blanket pins with which to make a bedroll—gifts he kept for years.

While Bud was glad Lady had a great big pasture all to herself, it made catching her nearly impossible. Cajoling her into a bridle was beyond the boy's impatient young ways. In his small arsenal of tricks he had only an oat-filled cowboy hat, which was creased with a slanting dent in front, like Tom Mix's. Naturally, the young mare viewed Bud and his hat with caution. He meant to ride her and she knew it. He chased her all over that pasture, cursing like a sailor, in a game that took half an hour or so before Lady agreed that the oats required tasting.

Vic Noxon eventually mentioned his grandson's cussing—which neighbors blocks away reported hearing—observing that men who cursed and swore did so out of sheer poverty of language. *Poverty of language.* Bud mulled the construction. Like everything else the old man said, this remark made a big impact on him.

Lady had an unusual red roan coat, but Bud called her a "strawberry roan" because of a cowboy song about a bronc who could "turn on a nickel and leave you some change." She also had a beautiful, braided brown-and-white bridle, with a gently curbed aluminum bit—a highly desirable feature from Lady's point of view, for during winter aluminum warms easily in your rider's hands and won't freeze your mouth. On Lady's back, he rode over open country that is now, in the early twenty-first century, nearly all built up with roads, housing, and university buildings.

Bud and his friends, the Kelso sisters, roamed the mesas south of Boulder, followed Bluebell Creek into the mountains, and found shade and water. They watched the sun set behind the Flatirons and waited for the fireflies to begin their blinking in the twilight. They caught them in their hands and wove them into their horses' manes, which glowed as they cantered home in the dark. The fireflies stayed put, they reasoned, because they were intoxicated by the smell of horses. Yet it was the children who were intoxicated.

IN THE YEARS before World War II, the Pow-Wow was Boulder's big summer event, which celebrated the county's mining, ranching, and farming heritage, all fast disappearing. Naturally, the Summer Pow-Wow of 1938 found Bud aspiring to be a cowboy. There were the double- and single-jacking competitions, a nod to hard-rock miners. For the ranch hands and aspiring cowboys like Bud there were competitions in bull riding, saddle-bronc riding, bull dozing, calf roping, and calf riding. He rode down to the important events that summer on the back of his speedy new horse, his wild cowboy heart pounding. But membership in the rodeo fraternity, he soon saw, required the proper tools. He had everything except the lariat.

So Bud saved his money and bought a thirty-five-foot hemp rope—not the best choice for a lariat, but sometimes you have to learn the hard way. To keep it from unraveling he back-spliced one end, but then didn't have a clue how to splice a loop in the other end. Once again Bud turned to his resident walking and talking encyclopedia, Grandpa Noxon, the man who had taught him so many things.

Bud found him after supper in the rocking chair next to Grandma's bed, where she was resting. He interrupted their conversation. Would Grandpa show him how to splice a loop in the other end of the rope so he could have a lasso? He would, Grandpa said, but first his grandson would have to make him a marlinspike. A marlinspike! The thirteen-year-old was proud he knew what a marlinspike was, but surprised to learn that he needed something used only aboard sailing ships, for he had read about them in *Captains Courageous* and *Mutiny on the Bounty*.

"Whittle it," Grandpa Noxon told the boy. "Use a piece of wood under the workbench in the basement, as long as it's oak or hickory." Bud did have hickory, he told him. He was stalling: In order to whittle a marlinspike he needed a pocketknife, but once again he had lost the last one Grandpa had given him. Need triumphed over shame, and Bud asked if he could borrow Grandpa's pocketknife. Without a remark or a raised eyebrow, the old man handed over his knife. Bud headed for the basement, where he sawed the wood to the right length, whittled it down to a taper, and started back upstairs.

But as he passed the tool cabinet Grandpa helped him build the winter before, and already scarred by many previous attempts at knife throwing, Bud decided to get in a few practice throws. Grandpa's knife hit right for the first two or three throws, so he moved back two steps to see if he could get it to stick after *two* turns in the air instead of one. It stuck all right, but not straight on, and the off-center weight of heavy handle snapped the three-inch blade smack in half.

Numb with dread, Bud struggled up the stairs, the knife and broken blade in one hand and the marlinspike in the other. Grandpa was coming down the stairs. Stopping short of the landing, the boy looked up, it seemed, at God, and silently he held up the broken knife for his grandfather to see. "*Pshaw,*" the old man snorted, "I'll have it fixed up good as new tomorrow."

Home from the office the next day, he pulled out his knife. The blade, Bud saw with chagrin, was ground down to a pitiful nubbin. A few weeks later his grandfather had a brand-new knife.

As NEWSPAPERS TOLD of impending war, Colorado's hard-rock mines lumbered into service again. Vic Noxon laughed with delight, for it had always been the gold and silver for him. And when fellow investors suggested a Boulder County mine up Left Hand Canyon, near Jimtown, he mortgaged the big house in a heartbeat. He informed Clara in the chicken yard, where she fainted away. It was to her grandson and kitchen confidant that she divulged the dark news. Thereafter, under cover of night once a month, knocking at a Boulder door, Buddy stood on the stoop with an envelope containing the shameful mortgage money.

"WE WERE MUCH disturbed," Toye wrote her husband in October 1938, "over the war, and I, for one, still am scared. . . . It looks now as if it will come just when Bud will have to help fight it." But Berlin was a long way from Boulder. Bud's letters were filled with his usual boasts and questions. He was the "top student" in his class. "I got a 99 in a social studies test," he wrote his father that fall, "and a 92 in arithmetic."

The autumn of 1939, at age seventy-five, Vic Noxon still worked every day. When Dr. Gilbert noticed a purplish blotch on his lip and blamed his pipe smoking, the old editor switched to cigars. He carried in his jacket pocket a small bottle of strychnine pills for his chest pains. The previous spring he had been ill with a kidney stone and made a visit to see his sole surviving sibling, Gertie, who lived in Tampa, Florida. Afterward, on a Sunday in October, he stood on the front lawn, speaking with old friends. He was working, he told them, on a story about his parents, Dr. and Mrs. A. M. Noxon—wanted to get the history down so no one would forget. In his head, too, was a first draft of his editorial that week. It concerned Lindbergh's controversial trip to Nazi munitions factories. His heart had troubled him the day before, so he accepted a car ride downtown, to his office at the *Miner*.

Bud was just then returning from the pasture on Lady's back, and tore around the corner at a gallop. Seeing Grandpa, he brought Lady to a dramatic, clod-flying stop on the front lawn, a bit of front-yard showmanship forbidden by Grandma Noxon. "Bye, Grandpa," Bud said as he waved. The old man took the cigar out of his mouth and waved back before getting into the car. His words made Bud's heart nearly burst: "Best kid rider I've ever seen."

GRANDPA NOXON DIED on the eve of World War II, succumbing at his typewriter. Grandma followed him eighteen months later, dying in her bed, surrounded by her children. For Bud it had seemed he would always be seven going on eight and always his house would sit on the hill, with Grandpa in his den, Grandma in the kitchen, Mom upstairs on the sleeping porch. But there was the mortgage now, and the two sisters, Alice and Toye, forced to sell the house as the world plunged into war. That last summer of 1941, the sisters clipped Clara's yellow and red roses. The dried petals they placed in a Chinese ginger jar. One can still smell the roses.

PART

TWO

SKY

5

I Am Now a Naval Aviation Cadet

*It's your opportunity to be a Flying Officer of the Navy . . . your chance
to get into action as a pilot in the finest, the fastest, the most powerful
warplanes in the world—the Navy planes that strike first, strike hardest
wherever the foe is found.*

*The Navy needs men to fly these planes. Needs them urgently—today.
It wants men of officer calibre—physically fit, mentally
alert—men trained to act, to command, to be leaders.*

—U.S. Navy recruitment advertisement

"I have tried for months," Toye wrote her husband, "following every lead and using all my ingenuity, to find a way for Bud to do some real skiing." Trying for months with all her ingenuity led Toye to Kirk and Libby Kirkendahl. They taught Bud to ski: "He should become an expert," she reported with some pride, "because apparently he is quite good already."

The Kirkendahls were a new kind of Colorado pioneer. In the late 1930s they were building their own ski slope west of a place called the Idaho drift. And in the sad years after Grandpa's death, Bud found a freedom and beauty that changed his young life. On skis in Colorado's back country, he found the world was much larger, and far grander, than Flagstaff Mountain, or downtown Denver, or the street where his house stood. More important, with skis on his feet, his world became thrillingly fast.

In the mountains, too, he could witness first-hand something new and important: the practical application of engineering know-how in the service of an enterprise larger than himself. He watched Kirk and Libby solve, on a small scale, two of recreational skiing's biggest problems. The first was shelter for an overnight; the second was getting to the top of the mountain. For shelter, the Kirkendahls located an old miner's cabin, which sat on an abandoned claim west of Caribou, a ghost town in the mountains behind Boulder. After two summers of work, it became everything a ski cabin should be: cozy, weather-tight, and able to sleep at least twelve skiers. Four wooden bunks stacked two high (with canvas curtains, to keep in the heat) were each wide enough to sleep three adults. Wooden sideboards held straw bedding, atop which everyone put their bedrolls. Filling a corner was a huge wood-burning stove. It had a water well that provided hot water for washing up in the morning. Ten yards from the front door was the outhouse.

Getting to the top of the mountain was achieved with the help of a 1928 Chevy sedan—and a lot of ingenuity. In the late summer of 1937, the Kirkendahls drove the Chevy up to Caribou, past the Idaho mine. Beyond the end of the dirt road and three miles farther west, Kirk and Libby drove the Chevy over the ridge, down across the valley, past the peat bogs, and finally to the flat top of a mine dump above the miner's cabin. After removing the Chevy's wheels and body, they anchored the engine and chassis to the ground. Attaching a large spool of cable to the rear axle, they ran it to a huge pulley anchored to yet another mine dump up the mountain. The cable was then brought back down the mountain to be attached to the body of the Chevy, now mounted on skids. Come winter, all they needed was to have someone up the hill fire up the engine, put it in gear, let out the clutch, and allow themselves to be hauled up the mountain on comfortable, upholstered car seats.

Bud skied every chance he got, November through June, and on Sundays wore ski boots beneath his altar boy's cassock to make for faster getaways to the slopes. He could easily have spent the rest of his life skiing were it not for Pearl Harbor, which changed everything.

The day of Japan's surprise attack, Sunday, December 7, 1941, Bud and his pal Merle Skipp were standing on the front lawn at Bud's house. Toye ran out the front door to tell them that Japanese planes had attacked the fleet at Pearl Harbor, in the Hawaiian Islands. The boys looked at each other with that focused, we-will-not-die thrill boys feel when a glorious war is at hand.

They would have signed up right then and there, but they were juniors in high school, trapped in a birthday-imposed limbo. In the meantime, Bud could only watch and wait while his new heroes, Navy and Marine fighter pilots, died at Wake Island, flying F4F Grumman Wildcats, and died some more during the Battle of Midway, flying Douglas TBD Devastators. He clipped out everything he could find about combat aircraft, filling a scrapbook with illustrations and photographs from every imaginable source. The United States had the finest aviators in the world. But that first year of the war they flew aircraft that cost them their lives.

Bud had always wanted to fly. Before Pearl Harbor, however, flying was but one among many glamorous occupations he imagined for his future. Olympic-level skiing, the downhill, topped the list of dreams, followed by cowboy or rodeo work—even lumberjacking. In the gym he pursued gymnastics, weight lifting, and wrestling. He competed in both swimming and diving. The outdoors offered archery, tennis, and horseback riding. He excelled in marksmanship, either rifle or pistol.

But Pearl Harbor had been attacked, fighter pilots were gods, and Bud's course was set forever. He and his high school classmates all expected to be "in it" before too long, so he began considering his options. There were three different air corps to consider—Army, Navy, Marines. In his view, the Army Air Corps had superior fighters—particularly the P-40s that General Claire Chennault's Flying Tigers had already made famous in China.

But for Bud it was the Navy Air Corps or nothing. With its battle cruisers, destroyers, and aircraft carriers (the latter being deployed for the first time in war), the Navy could bring the battle *to* the enemy. In this view the boy was powerfully persuaded by a pivotal battle, waged on his last day as a high-school junior, June 4, 1942. It came to be called the Battle of Midway, and it changed the entire course of the war. But he needed extra coursework to prepare for the Navy's tough entrance exams, so that summer Bud took courses in radio work and an extra-credit aeronautics course his senior year. The Navy took only the best. So the best was what Bud determined to be.

Pearl Harbor changed sleepy Boulder forever. High-school seniors, plus nearly everyone at C.U., signed up en masse. As the university converted its facilities into military training centers, the campus filled with sailors. Bud wrote his father long letters about his studies, taking pains to justify his interest in flying. He wanted his father to know how well he was doing in school. He was one of three juniors, he explained in one letter, nominated to be student body president senior year. Twenty years—to the day—before he made his spaceflight, the high-school junior was feeling grown up and, in his own modest way, accomplished:

May 24, 1942

Dear Dad,

I waited so long to write this letter to you so that I could give you the results of the school elections.

The Head Boy elections were first and I was one of the final three candidates. We had to get up before the student body and give talks, Henry Hutcheson and I sorta split the major vote and Warren Foote got it. They then had Cheerleader elections and I got that.... Also, I got on the editorial board of the Junior edition of the *Owl*. All in all, my Junior year has been very successful. Now that I'm through with my bragging, I'll get on to some news.

About this summer: they are offering two new courses at B.H.S.... They are brought about by the war ... to give the future pilots better training.... I could take the primary radio mechanics course in summer school and then I thought I could drop Spanish III in winter school and take the Aeronautical ground school course in its place. I had planned to take a CAA course in C.U., and this is the approved ground school course for that subject, and then when I got to C.U. I could start right in flying without having to take the ground school over again

and I'd be a long way ahead of everyone else. CAA mean Civil
Aeronautics Association.

   I think these courses would be very good for me even if I
don't get in the air corps. I would be very happy to have you
write me and tell me what you think of this plan and whether
you think it would be wise to do that.... Other fellows have
their dads right handy when they can have long talks with
them about this but I don't, so write me a long letter....

Bud's father didn't reply. Again, the son wrote: "I'm taking the
aeronautics course in winter school and already have the books published by the government called Math for pilot trainees and Physics for
pilot trainees. They're a cinch." He wanted a pat on the back more
than anything: "I really like to write you and tell you all about things,"
he confessed, "but you don't ever tell me what you want to know."

A new draft law took effect as Bud, class of 1943, began his senior
year at Boulder High. Toye wrote a long letter to Carpenter, trying to
explain how it would affect their son. Still no answer. Bud felt frustrated. He resented having to expend so much energy on a mute
ghost. He wanted his father's blessing, if nothing else. Again he wrote,
in December 1942. A year had passed since Pearl Harbor, and in six
months Bud—Scott—would turn eighteen:

   You see, I've decided after a lot of deep thought that I want to
   fly.... That simmers it down to which branch of the armed
   services I want to go into. Nothing can sway that decision....
   The Army Air Corps has the best planes, I think. But they're so
   crowded. Then, too, if you flunk the enlistment exam... they
   draft you into anything *they* think you are suited for—
   bombardier, navigator, or anything else, even a buck private
   (and I don't like that so hot). That only leaves the Navy Air
   Corps. They by all means give you the best training because
   when you come out of that you are not only a good pilot but
   also a good bombardier, navigator, gunner and everything else
   that an airplane needs.... If you make the grade, you can go
   into the Navy Air Corps as an Ensign or into the Marine Air
   Corps as a Lieutenant Junior grade. Now I *like* that.

Now the Question is What to do?...I could enlist in the
Navy now, with Mom's permission and yours, and give them all
my papers. Then when I am 18 I could take the test and start
basic training immediately....I want to get in the war now.

After reading through all this three times I can say that it
pretty nearly presents my side of the problem. Now I want
yours. Tell me everything you can because you're the only
fellow I can talk to....

More later. This is all for now but please please write me
soon.

Two months passed and still his father hadn't responded. Bud
blamed himself. His letters weren't persuasive enough. His desire to fly
airplanes (the extent and intensity of which he carefully disguised as
sober career decisions) must have seemed foolhardy and childish. So
he wrote his father again, on February 11, 1943:

Thursday night

Dear Pa,
Long time no hear, and you owe me the letter too. I think that
if we had one thing in common we would get a lot more letters
written and we would get along better too. So much for that.

Tomorrow I leave for Denver to take my primary physical
for entrance into the Naval Air Corps reserve. If I pass all the
tests I have to go through he said I would probably be called
before the first of August. This may be a shock to you but let
me assure you that a lot of thought is behind it....Professor
Hutchinson at the University said he thought it was the thing to
do and he recommended the Navy Air Corps....In short,
everyone I have talked to seems to think that without doubt it
is the thing to do. Here are their reasons.

In the first place they all say that I am going to be in it
before a year is up anyway, so get in now while I can get what I
want. I've decided that what I wanted was the Naval Air Corps.
People have told me that I am the kind of person they want for

a pilot and from the very little you know of me you should be able to see that. In the recommendation letter, Mr. Easley my aeronautics teacher said I was especially adept at the kind of sciences and was top man in his aeronautics classes, and he teaches two of them, so even though I do do a lot of things that you don't approve of, I do all right in *anything* that I am interested in and really try to accomplish. I do a lot of messing around and I really shouldn't but I don't suppose that I ever will be very sorry about it. I would rather be a moron than one of those fellows that studies every minute of the day.

Bud had just devoured Charles Lindbergh's autobiography, in which, with no shame, the great aviator confessed to having been an indifferent engineering student, never applying himself—until his studies were linked with flying airplanes. Finally, a *role* model! Bud knew he was the same—all the book and head work unbearable if not tied to the flying in his heart and soul.

In this letter to his father, the high-school senior mentioned several important adults in his life: two uncles; two men at C.U., Professor Hutchinson and Coach Vavra; and his teachers at Boulder High. All of them thought well of the young man. But still his father's good opinion eluded him. Bud wracked his brain, castigated himself and his lazy ways, read and reread his draft letters to find the hidden flaw so glaring to his old man:

As I look over this letter I can see what you are going to think. When I get started, I don't take time out for spelling or punctuation. I'm really not so illiterate as the letter would have you think. Mr. Wardner, my lit teacher, said I wrote interestingly and fluently and he thought it was a pity that I didn't try to write the whole story of my life. That's what he wrote on my autobiography paper.

More Soon

Please Write

Folded in the same envelope was a note from Toye. From its tone, it is clear she was unhappy about their imminent divorce. She also knew more than she was telling Bud. Carpenter thought their son could avoid serving! Toye, again, took up her son's cause:

> Naturally he does not wish to avoid service, and naturally he
> does not consider it in the same light we do. Our age, our
> temperaments, our circumstances make each of the three of us
> look at it differently. To avoid service by reason of occupation
> would be humiliation to one of his temperament, and by
> temperament I do not mean that which is the result of his
> youth but his basic manner of thought and action.

Since Carpenter did not seem to grasp the facts of the new draft law, she wrote with emphasis:

> He *is* going to have to enter some branch of the service, there
> is no getting around it so far as I can see. He wants naval
> aviation.... He really has considered it as sanely as it is possible
> for him to do so. I have left it for him to work it out with the
> men of his acquaintance and with the military liaison officers at
> the university. I have told him that he can have my permission,
> for to me it seems unavoidable. Does he have yours?

> I am sure you will realize that with his going from home the
> purpose for my life will be ended and that I have not given my
> consent without grave consideration. Selfish love must not
> prevent his chance to live his own life. Fate alone has the right
> to do so.

BUD PRESENTED HIMSELF the next day, February 12, 1943, to the U.S. Navy's recruiting office at Lowry Air Field in Denver. Still his father had not written.

"I was accepted." With those words Bud informed his father about the satisfactory outcome of his preliminary exams at Lowry. He enclosed papers for Carpenter to sign (Bud was still a minor) and explained that the situation was getting complicated. The Navy had informed Bud that for him to become an aviation cadet, he needed to take some additional exams. For these he needed to report to Twelfth Naval District Headquarters, in San Francisco, California. The tension was too much for the teenager's roiling emotions: "I lay awake nights thinking about getting in," he wrote his father, adding, "if I don't make it, I'm going to commit suicide."

Finally, a month later, an approving letter! Bud answered right away with a puppyish-sounding confession:

> You know, a lot of times I'm inclined to think that you are a rather narrow-minded individual who simply refuses to think about things the way I do. . . . But your last letter was really swell. I am sorry truly if I seem to defend myself and my ideas against you and I will try not to let it happen again. The letter made you seem very open-minded and made me feel good. The way you started the letter by saying "Dear Son" also made me feel good because I have always wanted someone to call me son and I would rather have my father call me son than by my own name.

Bud's good news about a free trip to San Francisco was soon complicated: It would take weeks for the Navy-issued scrip (a check) to reach him. He had no money and virtually no time—in twenty-four days the high-school senior would turn into an eighteen-year-old pumpkin. The news destroyed him. But Boulder was then a small town, and Toye knew everyone. She quickly located a young woman driving to California the next weekend to visit her sweetheart before he shipped out overseas, and arranged for Bud to go along. Ever the risk-taker, she borrowed the sixty dollars her seventeen-year-old needed for the trip, writing her husband with news that he, Carpenter, would pay her back: "There is, of course, the chance that he will not qualify, but it was a chance worth taking. He was elated over passing the physical," she added with a mother's pleasure, "for it is generally conceded that to pass the physical for V-5 one must be perfect."

IN 1943, TWELFTH NAVAL District Headquarters was housed in the Ferry Building, on San Francisco's Embarcadero, then a tough neighborhood catering mainly to sailors on liberty. Bud arrived on a Saturday and checked into a cheap hotel in the area. Early the next morning, when he would normally have been in his altar boy's cassock for the nine o'clock service, there he was, wandering through the Embarcadero. He stepped into an empty bar and watched while the rubble was swept out and the place aired. He would never forget the smells that bright Sunday morning—drunken sailor breath, stale cigarette smoke, spilled beer, and the ocean.

Feeling a little like a hayseed, Bud toured the city—walking around, taking buses, and checking in with family friends, as his mother had requested. He began to feel more at ease. On Monday the various examinations began. There were two "mentals" and two physicals. The physicals had gone well. He knew he had good eyesight, but 20-10, the doctor said, was something rare. The intelligence tests covered the usual subjects: vocabulary, reading comprehension, mathematical and mechanical aptitude, and some physics.

Bud passed, with scores in the high nineties. His spirits in the stratosphere, he began composing a triumphant mental draft to his father. On April 11, 1943, at 7:38 P.M., he wired his mother the great news:

MRS M S CARPENTER=

714 LINCOLN PL

DEAR MOM I AM NOW A NAVAL AVIATION CADET WAS SWORN IN SAT-
URDAY 430 LEAVE HERE MONDAY WITH CHALLENGER ON ORDERS.
SHOULD BE HOME WEDNESDAY LOVE=BUD.

He was strapped for cash—God, he was always strapped for cash—and sent another wire. When news reached his hotel that the money had arrived, Bud flew out the door in a delirium of joy and began running to the Western Union station, blocks and blocks away. He ended up sprinting the entire distance. All the while he marveled at his endurance, for he kept expecting to tire yet felt no fatigue, only strength. So on he ran. And as he ran it struck him as a kind of miracle or vindication: "I'm not only an aviation cadet," Bud thought with joy, "I'm a *superhuman* aviation cadet."

He still had braces on his teeth. Years passed before he realized his race that April day during World War II was fueled by sea-level amounts of oxygen. He had been training at altitude all his young life.

IN DECEMBER 1941, when the United States entered the war, the Navy had a combined total of 6,600 active-duty aviators (Navy and Marine). This number ballooned to 26,453 by the time Bud's class of 1943 received their high school diplomas. Not all of them could be trained, and serve in combat, at once, so the Navy created the V-12a program, essentially a college scholarship for cadets that allowed the Navy to warehouse its V-5 recruits—officer-caliber aviation cadets. Some young men, like Bud, entered V-12a straight from high school, others transferred from civilian college programs, and still others were enlisted men who sacrificed their active-service ratings for an education and officer training.

By the end of 1942 the Navy had reached its recruitment goal, which was to have 2,500 new flight students enter training each month. On April 15, 1943—four days after Scott Carpenter was sworn in—word came down that the Navy had a surfeit of recruits. Although it continued recruiting (no one knew how long the war would last), the Navy began to institute longer training periods for each phase of the aviation curriculum: Pre-flight, Primary, and Advanced flight training.

Intensive drilling was a constant.

For Scott, World War II would therefore be three semesters of college in the V-12a program at Colorado College, followed by Pre-flight in the spring of 1945, at St. Mary's College, in Moraga, California. He had just begun Primary flight training, at Ottumwa, Iowa, when the Bomb was dropped, in August 1945.

But in April 1943 the end of the war was nowhere in sight, and Bud knew only what the Navy was telling him:

April 20, 1943

Dear Dad,

Well I'm back from Frisco and boy did I have a good time. I went through a lot of stiff tests..., but I got a 97 on my mental.

I was sworn in on the tenth and maybe you got a letter like the one Mom got. I saw the whole darn city and everything in it and came back on a Pullman, which was my first train ride that I can remember. I also passed my V-12 tests (V-12 is the officer training program) and was asked to go to Denver for an interview. The Navy's really fighting to get me, aren't they?

Your loving son,
Bud

Bud returned to Boulder feeling like a hero. There were huzzahs and claps on the back from buddies. Getting into the V-12a program was a great coup. However, for Merle, Bud's best friend, there were no hurrahs. The phenomenal athlete was declared 4-F because of a football injury to his knee. In 1962—after another injury ended his cycling career—Merle took his life.

IT WAS FEAST OR FAMINE with Bud's father, who for his son's graduation had sent him a nice watch. But, as Bud explained, the timepiece was entirely inadequate for his impending combat missions. He knew what he wanted: "It is stainless steel, nonmagnetic, shockproof, waterproof, dustproof, and has a sweep second hand, minute hand, hour hand, and numbers that are coated with radium so they shine at night.... Then I can tell the zero hour at night to the very second."

Now mad with the power of youth and the Navy's recent vindication, the graduating senior asked for a car. "There comes a time in every boy's life," he explained, "when he would give everything he owned to have a car." As with the watch, he knew exactly what he wanted: "The best Ford V-8 in town." It had new tires and got 23 miles to the gallon. In short, Bud concluded, "it's just the slickest car a fellow could ever want."

His father declined to feed the spending conflagration, so Bud sold his Penzel-Mueller clarinet for one hundred and fifty dollars and earned the remaining fifty dollars working two summer jobs. For a few months he owned, drove, and was seen in his very own car—a 1934 Ford V-8 coupe. He could take a girl dancing at the Dark Horse

Tavern, in Estes Park. He could drive to Denver to see his grandparents and have his braces removed. He could roar down to Pearl and Broadway at two in the morning, pull a one-eighty in the intersection, and race back up the Hill. With fuel rationing in effect, he rated only a low-priority A-ration card—and, at ten cents a gallon, gas was expensive the summer of 1943. But with a quarter from Dot Reed, his girlfriend, and a quarter of his own, they could put five gallons in the car, which meant a hundred miles of driving and freedom only an eighteen-year-old can imagine.

The Ford was black, with solid hood sides, and had SUPERCHARGED painted on the back as part of the trim. Because the trunk was machined for a rumble seat, Bud located old seats and the proper hinges at the junkyard, and turned the trunk around. Now the car could carry six instead of just three. Next he cut down the gearshift lever to a hot rod–style five inches, added Smitties (mufflers that gave the car a roaring sound), and sanded the dashboard down to a bright, polished steel. It had a dandy radio.

One of Bud's jobs that summer, as he was awaiting orders, was busing tables for V-12 officer candidates training at C.U. for service in the "black-shoe" Navy. Fleet officers wore black shoes. Scott (as he was known to the Navy) was to be "brown-shoe"—so-called for the brown shoes only aviators wear. His second job was driving an ice truck. Even the most menial jobs impart lessons. While busing tables Scott saluted one sailor he particularly admired. But he was holding a stack of dirty trays in his right hand and received a stern reprimand. Not only was the eighteen-year-old out of uniform, he had used his *left* hand for the salute.

Meanwhile Scott waited for orders—for something to *happen* to him. "A lot of my buddies who joined the Marines and Sea Bees 3 or 4 months ago are *already* overseas," he wrote his father in frustration. "I just about jumped out of my shoes," he added, when he saw that "one of the guys at Boulder High was on Bougainville and is now on Tarawa." He'd seen his classmate's picture in *Life* magazine.

Not until November 1943 was there room for Scott at the V-12 program at Colorado College, where he roomed in Jackson House with about seventy-five other enlisted Marines and sailors. A classmate had four major Pacific engagements to his credit. "I learn more from my mate from Guadalcanal," he wrote his father with disgust, "than I do from a whole month of classes." He would have complained more, but he was too tired and too busy being drilled to within an inch of his life. Scott may have thought he was fit, but the Navy found ways to exhaust the fittest eighteen-year-old in the world. He looked "very tired," Grandma Carpenter reported to her son after one of Scott's visits through Denver. She'd begun preparing dinner, she wrote, and her grandson just "lay down on the floor and went sound asleep."

He hitchhiked everywhere, like everyone else in the service. Toye now drove the Ford. On a trip home to Boulder, standing on Aurora, Scott saw his mother in the Ford coupe, turning west onto Aurora Avenue, the Smitties roaring. He started to wave, but she just dropped from sight, disappearing below the dashboard. He laughed out loud, knowing immediately what had happened. Toye was so frail that to shift gears while keeping her foot on the clutch, she had to hunker down so she could put all her weight into that modified, five-inch shift lever. But she loved driving that car, and never once complained.

Scott also saw his father that fall in Palmer Lake. In all this time the man had not once commented on the war, or on his son's role in it. At the train station, saying good-bye after their visit, father and son were mindful of how strained their relationship had become and pledged each other a new, more regular correspondence. Their letters were different after that—still sporadic, but more grown-up. Scott's envelopes, which his father saved along with the letters, began to sport new, Navy-type braggadocio, some with "Sailors Mail—Rush Like Hell" written on the flap. The letters themselves, to his mother and his father, were laced with a new lingo: "Well, long time no-um hear-um from-um you-um," and "Hey, pal!" "Hey, frien!' "—pidgen from far-away ports. Behind the braggadocio, of course, lurked homesickness. Scott had never before had to correspond with his mother.

She wrote wonderful letters. The first ones she signed "Mom." But Scott was so homesick that memories of sounds and sights from Boulder besieged him, especially the sound of a particular bell his mother had always used to call him home. She hadn't the lung strength to call his name. He finally broke down, asking her, please, to sign her letters "Tinkle." And she did, drawing a small bell ("Come home!") alongside her new pen name.

When Scott next wrote his father, he was a seaman second class serving at Alameda Naval Air Station, Oakland, where the Navy had parked him and some classmates until spots opened up in Pre-flight. The envelope was postmarked November 29, 1944:

Dear Dad,

...

I took the train to Alameda. We are attached to a transport squadron here and the duty is pretty good, chow excellent, but this base is so big you have to walk 2 or 3 miles to get anywhere. I've been in the cockpit of every Navy plane and a few Army planes too, P.-51, P.-47, B.-26, B.-24. These little Mustangs (P.51's) are the sweetest little ships I have ever seen.... In the morning we have classes in engine construction and operation, swimming, football, and gymnastics. In the afternoon we are all given special details. I got to load some mail on the Mars, the Navy's largest flying boat. The Mars is longer, wider, and heavier than the B-29.

Before the end of 1944 he wrote his father once more, this time from the long-awaited post at Pre-flight, St. Mary's College—one of the happiest times in Scott's life. It showed in his letters, written in a distinctive, nearly beautiful, adult cursive. He was almost twenty years old. By April 1945, from the sound of his letters, Scott was ready for an acorn battle, fair or otherwise, with his father. He related his accomplishments, sounding both surprised and nonchalant about having endured Pre-flight, where the competition got even tougher and the washout rates were legendary. Adopting the all-business tone of a Navy man, he wrote: "Received the request for more information on how goes it at USN Pre-Flight West." In the "first shooting we've done here...my target was the best in the Third Battalion." He lost a wrestling bout "by points in the third round." But the victor, he explained, had a wrestling scholarship at Michigan, "so at least I lost to a good man."

Scott went on to win the regimental wrestling championship in the 155-pound division—breaking his thumb in the process. It was a small price for getting his picture in the hometown paper. Writing to her husband, Toye reported how happy their son was "to have made the grade. He . . . and one other Third Battalion boy had broken the station record," which for three years had been 3.87. They earned a 4.0.

Half of Scott's classmates washed out at St. Mary's, which for him was the endurance and academic test of a lifetime. He met George Nissen on the mats and trampolines at St. Mary's, where Nissen was already a famed gymnastics coach, forming a lifetime friendship with the man. Scott also found that when he really buckled down, he could do well—as well as the best. He tried to explain it to his father in a short letter written on the Fourth of July: "I was one of 70 out of 141 in the third battalion who came through." He was proud to have excelled at Pre-flight, but Pre-flight wasn't war or combat flying. While he had been wrestling and studying and celebrating his twentieth birthday at St. Mary's, U.S. Marines his age and younger had given their lives to secure Iwo Jima.

THE TAIL END OF THE WAR was near, but still Scott was ordered to Ottumwa, Iowa, home to one of the Navy's sixteen Primary flight training schools. He arrived in mid-July after hitchhiking with a friend through Colorado all the way from St. Mary's. On July 22 he reported his new whereabouts to his father. He was "on watch" and it was "0200." He was finally getting some flight time: "I just finished my first hop and I really (I *mean* really) got what the Navy calls 'wrung out.' We did every aerobatic maneuver in the books and then some. I had a lot of fun and I think I'm going to like this flying business a lot."

At Ottumwa, Scott learned how to play hearts, dated WAVEs, and broke his foot. It was because of the WAVEs that he broke his foot: He had had enough beer, one night, to ruin his better judgment, so when he and his date walked through the gym on their way to see a movie,

Scott decided to show off his trampoline ability. But when he hopped up, he discovered the mat was split right down the middle. Naturally, he still had to perform the double back flip he told his date he could do. But he landed short, jammed his foot into that mat, and broke his metatarsal arch. He went through with the rest of the date that night, watching the movie in a lot of pain. But the next morning the pain was even worse. They wouldn't do anything at sick bay. X-rays didn't show the break until a year later, after he was in another, more serious, accident.

At Ottumwa, Scott accumulated eight hours in a Stearman N2S, an open-cockpit biplane. Called the "Yellow Peril," it had been the standard Navy trainer since the 1930s. The instructor pilot sat in the aft cockpit and spoke to the student pilot (who occupied the front seat) through a Gosport tube—a Royal Air Force term for the primitive mouthpiece that transmitted the instructor's voice to earpieces in the student's helmet. Students could listen to the instructor, but not reply. It reminded Scott of the speaking tube his mother used in Boulder.

The N2S has a tail wheel instead of a nose wheel and is called a tail dragger. It is notoriously susceptible to ground loops. For example, if on takeoff the nose begins to drift left—because of torque or crosswind or other reasons—the pilot has to catch it in a hurry, with *right* rudder, so it doesn't overpower what little directional stability the plane has. If he does not, he just does a spin in the middle of the runway, or the tarmac, or the dirt (whatever he happens to be taxiing on). The spin can get up fast enough that trainees end up dragging a wing tip—resulting in a damaged airplane, which is bad on their record.

Tail dragging is easy to remedy, if you haven't grown up sledding. Scott's story is that his Colorado upbringing, the sledding in particular, served him badly with the N2S. He had established a habit with sledding that had become pure instinct: Push the right runner with your right foot, which forces the runners around to the left, and you turn to the left. If you push the runner with your left foot, this bends the runners away from your left foot, so you turn right. It's just the opposite in an airplane, and he had to unlearn a muscle instinct. You push on your right foot, you turn right. Left foot, turn left. On almost all his takeoffs at Ottumwa—maybe all of them—the instructor pilot had to take corrective action because Scott instinctively added left rudder to counteract the torque, which only made it worse. He thinks he may have scared everybody who first flew with him.

"THE WAR IS OVER," Scott wrote his father on September 1, 1945. Obviously his father knew the war was over. Writing his father somehow made the news more real. The Navy was about to demobilize all of its aspiring aviators. As a consequence, the young man was in a funk: "I don't know what to think....I haven't done a damn thing for the war and I feel sort of yellow for getting out now, with two out of three years toward my goal under my belt with nothing to show for my efforts."

The prospect of returning to Boulder afforded him little cheer. There was no home for him there. College life seemed tame, and fraternity life juvenile, after his two years of preparing so intensively for war. Again that old feeling of dislocation returned. He thought he'd found something greater than his own life, and now it was evaporating. Like most other World War II veterans, with or without time overseas, Scott was confused and not a little depressed. Worse, he was having to make decisions about the future, which had been the Navy's job since he was eighteen—and that future, moreover, had always meant flying.

IN SEPTEMBER 1945 Scott was demobilized in Shoemaker, California. On a spur he hitchhiked to New Jersey to see his father, knocking on his door at six-thirty in the morning. Carpenter was shaving. "Great Scott!" he said in surprise. It was one of the man's favorite expressions. He took his son to the Givaudan plant at Delawanna, introduced him around, and said he had been flying planes for the Navy. Then the senior Carpenter stood back, hooking his thumbs into the armholes of his vest—the picture of paternal pride. He and Edyth took the young man to Radio City Music Hall and afterward to some nightclubs. Before he left for Colorado—he had to register for courses—his father took him to Saks Fifth Avenue and bought him a fifty-dollar camel-hair sport coat.

"I am very glad he is to be with you for a visit," Toye wrote on October 2. "You can do a great deal for him in his readjustment out of the service—which by the way is not going to be too easy for any of them." She had good news, though. Boulder Community Hospital had hired her as medical records librarian, a part-time job, in view of her part-time strength. "I like it," she said, "and they haven't fired me yet, and I really don't think they are going to."

Upon returning, Scott visited his Carpenter grandparents and his Uncle Claude, still living on Quince Street, in Denver. Grandma's health had declined—not in body so much as in mind. Grandpa described her as "forgetful" and "nervous." She began misplacing her purse, although in truth she had taken to hiding it, in her fits of paranoia. Then she could never find it, convenient proof that it had been stolen. Worse, every afternoon Ruby became fretful, suddenly remembering "an appointment." The police would find her hours later, lost and agitated, and bring her home. Worst of all were her tirades and rages against her gentle, quiet husband, Marion. Eventually even son and husband together couldn't manage her care, and Ruby Frye Carpenter was committed to Pueblo, where Colorado maintained its enormous state asylum. She died there in 1954 at the age of eighty-two—a sad end for Buddy's early, fierce champion.

BACK IN POSTWAR Boulder, and back in school, Scott wrote his father, sounding not a little like Holden Caulfield.

November 23, 1945

Dear Dad,

...

Not much exciting around here has happened. I have been
a pretty active fraternity man since I got here. It is a good way
to meet people but the shallowness of the friendships at first are
disgusting to me now. All these nicely-nice people... when
nobody really gives a damn are beginning to get me down. This
is no thing to get started on in a letter so I'll quit. It is just a

little new to me now and I'll get used to it I suppose. I can't be independent any longer is all.

C.U. reviewed Scott's Navy transcript—three semesters of V-12 education—and declared him a junior. He was back in college in an altered hometown. "School goes as follows," he penned a disconsolate report to his father: "4 hours of beginning calculus, 2 hours of astronomy, 5 hours of.... My goal at present is Engineering and that is all I know.... everything I do looks hopeless—I don't know what I want to do and it is a *hell* of a feeling." Toye concurred: "What he left at home was gone with the winds of war and the two years." Their son, she wrote, had "no hold on the future."

Scott's postwar fog continued, enlivened periodically by love squalls kicked up by an entrancing High Plains beauty, Mary-Ellen Wait. C.U. had gone so far as to confer a full academic scholarship on her—in "P Chem," his father's field. Scott was jealous. He was living more or less independently, renting the basement rooms at the Skipps' house on Sixteenth Street. His mother saw him enough to know his state of mind, which was unraveling. He hated school and worked three jobs—never more than thirty hours a week, to comply with the G.I. Bill restrictions. Never enough to do anything.

All that summer of 1946, in his spare time Scott poured every cent he made and every cent his father sent him into his 1934 Ford coupe. The heater was exhaust-powered, with a custom-made air scoop of sheet metal that picked up air from behind the fan. He devised a way to duct it through another compartment, which went past the exhaust manifold, where it picked up red-hot air and vented it into the car through a little hole on the passenger-side floor. A little flap that pivoted on a screw turned the heater on or off. That metal flap and the ring were always red-hot, and his friends learned the hard way never to ride in the Ford barefoot.

Finally, when Scott ran out of engine parts to fuss over, he began to paint them. Soon the oil-filter can in the engine compartment was a glorious enameled red, and then the generator, too. When he finished painting selected engine parts, he sat and ogled the car in the driveway, its hood open.

It had been that way his whole life—Scott and his *things*. A pocket-knife, a willow whistle, the Penzel-Mueller clarinet, his priceless L. E. Stemmler bow and arrows, a cherished bridle, an eiderdown sleeping bag, and Boer war blanket pins. His Tom Mix cowboy hat. All of them talismans that conferred—*what*? Love? If so, Scott certainly loved them back. He polished, oiled, sharpened, tinkered with, painted, and improved all of them. Now it was the car. But for all his energy and attention and care lavished on the car, he remained a discouraged, drained, dislocated twenty-one-year-old veteran who hadn't done one damn thing in his life.

On Friday, the thirteenth of September 1946, Scott worked all day at a campus construction site. The night before Mary-Ellen, his on-again, off-again girlfriend, had angrily backed out of their Friday-night date, and he was miserable. She listed all the reasons she was unhappy with him. She fumed. Scott fumed back. He went to the Dark Horse anyway, taking instead Vicky Brunette, who had written him so many letters when he was away in the service. Afterward, past midnight, he drove Vicky to her home in Estes Park, where she lived with her parents, and headed down the mountain for Boulder. It was about one-fifteen and he was tired. Construction all day, a nasty lovers' quarrel, and then dancing all night. He was sleepy and did everything he could think of to stay awake: played the radio, smoked cigarettes, rolled down the window. The Colorado night air is cool in September. No one was on the road. He remembers approaching Strawstack Mountain for the final curve, and then the next thing he knew, he was jerking awake to hear a *thump-thump*, the sound and feel—he knew in that instant—of guard posts being sheared off at their base.

A Navy wife saved his life. Dot and her husband, Don Beeson, were driving down the mountain from Estes Park about an hour after Scott's car had left the road at what a patrolman later calculated was 80 miles per hour, crashed into the far side of an embankment, turned around, flipped over, and landed upside down at the bottom of a culvert. When Scott came to the first time, he found he was already outside the wrecked car. But he passed out.

He came to again, and this time was perplexed about a couple of important matters. *Why only one shoe?* he wondered before passing out again. When he came to a third time, he heard the sound of an approaching car. It was then or never, Scott knew, and he began clawing up the steep scree slope. The force of the impact had collapsed one lung. His ribs were cracked; he was bleeding internally. At six thousand feet, in the cold night air, with these injuries, Scott's blood pressure had plummeted, which is why he kept passing out and, without medical attention, would soon die. Still he scrambled up the scree slope. His left foot was broken and mangled, his right knee sliced open and up through his quadriceps. He was bleeding profusely from face and scalp lacerations—he had, in fact, been neatly scalped. His entire scalp hung, inside out, off the back of his head. As he got to the top of the slope and prepared to be presentable to his saviors, he flipped the bloody flap into place atop his head, like a hood, just in time to see the car speed past him in the darkness.

"Help!" he yelled. "Help me!"—now to taillights disappearing around the bend. He lay face-up on the road and prayed aloud, "Please, God, send someone out here."

Inside the car, Dot Beeson had awakened with a start. "There's a man calling for help," she said to her husband. She was silly, he told her. She'd been asleep. "No," Dot insisted. "*Turn* this car *around*!" she ordered. Don Beeson had flown Grumman TBF Avengers off the carrier deck of the *Essex,* and on April 7, 1945, earned the Navy Cross for sending the *Yamato,* pride of the Japanese Imperial Fleet, to the floor of the Pacific. His was the last torpedo to hit her amidships. Don followed orders and turned the car around.

Ghost-giants had stalked Scott's childhood. But this time living giants, Navy ones, were awake and driving cars in the middle of the night, just as he was fixing to die. The Beesons helped the young veteran into the back seat of their car, where to his mortification he continued spilling blood. Apologizing for the mess, he gave them directions to Boulder Community Hospital. His mother worked there, he told them proudly, as medical records librarian.

He knew she would be surprised to see him there in the morning.

6

A NAVY WIFE?

ON HIS THIRD DATE with Rene Price, Scott tested his future wife: "Can you make oatmeal?" "Cold or boiling water?" came her canny reply. Only cheaters started with boiling water. The two under-graduates had a lot more than oatmeal in common.

Rene was born in Clinton, Iowa, in 1928, making her three years younger than Scott. Her parents, too, had separated when she was little. She, too, had grown up in a household of loving adults—among her mother Ollie's family. She saw her father perhaps twice in her childhood. And, like Scott, Rene had watched her mother contend with the lifelong debility brought on by T.B. As the Depression began to strangle the railroad town, the Olson kitchen and back porch became a haven for neighbors—most of them out-of-work railroaders who traded clothing, quoted Will Rogers, praised Roosevelt, and reviled Colonel Robert R. McCormick, the editor and publisher of the *Chicago Tribune*. "What does the son-of-a-bitch say today?" Ollie harrumphed each morning, as the *Tribune* thudded on the front stoop.

Like Scott, Rene remembered her family's stories and good times with a kind of yearning, her childhood defined by a transcendental summer day and night that began when her Uncle Feather returned from the Mississippi with a huge mud turtle. Word of the catch spread among the neighbors on Eleventh and Twelfth avenues. They drifted into the backyard, where already he had started a fire under the black iron kettle and was cutting the precious meat from this river behemoth to make his famous Mulligan stew. Dinner was served that night, with all invited.

Kitchen chairs appeared, and home brew from secret places, the entire neighborhood and the Gifford cousins with ukeleles, lemon pies. They ate and sang through the night—Al Jolson songs, Ruth Etting showtime tunes, and finally Feather on the banjo singing his fifteen raunchy verses of "Frankie & Johnny." Rene, long since sent to bed, listened from the second-story window, wanting the night to last forever. As World War II began, Ollie's ill health forced the family—recently fortified with husband and two young children—to decamp for the salubrious West. One more convalescent for Boulder, Colorado.

Graduating from Boulder High School in 1946, unfazed by her selection as "most beautiful girl," Rene had studied voice for five years and had sung principal roles in the Gilbert & Sullivan operetta productions staged by Warner Imig, head of C.U.'s School of Music. As part of the Pep Squad she organized paper drives, and as a Rainbow Girl she and three of her fellow officers invited a Negro couple, as they were then called, to the Spring Dance. The invitation shocked the town, nearly cost the students their posts, brought a visit from the head of the national chapter of the Rainbow Girls, and caused the association bylaws to be rewritten restricting guests by race. No Negroes allowed! Rene was stunned by the action and the punishment meted out to her. Worse, she was not allowed to cover the story for the high-school paper, *The Owl,* where she was also girl reporter.

Rene and her fellow co-eds entered C.U. alongside nearly seven thousand returning G.I.s in 1946—outnumbered two and a half to one. Most of the men had seen some version of Paris during the war and had little interest in Boulder's prewar status quo. Rene, as usual, jumped in with both feet. A history major with a music minor, she was pledged to Delta Delta Delta. TriDelts were eager that year to be the first Greeks on campus to break the Aryan-only code. They invited their Phi Sigma Delta brothers, C.U.'s Jewish fraternity, to Thursday Afternoon Tea, a self-important social event weighted with social significance.

With an energy that matched that of her future husband, Rene was writing a paper on Milton's *Paradise Lost* while working part-time at the student bookstore. Here she helped organize a campus protest march against the Board of Regents, then conducting a witch hunt for Reds (there were, in fact, Communists on campus) and demanding that the music school withdraw its invitation to Paul Robeson and his production of *Othello*. Three thousand students marched and Robeson sang.

She was shelving textbooks at the Colorado Book Store when Scott walked in, scanning the store. She stepped up on her ladder, the better for him to see her. They had met once before, briefly—a fateful eye click in the lobby of the Boulder Theater, he in a black tux and bow tie, taking tickets, she with someone else. Rene was convinced he would find her, but his car accident had intervened.

"What, no bow tie?" she teased him. The scars across Scott's right cheek were fading. He invited her to his fraternity dance, where Stan Kenton would play something called New Jazz. Rene accepted, and they quickly began to fit their lives together in a two-year walking, talking courtship. He told her his Grandpa Noxon stories; she gave him Uncle Feather in return. He wanted to fly airplanes; she wanted to write. Their love affair was nourished by similar childhoods: ailing mothers, absent fathers, and above all the hurt they'd endured because of fatherless homes that had left them with gaping holes in their hearts—odd children out. "You're the best thing that ever happened to me," he told her.

Scott and Rene planned their children, and the kind of family they would be, before they were married. Healthy, smart children, of course, and lessons in all sports. Their children would swim dive, ski, and play tennis. Music was important—piano lessons a *must*, but the guitar was even better: they were portable. Guitars fit in the car. There would be *no* doctors, he insisted. They would raise their kids not to be sick.

Postwar Boulder offered few opportunities for recent graduates. Scott's friends drifted back into their father's businesses, men's clothing, used cars, teaching. A few enterprising souls headed up into the Rocky Mountains to start ranches, install a ski-tow line on a leased hill, or pursue that million-dollar pipe dream, a mink farm: "Make a million in five years!" The valley of broken dreams, the wags called it.

At the university, it was hard to stay optimistic. The engineering and geology schools were crowded with students, yet the country's once-booming aircraft industry had few orders for aircraft and even fewer job openings. Graduating geology students left for jobs in South America to seek their fortunes. Standing around countless wedding-reception punch bowls, everyone trotted out the same topic: "What will you do?" "Where will you go ?" Scott plugged away at school. Getting married meant earning money, so Rene moved to Estes Park, where working at a resort restaurant netted her fifty dollars a night in tips, on top of her base salary of thirty-five dollars a month. Up at Red Feather Lakes in northern Colorado, Scott was working, too. He wrote his father with momentous news. It was June 22, 1948.

> Guess where your wandering Son has turned up this time—
> a lumberjack at a lumber camp—Yessir—me and the other
> Swedes, Yumpin Yiminy! We...saw trees for a solid nine and a
> half hours with an extra 45 minutes out for lunch. They pay us
> $6 for a thousand board feet, so the harder you work, the more
> you earn....I am planning to marry the little girl whose cheek
> you kissed last fall....
>
> I don't expect your blessings...but I'm quite sure it's what I
> want to do—I hope you like Rene.

A month later, his father's reply in hand, Scott responded by the light of a kerosene lamp: "Your attitude toward my marrying is exactly as I expected....But hear now my side." Toye had meanwhile borne the brunt of Carpenter's assault. She replied on July 8: "My Dear! My Dear! Let's be practical about this. Let's put ourselves in Bud's place.... Think back to 24 years ago.... Did you not face the more distant future with confidence based solely on your faith in your own ability and faith in the love of your wife?" As for the merits of their son's decision to marry, Toye was "neither in favor of it nor opposed to it." This did not mean she was "indifferent," insisting it was "their problem and *their* life to live … and, in so far as I am able to do so without interfering with their growth and development, I shall try to help them make of their marriage what I had wanted so desperately to make of my own."

Scott and Rene were married in mid-September at St. John's Episcopal, nearly two years to the day after his near-fatal car accident near Strawstack Mountain. A Methodist (if culturally Lutheran down to her DNA), Rene nevertheless took confirmation classes with Father Walters, still rector at St. John's after thirty years, and became at least a nominal Episcopalian for her twenty-odd-year union with Scott.

THEY STARTED THEIR LIFE together well outside of town, in Left Hand Canyon, where they rented a white clapboard house. In 1948 it was a thirty-five-minute drive to campus. Rene sang while Scott whistled her accompaniment. He studied every moment he was not chopping wood. Yes, it was "remote," they said, and exactly what they wanted, along with a bathroom of their own. The notorious "Vetsville" had only public toilets, Toye explained to her former husband, defending another of the newlyweds' decisions.

That winter of 1948–49 broke the county's snowfall records. Nevertheless, Scott and Rene made their way down the hill toward Route 36 in their '38 Ford convertible coupe, honking and waving at the miners headed the other way up to the fluorspar mines at Jimtown. "We've cleared the drifts up above!" they called out, and the miners responded in kind: "We cleared 'em down below!" Regardless of the snowfall, Scott missed not a single class, and the Carpenters established a routine: After classes he met Rene at the bookstore, where she earned thirty-five cents an hour—forty-two dollars a month, more than enough to cover rent. Together with the G.I. Bill (which covered tuition and expenses) and a seventy-five-dollar monthly check from Scott's father, they could afford a Coke at the Sink, a hangout for C.U. students on the Hill, where they fed the jukebox to hear "Heartache," by Ted Weems.

They brown-bagged their lunches, often meeting at Toye's apartment, where they could "heat up some soup," Toye wrote, adding they "always come in the door laughing."

Having succumbed rather quickly to Rene's letter-writing campaign, Carpenter wrote "something *very* nice about Rene," Toye noted with gladness. He was also interested in what his son might do upon graduation, suggesting a career with New York Life, where he had set up his own annuity. He wrote Toye that he had even arranged for an interview with the company, followed by an aptitude test.

Insurance? they said, jaws dropping, upon hearing the news from Toye, who prepared her former husband for the difficult news that Scott might not be suited for the white-collar work of insurance. He was "quite concerned, of course, about what to do come June and graduation," the mother wrote, and "did appreciate your suggestion," but his "aptitude test...as you no doubt know" had not been "favorable, which did not surprise me in the least."

Scott had meanwhile learned the Navy was recruiting engineering students through something called Direct Procurement, a program that offered an officer's commission in addition to flight training. Because of his World War II service, he could enter as an ensign. Like Scott, Rene knew immediately that this was what her husband had to do and drove with him to Denver the summer of 1949. The recruiting officer wanted to meet her. She was four months pregnant.

A month before graduation, Scott informed his father of his decision. First he listed advantages he thought his father would appreciate: the training, the pay, the opportunity to get an advanced degree. Finally, the truth: "Flying is my first love." It was not a "sure thing yet," he cautioned—"I took the physical and the Officer Qualification Test today and did OK"—but his application still had to be approved by the Officer Procurement Board in Washington, D.C. He invited his father to his commencement. "Try it, will you? You have a considerable investment in me. I can never begin to make you know how much it has helped, nor how grateful I am for your kindness." He closed with a hopeful, "See you in June."

Carpenter's withering reply charged among other things that his son would be nothing better than a "flying bus driver." Scott took it hard. Rene, who had long since identified the man as a bully, was appalled at the damage. Still, she admitted to misgivings of her own:

> A Navy wife? A nomad? Horrified thoughts of packing and
> unpacking, meeting train schedules, postponing a much-
> wanted family, and months of being husbandless came to
> mind. But I gulped and started a quiet investigation of my
> own. This is what I found out about the Navy: By act of
> Congress a Naval officer is a gentleman, and the braid he wears
> is his badge of honor, his "press card" to anywhere in the
> world. The Navy's traditions are the mightiest, its background
> unimpeachable, and its performance in all matters 4-0 (that
> means "perfect" in the Navy vernacular). Or he might be
> assigned as a technical advisor to a friendly foreign country
> whose air power must be built up to ensure our safety against
> aggression from Soviet Russia.

"Above all," Scott was "excited and happy," she stressed, about his decision and "itching" to be back in an airplane, and the "stick and rudder efficiency" of the Navy.

Late that spring Scott and Rene drove out of their canyon one final time. The winter snows had not once kept the newlyweds from classroom or workplace. But the record snowfall reappeared as a torrent of snowmelt in May, roaring down the Front Range and washing out their bridge one fateful morning: Scott's final exam in heat transfer, a required course. He would have to take the entire course again. But one thing or another intervened. And then the Navy called— the long-awaited affirmation. He was in. *Incredible,* thought Scott, the Navy would *pay* him to fly. With a five-hundred-dollar loan from his father-in-law for uniforms, he was off to Pensacola. In a postcard written on November 4, 1949, he told his father: "I'm as happy now as any person could possibly be. Rene will be down at the first of the year and then we'll start on the career in earnest. This is what I've wanted all along."

———

IN THE UNSETTLED peacetime year of 1949, the U.S. Navy trolled the country's colleges and universities for promising engineers who wanted to fly airplanes. Called the Direct Procurement Program, the recruiting effort identified five hundred recent college graduates on a rolling basis throughout the year. Scott Carpenter was the U.S. Navy's five hundredth DPP candidate, and he reported, as ordered, on October 31, 1949, to Naval Air Station Pensacola, on Florida's Gulf coast. Such a talented young recruit, the Navy assumed, had his degree.

In so reporting, Scott was literally steps behind Jim Williford, a lanky Georgia Tech graduate. They and a third fellow named Dick Brooker went through flight training as the only three ensigns in a battalion otherwise composed of young aviation cadets, one of whom was an African American named Carter, the country's second black naval aviator, thanks to President Harry Truman's order to desegregate all the military branches.

Upon their arrival at Pensacola, Jim and Scott were told to purchase uniforms, but these couldn't be bought without ID cards, and ID cards could not be obtained until they had uniforms for the ID photo. They borrowed an ensign's shirt, complete with insignia, and after posing for their IDs were able to purchase their uniforms.

Basic training at Pensacola begins with six months of ground school. Classes, held at Mainside, cover celestial navigation, communications (radio procedures), and aircraft recognition. Scott and his classmates studied the rules and principles of flight, flight procedures, naval history, and a book called *Stick and Rudder*. They learned about lift and drag and engines, in this case only reciprocating engines (called recips), which drive the propellers. Propeller-driven airplanes were the only kind of plane they would be flying for a long time.

Scott lived at the Bachelor Officer Quarters. When Rene and the baby arrived on January 20, 1950, the small family repaired to the Willifords for a night; Jim and his wife, Pat, also had a new baby boy. The next day found the Carpenters in their own place, at Navy Point, with a monthly rent of seventy dollars. Although they often returned to Boulder for visits, the Carpenters were now committed Navy nomads and would rarely have the same address for more than a year.

Rene's basic training began in a classroom on base filled with her new colleagues, Navy wives. "Ladies," began the flight surgeon, "your husband's life is in *your* hands." Rene sat up straight. "It is therefore *essential* he have a nourishing breakfast every morning he flies. Without a hot, nourishing breakfast, your husband will, at approximately eleven hundred hours, experience plummeting blood-sugar levels. He will become less alert. He may not notice the red light flashing in his cockpit. He will not see the airplane approaching on a collision course. You, ladies, will have killed your husbands."

Looking around the room for nods of assent, Rene heard instead one woman muttering: "He can make his own damned breakfast." As a patriotic teenager during World War II, Rene was well-versed in the dictum that they "also serve who stand and wait." More so, she reasoned, those who stand and prepare hot breakfasts. She'd been rising every morning at five since she arrived to brew coffee, make oatmeal, pour whole milk, slather toast with butter. She quartered oranges and then started on lunch, usually a triple-decker meatloaf sandwich, wrapped in waxed paper.

Jim and Scott and their classmates who passed were graduated from Pre-flight on March 6, 1950. Finally they could begin Primary flight training, which in 1950 took place at Whiting Field in the back seat of an SNJ. Called the Harvard by the British, the SNJ was a dual-cockpit trainer, with retractable gear and a single 225-horsepower engine that drove a two-blade propeller. The North American–made trainer was the mainstay of Naval aviation training for years. Scott's instructor was Lieutenant Van Trane, a twenty-six-year-old World War II veteran with a tour of squadron duty under his belt.

By 1950 the Navy was using radios between the fore and aft seats instead of the World War II–era Gosport tube. Scott improved the radio system by buying a lip mike at the surplus store and mounting it on his headset; he could trigger it with a button on the stick, an innovation that saved both time and motion.

First flights are gentle affairs, just for familiarization. Trainees occupy the SNJ's aft seat, listening to the instructor describing and demonstrating basic procedures. Out of the airplane, there were also "bearing and conduct" issues to master: work khakis, dress blues. Summer whites, working greens. Scott was determined to display all the spit and polish of a properly turned out officer, and he kept his uniforms in impeccable condition.

When the Korean war began, in June 1950, Scott was two months into his flight training. Before the war ended, Pensacola would turn out more than six thousand Navy and Marine pilots. At Pensacola, instructors drum into the trainees that flying airplanes is not inherently dangerous, only mercilessly unforgiving of human error, with the Navy figuring a pilot needs about five hundred hours of flight time, give or take a hundred, to lose the poor judgment, clumsiness, fear, recklessness, and sloppiness that invite fatalities. Most accidents are caused, Scott learned, because of *pilot error,* not by bad luck, engine failure, or weather conditions. The Navy does not encourage, tolerate, or wink at risky aircraft maneuvers, as the adage suggests: "There are old pilots. There are bold pilots. There are no old, bold pilots."

Toye visited Pensacola just before Scott soloed at Pace Field. "The entire set up is different in so many ways," she wrote Carpenter, "from anything you or I have ever done that a word report is really inadequate....He talks it *all* the time." Her relationship with the man continued to defy categorization. They had been divorced five years. He had remarried. Still, Carpenter had just sent her two dozen red roses to commemorate their twenty-fifth wedding anniversary. She thanked her former husband for the roses but remarked on the end of an era. She was no longer the steward of the father-son relationship. Still, she encouraged him to visit Pensacola so the father could see for himself their son in his element—the sky.

AFTER PRIMARY CAME flying solo, followed by acrobatics, gunnery, night flying, formation, and carrier qualifications (CARQUALs). More than three downs at any stage in this process and you're "washed out" of the program. It is at this stage of flight training that one's feelings of intense gratitude suddenly give way to equally intense fears, not of dying, but of screwing up. These fears are magnified by the Navy's oft-voiced perplexity that washouts came with no warning labels. Six months of valuable ground school, thirty-six hours of Primary flight instruction, and no way of telling beforehand whether or not a recruit could safely fly solo. Pace Field, where one soloed in those days, was just a grass field with a windsock and a fire truck standing by.

On the scheduled day, Scott went out to Pace Field to practice touch-and-go landings with Van Trane until the instructor said, "Okay, let me out." This was it—solo flight—the big moment. He flew alone for about twenty minutes, practiced a couple more landings and take-offs, and finally returned uneventfully to the landing field. Van Trane cut off his necktie, in keeping with half of a Navy tradition, the second half of which dictated a bottle of scotch for the instructor. Scott gave him a bottle of Chivas.

The Korean war, now six weeks old, was affecting plane assignments and thus Scott's choice of advanced aircraft training to come. "There are no more F-8 or F-4U billets available at Corpus," he wrote Rene, in Boulder visiting. "All of the ships are in action, so if I want single engines I will get F-6's. I will get F-8's later, of course, and in the long run I will get better training in two different types, so I guess it won't be so bad." The couple hadn't talked much about the war, nor about the fact that Scott would be "in it" before too long.

"FLYING GOES ON," Rene wrote her father-in-law. "Scott is flying formation now and next is gunnery. After he makes his carrier qualifications, we will be on our way to Corpus." She meant Corpus Christi, Texas, and Advanced aircraft training. Rene was pregnant again. Everyone was pregnant. With little instruction from family doctors, young women were left basically guessing how to use their mysterious contraceptive devices. Whispered kitchen conferences—"You mean, you actually *fold* it in half?"—that dissolved into whoops of laughter generally helped matters, after a surprise pregnancy or two.

For fun at "Pensy" there were spaghetti parties and games of bridge with other couples. The hostess would make the pasta, while guests each brought something: a sauce, a salad, rolls and butter, Jell-O for dessert. The Willifords made beer in their closet. Babies were laid out in back bedrooms to sleep while their young parents played cards and yelled stories in the tiny living rooms. Something new—a roadside burger stand—had recently opened for business across the state line in Alabama. Rene and Scott would drive there for the novel dining thrill of a freshly grilled, custom-made burger with bacon and cheese on a bun, eaten right there in their 1941 Mercury, which was always washed and polished on weekends.

Night flying and instrument flying took place at Corry Field, just over the hill from their Navy Point apartment. At the beginning, it was a simple procession of airplanes circling the airfield. The sight of cities at night, and of lights on the ground, was beautiful to Scott, who was equally entranced by the blue flame he saw issuing from the exhaust stacks of the engines—thinking, there was his heart and soul out there in the engine, breathing this powerful blue light.

With some fiddling on that first night-flying exercise, he found a way to change the color of the fire. The engine is controlled by the throttle and the propeller-RPM control. The fuel–air ratio delivered to the engine is controlled by the mixture control. If the control were set at "FULL RICH," out shot a long, flaming-red exhaust plume, the fuel still burning as it roared out of the engine. But pulling the mixture control back toward "LEAN" made the red disappear and the flame diminish. Moving the mixture control still farther back, he could see the flame turn the deepest blue, then the palest, a sublime sight accompanied by the unsublime sound of a choking, starving engine.

He loved night flying.

Carrier landings would follow. This was where Navy pilots, Scott knew, left their Air Force counterparts in the dust. Air Force pilots never have to learn how to fly low and slow, when control is not quite as good and the aircraft not as responsive as it is at higher speeds. The Navy way meant an entirely different flight regime, called flying the "backside of the curve." It especially impressed him one day when he was turning on the base leg of the landing pattern, which is the final 180-degree turn prior to landing. He happened to look down to see a young kid on a bicycle looking up at him. Scott waved at him and the kid waved back. Cars sped past them both, while he in his plane and the boy on his bike maintained about the same speed. The kid was pedaling about as fast as he could, while Scott was shy of a stall. Low and slow, which is exactly how one lands on a carrier.

TOYE, WHO HAD long ago made her peace with death, had also prepared, once the Korean war began, for her one child to die. Gloom had recently descended over Boulder, she wrote Carpenter, because a local boy had just died during flight training at Pensacola. But as for their son, "his ecstasy in flying, and in flying so well, and the fullness of his life with Rene and Scotty, have lifted my spirits to almost equal heights.... The world being in the mess that it is"—some things never change—"this living must pretty much be on a day-to-day basis, and his day-to-day life is full. No matter what may happen, he has had that."

She could also report to the famously critical father, as both Scott and Rene would, that the young aviator had made "six of six" perfect landings during the CARQUALs. "No doubt you are now convinced," a proud mother wrote, "that I am crazy to be buoyed up by anything which has such dire consequences." But she was a soldier's mother now and explained her thinking: "Length is not the only dimension to life, and I *still* think it helps to be crazy."

In early December 1950, before everyone in the class left for Corpus, Scott arranged a graduation party and selected a popular restaurant just a couple of blocks from the main gate. But upon learning that the group included something new, a black naval aviator, the restaurant called Scott and reneged. A quick call shifted the celebration to a hotel, where it went on without incident. The Navy's first black aviator, Ensign Jesse Brown, had just lost his life providing close ground support, flying an F4U-4 Corsair, to Marines fighting their way out of the Chosin Reservoir.

UPON THE SUCCESSFUL completion of Advanced aircraft training at Corpus Christi, Scott could expect to be designated a naval aviator, given his wings, and ordered to squadron duty with the fleet. In 1950 aviators had three choices in Advanced training, and in choosing they were defining their aviation careers for the remainder of their military service. These three choices were fighters, patrol planes, and helicopters. Of course, the fighter pilot occupies the top of the pyramid of respect.

On the long, solo drive to Corpus that December, Scott chose patrol planes in one of the most difficult decisions of his life. His boyhood dream, held all through high school and beyond, was to be a fighter pilot. But he was now twenty-six years old, a husband and a father, with a second child on the way. His ego, he knew, demanded he be a fighter pilot, but he remembered as a boy how he had hated being fatherless. He wanted his son to know and love him. He wanted to be there to know and to love him—to teach him all the things he had learned from his Grandpa Noxon. At the relatively sober age of twenty-six, Scott realized that his personal need to be a hot shot was being outweighed by his growing sense of responsibility as a husband and father. The choice he made still haunts him.

Rene was always clear: Scott should choose fighters. She was stunned by his decision, which he laid out for her in a letter and then confessed he had wanted to tell her in person. "There would still be the chance to change," he offered on December 6, 1950, "if *we* decide that is best. . . . So much for the situation—it's driving me batty." And it was.

The second Carpenter baby was due at Christmastime, so after two solo weeks at Corpus, Scott returned to Pensacola on leave. Navy wives were doing their part for the country's postwar boom in babies. The base hospital, however, didn't have room for them all: women in labor were lined up in hallways and anterooms, separated by hanging blankets. Rene had enjoyed an easy first delivery in Boulder, helped by an experienced delivery-room nurse and, for the pain, a saddle block, a postwar obstetrical innovation. But the mid-twentieth-century hypodermic was a blunt tool; an errant injection into the conus media could just as readily paralyze, not numb. It could also not work at all, which is what happened to Rene, with her second baby presenting breech and the obstetrician attempting a radical caudal block. Then his overvigorous, internal attempt to reposition the baby caused Rene to scream. This in turn caused the doctor to slug her, *hard,* in the jaw.

Recuperating quietly afterward, Rene heard another woman, just delivered of her seventh child, wheeled into the next partition. "Your *seventh*?" the twenty-two-year-old said in wonderment through the hanging blanket. "Yes," her neighbor replied, and her husband, a chief petty officer, was shipping out that night for Korea. Later, as the flow of visitors slowed throughout the ward, the chief arrived for his farewell: On the floor, visible under the blanket-curtains, Rene saw his shoes coming off, heard the unmistakable sounds of coitus, followed by the valedictory zipping and buckling of pants and, finally, footsteps away to war.

For Advanced training at Corpus, instead of flying the speedy, single-engine F8F Bearcat, which was the hottest Navy fighter in the Pacific during World War II, Scott would be flying the lumbering, old four-engine PB4Y-2 Privateer, the Navy's single-tail version of the U.S. Army Air Corps B-24 Liberator, the slowest and most ungainly heavy bomber in use in the European theater. This was the downside of his decision. Gone forever, he thought, was his dream of streaming his silk scarf out the canopy.

Advanced flight training in the months that followed was much the same in both fighter and patrol airplanes. Each involved extensive practice in instrument flight, the kind of training required to fly safely at night, or in bad weather, when the pilot has no visual reference to the world around him. Armed with the rudiments of instrument flight, pilots go on to the second phase of advanced training, called "fighting your airplane," learning how to use the plane's systems and capabilities in combat. This is where flight training for the patrol plane pilot and the fighter pilot begins to differ drastically. Both programs, however, made relatively safe and experienced fledgling naval aviators.

True to Scott's expectation, he was soon in further training with a fleet patrol squadron, but in the P2V Neptune ("V" is a U.S. designation, roundly detested by allied nations, that stands for Lockheed, the manufacturer). A successor to the PB4Y-2, the airplane was superior in almost every conceivable way. Learning to "fight" the P2V turned out,

Scott found, to be a demanding but tremendously fun job. Best of all, the Lockheed patrol plane had the finest reciprocating engine ever mounted on an airplane; the turbo-compound R3350 never had a superior successor. He was delighted with the assignment, despite the fact that the P2V was a big airplane—91 feet long, with a 103-foot wingspan.

The crew for combat flights generally consisted of three naval aviator officers—pilot, copilot, and navigator, sometimes with a fourth officer serving as second navigator. The rest of the crew were trained as system technicians who operated the electronic surveillance equipment—radio communications, radar, and Electronic Counter-Measures—which comprised most of the plane's on-board "weaponry." The P2V also carried aerial mines and torpedoes as well as sonobuoys, small listening devices dropped in the water to locate submerged submarines.

Some versions of this multifaceted airplane had 20-millimeter nose guns, operated by the pilot, in addition to tail guns, operated by an enlisted man. The copilot also controlled a powerful searchlight located on a wing-tip tank for locating surfaced submarines at night. Other versions replaced the tail guns with an extended tail called a stinger, which enclosed Magnetic Airborne Detection equipment (MAD). The MAD could detect a submerged submarine from the way it altered the earth's local magnetic field. This appendage, which appeared on the P2V-5, became known, of course, as the MAD tail.

RENE PINNED ON her husband's Navy wings of gold on April 19, 1951; a press release was sent dutifully to the hometown paper. They were soon at Naval Air Station San Diego, where Scott would get additional electronics training and where their six-month-old, Timmy, died in his sleep. Rene found him early in the morning; Scott had already left for work. She called the airfield in a panic and he rushed home, but there was nothing to be done. Unable to call his mother, Toye, with such terrible news, Scott spoke with Father Walters, still rector at St. John's after all these years. It was he who told Toye. The pathologist had found "interstitial myocarditis and pericarditis," Scott wrote his father. "It means a virus infection and subsequent paralysis of the heart and the muscles surrounding it." Timmy had been, he wrote, "the happiest baby boy you ever saw. He'd laugh at me and grab onto my fingers and I'd lift him to a sitting position, and then he'd open his mouth as wide as it'd go and laugh some more. I burped him after his bottle and put him to bed....If he had cried out once, Rene would have heard him, so he must have passed away very peacefully in his sleep."

It was "difficult to talk about," the young father added, saying he hoped the "letter of explanation" would suffice. Anticipating a question, he wrote, "We plan to try for another as soon as the doctor thinks Rene is able." By the time the young Navy family got their orders for N.A.S. Whidbey Island—more electronics training—Rene had gotten over her morning sickness. The grief took much longer.

7

LOVE, WAR, AND QUONSET HUTS

On November 17, 1951, the Carpenters and the Gunckels, another Navy family, disembarked into the aromatic wonder of Honolulu, after a rough crossing of the Pacific aboard a darkened transport ship thought to be stalked by enemy submarines. Recently assigned to a maritime patrol squadron designated VP6, Navy lieutenants (junior grade) Scott Carpenter and Dave Gunckel had forty-eight hours in which to settle their wives. They quickly located two apartments in a small, three-story garden apartment complex, called the Royal Grove, only two blocks from Waikiki Beach. Scott and Dave, an Academy man, cemented their friendship at N.A.S. Whidbey while vying for the Navy's expert marksman badge. They both won, and now the two new dead-eyes would be the last to join their first squadron, at N.A.S. Atsugi, Japan. There they could expect to be trained as navigators by pilots moving out of the navigator's seat and into the cockpit, replacing, in turn, pilots rotating out when VP6 returned to Barber's Point, their home base.

This is the Navy way: constant turnover and constant training, constantly moving worthy pilots from right seat (copilot) to left seat (pilot) and promoting a few to Patrol Plane Commander, or PPC. Newly minted Navy pilots, like Scott and Dave, are brought in as navigators or co-navigators in a crew of up to ten men. No matter how glittering their records at flight school, naval aviators always start at the end of the chain—in the navigator's seat. Their wives, too, started at the end, or bottom, of the great Navy food chain.

Having recently mourned the loss of her second child and now pregnant with her third, Rene was due in early March. Ginny Gunckel, also expecting, was four weeks behind. Two-year-old boys clung to their legs. The two families walked to the beach that first evening to hear the ukelele playing and to say their first sad good-byes before the men flew off to Japan. The next morning meant a trip to Pearl Harbor, where they paid their respects to the *USS Arizona* and the men still entombed there. Their husbands left them early the following morning, on an airplane bound for N.A.S Atsugi, the squadron's forward base in Japan. In 1951 the journey required three refueling stops—Johnson Island, Kwajalein, and a fourteen-hour layover in Guam, its palm trees, Scott wrote, "still stumps" from World War II naval artillery.

Japan, too, was still devastated in 1951, a sobering sight for U.S. naval aviators fresh from a visit to the *Arizona*. Still, there was no hint of triumphalism in Scott's first-hand account of Occupied Japan. How triumphalist could one feel, as wounded soldiers, fresh from Korea, were being unloaded at the Haneda airfield? Airmen were dying, too. Scott's new squadron had just lost a P2V-3 while on a U.N. weather reconnaissance patrol—the Lockheed Neptune with a full crew of ten just vanished from the radar over international waters in the Sea of Japan. No survivors, no remains. The downing wasn't announced until Thanksgiving.

Until then, scuttlebutt alone confirmed the catastrophe. Then the Navy visited the crew's families and told them to pack—nothing more. Within four days the families were off the island and gone in an institutional reflex that would persist through the Vietnam war.

IN FULFILLMENT of a pledge, Scott wrote Rene detailed letters about everything he saw. On the approach to the airfield at Haneda, he recognized the Palace, the one-man sub factory, "with bomb craters still visible," he wrote, and the big Mitsubishi aircraft plant, where the infamous Zeroes were built. There were "steel mills, canals, junks, ships of every description, old submarine barriers over the mouth of the bay," and a few big, wide concrete freeways with "not an automobile in sight."

The squadron would be forward-based at Atsugi until January 1952; there he was assigned to Crew 5 of VP6, a maritime patrol squadron of P2V-3 Neptunes. The term "patrol" in times of war is something of a misnomer, especially for VP6—the first operational squadron to fly the Lockheed P2Vs into combat. Nicknamed the "Blue Sharks" after a thrilling *Collier's* war story entitled "Blue Sharks off the Red Coast," VP6 crews had provided cover for the Inchon landing, attacked railways, conducted antisubmarine warfare over the Yellow Sea, and, as always, as the Navy's priceless eyes and ears, gathered ELINT, or electronic intelligence, on their long reconnaissance and surveillance patrols. But aircraft losses forced Commander Guy Howard, the skipper on that deployment, to order an end to "active" combat flying. Their planes were too expensive, too large, and too vulnerable—and the patrol, reconnaissance, and antisubmarine roles too important.

Too large for carrier-based operations, the P2Vs were by necessity land-based maritime patrol planes. Because of this they relied on "forward" bases like N.A.S. Atsugi to get them as close as possible to the fighting and related patrolling. Home base was different. Home base is where you have a life. For most patrol squadrons during the Korean war, home base was N.A.S. Barber's Point, in Hawaii—a plum assignment even when you factor in war. During his first squadron duty with VP6, Scott would have three separate deployments at forward bases out of Barber's Point. N.A.S. Atsugi was the first. The second was N.A.S. Kodiak. A postwar deployment at N.A.S. Agana, Guam, was the third and last.

Most naval aviators have fairly simple career goals, particularly when they are navigators aboard the P2V: (1) earn the highest possible marks and fitness reports, (2) move up to right seat (copilot), (3) then to left (pilot), and (4) hope to make PPC, Patrol Plane Commander, before the entire four- or five-year tour of squadron duty is over. It is a thrilling, harrowing experience.

Scott's first deployment was followed by a return to Barber's Point. The squadron was redeployed about six months later, in July 1952, and forward based at N.A.S. Kodiak, in the Aleutians. This seven-month wartime deployment lasted until early 1953, as the Korean war wound down. The squadron flew lengthy reconnaissance missions around the Aleutian chain of islands, then down along the Red coast—Soviet Russia and China—and then back up the chain to Alaska, where high, gusting winds often made take-offs and landings very tricky.

Of his patrol missions during that first deployment, flying out of Atsugi, Scott wrote only that they were "ten to twelve hours" long, and "very interesting." They patrolled "the area," never specified. They were flying low and slow over the Yellow Sea, listening, watching, and reporting without letup in unsung, unglamorous assignments that saved countless lives—and caused the deaths of untold others.

GINNY AND RENE were, in the meantime, at the Royal Grove apartments with ninety-six dollars between them. So they joined forces, moving into Rene's ground-floor unit, where there was a patio. They decided they'd call it two rooms—the outside patio was one, and the other was the inside room with the kitchenette. There was a double bed, so the women separated the mattress from the box springs and put each one in a corner of the room. For a week Rene took the box springs while Ginny took the mattress. The following week they switched. Scotty and Davey each had their own bed, which their mothers constructed from pads of blankets.

They maintained their mutual sanity by taking turns at Waikiki beach—then a beautiful expanse of sand and palms where you could see all the way down to Diamond Head. Rene and Scotty had the morning shift; Ginny and Davey the afternoon. They talked about the fathers fourteen to forty times a day on matters ranging from plane recognition and literacy to personal bravery: "Oh, *look* at that plane," mothers claimed, pointing overhead to a P2V. "Daddy flies that kind of plane." Or at night, "Now let's write—we're going to write our letters to Dad." Or when disciplining, "Now, *Dad* wouldn't *like* you to do that." Or encouraging, "Oh, Dad would be *proud* that you put your foot in the water, yes!" It was *Dad, Dad, Dad* day and night.

By way of modest compensation, the Moana Hotel with its famous banyan tree was just around the corner. And just down the street, still on the beach, stood the Royal Hawaiian, the pinkest and most minareted palace fabled from prewar social doings. They were living in paradise, Rene thought, only they were poverty-stricken.

The two women wrote to their men, allowing the boys to write something at the end of the letter. It was that, or a picture. Then they made grilled-cheese sandwiches on the two-burner stove in the kitchenette. Each day proceeded in this fashion, culminating in the equally routine night-time "crazies" when the toddlers went berserk for approximately one hour.

But eventually they went to sleep, and once this happened, Rene and Ginny ventured outside in the falling darkness to take in their exotic new surroundings. Postwar Honolulu was beautiful, small, and pristine, its cottages and bungalows marching almost primly up the hill with their fences covered with effortlessly flowering vines. A great canal, called the Ala Wai, ran through it. Behind the entire vista rose the Pali mountain divide.

Few Americans had traveled during the Depression. Fewer still traveled during the war. But now Hawaii was receiving its first postwar tourists, and the full effect was both charming and electric. There were extraordinary-looking women, Hawaiian, Eurasian, White Russian, Japanese, and Chinese-Filipino beauties who danced the hula and wore eye makeup in ways not thought permissible—at least to Midwestern girls like Rene and Ginny.

THE CARPENTER-GUNCKEL living arrangement at the Royal Grove didn't last much beyond Thanksgiving 1951. The management had stopped exchanging greetings after two weeks. Allotment checks still had not arrived. Their car had not been released from Customs, nor had they located permanent (and separate) housing. Now viral and bacterial illnesses joined this desperate scene. Ginny came down with a fever, so Rene was writing to Scott every night, having to relate how sick Ginny was and how there was no money and no car. Each day Scott would ask his PPC, Frank Barlow, if there were anything his wife could do. "I hate the Navy!" she finally wrote. "No one cares how or where we live!"

Scott, in the meantime, was making the rounds of the various Allied air forces. He described a memorable visit to the Royal Australian Air Force hangar, where he talked shop with a couple of Aussie pilots. "One of them showed me all through an MK VIII Meteor (British) twinjet fighter. I sat in the cockpit and got a pretty good check out." He made arrangements "for a hop" in "their MK VII, which is a 2-seat trainer," and then added, with some astonishment, "Those guys are the swearingest outfit you ever saw."

He was joining a "first-rate" outfit. His skipper, Guy Howard, was a dashing World War II hero, the grandson of Maine's own General O. O. Howard, graduate of Bowdoin and West Point, founder of Howard University, in Washington, D.C., and famed one-armed Civil War soldier and Indian fighter. As part of Patrol Wing Ten during World War II, Guy had flown two hundred combat missions, evacuating civilians, plucking Allied airmen out of the Celebes, Banda, and Sulu seas, patrolling Java, and avoiding Zeroes while flying the highly vulnerable PBY-4s, not one of which survived the war.

Under Guy Howard's command in the war that followed, VP6 would earn a Presidential Unit Citation.[1]

THANKSGIVING NIGHT of 1951 the two pregnant Navy wives, all of twenty-three years old, put their sons to sleep, went to the lunch counter at their corner drugstore, and ordered Thanksgiving dinner. Rene mailed her receipt for $2.15 to Scott's fleet post office address. A note said, "Having wonderful time." Come Christmas, Scott replied in kind, enclosing a picture of him and his Patrol Plane Commander, a "prince of a guy." They were in their aviation greens with their backs to the camera, legs crossed, arms outstretched toward their solitary drinks perched on empty tables. Beyond was a dance floor sparsely filled with couples. The tables were empty. The caption read: "Having wonderful time. Wish you were here."

The next day, December 26, irony was dead, along with the squadron's Executive Officer, Commander Robert J. ("Perk") Perkinson, and a radioman. The aircraft and its crew were conducting antisubmarine warfare during a night patrol when "they lost one engine and the prop wouldn't feather." Scott described the incident to Rene, writing on Nikko Kanaya Hotel stationery. They were forced to ditch at sea, he explained, and the impact caused the airplane fuselage to break in two. "Perk" and his copilot Tony Garland were trapped in the cockpit. The yoke had hit Garland so hard his intestines ruptured. " 'God, Scott, it was rough out there,' " Garland told Scott in sick bay, "so cold I wished I were dead.' "

"Try not to get too discouraged," he wrote Rene afterward, adding by way of apology: "This Navy life is just about all I am qualified to offer you...." Before she knew it, though, he would be home "on shore duty, and the casualty lists won't have to concern you for a while."

EXECUTIVE OFFICERS' wives usually took care of the kind of problems Ginny and Rene were having. But the Korean war had turned the re-servists' lives upside down, too. Called back into active service, one se-nior officer's wife worked full time and could not manage the full-time volunteer duties once expected of a Navy wife—all of which she con-fessed to Rene, between profuse apologies, when she arrived at the Royal Grove to collect Ginny for the drive to the hospital. A throat culture confirmed a serious strep infection.

With the old Navy safety net tearing, Rene was determined to act. Then both boys came down with diarrhea, first Scotty and then Davey, both still in diapers. Now they had a terrible, constant mess, changing diapers every twenty minutes, rinsing them out in the toi-let. The boys were vomiting, too, although they felt well enough to play in the toilet, now a marvelous place to wash and flush their wooden cars and engines, as they had seen their mothers wash out their diapers. The toys got stuck in the plumbing. The plumbing in the complex broke down. The mothers informed the managers. The managers asked them to leave.

But at long last the car arrived, so Rene began to hunt for housing in Waiamea. But by 1951 the reserves had all been called up; the war was reaching its manpower peak. Oahu housing was worse than ever. Rene still found a little house with a sign with a telephone number. When she met the landlord, she was on her best behavior: "Yes, yes, I promise. I raise my right hand to God. No, just a single family—just a mother and son." She signed the application form, paid the money—two months' rent, scraped together with funds borrowed from the PPC's wife.

Then Rene moved in with Scotty, very obviously. That night she drove back to the Royal Grove for Ginny and Davey, who hid in the back seat while Rene drove into the garage, and they sneaked inside undetected by neighbors. So for the next two weeks only one mother and one child went into the yard at a time while the other mother-son pair hid inside the house—to prevent anyone from suspecting that two families, God forbid, were living in that house against the rules and regulations and covenants of Hawaii 1951. Until someone ratted on them.

They got a call from their Chinese landlord, who said simply, "Two families living there." Rene said, "No. That's my sister's visiting me!" And he said, "I'll give you until the end of the month." But they were *expecting*, Rene protested, and would have their babies "any day," and argued hardship and handicap. This failing, they begged mercy: "Our babies are due. We can't even *lift* anything."

This was January 1952. Rene would deliver Jay on March fourth, and Ginny would follow April second, and they'd just been thrown out of their second place. The women had to find another house. This was two weeks before their husbands would return home.

FINALLY, CUSTOMS RELEASED most of the Carpenters' and Gunckels' belongings—all the household things that had come by transport ship. Still, there was no available housing at Barber's Point. They were on the list for base housing, but they weren't going to get it by the time their husbands came home. So Rene watched the two boys while Ginny looked for a place out near Barber's Point. Then Ginny would take the boys, and Rene would go look. Ginny found her house first, and told Rene about the road. "Go check this little street, it's divine... sand on either side of the road and right near the beach." Rene stumbled on a beach cottage in the process, owned by the Chee family. Ginny had found a little cottage a block and a half down the sandy road. There, at least, they were closer to their lifeline, Barber's Point, which was home to the clinic, the day-care center, and the other squadron wives.

Truce talks had recently established a demarcation line on the Korean peninsula at the 38th parallel, where a stalemate had developed. Then President Dwight D. Eisenhower was sworn in, and in mid-January 1952 the whole squadron came back to Hawaii. The first thing everyone did was to celebrate Christmas, which was done in two shifts at the Waiamea house. The tree was still up, so while Dave and Ginny and Davey had their celebration, the Carpenters headed out with Scotty for a drive around the island. Then the Gunckels took their big trip around the island and the Carpenters celebrated.

ONCE A SQUADRON returns, Navy tradition dictates a tremendous round of parties. There are parties to say good-bye to the pilots who are leaving, parties to gather in the new people. There you heard the great stories from the forward area, stories about flying, stories about who snored and who didn't, personal quirks, aggravations—all of them softened or made funny as a way of smoothing out the deployment's real hardships and annoyances. Parties were held for outgoing skippers to say good-bye, and to welcome the new skipper, who would hand out new assignments and prepare everyone to be broken in.

The U.S. Navy had a contract with Tripler, the great U.S. Army hospital, to provide obstetrical services. So on a rainy night, when the new Carpenter baby decided to be born, Rene and Scott barreled down the King Kamehameha Highway, Scott driving ninety miles an hour, honking as they pulled up in front, orderlies running out to the car, one of them commandeering Rene, telling her: "Pant, pant, pant, pant—we're going to get you there."

Jay was born in the lobby, and his mother managed seven days of heaven at Tripler, during which the parents had their usual terrible time of naming the babies. With Jay it was excruciating. Rene had written up lists of names she had been considering for months. Scott would arrive for dinnertime visiting hours and they'd attack List A: "All right, now, who in the family...?" or "What friend do we...?" agreeing after four days or so: "Let's try Robert." "Should we call him Robby?" "Well, I don't think Robby is—Robby's not traditional enough." Each objection took an hour to thrash out.

But then they brought the newborn home to Ewa Beach and its barefoot, sandy paradise of children in shorts and shirts and bare feet, superintended by parents and doting landlords, the Chees. Soon after the squadron returned to Barber's Point, the four Chee sons invited their tenant to go fishing on the long skiff they owned. Each of them was very adept with a spear gun called a Hawaiian sling and promised to teach the Navy pilot how to use it. So out they went on a Saturday, provided Scott with a spear gun, and spent the entire sun-splashed day fishing underwater. On that first trip out, the youngest boy speared a giant moray eel, came to the surface, and excitedly displayed the writhing creature to everyone in the boat, as it grimaced and gaped and flipped about, dying impaled on the boy's spear.

His brothers shouted instructions, waved their arms. But no one wanted either the spear or the eel. Naturally, he threw them both into the boat—the spear and the thrashing eel—whereupon everyone in the boat dived into the water. Luckily they had also caught some snapper, and that night the Carpenters were invited for dinner—snapper, of course, steamed in whiskey, one of Mrs. Chee's favorite recipes.

The Carpenters lived on the beach for another five months, until finally assigned to base housing, and their first Quonset hut, at Ewa Beach. At Ewa (pronounced *EV-uh*) they would pay only the prorated amount of money required of an officer of Scott's rank, in this case, lieutenant junior grade (j.g.). They would also be joining the larger community of Navy officers, many of them VP6 squadron members. They left the Chees' with hugs, tears, and recipes, one more farewell in a long chain of good-byes. Scott's experience with the Chees in the waters off Hawaii had opened his eyes to an entirely different, and new, world. His fascination with that world would culminate a decade later in the U.S. Navy's "Man in the Sea" program, called Sealab.

Ewa Beach was a reactivated Marine base from World War II. It had double Quonsets in long rows and streets, but with picnic tables and luxuriant grass lawns separating each one. For evening walks, there were crumbling runways from the previous war and row upon row of old revetments where U.S. Marines had concealed their airplanes from Japanese attack. Although primitive-sounding, Ewa Beach and its Quonsets of the early 1950s were perfectly acceptable to the needs of squadron families. Inexpensive, convenient, and even, in a Navy kind of way, exclusive: This was officers' housing, as serviceable and public-spirited as their husbands' uniforms. It was also infinitely better than no housing at all. The Navy's strict class system ensured that officers' families lived apart even from chief petty officers, the highest-ranking enlisted men who are thought actually to run the Navy.

Slowly the squadron prepared to leave for its second wartime deployment, forward-based at N.A.S. Kodiak, Alaska—a long tour of six or seven months. In June, a month before the squadron left, the Carpenters moved into their two-bedroom, double Quonset. It was draped with a luxuriant Cup of Gold vine whose flowers, when they burst into bloom, were like huge yellow magnolias. Inside the Quonset was a big living room and then an L-shaped dining area. Rene bought fifty yards of industrial burlap, the kind used for bagging pineapples, painted the burlap with a haphazard fish design, using primary colors, and then draped the fabric ceiling to floor, leaving two openings for the windows. A fire hazard for sure, but cheap at the price of two dollars. The kitchen was small and opened onto a long stretch of green commons, with twin double Quonsets stretching away as far as the eye could see.

Scott's first weeks at N.A.S. Kodiak, away from the idyll at Barber's Point, combined intense flying, readjusting to a bachelor's existence, and hunger. He wrote frequently about "chow." There was never enough food for Scott, still whippet-thin to judge from his request for

Jockey shorts, which Rene kept neglecting to send him. "*Write it down,*" he told the frazzled mother of two, "so you don't *forget!*" He was adamant about the brand: "they *have* to be Jockey shorts—size 30."

As a member of VP6 Crew 7, Scott moved up to right seat, copilot, and flew the Aleutians, down the Russian and Chinese coasts, sometimes back to Whidbey Island, and then back to the Aleutians. On arrival at Kodiak he wrote Rene that he and John St. Marie, his intense Patrol Plane Commander, got along well together—he was pleased when John suggested they room together at Kodiak. They ended up sharing two nice rooms at Bachelor Officers Quarters, sharing a bathroom with two other VP6 pilots, A. J. Smith and John Clifford. But two weeks later he was "fed up" with his senior officer: St. Marie should have "joined a monastery instead of the Navy." The PPC's alarm clock "ticks too loud—keeps me awake." No radio in the morning, none in the evening. "His radio! That's why I need one of my own." More complaining about life at a forward base and closing with a resigned "Ah, well—."

During each three-day tour down the chain they would spend two nights at N.A.S. Adak with one other crew in a two-room shack called Chuginadak. The big cook-stove kept them warm, heated their rations, and kept everyone close at hand. Kerosene lamps and cookstoves served as inspiration for camaraderie and sea stories. It was even better than camping out. The family separations were made worse, sometimes, by weather so bad that mail planes, with letters from home, could not land. But Scott had begun flying right seat to St. Marie's coveted left-seat spot as pilot. "John said I did real well, so I guess I am getting closer to being a good Naval Aviator," he wrote. And then, "I made all the voice reports." At Adak, with the U.S. Air Force manning the control towers, Scott was prompted to add, in a private bit of inter-service gloating, that he "showed the Air Farce (as we call it) how voice reports should be made."

RENE AND THE BOYS moved outdoors, along with everyone else at Ewa, gravitating to the commons and the picnic tables where mothers drank coffee, watched their children play, and talked. But not about everything. Squadrons are competitive units, and the women quickly learned never, *never* to talk about their husbands, except for what were generally regarded as funny stories. Those who stepped over this subtle but unmistakable line invited immediate group shunning. So the women talked about their babies and their menstrual cycles. It was fair to talk about labor and delivery, other women's labor stories, other people's health problems. Health, children, and the mail. Personal problems, or a husband, were rarely discussed. An indiscreet remark was a kind of disloyalty—bad form in the Navy.

As Jay grew older, Rene began bringing him outside in a cardboard box, where he amused himself for hours simply trying to topple it over. But for every sweet and tractable quality the new baby possessed, Scotty embodied its opposite: a factory-issue, hell-on-wheels two-and-a-half-year-old, particularly on trips to the clinic. For vaccinations, in self-defense, he began donning his toy cowboy pistols, complete with leather holster, a present from his Grandma Toye.

When the nurse announced his turn, Scotty simply threw one of his trusty pistols at her. Still he was not spared. Vaccinations were important, and mothers were more fearful about polio in Hawaii because of the midday heat. Conventional wisdom held that overheated children were more susceptible to the polio virus. Hot afternoons. Children becoming "overheated." Mothers heard that word a lot. So children were allowed to play hard in the morning, but after lunch were brought inside for naps and quiet time. By three or three-thirty in the afternoon, they were again released to the outdoors.

The men at Kodiak were up-to-date on their child-rearing literature—a new genre for parents on the move and far from their own parents in the years after World War II. Scott had heard about an expert he called "Dr. Spahk." Get a copy of his book, he counseled Rene, and "start a system of rewards" for "good behavior." Perhaps a visit to the Officer's Club? Scott was disconsolate after seeing "some parents and their two boys," he confessed to Rene: "I had an almost irresistible desire to go ask them if I could play with their children. I miss you all so terribly."

He also supervised, from Kodiak, Rene's dealings with car mechanics and auto-body repairs: The car looked "crummy to begin with," he lamented, but "the recent dent is the *last* straw." There were the household finances, too: "Keeping a checking account is an exact process," he scolded his wife, "not something to be compared with a squirrel hiding nuts. If you have $217.43 in the bank, then carry $217.43 in the checkbook." Rene had complained in a letter that she didn't even know how much he earned. "You *should* know. I thought you did," he replied. "I draw $124.00 each month, and the mess bill is $45.00, leaving me with $79 each month."

Squadron wives also found ways to make time pass in valuable ways, and volunteer work at Tripler was an important commitment: twice a month a coordinated, island-wide effort drew on thousands of women from every military base on Oahu. Tripler served the Army, the Navy, and the Marines. Many of the Korean war wounded were brought there—men airlifted there straight from their MASH units, or the front lines, still in their battle clothes. Squadron wives were always there to write letters for the guys coming from Korea, either to help them with phone calls or with their letters.

"You smell so *good*," one young soldier told Rene as she sat down to help him with a letter home.

ALL THESE DEPLOYMENTS took the men away for holidays and birthdays, making the separations doubly hard. As a consequence, there were problems with alcoholism, depression, and anger. Fueling these difficulties was a grapevine of rumors reporting on whose letters were or were not coming in, scuttlebutt that took on the force of fact through, "They say…,"massaging every possible variant until it rolled and grew and took on a life of its own, fueled by a few unhappy women working the phones.

Some women became unhinged. During the long Kodiak deployment, one mother stopped appearing in the mornings. Her children would come out, go back inside, yet no mother. Topsy Franco, a good friend, called Rene on the phone to say she had knocked at the door. "She—I saw her wave," Topsy said, "but she doesn't open the door." And then the dread, unavoidable decision: "We have to go in."

This was a dilemma, for the unwritten rules forbade any interfering, or trespassing, in another person's life. But together Topsy and

Rene entered the house and found their neighbor in the bedroom, underneath the bedclothes. Clothes and dishes were everywhere, under the beds, in the bathroom and the living room. With no real knowledge about mental illness, Topsy and Rene nevertheless knew their neighbor was very sick. Going through the chain of command, they called their Executive Officer's wife, a savvy, can-do leader who immediately called the chaplain's office.

The woman was hospitalized and her husband ordered back to Barber's Point. Meanwhile, Topsy and Rene set about washing dishes, bathing the children, putting things in order—doing the simple things.

AT THE SIXTY-FOURTH latitude north, near Fairbanks, Scott wrote, "the sunset colors never leave the sky. They just move around the horizon and become sunrise colors." They hit the bars in town one night, encountering, Scott confessed, a lot of "drunk Eskimo B-girls trying to pick up a few bucks." But the mess sergeants won their hearts that night. Who could have said no? "They took us back to the chow hall and cooked us some french fries and southern fried chicken....Got in at 0430." Scott closed, as always: "Time for chow—more to my sweet when I get back."

VP6 was earning its chow up near the Arctic Circle, where magnetic north wreaks havoc with compasses. That together with the trackless expanses of snow, ice, and water make or break aviators training in the navigator's seat: "We missed our point by just a few miles," Scott explained with immense pride, "with the compass swinging like mad—we hit the ship right on after about five hours of flying. Proud??" His squadron mates, he wrote Rene, congratulated him: "'Say, I hear you're pretty hot on the navigation,'" they told him. Even St. Marie was impressed. So impressed, apparently, that the PPC moved Scott to left seat for a "test hop." He made "one good landing out of one try." Yet another test hop the day following: "Did well today too—one bad landing, two good, and one excellent." His next letter home, August 28, 1952, has Scott once more in the left seat for a hop "up the Chain."

Lightning hit their plane during a patrol in late October. St. Marie, in the right seat, thought a gas explosion had broken the wing. The copilot, momentarily blinded, didn't hazard a guess. The ordnance-man, Van Cleave, who had been up in the bow working the guns, thought all the guns had gone off. No, said Scott, the "wing heater" had exploded. Charles Pomeroy, the radioman, remarked only: "Pass the toilet paper." Upon landing, they could see where the main bolt of lightning hit. It left a big dent in the nose, with many holes and nodules where the heat had melted the aluminum.

At Ewa Beach it was month after month of squadron life, with or without husbands, playing bridge, telling stories, making and playing music, and every so often rousting illicit lovers from behind dumpsters in a bit of impromptu moral policing that Rene and Jim Williford conducted for laughs. There were also USO shows, one of them with Frank Sinatra. Rene took Scotty, now old enough to sit still, to see him perform at Pearl Harbor. Sinatra was at the low point of his career. Crooners were going out, and his voice was going, and when he closed out his first set with "Ol' Man River," he could not hit the low note. The sailors booed and began chanting: "Ava, Ava, Ava!" Ava Gardner, Sinatra's new wife and at the moment Hollywood's most glorious star. The curtains closed and after an intermission Sinatra came out, announcing, "Well, you wanted Ava. You've *got* her." Out from behind the curtain she appeared, in high heels and a gorgeous, full, circle skirt on her beautiful figure. The sailors went *crazy*.

Scott, too, listened to music—and propaganda—on Radio Moscow. "We're using P.O.W.s for running rifle targets and bayonet practice," he informed Rene drily, on December 14, 1952. "We have just gouged out the eyes of 48 North Korean prisoners. Killed 800 Chinese prisoners who were subjected to atom bomb tests in the U.S."

But the Radio Moscow propaganda featured "program breaks," Scott wrote, "that are always preceded by some sort of bells or chimes, rung in an echo chamber or something." The effect, he told Rene, was "beautiful," as was the choral music, "the most beautiful I have ever heard—even the women's choirs sound free and strong and lusty...."

We listen to American Radio stations," which themselves broadcast propaganda, in Russian, "but it only lasts for a few seconds after it starts, because," he explained, the signal was "immediately jammed by Russian static and noise transmitters."

WHEN NOT LISTENING to the deeply northern, snowbound sound of Russian chorales, the crew also picked up the unmistakably Pacific and Hawaiian sound of steel guitars—music from Waikiki beach. And they heard another squadron, VP4, making voice reports to Barber's Point. *Home.* On these memorable winter patrols, with sounds of steel guitars commingling with Russian chorales and punctuated by the awesome sight of erupting volcanoes, Scott wrote Rene only that it defied description. Crew 7 had just broken the P2V-3 record for altitude: "28,250 feet," Scott boasted. The air was so rare that a crewmen nearly passed out while climbing back to the tail guns to take photographs of "our vapor trails." At minus 60 degrees Fahrenheit, outside temperatures on these winter flights were so cold that "oilcicles" developed in something called an "oil breather tube" mounted outside the airplane.

JUNIOR OFFICERS like Scott plot, pray, and plead for a PPC willing to cede the left seat for the all-important time spent actually flying the plane. The fitness reports written by Patrol Plane Commanders and C.O.s, or Commanding Officers, are based largely on an aviator's ability to assume and eventually master increasingly demanding assignments. Junior officers try *very* hard to be good. On the long Kodiak deployment, Scott's prayers were answered in John St. Marie, a fine man, a great pilot and teacher, generous with the controls of the sophisticated and hugely expensive Navy patrol plane.

After a separation of nearly six months, Scott wrote Rene how "terribly lonesome" he was for her. It was Christmastime 1952, and the squadron had taken a hop down the coast for a shopping trip. "Buying the things in Seattle," he wrote, "talking to the girl who had so recently seen you, and seeing the two guys with their wives all combined to make me blue tonight." He wrote in words that every serviceman, every servicewoman, away from home has written a million different times—saying the same thing: "I am still weak from thinking of you so steadily yesterday." Christmas carols playing on the Seattle streets made the Navy pilot's heart "almost stop," he confessed, "for the want to be with you, to hold your hand, to hear your voice, to show you something, or to do any of the little things I take for granted when we're together."

The season, the long separation, he confessed, had made him short-tempered with the enlisted men and other officers. He often caught himself with his eyes closed, "pleading, crying out...for time to pass, quickly...I can't go on—I can't live without her."

THE SQUADRON RETURNED to Barber's Point, in triumph and formation, after New Year's. Together they flew their blue P2Vs down the west coast of the United States and then across the Pacific to their families waiting on the tarmac for hours, scanning the skies, anticipating the embraces and happy reunion tears. Rene was getting her teeth straightened. She had hoped to have the braces off by the time Scott returned, but swooping in for the first clinch, Scott jerked back and felt his nose in alarm. Rene's braces had drawn blood.

The customary round of parties ensued, followed by rest, repairs, training, and new assignments. For Scott this included a wildly unanticipated promotion to Patrol Plane Commander. He tried to explain the accomplishment to his father in the family-eyes-only sort of boasting every proud young professional understands: he'd made PPC with "fewer hours and less time than anyone I know of," admitting to his father he really was "quite pleased since I didn't expect even to make First Pilot." Out of fifty officers in the squadron, only twelve were PPCs, he told his father: "One is the skipper, a commander, four lieutenant commanders, six lieutenants, and me," the only lieutenant (j.g.) PPC in the squadron.

With such a feather in his cap, Scott could now hope for orders to Test Pilot School. This meant Naval Air Station Patuxent River, Maryland. It would have to wait, however, for 1954. The squadron's next forward base, and the final deployment in the tour, would be N.A.S. Agana, Guam.

As it happened, Guam would be a hot, dull, difficult, heavy-drinking tour. The war was over, hence the morale problems. The new skipper was a difficult man, whom Scott had already pegged as "an eccentric" in his first letter home. After two weeks and some incidents not described, he wrote only that "some of this would outshine *The Caine Mutiny.*" Perhaps it was Scott, maybe Frank Franco, but someone sent fifty copies of the skipper's memorandum on Coca-Cola and base hygiene to Barber's Point.

UNITED STATES PACIFIC FLEET

AIR FORCE

PATROL SQUADRON SIX

3 August 1953

PATRON SIX NOTICE 1701
From: Commanding Officer, Patrol Squadron SIX
To: Patrol Squadron SIX
Subj.:   Coca Cola Bottles, instructions for disposition of

1. <u>Purpose</u>. This Notice is issued to promulgate instructions for the handling of opened Coca Cola bottles in order to maintain a maximum condition of health and appearances.

2. <u>Background</u>. Coca Cola Bottles, after being used, normally contain a small residue of Coca Cola in the bottom of the bottle. This residue attracts ants, roaches, and various other insects which are a menace to health and precipitate poor working conditions. It is considered that the Coca Cola bottles are a menace to personnel who may inadvertently step on the bottles and fall. In addition, open bottles in the office spaces present a highly unmilitary appearance and constitute additional workload for personnel assigned clean up duties. It is emphasized that each misplaced or lost bottle costs the Recreation Fund approximately three cents and over a period of time, unless the empty bottles are properly stowed and returned, the loss can amount to several hundred dollars. This money we cannot afford to lose for the Recreation Fund.

3. <u>Directive</u>. All Coca Cola bottles will be consumed in the immediate area of the machine. This area is defined as extending not over ten feet from the machine. Bottles will not be taken into any office or shop space. Empty bottles will be placed in the cases provided and will be in an upright position to prevent spillage.

4. <u>Cancellation</u>. This Notice will be considered cancelled upon the departure of the squadron from the spaces where Coca Cola machines are installed or upon removal of the machine from the squadron spaces.

The Skipper

The memo was pasted into the family scrapbook, along with other mementos of service to country. At the bottom is scrawled in Rene's looping hand: "Topsy and I laughed till we cried."

For Scott and his fellow pilots, the Guam deployment was periodi-cally enlivened by typhoons, skin-diving, spear fishing, and some memorable bar crawls through Mabini, Manila's famed red-light dis-trict. But generally speaking, at Agana, morale was abysmal. As the duty officer on watch one night, Scott had had to intervene in a bloody brawl in the enlisted barracks. He was genuinely anguished by the sailors' living conditions: "They live six men to a cubicle. They don't have sheets.... They have one locker apiece to stow their gear.... What do you expect? What sort of a chance do they have? So what happens," he wrote Rene, "but Scott Carpenter comes in, says, 'Stand up, M———! You're on report.' Scott Carpenter, who has had everything go his way all his life, condemning an enlisted man to Captain's Mast...."

"Put this down," he wrote Rene, "for later discussion." The Navy couple kept a list of conversation topics, for when they were together again and could hash things over. Also, "you must tell me about this new game called 'Scrabble.'"

Scott survived the Agana tour by taking Navy correspondence courses on the P2V; he also spent a lot of time with the P2V-3 mechan-ics. The work and study paid off: On a night check, one of the mechs pulled the salvo handle on a squadron plane only to see the bomb-bay tanks drop down on the partially opened doors. The planes were grounded until Scott came up with a fix. "Ordnance came to me," he told Rene with pride. "Electric came, and even the leading chief came to me." Together they "wrung out the system," he reported, and discovered it wasn't properly rigged in any of the planes. "I devised a way to fix it," he told Rene. "I am proud of this." Growing confident, now, about what he described as his "peculiar combination of talents" (among them, he wrote, were "thoroughness and mechanical aptitude"), the Navy lieutenant concluded he was a good naval officer. He had an "awful lot yet" to learn about flying, he confessed, "but I know the P2V-3."

His senior officers appeared to agree, for as the deployment wound down in December 1953, Scott was named one of the instructor pilots, which meant he would be training the pilots rotating in to replace them at Agana. None of them had flown the P2V. On the first day, he told Rene he had given a five-hour "impromptu" lecture to incoming "pilots and mechs." It was a little "hard on the throat...but I could answer *all* questions," he wrote, underlining "all" twice. He complimented the new group: "I had my first instruction hop today—the pilots are good and should be safe for solo pretty soon."

"You know something else?" he told Rene. He wanted "another little baby—soon." Jay's second birthday was approaching. This time, "a little girl."

Late-arriving replacement crews meant more work for the crews planning to rotate out. The skipper was adamant, for some reason, that the PPCs take on lowly navigational chores on top of the work they were already absorbing because of the overdue crews. "How's that navigational work coming along?" the skipper wanted to know, yelling into the showers. Scott and Franco, both PPCs, had just returned from a long hop and were showering before chow. They exchanged glances. "We're not *doing* navigational, skipper," Scott yelled back over the steam. "Got too much to do as it is."

Come time to write up the fitness reports, at the end of the tour, and the skipper was still fuming about Scott's remark in the shower. His draft report had downgraded the PPC of Crew 7 to excellent; the lieutenant had never garnered anything lower than an outstanding in his five-plus years of U.S. Navy fitness reports. But as it happened, Commander Frank Franco was the squadron's administrative officer, privy to fitness reports as they were drafted. "You can't do that," Franco told the skipper to his face. "You can't downgrade an officer to excellent because you didn't like what he said in the shower."

Commander Franklin Aloysius Franco II (USN), husband of Topsy and captain of the last football team ever fielded by Providence College, prevailed. Outstanding Scott was, and outstanding he remained.

Scott's first squadron duty was coming to a close. The skipper, in a surprise benediction, submitted a "glowing" fitness report for him in October, "the very best" of the lieutenant's entire three-year duty. On December 5, 1953, Scott was, "at the skipper's request," completing "a rough" of his nomination to test pilot training. In 1954 only thirty pilots out of the entire air arm of the Navy could expect to be selected.

Back at Barber's Point for one last time, Scott enjoyed a long-postponed shore leave with Rene and the boys. They had twenty days of vacation, three days of which the couple spent alone at the Royal Hawaiian. Then, eagerly anticipated work on brand-new P2V-5s: "They are right off the line at Lockheed and will be a joy after our old, worn-out P2V-3s," he wrote Toye. In May came the welcome news that Scott was being promoted to full lieutenant. Then more happy news: Guy Howard, the finest skipper to command a Navy patrol squadron, told Scott he was recommending him to the Test Pilot School at N.A.S. Patuxent River, Maryland.

Nominations to Patuxent are one thing. Appointments are another altogether, and soon Scott had even that, a week after his twenty-ninth birthday. By June 1954 the Carpenters had departed Honolulu for a triumphant cross-country family tour, through San Francisco, Boulder, and Iowa. In New York that fall, Scott's father and Edyth arranged for baby-sitters and treated the couple to an opening-night performance of *Fanny*, the Broadway musical of the season. Rene was twenty-six years old, tanned, blonde—and eight weeks pregnant with their first daughter. With no suit to his name, Scott was resplendent in his Navy uniform. Heads turned as the couple took their seats. Ezio Pinza's splendid tenor filled the theater. He sang one of the sweetest homecoming songs ever written for the stage:

'Welcome home',
Says the door,
'Glad to feel
Your hand once more . . .'

The couple glanced at each other in the dark of the Majestic Theater. Home was now the famed Patuxent River Naval Air Station, on the humid, green Maryland shores of the great Chesapeake Bay.

PART

THREE

STARS

8

FOR SPACIOUS SKIES

The starry skies above me and the moral law within me.

—IMMANUEL KANT, INSCRIBED ON A PLAQUE AT THE PEËNEMUNDE MUSEUM

"SURE, I'VE FLOWN that airplane." Every aviator wants to be able to say those words when the conversation turns, as it always does among military pilots, to the latest, fastest, and most advanced airplanes. Scott could say those words at Patuxent, where he now belonged to an elite group: military test pilots. His difficult decision to fly multi-engines, made four years before, had not meant, after all, the death of his boyhood dream to fly fighters. For three years he would fly nearly every type of Navy airplane in active service, as well as many older champions retired from active fleet service. As it turned out, his three years at Patuxent would soon qualify him for membership in the most elite group of them all: Mercury astronauts.

When the Carpenters left N.A.S. Barber's Point for stateside duty in July 1954, they shipped aboard the old troopship *Constitution*. In the hold was their new '54 Mercury Sun Valley, which they had bought after selling the roomy old '49 Mercury convertible. The Sun Valley was a classy little car with a sun roof and other nice features, the best of which was that it was *new*. Yellow and green, but new.

Over the next four years the family of four would become six, expanding to include two daughters—Kristen, born in 1955, followed sixteen months later by her sister Candace. The Carpenters would make four permanent change-of-duty stations in those years, moves involving coast-to-coast trips with a sixteen-foot trailer in tow. But at the beginning of this busy period the family would have three solid years at Patuxent. They found a two-story house on Kearsarge Street, where, for Rene, with two infant daughters plus the two small boys, life became a blur of domestic triage. But in the classrooms and hangars, on the tarmac, and in the air over the Chesapeake Bay, Scott's world of military aviation came into sharp focus.

MILITARY AVIATION begins with a strategic vision: designers perceive the need for a certain capability ten years in the future, and then, appropriations allowing, industry follows through with design and manufacture. At Patuxent these new planes are tested and modified, tested and redesigned, and then retested and evaluated in all the flight regimes for which the Navy thinks they're needed, including some unforeseen at inception. Of course, the same thing happens at the Air Force's counterpart flight test center at Edwards A.F.B., in California.

This development cycle naturally comprises repeated failures and triumphs, of both man and machine, but eventually it culminates in a brand-new flying system and capability. Driving this development cycle—powerfully motivating everyone at Patuxent in the mid-1950s—was an intense U.S.–Soviet rivalry for air supremacy. Few had the slightest idea that this rivalry would soon extend into space.

APART FROM THE intense personal satisfaction Scott felt in flying with the Navy's top pilots (first-rate Air Force, Marine, and civilian pilots, too), he also knew he was contributing to a vitally important development cycle. Finally, the pursuit of engineering perfection he found at Patuxent meshed with his love of all flying machines. It would come to define his life.

Scott was a member of Patuxent's Class 13 (designated "Thirsty Thirteen" because of their drinking habits) and ended up in the top third of his class, even garnering a perfect 100 in his old *bête noire,* heat transfer—called Thermodynamics at Patuxent. But he had a lot to learn. He was not only one of the youngest guys in Class 13, but also one of only two multi-engine pilots there. He had plenty of hours—one earns these on patrol missions—and his P2Vs had flown through typhoons, been struck by lightning, lost engines, flown higher and heavier and colder than most. But they were still P2Vs—great big airplanes. He had never flown a jet airplane solo. That would soon change.

His first memorable flight at Patuxent was in a propeller-driven, single-engine attack airplane called an AD. It had little, short wings and a big, powerful engine up front. The beautiful and rugged F9F-6 Cougar was Scott's first jet fighter, made by Grumman, then nicknamed the Grumman "Iron Works" because their airplanes were so sturdy. The F9F-6 Cougar was very fast and powered by a superb jet engine, which just went round and round with a whirr, instead of reciprocating and making the staccato roar common to most propeller-driven airplanes.

Scott learned to fly jets by flying jets. Once, on a night takeoff in the Cougar, he scanned his instrument panel in the instinctive way pilots develop, only to notice that among the six or so dials, his "rate of climb" showed he was in a descent. He was over the bay at the time, at night, with no visible lights on the ground or water, and could have been five hundred feet from the water or five. Scott never knew for sure. "Rate of climb," he learned that night, was the instrument to watch during jet takeoffs at night over dark water—knowledge he would have gained much earlier had he been trained the regular way in jet fighters.

For about six months he slept during the day, and at night, between the hours of two and five, flew Martin P4Ms, ferret planes equipped with secret electronic countermeasures equipment and an experimental antenna called a Yagi, after its Japanese inventor. In 1955 Soviet and Chinese radars were transmitting in the same frequency band being used by American television, so Scott and his crew had to test the Yagi and its electronics between the hours of 0200 and 0500, when the American television stations weren't transmitting. Once they were over the Chesapeake or the Eastern Shore, the huge antenna secreted inside the fuselage, a crewmen would open the bomb-bay doors and begin cranking out the huge antenna by hand until it was in the proper position.

Martin made only fourteen P4Ms. They had two of the biggest reciprocating aircraft engines ever made, with a separate jet engine enclosed in the same nacelle. The P4M was a dream to fly. Although it featured a number of advanced design concepts, the airplane had operational shortcomings that made it unsuitable for fleet use. In any event, its design was better than its antenna system, which is to say there was no stop on the crank-operated rack, so on one flight when the crank got ahead of the crewman, the antenna just kept going straight down out of the airplane. The Navy never knew where, when, or what the top-secret Yagi antenna hit after it was inadvertently jettisoned from the P4M.

Scott's favorite little airplane at Patuxent was Grumman's F11F Tiger Cat. A mystery surrounded that machine when it first showed up at Patuxent because at first it was called the F9F-9, meaning it was the ninth modification of the Panther/Cougar series. But it clearly had a brand-new airframe/engine combination that required a brand-new designation to match. The pilots were told that appropriations provided money only for modifications of an existing type, so the Navy spent money earmarked for Cougar modifications on Tiger construction until the next fiscal year brought in money for a new airplane type. Only then was the airplane called the F11F Tiger Cat.

Richard T. Whitcomb, an engineer at the National Advisory Committee for Aeronautics (NACA), came up with the first major modification of the F11F fuselage. His redesign essentially fooled the air into thinking the airplane wasn't going as fast as it really was. The aerodynamic ruse not only reduced drag and fuel consumption but also increased top speed and established what became called the "area rule." This in turn produced what was called a "Coke bottle" fuselage, and with that modification the airplane became the F11F1. It carried a radio call sign Scott always loved to say: "Foxtrot One One Foxtrot One." It had such a nice ring.

Test pilots can be a vain bunch, often hopping into new jet airplanes without referring to the manuals ("I can fly anything"). Scott was no exception. His second flight in the airplane brought the first Tiger Cat to Patuxent for electronics testing. After landing, he put out the speed brakes to help the plane slow down—standard practice on the F9F series. It's *verboten* on the F11F series, he discovered, because the brakes on the bottom of the fuselage ran into the ground, leaving a cloud of brown smoke and orange sparks on the runway and a red face on the pilot. He thinks he may also have alarmed the guys in the tower, who thought he'd blown a tire or caught fire. Had he landed with the brakes out, the fuselage could have been damaged, but in this case there was no damage other than to the speed-brake panels, which had to be replaced.

The lesson? Read the pilot's handbook.

The F11F also became famous for shooting holes in itself. It happened during supersonic, high-angle-of-attack, gun-firing runs on a target sleeve towed by another airplane. The bullets were fired well above the horizontal, arced upward, and began to slow down. The pilot pushed the F11's nose down, maintaining supersonic-level flight, and overtook his own bullets, which then went through the canopy. Damage to the airplane wasn't severe, but the event was precedent-setting.

Scott never managed to shoot at himself, but he was involved in an interesting incident in an F2H, a little twin-engine fighter by McDonnell. After landing, and on the way back to the hangar, his left brake gave out. He happened to be headed straight for a line of parked airplanes. The only way he could stop without turning right was to let the left wing tip ride up the blast fence behind those airplanes. That kept him going straight as he came slowly to a stop, and prevented him from running into any of the other airplanes. It was a bad place to lose a brake. It's safe to say, however, that there are no *good* places to lose a brake.

In the mid-1950s, everyone's favorite big airplane at Patuxent was the A3D, a single-piloted, twin-engine attack airplane that flew like a fighter. Scott got into some trouble with his superiors because of his exuberance on one flight, which led him to barrel-roll the airplane on the way back to the base after a test flight, a maneuver forbidden by the manufacturer. Someone saw it happen, or heard about it, so Scott spent some time on the carpet. Fortunately, the airplane controlled beautifully and didn't break, but it is a big, heavy machine, and airplanes like that are not frequently rolled.

The A3D was a long-range airplane, which means a heavy fuel load, which means strict landing-weight limits. When the wings are heavy with fuel, a rough landing can do serious damage to wing spars. In extreme cases, rough landings in severe weather can even break wings. Again, Scott chose (or likes to think he was forced to choose) to extend the published limits of the airplane. He had just taken off for a long test flight in an A3D, which means the wings were nearly full of fuel, when he got a call from base operations: His six-month-old daughter, Kris, had suddenly taken ill. Her veins had collapsed, doctors weren't able to introduce an I.V. at the base hospital, and no ambulance was available at sick bay to take her to the naval hospital in Bethesda, Maryland, a two hours' drive north.

Scott landed, way above the landing-weight limitation. Fortunately, the weather was good and the winds were steady. He made a smooth landing and the wings held. Scott drove madly to the Bethesda Naval Hospital, Rene in the front, with an orderly holding the infant girl in the back of the car. At Bethesda, with great difficulty, doctors performed an ankle cutdown, found a vein, and with a tiny I.V. were able to rehydrate her. Like all the Carpenter children, Kris had been born with a full head of black hair. It fell out in handfuls at Bethesda, growing back in an unusual shade of strawberry blonde that gradually lightened to platinum in the summer swimming pools of Texas—their only fair-haired child.

Patuxent was a sustained three-year epiphany for Scott. But in 1957 it became time, the Navy decided, for him make room for new disciples eager for their own epiphanies on the shores of the Chesapeake. The Carpenters had orders for Monterey, California, where the Navy's Line School awaited. Lieutenant M. Scott Carpenter, whose only wish was to fly airplanes, was to become a well-rounded naval officer.

IMPORTANT TEST PILOTING takes place at Patuxent and Edwards, but the civilian National Advisory Committee for Aeronautics was the creative and intellectual force behind most of the aircraft being flown and tested in the United States. And without the NACA, this story would pretty much end here.

The NACA was chartered by the U.S. Congress in 1915, after an investigative trip across the Atlantic revealed that wartime Europe possessed fourteen hundred military aircraft. The United States—where airplanes had been invented—had fourteen. The agency's mandate was "to supervise and direct the scientific study of the problems of flight with a view to their practical solution, and to direct and conduct experiments in aerodynamics." By the mid-1930s, with guidance from the NACA, the United States had overtaken transport aviation with the revolutionary DC-3.

But on the eve of World War II the country had little in the way of fighter aircraft. Willy Messerschmidt and Claude Dornier had meanwhile presented Nazi Germany's Luftwaffe with the most advanced fighters in the world. Mitsubishi was also doing its part, in Japan, for fighter design and manufacture. Charles A. Lindbergh brought the bad, and unpopular, news home in 1939. The NACA then had only seven hundred employees. Soon, however, it was hiring like mad. By the end of the war, the agency had expanded to nearly eight thousand employees. Working with great American companies, among them Boeing, Chance-Vought, Curtiss, Douglas, Grumman, and others, the quiet civilian agency helped to win not only the war but also the cold war to come.

WHEN THE NATION was born, Thomas Jefferson envisioned America as a pastoral, agricultural bastion, a nation of smallholders and prosperous farmers. Alexander Hamilton, more familiar with the rocky soil to the north and its seasonal poverty, touted instead the virtues of a manufacturing, mercantile system. Trade was the key; the United States would be a nation of merchants. The Founding Brothers should have asked their confrere, Benjamin Franklin. He would have told them that, although it was nice to farm and trade, America (itself an invention) would go nowhere without its entrepreneurial, genius inventors.

By the mid-twentieth century, nowhere were Franklin's intellectual descendants busier or more inventive than in the machine shops, offices, wind tunnels, pinochle games, cafeterias, and car pools at the NACA research centers: Langley Field, Lewis, and Ames. Langley was the oldest of the three and focused on aeronautics; the propulsion experts worked at Lewis Research Center, near the Cleveland airport; and the aerodynamicists and theorists labored at the Ames Research Center at Moffett Field, near Mountain View, California. Eventually, Wernher von Braun's operation (launch vehicles) at the U.S. Army Redstone Arsenal, with its six thousand employees, was absorbed by a reorganized NACA and renamed Marshall Space Center. Dr. von Braun remained in charge.

Primus inter pares at the NACA, however, was the Pilotless Aircraft Research Division (PARD) and its trio of Louisiana State University friends and stalwarts, Max Faget, Paul E. Purser, and Guy ("Tibby") Thibodaux, who have recalled their years there in oral histories that crackle with intelligence, fondly remembered goofs and triumphs, and a wee bit of scorn for their rivals (von Braun excepted). Most of all, however, they express an abiding affection for each other, for pioneers now gone, and for the early days.[1]

Although Purser, Faget, and Thibodaux were all products of the engineering department at Louisiana State University, a land-grant institution, they readily concede that no one needed an academic credential to excel at the NACA. But you did need talent—lots of it—which for decades the agency had been accustomed to finding at national model-plane competitions. According to Thibodaux (the sole Cajun of the three), one of the agency's top aerodynamic scientists began as an elevator boy at headquarters.[2] Thibodaux himself was born at a cypress-logging operation in the Atchafalaya Swamp, not far from Thibodaux, Louisiana, named for his Acadian forebears. He moved to New Orleans with his family as a five-year-old.

A native of southeastern Louisiana, Purser was the son of a New Orleans attorney. The Great Depression ruled out Tulane as an educational option. That left LSU. His friend Max Faget was born after World War I in British Honduras. Max's father was Dr. Guy H. Faget, a tropical diseases specialist there, filling in for British doctors serving in France.

As head of the Carville Leper Colony, in Louisiana, Dr. Faget would develop the first practical cure for leprosy.[3]

All of them served during World War II. Purser signed up with the U.S. Army, only to be lent back to the NACA for defense-related research. Faget served aboard a combat submarine in the Pacific as a U.S. Naval Reserve officer. Thibodaux had the most exotic military career, in the China-Burma-India theater, as a second lieutenant in the still-segregated U.S. Army, a white officer in the all-black Forty-fifth Engineering Regiment that built advanced fighter strips in the Burmese jungle and the road from Lido, India, to Kunming, China.[4]

Faget and Thibodaux pledged each other that if they survived the war they'd join forces and look for jobs together. So in 1946, with their friend Purser at the NACA, there was only one place to look. They borrowed Dr. Faget's canary-yellow 1941 Chevrolet coupe and drove up to Langley Field, Virginia, where Purser met them in the lobby and promptly offered them jobs in the newly created Pilotless Aircraft Research Division. They remember the day vividly. Not as vividly as their boss, Dr. Robert R. Gilruth, who claims he "never had a luckier day in my life than when I picked up those two guys."[5]

Thibodaux, the chemical engineer, was immediately put to work on rockets and solid-fuel propellant systems. He would come to dominate the field for the rest of the century, explaining later that his two greatest professional assets were laziness and lack of ambition. Of course, you need to be brilliant to make these attributes work for you, and Thibodaux was brilliant.[6] Faget had a degree in mechanical (and aeronautical) engineering, so he was assigned to ram jets. Purser was that rarest creature among engineers, a rapid, meticulous writer and editor, and a whiz at administration. He had already snagged a position as assistant to Gilruth, the director of PARD and also, it would turn out, the finest research administrator of the century. "He called me his special assistant," Purser explains, "because I had the task of doing almost anything he felt he couldn't do, didn't have time to do, or didn't want to do."[7]

The three LSU graduates had found a kind of engineer's paradise, not least because Gilruth ran PARD as though it belonged to the lowliest technician there. It was "a bottom-up organization like you never saw before!" Faget says. "A bottom-up organization with a big free ticket." ("The ticket wasn't *that* big," Purser clucks. "We still had to go to headquarters for anything over $5,000.")[8] By "bottom-up," Faget meant any notion had merit if anyone in the organization thought something was "a good idea." Caldwell Johnson, another renowned designer, remembers that collaboration across divisions was so intense and free he often forgot which division he worked in and whose boss was his.

Gilruth wandered through the PARD offices, sitting on trash cans (turning them over if they were empty), asking questions, listening to answers, and preaching the gospel of absolute simplicity. To a worker stuck on a problem, he exhorted, "Use your *head*!" Thibodaux learned to do just that. *Passive systems,* he found, those that rely on immutable physical and chemical laws, were the perfect expression of the Gilruth gospel. Active systems break. They're expensive. They fail. Passive systems are reliable and cheap. And absolutely simple.

Everyone in Hampton, Virginia, Purser remembers, called them the NACA Nuts—which in Tidewater parlance came out "Nakker nuts." Faget was famously distracted, even by NACA standards. His first year at Langley Field, he called his friend Thibodaux every morning to get directions to work. "If you think *we're* weird," adds Purser, "there was one guy who had a piece of white adhesive tape on the top center of his steering wheel, and he would drive along solving mathematical equations in his mind and just glance down once in a while to see if the white was still in the middle!"[9]

THEY WERE WORKING on lots of different problems. In the immediate postwar period, one problem concerned the propeller-driving reciprocating internal-combustion engine and the turbo-jet engine. They required oxygen, which was in short supply in the stratosphere, where the newest planes were trying to fly. Without oxygen, combustion can't take place; fuel needs oxygen to burn. The solution was the rocket engine, which provides its own oxygen in addition to fuel. Soon these new airplanes powered with rocket engines were approaching the never-never-land of flight beyond the speed of sound (Mach 1). Some said it couldn't be done. But on October 14, 1947, Captain

Charles E. ("Chuck") Yeager, USAF, became the first to exceed Mach 1 aboard the rocket-powered Bell X-1. Supersonic flight was not impossible, after all.

Exciting, yes. But also sobering. Emphasis began shifting toward the intercontinental ballistic missile (ICBM). Called a "stand-off" weapon, ICBMs could deliver a nuclear device five thousand miles away, the distance from North Dakota missile silos to the Soviet Union, or vice versa, from Siberia to the Eastern seaboard. The ICBM's stand-off capabilities notwithstanding, everyone knew that few creatures would be able to stand off quite far enough from the resulting radiation blast. Welcome the dawn of global uneasiness.

Yet the search for measures and countermeasures continued. Always has. Always will.

THE QUEST FOR stand-off weapons has gone on ever since a caveman first hefted a rock in self-defense and contemplated the long stick, or sharpened flint, his enemy was brandishing. Experience brought not only episodic wisdom (peace is preferable to war), but also more knowledge about weapons themselves. Those that can be used at some distance from the enemy are superior to those that expose you to harm. Skilled users of these stand-off weapons (like the slingshot) can sometimes prevail over a superior foe, as David prevailed over Goliath, the Philistine giant.

Speed is important in warfare. With speed comes the element of surprise and the ability to attack, and withdraw, quickly. In this regard, the horse was key. Teams of horses can be trained to pull highly maneuverable chariots, filled with armored archers, around a battlefield. A mounted warrior has an advantage over a foot soldier, better still a mounted warrior on a stirrup-equipped saddle, a modest contrivance that revolutionized European warfare. Battlefield tacticians maximized horse and human power with the phalanx, a wedge-shaped cavalry formation that split the enemy's forward line, making it more vulnerable to a secondary offensive.[10] Metallurgists and armorers conspired to create a truly daunting military sight, described by Charlemagne's biographer: "That man of iron topped with his iron helmet, his fists in iron gloves, his iron chest and his broad shoulders clad in an iron cuirass. An iron spear raised on high against the sky was gripped in his left hand. In his right he held his still unconquered sword."[11]

Every era has its man of iron and his "unconquered sword." The fighter pilot and his flying machine is probably our own.

WAR IS A NASTY business, but the clearest thinkers tend to bring conflicts to a quicker conclusion (if they cannot prevent them in the first place), sustain fewer casualties, and gain their military and political objectives. This raises the invention- and industry-provoking aspect of war: namely, for every new lethal measure there is a countermeasure—witness the longbow's decline after the introduction of heavy defensive armor.

Inventions and innovations sometimes came so fast and thick that battle tacticians couldn't manage, as happened during World War I, when generals sent millions of soldiers onto killing fields, not fields of battle. More to the point, here, is the invention of the airplane in 1903. To the delight of civilians, airplanes sped them to new places. Mail and medicine could be transported more quickly. The military mind was equally delighted, observing that the plane, like the horse, could be adapted to war. Equipped with proper guns, it could shoot down an enemy's air assets. With explosives, it could bombard railways and munitions factories. To this day the airplane remains a superb stand-off weapon, although it, too, is vulnerable to countermeasures and its standoff distance is exceeded by that of ballistic missiles.

So, THE STORY of invention brings us to the cold war, missiles, rockets, unsuspecting Navy lieutenants, and space. For on October 4, 1957, the Soviet Union launched into orbit a small, pinging radio satellite called *Sputnik I*. Speculative comparisons about technological superiority were over. Soviet rockets could do what American rockets could not. The United States was behind, once again, in a deadly serious technology race.

In October 1957 Scott and his two sons, Scotty, seven years old, and five-year-old Jay, were driving east across the country in the yellow and green 1954 Mercury Sun Valley. The tour of duty in Monterey, California, at the Navy Line School had ended; Scott had orders to the Air Intelligence School in Washington, D.C., for eight months of classroom instruction on the duties of air intelligence officer, after which he could expect a three-year assignment to sea duty. Although photo interpretation would be an interesting part of his studies, Scott's main assignment would be briefing and debriefing the pilots on their missions. No flying of his own.

Rene had flown with the girls to Boulder, where they would stay while the boys and their father enjoyed a cross-country trip with their bedrolls. The plan was to meet up in Boulder, after which the Carpenter men would press on for Virginia and house-hunting duties. They camped out every night by the car (waking up one morning dusted with snow) and saw a lot of night sky. In Nebraska, however, was something altogether new. They had heard news of the Soviet satellite on the radio, so Scott knew what it was.

"There's *Sputnik!*" Scott said to the boys, pointing to the satellite. They were unimpressed. To them, it was simply a white light on what appeared to be a low, fast-flying airplane. But when their father explained what they were really seeing, where it had come from, how far away it was, how high it was, and how fast it was moving, they perked up. Scotty asked why the light didn't flash like other airplanes. His father told him that the satellite possessed no light of its own but was so high it could still see the sun, so the three of them were looking at reflected sunlight. There was a long silence while they contemplated a brand-new world.

At the same time, Faget, Purser, and Thibodaux were attending something called the Round Three Conference, mulling a Boeing proposal for something called the Dyna-Soar, a successor to the Air Force's X-15 rocket planes. Everyone was trying to figure out how to get to Mach 15. The conference was held at NACA's Ames Research Center, in Mountain View. All year the Langley hands had been flying back and forth across the country, playing lots of poker, while Faget used the NACA's unpressurized plane to tactical advantage. Over the Rockies, he cannily watched his card-playing buddies for signs of hypoxia, oxygen deprivation. When their fingernails turned blue, Faget's practice was to bluff outrageously. He almost always cleaned up.

No one was the least bit addled at Ames, however. They listened intently to the Boeing proposal. The Dyna-Soar, Purser recalls, was going to be a "long, slender, triangular aircraft that would be flown with power to very high speed, and then allowed to coast, or glide, with an eventual range of 12,000 or more miles." It was "either a winged bomber," Thibodaux recalls, "or a winged orbiting space-surveillance aircraft." As the former, Dyna-Soar could fly, or glide, halfway around the world at speeds of Mach 15. With the newest propulsion technology, the Air Force thought the hypersonic glider might achieve earth orbit. As the latter, a space bomber, it was supposed to be able to fly and bomb anywhere in the world.

Attending the discussions were two Ames theoreticians: Alfred J. Eggers, Jr., and his boss, H. Julian ("Harvey") Allen. Both men had been thinking about the aerodynamics of reentry bodies since the early 1950s. Eggers in particular had developed deep misgivings about the glider-bomber, and during the Round Three Conference, in October 1957, stood up and objected rather forcefully. Faget was familiar with Eggers's theoretical work and also spoke in opposition. The hypersonic glider had no strategic utility, Faget said: "Zero. *Zip.* We weren't going to do that." Even at Mach 15, the behemoth would be identified by Soviet radar and shot down by Soviet air defenses well before it reached its target.[12]

So there they were, Faget, Purser, and Thibodaux, all sitting in the Ames auditorium, pondering the extinction of the Dyna-Soar, when someone came in and announced the launch of *Sputnik I.* NACA director Hugh L. Dryden was there, along with most of the Ames people. So was a young civilian pilot named Neil Armstrong, who would soon fly the X-15 and eventually push it to speeds of almost Mach 6.[13]

"Scared the hell out of everybody," remembers Faget. Here the Soviets were, "putting up a gallon jug," and all the Americans could do was "launch a grapefruit." The Dyna-Soar died that day. *Sputnik* changed "all the rules," explains Faget. The United States wasn't going to *fly* into space in an airplane. It was going to get there, he knew in an instant, on a rocket and return to earth along the lines that Al Eggers and Harvey Allen had been suggesting since 1952.[14]

Allen had two interesting hobbies. One of them was the Mayans; he was always traveling to British Honduras (now Belize) to look at the ruins and ponder their star-gazing habits. His other hobby, somewhat related, was gathering meteorites. Faget says these meteorites gave Allen the unconventional idea of a blunt-nosed, high-drag (rather than a pointed-nose, low-drag) capsule design:

> He noticed that the little meteorites, the ones that were of any size at all, could get all the way to the ground, but they were pretty small. And they had a rounded nose. The nose had gotten round because the surface had melted, and it had melted in the position that made them, apparently, aerodynamically stable, as clear as he could tell.

So the meteorites had a nose, or leading edge, that was a section of a sphere and therefore aerodynamically stable. Add a small afterbody, shielded by the nose so it won't melt, and you have the basic shape of a reentry vehicle. "And he got to looking at these things," Faget explains, "and he said, 'The reason they survive is that they have a very high drag-to-weight ratio. So the way to get down from orbit is to slow down!' "[15] In short, a blunt-end reentry shape—the eventual design of the Mercury capsule.

THIBODAUX WAS A solid-fuels man. Solid fuels were stable. No one did solid fuels except the Cajun. He even mixed his own synthetic rubber–based propellants with a commercial mixer he got from a bakery-supply company. In this he was bucking convention. Wernher von Braun had been using liquid propellants since Peënemunde, while developing a long-range bombardment system for Nazi Germany. A dozen years later, he was still employing the highly volatile mixtures at the U.S. Army's Redstone Arsenal. But PARD decided to go with Thibodaux's solid-fuel rockets, experimenting with them at the Wallops Island facility off the coast of Virginia. It also had experience with something called "staging" (stacking rockets on top of one another and programming them to go off in sequence) and achieving orbital velocity, or Mach 25.

So in the lobby of the Ames auditorium, maybe an hour after the *Sputnik* announcement, Thibodaux and Faget were buttonholing Hugh Dryden. Faget told the NACA director: "We're not going anywhere fast and if you just give us a chance, we could put a man in orbit." All they needed was authorization. Dryden demurred. Satellites, he reminded them, came out of the Vanguard program run by the Naval Research Laboratory.

"So we got back to Langley," Faget explains, "and talked to Bob Gilruth." The great PARD director said, "Well, you guys go ahead and work on it. We won't tell anybody." And that's how Project Mercury began.[16]

PRESIDENT DWIGHT D. Eisenhower greeted the news of *Sputnik* with his customary equanimity. He was a sensible, well-informed man, familiar with global conflict and not given to panic. He had fought and won a world war. He knew Hugh Dryden, the NACA director, and what the agency could do, if mobilized. He also knew the Soviets' launch capabilities grew out of a relatively crude nuclear science. In a technological irony, the Soviets had come up with big, heavy nuclear weapons requiring huge booster rockets. The United States' nuclear bombs were relatively light, and its booster rockets were as a consequence only as powerful as they needed to be. But with rocket technology now being driven by a cold war foe, the Soviets, the president conceded the wisdom of creating a single agency devoted entirely to space.

Until *Sputnik* all the space-related work in the United States was divided helter-skelter among the military services and all manner of government agencies, each one rather jealously guarding its meagre slice of the space pie. The U.S. Air Force was an obvious choice for the new job. But President Eisenhower wasn't so sure. The professional soldier and West Point graduate was more complicated than his résumé suggested. For one thing, he was a descendant of Plain people, Swiss Mennonites and German Pietists who along with their Anglo Quaker cousins had settled Pennsylvania in the eighteenth century.

David Hackett Fischer, a cultural historian, notes that the president's "forebears had refused to bear arms in the Revolution and the Civil War....Eisenhower remembered his mother quoting the Bible: 'He that conquereth his own soul is greater than he who taketh a city.'"[17]

Turning to his science adviser, Dr. James R. ("Jack") Killian, Jr., Eisenhower said he wanted a civilian space program. He "was certainly very strong on this point," Faget recalls. The president was also delivering speeches at the time on something he was calling the "military-industrial complex." The old soldier had two points to make in these speeches. The first was historical, to bear witness to what he had seen in Germany, where military and industrial interests had colluded with government to produce world war and a holocaust. The president's second point was cautionary. He saw similar forces at work in the postwar United States. Not fascist, perhaps, nor genocidal, but certainly too much of a military-industrial complex to suit his pietist sensibilities. He was particularly critical of an upstart U.S. Air Force intent on taking weapons to the ultimate high ground.[18]

If President Eisenhower had anything to do with the United States going into space, then the country would go there peacefully, with a civilian agency devoted to its famously spacious skies. We'd take the high ground, all right, and leave our weapons behind. If the president wanted a civilian program, Killian replied, then the NACA was his "best cadre" for the job. So in March 1958, Hugh Dryden, the agency's gentle, scholarly director, was summoned across Lafayette Square for a talk with the president and his science adviser. Dryden agreed. A civilian space agency was right for the country, but he had to talk with his people. He went back to his office in the Dolley Madison House and made some calls. He spoke with Abe Silverstein, head of the Lewis Research Center. He spoke with Bob Gilruth at Langley Field. They agreed. The NACA was the only real candidate for the job. The director conceded the inevitable, but reluctantly. His quirky, brilliant, anonymous agency was about to change forever.[19]

IF SPUTNIK SCARED the hell out of the rocket experts, then it caused something like panic among the American public. The first Soviet launch was soon followed by *Sputnik II,* which put a dog named Laika into orbit. The poor creature died, from heat and terror, during her fourth orbit of the planet. The ASPCA lodged a formal protest. But the second launch, dead dog and all, signaled "what the first *Sputnik* only implied." The Soviets were going to launch a human being into space just as soon as they could.[20]

It followed that the United States would have to beat them to it. Faget was already on it.[21]

So began the space race, with a burly Communist foe, a technological irony, nuclear weapons, a complicated, pacifist-soldier president, and the Gilruth gang. Still, Faget says, "headquarters was *absolutely unprepared*" to be the new space agency. Hugh Dryden and Gus Crowley, who worked at agency headquarters near Lafayette Square, were soon telephoning the three research centers, begging them to send people to help with the transition.[22] By mid-March a "space committee" of about a dozen people was formed—Faget, Purser, and Thibodaux were members—and from March to November 1958 worked out of the sixth floor of the Dolley Madison house, where no one was allowed to speak to them. The "space cadets" fanned out across Washington, striding the corridors of the Defense Department, the Atomic Energy Commission, the Advanced Research Project Agency (ARPA), and the Institute for Defense Analysis, sitting in on any meeting they liked—nerdy gods prepared to steal fire back from the mortals.[23]

The president of the United States, working hand in glove with NACA engineer Charlie Zimmerman, inventor of among other flying things the Captain Keds Rocket Belt, secured the best possible security clearances for the space cadets. "I think I had a badge," offers Faget, trying to explain his phenomenal security access for the epic eight-month period during which NASA was created. Thibodaux remembers only: "I showed up and they let me in." Every morning the committee members knew where to go because Charlie Zimmerman had "found out everything going on at the Pentagon. . . . He had a little petty cash fund we could throw chits in and take cash out for taxi fares and things like that."[24]

And off they all went to attend, listen, participate (if they wanted), and gather information on everything *everyone* was doing on space. At the end of each day, they'd convene at headquarters and then walk back as a group through Lafayette Park, down Pennsylvania Avenue until it became M Street, all the way to lower Georgetown and their flea-bag hotel, the Francis Scott Key, always stopping for a bottle at the nearby liquor store.

Gathering in the room Gilruth was sharing with Silverstein, who headed the Lewis Research Center, they passed the bottle around and "the young guys would tell the old guys how the cow ate the cabbage." No one took minutes. Nor did anyone particularly realize they were forming a space agency. Dryden did, Gilruth too, but they assured the Pentagon that their people were simply gathering information; no, of *course* they were not stealing programs. Nor did Dryden once divulge that, once the new agency was formed, the military's involvement in space would cease. Even then Paul Dembling, the agency's sole attorney, was drafting the National Aeronautics and Space Act of 1958.

This account of NASA's beginnings is not to suggest that Faget and Gilruth were keen about stealing *every* space-related idea floating around the Pentagon. At one presentation, they heard about a "Death-o-Meter," a control-room display that would chart a spaceman's biological status—respiration rate, pulse rate, core body temperature. Personnel were going to watch the Death-o-Meter in the control room, as far as Faget could tell, and "in case the astronaut got too close to death...we were supposed to bring him down, I *think!*"

But one could just as easily stumble across priceless information. Listening to one Air Force proposal, regarding the Atlas missile Convair was building, Faget learned for the first time what a spacecraft would have to weigh. "There was a guy from General Dynamics, Frank Dorr. So when we had a break," Faget recalls. "I said, 'Frank, what's this about putting two thousand pounds into orbit with the Atlas?' He said, 'Yeah, we call it the Bare Atlas. It'll put two thousand pounds into orbit.'" *Incredible* news:

At the time I knew we could do it without having to use a
second stage. Previously when we had a solid-rocket upper
stage, we also had an escape system in the event the Atlas failed.

Now suddenly we had no escape rocket. Shortly after we
decided to go with the Bare Atlas, Bob Gilruth said, "Max, what
are you going to do when the Atlas blows up?" I said, "I don't
know!" He said, "Well, you'd better figure something out!"[25]

Working with an existing idea for a tow rocket, Faget came up with
a design for a launch escape rocket, later adopted by the Soviet space
program and responsible for saving the lives of two cosmonauts; Faget
was later decorated, informally, with the Soviet Red Star.

While sleuthing space programs part of the week in Washington,
Faget was still branch head at PARD, hard at work on a capsule design
alongside Caldwell Johnson and Guy Thibodaux. The idea, thanks to
Frank Dorr, was to fit a medium-sized man inside a 2,000-pound ballistic vehicle placed atop a rocket.[26] After being launched into orbit, the
capsule would fire its retrorockets, slow down, reenter earth's atmosphere (keeping its occupant safe and alive inside), and splash down to
an ocean landing.

Faget and another NACA aerodynamicist, James Buglia, immediately began running some tests on blunt bodies. They determined that a

blunt body large enough to carry a man would return through
the atmosphere without overheating with a deceleration of
about eight Gs—a force that a man should be able to survive.
Along with a third aerodynamicist, Benjamin Garland, Faget
and Buglia wrote a paper recommending a ballistic capsule for
manned flight. The paper, a seminal one for the space program,
was a masterpiece of brevity: its text took up eight pages, and
drawings and references took up eight more.[27]

All well and good, except for the eight Gs predicted for reentry.
The military flight surgeons were unhappy. Faget explains that "some
of our most vigorous critics now became the Air Force medical
people." He describes the criticism as purely territorial: "They were
very concerned that they were not going to be in charge of this project, and they were criticizing everything we did." So Faget found biomedical stress data from centrifuge experiments with Germany's

World War II fighter pilots showing successful tests of up to eighteen Gs.[28] It may have been Nazi data, but it would help the United States beat a new enemy, the Soviets.

Faget showed this information to his critics and added that "as a tradeoff" for the high-G reentry, "a ballistic craft would come to an easily predictable splashdown," even if the astronaut were to black out momentarily. This is because a ballistic craft could take only one path, and therefore land in only one place. The M2, a competing design, would have a cross-range ability of fifteen hundred miles and could end up anywhere. Besides, it weighed in at four thousand pounds, while the ballistic design, because of its great simplicity—Faget's trademark—ran the best chance of being held down to two thousand pounds. According to Faget, the weight consideration is what eventually clinched the argument in favor of what came to be called the Mercury design, a name chosen by Dr. Abe Silverstein for this first American messenger to the gods.[29]

Faget remained concerned, however, about the effect of high Gs on the human occupant and that spring, while sleuthing space programs at ARPA and designing the Mercury capsule, he also got the idea for the contour couch. He explains his thinking at the time: "If you look at the body and put it under eight Gs, you say, 'That's not much different from whipped cream at eight Gs. It's going to sag.'" The contour couch—one custom-molded to a pilot's backside—acts as an exoskeleton during the rigors of liftoff and reentry, literally keeping the human body from extruding bits of lung, flesh, and vascular tissue.

The Langley machine shops began fabricating the couches in May 1958.

At the time, the U.S. Air Force was still running its important centrifuge tests at Wright-Patterson in a "G sub x" (G_x), or head-to-hip, mode, replicating the kind of acceleration orientation an X-series pilot at Edwards, for example, would experience during Mach 1 flight and beyond. Meanwhile, the U.S. Navy had recently built a state-of-the-art centrifuge at Johnsville, Pennsylvania, where medics were finding that human subjects could sustain much higher G loads if tested in a supine position called "G sub z" (G_z).

So Faget took his centrifuge studies to Johnsville. An NACA test pilot, Bob Champine, was on hand to help out, except he had been ordered not to exceed eight Gs, even in the G_z position with his very own contour couch. As it happened, a keen young lieutenant on the Johnsville centrifuge staff, Carter C. Collins, decided to help Faget out. And after each of Champine's runs, Collins said he'd take the same one, cheerfully modifying the contour couch made for the bulkier civilian test pilot with some foam-rubber padding. Having done his eight Gs, Champine left—for a hot new airplane at Edwards or a conference in California, accounts vary—while Collins persisted, saying, "Well, Max, let me see if we can go a little higher."

And in two-G increments in late July 1958, Lieutenant Carter C. Collins got all the way up to twelve Gs.

But while Lieutenant Collins was working up to twelve Gs, Faget had come up with some troubling test trajectories. "What happens," he asked years later, "if the Atlas fails at a velocity near to 18,000 feet per second?" At that velocity, Faget discovered, "the centripetal force from circling the earth at constant altitude would only be about one-half G." But then you start falling. When this happens, the ballistic capsule (and its human occupant) ends up "reentering at about a 10- to 12-degree flight-path angle." In other words, at least eighteen Gs of deceleration from drag.[30]

That's a lot of Gs. Only the Nazis had produced data on G forces of this magnitude—data Faget knew he *had* to replicate at Johnsville. So he put it to Collins this way: He promised to "be forever grateful" if the Navy lieutenant would ride the centrifuge up to twenty Gs. Collins said, sure, he'd give it a go.

"The next day, in two-G increments," Faget recounts triumphantly, "he rode it up to fourteen, then sixteen, eighteen, and twenty Gs." On his drive home at the end of that day, July 30, 1958, Collins pulled off to the side of the road three or four times to throw up; his internal gyros, the ears' semicircular canals, had been temporarily damaged by the G forces.[31] He was fine after a few days, basking in Faget's eternal gratitude and the elation of the entire Johnsville team. Collins's triumph at Johnsville, as it happens, occurred on the day the U.S. Congress passed the National Aeronautics and Space Act. The NACA was now NASA, the National Aeronautics and Space Administration.

FAGET CONTINUED TO tackle other knotty problems, such as determining the effects of a water landing on the human body. For these experiments, which began taking place both at Johnsville and St. Louis in 1959, NASA decided to use large Yorkshire pigs. Jack C. Heberlig, the engineer who had helped to design the contour couch, also made one for a pig, "who would be hoisted to a height of 16 feet and then dropped into a sandbox, where it would land at a velocity of 30 feet per second, the predicted rate for Mercury."[32]

One day they strapped one of the pigs at Johnsville into its custom-made contour couch for a drop. But then the guys broke for lunch. When they came back, their pig was dead.

"You can't leave a pig on his *back*!" explained the farmer who had sold them the pigs. He had to explain pig anatomy: their internal organs don't take to odd gravitational forces—G sub z *or* sub x—for longer than a couple of minutes. The weight of the organs, especially in the G_z configuration, pressed on his lungs. The poor pig suffocated to death—in a custom-made contour couch.

It was August 1958 and *still* Congress hadn't come up with funding for the new space agency it had legislated into existence. They wanted to see a model of the capsule. So Heberlig, the contour couch designer, got the Langley machine shop to build a small-scale model, bootlegging the order under "ATLAS WARHEAD REQUISITION NO. 263." Gilruth and Dryden were soon marching the model over to the House Select Committee on Astronautics and Space Exploration. They left the Hill with a $30 million budget.

Once empowered, Gilruth formed the Space Task Group (a makeshift name that first appeared in lowercase letters and then persisted, with capitals) to manage the manned-space part of the new agency. And on November 3, the "initial contingent of military services aeromedical personnel" reported to the STG for duty. They began working on "human factors, crew selection, and crew training plans."[33] They had a proposal prepared for President Eisenhower by Christmas.

THAT SPRING, while NASA was taking shape in the minds of Bob Gilruth and company, a devastating ice storm blew into Northern Virginia. The Carpenters had found a home there, in Pine Crest, for the brief tour of duty at the Air Intelligence School, in the Anacostia section of Washington, D.C.

Scott and Rene would be celebrating their tenth wedding anniversary that September. They were older, wiser, and four kids richer, which is to say more broke than ever. Still, Rene, who had been merely pretty at the age of twenty, was at thirty a beauty, with flawless skin and a lovely, slim figure. During the sometimes hard-drinking Navy parties, one could find her, a nonsmoker, holding her one cocktail of the evening, a watery Canadian Club on the rocks, laughing and talking about one rollicking topic or another. Neil Simon describes it best, for less than ten years later Rene and Scott would arrive at his home for a New Year's Eve party, as the guests of Leonard Lyons, the *New York Post* columnist. Paddy Chayefsky was also present that night, performing yeoman's service at the other end of the room, entertaining single-handedly more than a dozen guests. While Scott was buttonholed in the foyer by the curious, Rene "drifted quietly over to hear Paddy take center stage," Simon recalls. It was 1966. "After a while, this very attractive and intelligent woman interjected and disagreed with Paddy's thesis." Chayefsky was both startled and thrilled. He had just experienced the needle, which few have wielded more deftly, more gently, more sexily than Rene Carpenter, owner of the straight line:

> What made the exchange so unique was that there was an added dimension. She was so regal and so likable, that no matter what she said that irritated Paddy, you could see that Paddy was attracted to her. He was actively going toe-to-toe with her, giving her no quarter, slamming down her ideas as drivel and her politics as antiquated, dangerous, and balderdash, but he did so with a glint in his eye, almost furious with himself because he knew he couldn't help liking her.[34]

As the Carpenters prepared to leave the Simons' party, Chayefsky came over to say good-bye. He kissed Rene's hand, "On the other hand," he said, "I may be completely wrong."

The next day Simon sat down at his desk and wrote down some ideas for a play—about two political adversaries, a man and a woman, who are nevertheless attracted to each other. This germ of an idea eventually became Simon's *Star Spangled Girl,* a romantic comedy. It wasn't his best play. But then Simon never realized that Paddy and Rene's performance that night had been pure theater.

So, yes, Rene needled the blowhards, engaged the tongue-tied, encouraged a young wife. Everyone loved Rene, the star-spangled girl, her vices limited to a sharp tongue at home and a certain monthly irritability, during which her husband had learned to keep his head down.

As for Scott's domestic attributes, circa 1958, he was a little at sea about his duties, his grandparents' Victorian union his model: Grandma up before dawn, firing up the cast-iron wood stove; Grandpa at the head of the dining-room table, accepting her labor as one of life's givens. Seven days a week they both worked, until they dropped in their traces. Still, men did not prepare food, nor did they help to keep house. And so Scott committed a standard error in couples logic: inferring a universal truth from a unique upbringing. Rene, meanwhile, recognized no universal truth, only madcap chaos theory proved anew each day. Still, she managed well. She transformed her succession of dwellings into comfortable homes overnight. At five each afternoon she metamorphosed into a goddess, with some lipstick and a brush through her short blond hair, startling the children when she stepped out of her bedroom with a distant look.

Her priorities were unshakeable: during the day, the children and their meals and activities, then her appearance as evening approached, and if time permitted, finally, the housekeeping. The management of the food stock was a particular problem. Home from a hop or a briefing by mid-afternoon, Scott might end up with too much free time before dinner and so inventoried pantry items, not saying much. He didn't have to, with his actions so eloquent: closing left-open packages, arranging goods on the shelves. Oh, *God,* the refrigerator. Another inventory there produced a kind a physical pain for the orderly Navy pilot. There were cardboard-stiff bologna slices, the open jar of mustard sporting a helpful knife, long-forgotten what-looks-like lettuce in a corner. The garbage was next: Rene had short, soft fingers and did not collapse the empty milk cartons properly, which means, as he explained to the children, unnecessarily frequent trips to take the garbage out.

As the low-key marital drama unfolded in the kitchen, the children absorbed the obtuse scene: Dad's strong hands collapsing the stiff milk carton into a slim, square accordion, Mom silently wiping down the counter with a wet rag, her back to him. They were different; the children knew this much. Mom, a cheerful, freshwater spring of a woman; Dad, a deep, imperturbable river—all order and resolve heading somewhere.

Where wasn't exactly clear in 1958. The stint at Air Intelligence School was a prelude to a nonflying billet (as military assignments are called), probably two years of fleet duty in the Western Pacific, called Westpac duty. Sea duty means deployments, grinding, seven-month separations that try souls, marriages, and families to the limit. Youthful adventures with Quonset huts and sandy, sun-browned infants had by 1957 given way to mature knowledge. Ever since he could remember, Scott had lived for flying only. And despite the pay, the kids, the moves, the sheet-metal homes and burlap curtains, the separations, the danger, Rene had loved the flying in him.[35]

As it turned out, the stint at Anacostia was a boon to family life. Scott and the boys had located a roomy brick house in Pinecrest, Virginia. Sitting at the edge of a woods, it had two fireplaces and a huge yard, complete with a menagerie: two enormous white rabbits (which occupied a hutch), a large, affectionate duck, and a half-dozen hens monitored by a Rhode Island Red rooster, quickly nicknamed the Red Menace. The rent was high, more than they had ever budgeted for housing—even with the owner's allowance for diligent care of the animals. But they rationalized the cost and Scott saved money by driving on nearly bald retreads, which seemed never to last more than a week or two.

Home now, he parked in the driveway as children burst out the door to hug and be hugged: "Daddy!" The display was genuine and mostly spontaneous. He was the steady, irresistible center of the family. Shoelace knots, word pronunciations, fingernail cleaning and cutting done with his pocketknife (always very sharp), homework, table manners. They counted on him. Rene needed him. Scotty, as the eldest, conducted the official family debriefing between car and house: "Dad, the rooster pecked the girl down the road and her mother is mad."

The great spring snowstorm of 1958 arrived with two feet of sodden mid-Atlantic snow, the kind that snaps power lines, closes schools, coats streets with ice—the kind for building impregnable snow forts and for stockpiling lethal amounts of snow-based ammunition. Bronchial pneumonia felled the two brothers after the first day of snow war. Their mother made their beds next to the fireplace, the only source of heat in the house, while their father arrived with penicillin, driving the last car to make it down the hill as Northern Virginia was shut down for three days. For dinner there were hot dogs roasted in the fireplace and afterward a fresh retelling of "Shingebiss," the brave Chippewa duck who always triumphs over the fierce North Wind. With their sleeping children illuminated by firelight, mother and father talked quietly of the future. Orders were on their way for sea duty—Long Beach, California.

Packing day arrived once again. The '50 Lincoln was judged more reliable, so they sold the '54 Mercury, with the sun roof. The girls kissed the rabbits farewell while the boys said stoic good-byes to their pals. Red Menace strutted at the edge of the woods while the family piled into the car. "Bye-bye 'dis place," someone said. It was a rueful family joke, based on one of Scotty's early farewells, for no place was home.

The great road trip to California was planned with care. With the combined thirty days of leave and travel, the Carpenters had a generous allotment of time to spend visiting family in Iowa and Colorado. They towed a sixteen-foot trailer behind the Lincoln. In green Illinois, dusk approached after miles and miles without a single campground sign. Spotting a gate in the barbed-wire fence around what appeared to be an unused pasture, Scott opened it, drove in, closed the gate, and found a level spot to park the trailer for the night. Rene was preparing dinner when a car drove up. A man got out and said "Evenin'. How are you?" He turned out to be the owner of the farm. He didn't say "Get off my land" or "What the hell are you doing?" He and Scott talked some before he drove off home.

Before dark the farmer returned with his wife, and while he inspected the trailer, marveling over the miniaturization of stove and ice box, she brought cookies and ice cream to the card table set outside. The children found their manners—"Yes ma'am" and "Yes, thank you, I would"—as Rene watched, surprised. They told the farmer's wife about their menagerie left behind, especially Red Menace, the rooster. She laughed and listened to their stories, told in overlapping interruptions. They warmed to the moment and her attention, realizing as they listened to each other that no one else had this family story, or this trip, or this one night in Illinois.

Saying good night to their guests, the farmer and his wife drove back up the hill to their home, while the Carpenters, alone in the whispering field, prepared for bed and fell asleep. Awake before dawn, they heard a cock crow, and Jay said what everyone was thinking: "I miss the rooster."

Driving west onto the High Plains, the children strained to see the Rocky Mountains in the distance. (The first to spot them got a nickel.) Strange and familiar at once, they signified a kind of home to the nomads. In Boulder they visited with Grandma Toye and Grandma Ollie—like the Rockies, both strange and familiar and old, with wrinkles. They didn't know many old people.

Finally the Carpenters entered the Golden State, singing chorus after chorus of "California, Here We Come." The 1950 Lincoln Cosmopolitan, bought with fifty dollars from their Virginia landlord, puffed up the eastern hills of lower California, pulling the trailer, thinking it could.

UPON ARRIVAL IN Long Beach, Scott flew up the coast to Bremerton, Washington, to report for duty after finding a spot for his family at the Long Beach trailer park. Earlier that summer the USS Hornet, to which he had been assigned, was redesignated an antisubmarine warfare-support carrier (CVS-12); conversion was under way at a dry dock at the Bremerton Navy Shipyard in Puget Sound.

While he was gone, Rene found a house in the new Garden Grove neighborhoods sprouting up east of Long Beach. In the place of orange groves, board-and-batten-ranch houses now stood, three bedrooms and one-and-a-half baths, with sliding doors that opened onto level, grassy backyards, each adorned with a solitary orange tree.

Spotting one such house on Timmy Lane, Rene faltered, remembering Timothy, her six-month-old. But she kept moving down the newly paved street to the sale sign and knew she could live on a Timmy Lane, lost child and all. She and Scott promptly put fifteen hundred dollars down on the little house, listed at $15,500, and moved in before the end of the month: the kids, the beds, the kitchen stuff in boxes, and the indestructible monkeypod furniture and coco matting on the floor. Scotty and Jay were enrolled at the Crosby Elementary School. Although he flew down as often as he could from Bremerton, Scott would not return to Garden Grove with the *Hornet* until January 1959.

Scott spent his first five months of carrier duty in Bremerton aboard the *Hornet* in dry dock. Six months on sea duty as a member of the ship's company, five months of which were spent in dry dock. Every weekend he was off duty, Scott picked up an airplane at the Sand Point Naval Air Station and flew south to El Toro Marine Air Base, very close to home. Rene would pick him up there, and for a few hours they were a family again. He hated to fly back to Seattle.

Making matters worse, Scott learned that the *Hornet* was to be berthed not at Long Beach at all, as originally ordered, but at Coronado—North Island Naval Air Station, in San Diego. Rene had heard that the skipper's wife arrived in Long Beach, looked around, returned to her car, and drove south until she reached Coronado. The *Hornet* and her crew dutifully followed in her wake. It was hard to blame the skipper's wife. Coronado is beautiful. But now Scott had a two-and-a-half-hour predawn drive through coastal villages and fog banks, and then back again in the late afternoon. More than four hundred miles a day.

When the ship was finally ready for sea, in January 1959, the *Hornet* made her way down to San Diego for another period of training and sea trials. While they were at sea off the Channel Islands, Scott had the watch on the bridge, and as the eastern skies began to grow light, a cloud bank, hitherto invisible, became what looked like the horizon. Suddenly the lights of the few fishing vessels seen in the distance appeared much closer and thus in danger of being run over. Panic reigned on the bridge until the sky brightened and light peered beneath the cloud deck. The lights on the fishing vessels went back toward the horizon, where they belonged, and things quieted down on the bridge. Everyone present gained a new appreciation for the power of optical illusion.

The episode reminded Scott of another, spookier incident from the summer of 1945. He had just finished Pre-flight training at St. Mary's and was hitchhiking across country with a classmate. They had gotten a ride with a traveling salesman. Scott was in the front passenger seat, just watching the road go by. His buddy was asleep in the back. Then he saw something, like an owl, flying backwards, on the right side of the car, only to vanish and then reappear on the left side of the car—this time flying forward. It repeated this pattern at regular intervals. Scott showed the old man, and woke his friend up in the back seat, and they were perplexed, all of them, about that thing flying in circles around their car. Once they came to a rise, however, they saw an airfield to the north, its rotating airfield beacon shining brightly in the pitch darkness. Below the rise, they had seen neither the airfield nor the rotating beam of light—only its reflection on the mountain bluffs on either side of the road. But until then, for half an hour in 1945, Scott had seen an unidentified flying object.

BY THE END OF January 1959, the *Hornet* was out of dry dock and moored in San Diego. It was then that the Navy lieutenant encountered yet another optical illusion. He may even have rubbed his eyes. In his hands were the first of a set of four orders from the Chief of Naval Operations. To a junior naval officer, the CNO is one step above God.

9

YOU ARE HEREBY ORDERED

His difficulties will begin with the rocket launching. The acceleration pressure of 8 Gs will make breathing difficult. His respiratory muscles will strain to overcome the crushing force.... The heart will double its normal rate. The instruments before his eyes will fade from view in a brown haze. The feet and arms are now difficult to move.... Consciousness clouds, and for a moment he will wait in heavy, silent oppression.

—DR. NORMAN LEE BARR, 1959

ON JANUARY 26, 1959, Captain Marshall W. White stood on the foredeck of the "Fighting Lady" and contemplated yet another day in paradise. His ship, the *USS Hornet,* was moored at North Island Naval Air Base, California, and he was her skipper. Then someone interrupted his reverie with a teletype for his air intelligence officer: "You are hereby ordered to report to the Pentagon at 0700 on 2 February 1959...." He read the orders, again. No explanation. But then none was needed. The sender was Vice Admiral R. B. Pirie, Deputy Chief of Naval Operations for Air. Out of *all* the air intelligence officers in the Navy, why did the DCNO Air need Carpenter—just as White was preparing his ship for the West Pacific and himself for advancement to flag rank. That promotion depended on the aircraft carrier's performance under his command, which in turn depended on the officers and men who had been training under him for the previous six months. Damn it to *hell!*

Carpenter had no clue either, the skipper noted, watching the lieutenant absorb his mysterious orders.

Scott gingerly took his leave from the *Hornet* and boarded the train bound for Long Beach, where by prior arrangement Rene was waiting to pick him up. They drove home to Timmy Lane, where another equally mysterious letter awaited the lieutenant: "Do not discuss or speculate," it intoned, "lest you prejudice yourself and the project."[1] It too was from Admiral Pirie.

What project? He handed Rene the letter, and she searched her husband's face for clues. The Navy does not expect—unofficially, at least—husbands to keep orders like these from their wives, so on the way to the airport, the following morning, the couple discussed the various possibilities. It was a top-secret new plane. No, a top-secret air-intelligence program or mission. A top-secret *something*. They were excited, curious, and giddy. It was Thursday morning, January 29. Rene had brought her new issue of *Time* magazine, with Alec Cushing, of Sun Valley, on the cover—the Idaho resort where Rene had worked for a season, where they had skied as college students, and where their oldest child was conceived.

Scott drove. Rene read, and then suddenly she was jabbing at the magazine with her finger. "This is *it*!" she said. On page seventeen, *Time* magazine was explaining nearly everything. Not so top-secret after all. She read aloud: "As soon as the U.S. decided to go ahead with Project Mercury...the Pentagon's IBM machines began sorting through Air Force and Navy records for pilots with certain specifications, among them...." Their excitement mounted as they went through a list that described, well, Lieutenant M. Scott Carpenter. "Beginning this month they will go to Washington in groups of about 30 for full briefings...."

Scott bought his own copy of *Time* at the airport. Rene had refused to hand hers over. It sounded like about one hundred or so military test pilots were being considered—for spaceflight. Project Mercury was the name of the top-secret project, and soon the Navy lieutenant was lost in thought. The Pentagon said it had reserved rooms for the candidates at nearby motels. But he had made arrangements to stay with Liz and Dick Scott, Navy friends from Patuxent days who had recently moved to Bethesda, Maryland. So after landing at National Airport, he drove the small Opel the government told him to rent down along the Virginia side of the Potomac River, crossing over into Washington over Key Bridge, and then heading northwest into Maryland and the home of the Scotts.

They would have the whole weekend to catch up.

BACK IN SEPTEMBER 1958, Lieutenant Robert B. Voas, a thirty-year-old U.S. Navy psychologist, was told to report to Langley Field, Virginia, home of the new space agency called the National Aeronautics and Space Administration—NASA. He was to make himself useful to the Space Task Group, which was responsible, he was told, for the manned part of the country's new space program. Now that the NACA was morphing into a manned space program, expecting to launch humans into space, NASA needed flight surgeons, research psychiatrists, and aviation psychologists. They needed them right away.

So Voas was soon joined by two flight surgeons, the U.S. Army's Dr. William S. Augerson and Dr. Stanley C. White, from the Air Force. Later two research psychiatrists from the Air Force, George E. Ruff and Edwin Z. Levy, would arrive to help. Their first job was to select suitable candidates for space flight. As a protégé of Dr. Norman L. Barr, head of Pensacola's Naval Medical Research Laboratory, Voas suddenly found himself on the cutting edge of a brand-new field: space medicine.

Joining the medics on the Space Task Group's astronaut selection board, or evaluation committee, were NACA stalwarts Dr. Allen O. Gamble, Charles J. Donlan, and Warren North. Gamble had for years been the NACA's director of manpower. In 1958, however, pressing cold war priorities meant he was needed at National Science Foundation headquarters, assembling a national register of scientific and technical personnel. Charlie Donlan had been senior research manager at the old NACA; Gilruth named him assistant director of the Space Task Group. Warren North was a well-known NACA test-pilot engineer. At NASA, Gilruth named him chief of manned space flight. During the selection process, as an industrial psychologist, Gamble would labor alongside the medics at the working-group level. But toward the end of the three-month, five-phase selection process, the old NACA manpower director would rejoin his former colleagues, Donlan and North, to render the final decisions.

First, the Space Task Group needed a name, and a title description, for its spaceflight candidates. So on December 1, 1958, the committee members, now a dozen strong, brainstormed all day. Suggestions were chalked up on a Langley Field blackboard: *Spaceman, superman, space pilot*—one wag from Edwards Air Force Base proposed *man-in-a-can*. Another fellow found *aeronaut* in a dictionary, meaning "sailor in the air." Others piped up about Jason and his *argonauts. Astronaut,* or "sailor among the stars," was a logical leap from there, in addition to being a simple back-formation from *astronautics,* a term already ten or so years old. With no entry for *astronaut* in their dictionaries, they congratulated themselves on their historic neologism; someone later found the word in a 1929 work of science fiction.

The committee then set about defining the duties, qualifications, and recruiting sources for possible volunteers. Naturally, the Soviets were not sharing their data on Laika and other live-animal launches. The human and animal studies on which the evaluation committee did have data—human and animal experiments with high G loads, zero-G, cosmic radiation, sensory deprivation and overload—all pointed to extreme physical and psychological demands. Beyond the data there was only speculation, some of it wild. Perhaps in space, at zero-G, eyeballs would explode, hearts arrest, esophageal muscles constrict, peristalsis cease. Space radiation, unfiltered by earth's atmosphere, might burn retinas, sterilize gonads, crisp skin, or mutate DNA, discovered in 1953 and the source, still, of much concern.

Any volunteers?

"Proven toughness" was a key qualification, everyone agreed. A successful candidate must be able to withstand the hazards not only of a rocket launch but also of spaceflight itself and reentry. As for recruiting sources, that was simple. NASA was a civilian agency. Talent would come from the country's best available sources, civilian and military. Finally, Gamble drafted a bland-sounding Civil Service job description. It was published in the *Federal Register* under an equally unremarkable rubric: "NASA: Forty scientific specialists to be engaged on special research projects."

The draft announcement invited applications from what one committee member described as a "strange array of occupations":

> Listed were ... test pilots, crew members of experimental
> submarines, arctic and antarctic explorers, parachute jumpers,
> mountain climbers, deep-sea divers, and observers under test
> for extremes of environmental conditions such as acceleration,
> deceleration, zero gravity, high or low ambient temperatures,
> etc. As you can see, our basic concern at this point was with the
> feared stresses and hazards of launch, space flight, and reentry.
> *We were looking primarily for proven toughness.*[2]

But Max Faget had meanwhile determined that the Mercury spacecraft required the services of a test pilot. His engineering certitude led to a major policy decision, announced on December 15, 1958. The astronauts would be *pilot-engineers*.[3] The committee quickly retooled the job description. Pilots, "especially those with high-altitude jet aircraft experience," now had preference in the competitive selection process the committee was envisioning. Yet another change—an attempt to diminish what Drs. Ruff and Levy called "the lunatic factor"—was to ask "responsible organizations," military and civilian, to sponsor their best people.[4]

On December 17 the committee briefed T. Keith Glennan, the newly appointed NASA administrator. He agreed that everything looked "sound and reasonable" and said he'd see President Eisenhower in the "next day or two." Everyone waited for certain news of presidential approval. It was not to be. Still smarting from the disastrous Vanguard launch in December 1957, Eisenhower hated the proposal. The Navy rocket had exploded on national television and the press had been heaping coals on the president's head ever since. An open national competition for astronaut-candidates was a simple invitation for more coal-heaping.

How could the country, Eisenhower wanted to know, run an open search for volunteers weighing in the vicinity of 170 pounds when the biggest payload launched so far was the size of a grapefruit?[5] Add to that his basically conservative nature. He understood the space program had to go forward. He understood the stakes. But in the meantime, as long as he was president, the selection process would be kept secret and the finalists presented to the public as a *fait accompli*. Use military test pilots, the president said. They're qualified, easy to locate, and accustomed to following classified orders on short notice.

Gone was the open, national competition. Some committee members were disappointed, but one NASA official agreed: "the Mercury capsule is a job for a pilot, not a berth for a passenger."[6] After Christmas, the committee pared down the civil service selection criteria to seven items.

1. Age—less than 40.
2. Height—less than 5 feet, 11 inches.
3. Excellent physical condition.
4. Bachelor's degree, *or equivalent.*
5. Graduate of test pilot school.
6. 1500 hours of total flying time.
7. Qualified test pilot.[7]

The president had made the best decision he could—and an expedient one at that. The psychiatrists were relieved of an onerous and time-consuming weeding job. Dr. George E. Ruff explains the difficulty:

> What kind of people volunteer to be fired into orbit? One might expect strong intimations of psychopathology. The high incidence of emotional disorders in volunteers for laboratory experiments had much to do with the decision to consider only candidates with records of effective performance under difficult circumstances in the past. It was hoped that avoiding an open call for volunteers would reduce the number of unstable candidates.[8]

Preliminary screening, another time-consuming job, was also simplified because all the service jackets (military personnel files) were in Washington, D.C.

Voas was meanwhile stunned by an oversight made by the otherwise thorough committee. The old civilian agency had been quietly revolutionizing aircraft design since 1915. No one, at least outside aviation journals, had lauded its brilliant research administrators, its genius engineers, or its brave test pilots, all of them civil servants of the highest order. Publicity was not part of their organizational experience. Why would it be any different with NASA? But you haven't asked the obvious question, Voas explained: Think of Christopher Columbus. What happened after Charles Lindbergh's transatlantic flight?[9] These guys are going into *space*. Will they be able to handle the inevitable deluge of publicity? Voas asked. Good point, his colleagues said. The selection board agreed to evaluate public skills.

Voas and Gamble (who had served as a U.S. Naval Reserve officer during World War II) took charge of the computerized Navy records. The IBM machines made a first cut, leaving more than eight hundred service jackets to be processed by hand. They eliminated more than half of these: "494 who were not graduates of test-pilot school; 87 who were too old; 90 who were more than 5 feet 11 inches tall; and sixty-four who lacked a bachelor's degree." They were left with eighty-three files. A further records review cut the number to forty-seven Navy test pilots. But when they were done, Gamble realized to his horror that they hadn't seen a single service jacket from the Marine Corps. A quick call produced files on twenty-three Marine pilots, which Gamble went through himself. He chose four of them for Phase Two of the selection process, two of whom went on to become finalists: Captain Robert E. Solliday, twenty-seven years old, and Lieutenant Colonel John H. Glenn, Jr., a war hero ten years his senior.[10]

Meanwhile Drs. Augerson and White were having a bad time with the Air Force records, which had not yet been computerized. After two mid-January days, and an all-nighter, with Gamble and Voas pitching in at the end, the Air Force records ultimately yielded the names of fifty-nine astronaut-candidates.[11]

Fateful quirks in the process meant that both John Glenn and Scott Carpenter made the semifinal cut without their college degrees. Glenn's undergraduate education was cut short by World War II, and his records reflected this. But Gamble had gone through each of the

Marine records by hand, allowing the old manpower director to use his judgment. For his part, Scott may have been a heat-transfer course shy of an engineering degree, but his records said otherwise. Recruited through the Navy's Direct Procurement Program back in 1949, Scott and his fellow DPP recruits were by definition college graduates with engineering degrees. Back on the eve of the Korean war, when Scott was ordered to N.A.S. Pensacola by October 31, he'd neglected to mention those three pesky credits. But, then again, the Navy never asked.

THE WORKING GROUP ended up with the files of 508 military test pilots. It fell to Bill Augerson, the Army flight surgeon, to make the first rough medical evaluations and cuts. So he stacked all 508 medical files on his desk and combed through each one like a medical sleuth in search of certain childhood illnesses, evidence of lurking medical conditions, anything untoward. NASA was going to spend one million dollars training each astronaut. Working in this laborious fashion, Augerson was able to eliminate nearly four hundred men from further consideration. He was left with the service jackets of 110 men, each of them, he pronounced, "fully qualified on the basic requirements."[12]

It must have been a poignant task for the Army flight surgeon. A reorganization after World War II had cost the Army its vaunted Air Corps, now the United States Air Force. With the Army's air arm now consisting solely of helicopters (for which there were no test-pilot schools and no high-altitude flying), Augerson had not reviewed a single U.S. Army service jacket.

Phase One of the five-phase selection process for Project Mercury was complete. The committee began to prepare for Phase Two.

The working group placed the 110 men into three groups of about thirty candidates each; the plan was to have them report to Washington in three successive waves. The groups were ranked according to "the total flying time, the total testing experience, the ratings of the representatives of the test pilot schools, and the age and number of children of the candidates."[13] The most highly qualified candidates were therefore placed into group one and ordered to report on February 2. Men with large families were generally placed in the third group;

spaceflight was considered hazardous, and NASA was hesitant about creating widows and fatherless children. Despite his four children, then ages ten, seven, four, and two, Scott was assigned to group one.

He reported to the Pentagon on Monday morning, February 2, first attending a service briefing with his fellow Navy and Marine pilots. It was conducted by Admiral Pirie, the DCNO Air, author of the mysterious orders that everyone in the room had received.[14] An old patrol plane pilot, Pirie was a striking man with a full red beard and a kindly, protective manner. He assured the men that the Navy and the Marine Corps were "fully in accord" with the aims of NASA, the new space agency. There was no career downside, he promised, should the men decide to volunteer.[15] After the service briefing, everyone assembled— Air Force, Navy, and Marine—for three additional briefings. These were conducted by the Space Task Group. The first was a simple orientation on NASA—what it was and how it was organized. Warren O. North, a well-known test pilot, conducted the second and—probably for every pilot present—most influential briefing. Astronauts, he told the men, would be *pilots*:

> They would monitor and adjust the cabin environment. They would operate the communications system. They would make physiological, astronomical, and meteorological observations that could not be made by instruments. Most important, *they would be able to operate the reaction controls in space and be capable of initiating descent from orbit.* This was the key part, that the astronaut could take over control of the spacecraft itself.[16]

Lieutenant Voas discussed the training program, how rigorous it would be, and how, as engineers, successful candidates would be involved in the actual design of the spacecraft.[17] Before breaking for lunch, everyone was asked to sign up for private, ten-minute interviews during which they would have a chance to decline, or volunteer, to continue with the competitive testing; again, they were assured that their service files would contain *nothing*, no notation, in the event they declined to proceed.[18] Voas encouraged the candidates to discuss the project freely with one another during the break.

When the thirty-five or so pilots adjourned to one of the Pentagon's private dining halls for lunch, Scott sat down next to a young Marine captain, who introduced himself as Bob Solliday, from Pennsylvania—Test Pilot Class 20, meaning Patuxent. Scott replied in kind—Class 13, and from Colorado. Bob and Scott had more in common than Patuxent. They were distant cousins, but didn't know it, through the Landis clan. They talked, ate their lunches, and glanced around the dining room. Scott spotted John Glenn, whom he recalled from Patuxent. The Marine colonel had recently been in the news for a transcontinental speed record he had set, flying the F8U. Scott may have been the only representative from his Patuxent class, but Class 20 had a mighty representation—four men—and Bob pointed his classmates out to him: Wally Schirra, Pete Conrad, and Jim Lovell.

They talked shop: deployments, jet airplanes they'd flown, where they'd been stationed, their wives and kids. But most of all, they discussed the rockets they hoped to ride into space. Here, like a bolt out of the blue, Scott realized, was a chance to realize every test pilot's dream. He and Bob agreed: once you've had the indoctrination, training, and experience of the test pilot, you can never go back. Nor, if you fly for the military, where your job is not just to fly but to fight with your airplane, can you ever view the machine as other pilots do.

The military test pilot is part of a team that conceives, designs, and builds airplanes that fly higher, faster, longer, and with more and better weaponry (or a greater payload) than any other airplane ever built. You test and understand, test and fix, test and modify, test and improve, until you've helped to make the best war-fighting, machine-man combination possible given the state of the art. Once that process is complete, and you understand all there is to know about that airplane, then you get to start all over again, with another airplane, to advance the state of the art yet again. It's a never-ending process in the service of national defense, scientific advance, and human curiosity—a profession that serves all the noblest causes while providing the pilot the greatest possible sense of individual freedom and satisfaction. And here Scott and Bob were being invited to do what they loved, this time, incredibly, with rockets and a spacecraft, competing against a worthy adversary, the Union of Soviet Socialist Republics.

The room hummed with energy.

In their own lunchroom, Voas and his colleagues were passing an uneasy hour. Expectations were low about the volunteers, reflected in the bets they'd all placed, none higher than 50 percent. (One gloomy fellow bet that only 5 percent would volunteer.) But then the interviews began and gloom became astonishment as candidate after candidate walked in, sat down, and said count me in. By the end of the first day, three-quarters of the group, including Scott, Bob, and all of the Marine's classmates from Class 20, had volunteered.

Nearly all those who declined cited career reasons. Three naval candidates were expecting to be named squadron commanders, an exceptional achievement. Two Air Force officers had just been awarded full scholarships at M.I.T., at full pay, to get their doctorates. Voas recalls one officer anguishing over his decision, "twice rising from his chair and going to the door, his hand on the knob," only to return, sit down again, anguish some more, and finally decline. Another fellow opted out because his parents both had serious heart conditions. The shock might kill them, he said, if he told them he was going into space.[19]

Most of the men had taken motel rooms near the Pentagon. But Scott drove back to Bethesda and regaled the Scotts with accounts of the day. Richard Underhill Scott was one of the finest naval officers he knew. A dashing All-American center at the Naval Academy ('48), he had married Liz Hazlett, Professor "Swede" Hazlett's beautiful daughter. Everyone at Patuxent figured Dick would be CNO one day. But the year before, he had resigned his commission, citing the financial pressures the Carpenters were feeling. Still, Dick and Liz were as excited as Scott was about Project Mercury.

Rene would be waiting for news, so he called home.

"Well? *Is* it?" she said.

"It is," he answered, and heard her whoop of I-knew-it joy.

The next day she wrote Toye: "Just a short note to tell you of the excitement here—I actually can tell you nothing, but you must get last week's *Time*—page 17 under 'Space.'"[20]

Phase Two of the screening process continued the next day at the old NACA headquarters in Washington, D.C., at the Dolley Madison House. Dr. Voas had chosen to administer three IQ tests, one of them, Miller Analogies, was a graduate-level test of logical reasoning ability. Under Dr. Gamble, the NACA had identified engineering talent with a Civil Service engineering exam. And NASA wanted NACA-caliber engineers, and then some.

Like all U.S. military pilots, Scott was accustomed to constant training and testing, so the week of February 2 posed nothing unusually demanding. He had learned a lot from the briefings and the technical interview. It was pleasant, and even flattering, to be the center of such intense, friendly interest. All he had to do was to take tests and answer questions posed by very bright people who wanted to know everything the aviator knew about himself, about flying, and about aeronautics, especially during the technical interview run by Donlan, North, and Gamble.

McDonnell Aircraft had won the contract for the Mercury capsule, so Donlan had at his side the company's thick specifications book on the spacecraft, in addition to other materials on launch rockets.[21] A world map was nearby, and during the technical interview he showed each candidate the planned orbital trajectories and various charts and tables. Scott remembers detailed questions from North, the sole test pilot of the three inquisitors, about his technical background and experience. From the tenor of the questions, Scott inferred both urgency and high purpose. NASA was preparing to move technological mountains, and the Navy lieutenant commander knew his demeanor and answers were being analyzed with care. They knew Scott was a highly qualified test pilot—he and 109 other men whose files they were reviewing. But how extraordinary was he in comparison? What kind of man, and pilot, was he? What did he know? Could he say it quickly and well?

The three inquisitors, though tough, were also colleagues and peers—men who knew test pilots and aircraft inside and out. Flight surgeons, likewise, were another part of the flying fraternity. They had made careers out of examining and caring for people like Scott. The engineers were also brothers in design and flight-test. New to the fold, for most at NASA, were the research psychiatrists and psychologists, brought on board to study, evaluate, and write about their interesting new guinea pigs and research partners. All of them belonged, engineering test pilots included, to a tight-knit aeronautical, aeromedical, and flying community. All of them were committed to making better, faster airplanes, and now spacecraft, and to staying alive while doing so.

Staying alive was sometimes an iffy proposition. Gilruth knew one test pilot who flew the advanced airplanes coming out of Bell, one of them a fighter called the Aircobra. During a bailout the pilot had gone straight through the propeller disk.[22] Scott had never flown the Aircobra. Few had. But at Patuxent he had flown a photo-reconnaissance fighter called the F-9F-8P (Cougar). He was describing the experience during the technical interview—how the camera installation on the Cougar gave the pilot a view of the ground below and so on. Then he saw Donlan actually sit up.

It turned out that a similar device, more periscope than camera installation, was being planned for the Mercury capsule. The idea was to provide the astronaut with a view of the earth below for navigational purposes. Scott's sense later on was that his experience with the Cougar (a little airplane), in addition to his strong background in celestial navigation and communications while flying P2Vs (big airplanes), combined to make a favorable impression during that important technical interview.[23]

But other, more elusive impressions were also being weighed. Was a candidate likable—even funny? Articulate or tongue-tied? What were his motivations? With NASA then anticipating only three, four at the most, Mercury flights and a larger astronaut group of as many as a dozen engineer-pilots, it was important to identify relatively selfless astronauts, men willing to subsume their desire for individual glory to the needs of the team, indeed of the country. So it was Gamble's role during these interviews to ferret out clues about personality and motivation.[24] What were the candidate's "feelings regarding the importance of the program"? Could he work as "part of a team" without being guaranteed a flight? Some volunteers were candid: If NASA couldn't promise them a mission, then they weren't interested. This was just the kind of glory-seeking or other doubtful motivation, Gamble explained to *Newsweek* rather prophetically, that would be bad for group morale.[25]

Voas recalls that Carpenter, Glenn, and Shepard were standouts during the technical interview conducted by Charles Donlan, Warren North, and Allen Gamble. But almost every candidate, he conceded, tended to be "extremely socially extroverted and friendly," and very few were disqualified on the grounds that they might not bear up under the intense public scrutiny to come. Interestingly, few candidates fit the stereotype of the daredevil test pilot. On the contrary, they appeared to be mature, careful aviators who acknowledged the dangers inherent in their profession, but expressed the "intellectual conviction" that "knowledge and caution" would prevent most accidents.[26]

The Phase Two psychiatric interviews were tame affairs. One psychiatrist reviewed a candidate's life history and "current life adjustment"; the other ran an unstructured interview. They compared their notes after both interviews and came up with a combined score. "Subsequent investigation," it was agreed, would resolve any "doubt and disagreement."[27]

Scott was fascinated by the psychiatric interviews and by Dr. George E. Ruff. All the other interviewers were people he could understand, or at least relate to. They asked straightforward questions. Scott provided straightforward answers. But Ruff asked questions that simply had nothing to do with airplanes, physics, or science. Worse, he was completely unreactive to each of the pilot's answers. At one point in the interview, Scott knew he had badly mangled the pronunciation of a word he needed for one of his answers. Ruff was expressionless. After a while, Scott became convinced that he might have whined about his two imaginary friends, named Magoo and Oglethorpe, who played only with each other, and that Ruff would not have blinked.

So after a while, he relaxed a little and began to study this interesting new person, who, he had been told, was the kind of doctor who knew if you were telling the truth. Which meant he knew when you were lying. Then Scott grew tired of the covert mental duel, concluded he was no match for the young psychiatrist, and decided to provide transparent, but careful, answers.

Like Bob Voas—and for that matter, the elite military pilots he was studying—George Ruff was in an extraordinary place at an extraordinary time. The Philadelphia native had been studying the biophysics of stress ever since his medical residency. In 1957, at the age of twenty-nine, he had been named head of the stress and fatigue section at the Aeromedical Research Laboratory at Wright-Patterson A.F.B. There he designed stress experiments and studies, monitored centrifuge training, and measured heart rate, blood pressure, adrenal corticosteroids in the blood, temperature, respiration, and skin resistance. He was helping the Air Force identify "premium men for the premium mission." This meant the very dangerous U2 surveillance flights the United States had begun to conduct over the Soviet Union.

The U2 was a lightweight, single-engine, single-pilot, jet-propelled airplane developed by the Lockheed "skunk works" program. Because its mission was surveillance, it flew slowly, at speeds of about two hundred or three hundred miles per hour, making it highly vulnerable to interception. To compensate for

---

**THE SELECTION PROCESS:
PHASE TWO (Feb. 1959)**

• Personal history statement
• Short-answer biographical inventory
  (a NASA personnel testing tool then
  being developed)

TESTS
• Miller Analogies Test
• Minnesota Engineering Analogies Test
• Doppelt Mathematical Reasoning Test
• Stanford Binet IQ Test

INTERVIEWS
• Technical interview
• Psychiatric interview
• Flight surgeon interview
• Exit interview

Source: Robert V. Voas, "Preliminary Draft of Astronaut Selection Section, Mercury Technical History," NASA Memorandum to Mercury Project Office, Mr. Robert T. Everline, MEO, August 28, 1963.

this vulnerability, the spy plane flew very high, at altitudes beyond the reach of any Soviet weaponry. But depressurization at fifty thousand feet is fatal. If a pilot managed to survive, and to bail out at lower altitudes and parachute to safety, capture was to be avoided at all costs. U2 pilots, the Air Force's "premium men," were therefore equipped with fatal doses of cyanide.[28] So when NASA approached the Air Force asking for help, Ruff and his colleagues at the Aeromedical Research Laboratory were ready.

Under the direction of General Don Flickinger, the Air Force physician who had developed the "premium man" concept, "psychophysiological response patterns" were of particular interest. NASA, and the country, was the direct beneficiary of this extraordinary concatenation of national talent and foresight. By 1959, as the fledgling space agency cast about for national expertise in a brand-new field, astromedicine, the Air Force had already devised and tested exhaustive psychological and physiological workups.[29]

For the medical interview, each of the candidates presented his most up-to-date medical records to Dr. Bill Augerson, the Army flight surgeon who had culled through the original pool of 508 medical records. Several suspiciously lanky volunteers caught his attention. Although their medical files showed they were five-eleven and less— sometimes far less—a quick measurement said otherwise. Some of the men had grown since enlisting, in their late teens and early twenties, but other errors had crept in as pranks during hasty enlistment exams, with clerks asking for height without a glance at the six-foot-two jokers claiming they were five-eight.[30] Six "very promising" candidates were disqualified because of their height. It is not known whether these same candidates reapplied after height requirements were modified for subsequent astronaut selections for the Gemini and Apollo programs.

The Space Task Group's second group of astronaut-candidates arrived on February 9 and went through the same process as the first. By then, sixty-nine of the 110 military pilots initially identified as "fully qualified on the basic requirements" had reported to Washington. Gamble and Voas stayed late at headquarters during that second week, toting up scores. They found a whopping thirty-two of their volunteers had passed every test "with flying colors." Of the sixty-nine volunteers, sixteen declined to proceed, fifteen were disqualified by one or more of the interviews or tests, and six were too tall.[31]

Complaining of "an embarrassment of riches," the selection board called a halt to Phase Two, never summoning the third group of candidates from the original pool of 110.[32] The working group still had an unbelievably generous "selection ratio," which to a psychologist like Bob Voas meant they had many highly qualified applicants and only a few slots to fill. With so much data to collect in a short time, the working group—now comprising NASA psychologists Voas and Gamble and psychiatrists Ruff and Levy—placed the thirty-two finalists in five unranked groups of six candidates each and one group of two. The first group went straightaway from the Pentagon trials to Lovelace Clinic, in Albuquerque, New Mexico.

Scott returned to the *Hornet* to await news, he hoped, of his advancement in the selection process. When it arrived, this second time, orders came not through the chain of command but via civilian channels and the U.S. mail—to the Carpenter home in Garden Grove. Rene immediately opened the envelope, marked special-delivery, registered mail, and basked in the historic language: "You have been chosen to proceed with further interviews and tests in connection with Project Mercury. Please call ———— in Washington, D.C., by noon Monday if you wish to continue."

Rene thought, *I knew he'd make it! How incredible!* She reread the happy letter in a rush until her eyes snagged on the phrase "by noon Monday." *It was Tuesday afternoon!* She screamed and dialed the telephone number.[33] "We volunteer!" she told a startled Dr. Allen Gamble, whose office she had rung. She described the conversation to Toye:

> Scott "and his record made a great impression upon the
> examining board" and he's been asked to continue on to the
> second and third phases . . . also asking us to call Dr. Gamble
> ("The Chief Inquisitor") collect in Washington. I called
> immediately and jokingly told him—"you couldn't have

chosen a better man," and he answered, "I'm inclined to think you're right, Mrs. Carpenter." But what *else* could he say? The physicals begin March 6—last for two weeks.

The field has now been narrowed to about 30 men. Out of this 30 will come the 10 or 12 who will work as engineers on the project and ultimately take the "rides."... It's on our minds almost every single minute. Scott has been waiting all his life for something like this—but this exceeds *wildest* dreams....[34]

Scott now faced the unpleasant job of busting out yet again from the *Hornet*. Captain Marshall W. White, his skipper, issued a flat-out no. The *Hornet* was due for a training cruise. But he was scheduled, Scott replied, to report to Lovelace on March 6. He showed White the letter. The skipper was immovable: "You are not leaving this ship."

He had no choice but to call Washington. Scott had Gamble's home number and rang him from a pay phone on a North Island wharf. It was midnight in Washington. Gamble assured Scott he'd take care of it. "So then and there I called Admiral Arleigh Burke," he recounts, rousing the CNO out of a sound sleep. The admiral used some "real sailor language," Gamble recalled, "directed not at me but at that skipper." The CNO then called the skipper, who went on that training cruise without his air intelligence officer.[35]

THE ASTRONAUT selection process, circa 1959, drew on the growing institutional wisdom in both the Navy and the Air Force about premium men and how one identifies them. Anticipating that spaceflight would be more stressful than U2 flights or test piloting, the Space Task Group asked Ruff, Levy, Voas, and Bryce Hartman (a researcher from the School of Aerospace Medicine and inventor of the Panic Box) to structure the medical and stress tests accordingly. These tests became Phase Three, to take place at Lovelace Clinic, and Phase Four, to be held at Wright-Patterson A.F.B.[36]

After combining the screening instruments used at Wright-Patterson and Pensacola, the four behavioral scientists found they would need

Bud (*seated*), with grandparents Ruby Frye and Marion Ernest Carpenter (son of Cass), Denver, Colo., ca. 1940. Standing are Bud's uncle, Claude Morrison Carpenter (*left*), and father, Dr. Marion Scott Carpenter.

Vic and Clara Noxon (*b.* 1864, Compton, Ontario) with grandsons David Corbin (*in arms*) and Buddy (Scott) Carpenter, Boulder, Colo., 1927.

The Noxon family home, Boulder, Colo. Bud lived here until 1941, when he was a freshman at Boulder High School. The house still stands at the corner of Seventh Street and Aurora Avenue, now well inside Boulder city limits. Toye's sleeping porch, constructed in 1927, is visible on the second floor; the Flatirons are visible in the background.

Toye with year-old Buddy, her son, 1926, probably Inwood, New York City.

Scott and Toye, University of Colorado campus, ca. 1962, Boulder, Colo.

Victor Irwin Noxon (*b.* 1864, Idaho Springs, Colo. Terr.), outside his offices, Fourteenth and Walnut, Boulder, Colo., 1937. One of C.U.'s earliest graduates (1886, civil engineering), Bud's "Grandpa Noxon" was a Democratic party activist, beloved editorialist, and publisher of the *Boulder County Miner & Farmer* from 1909 until his death, at his typewriter, on the eve of World War II.

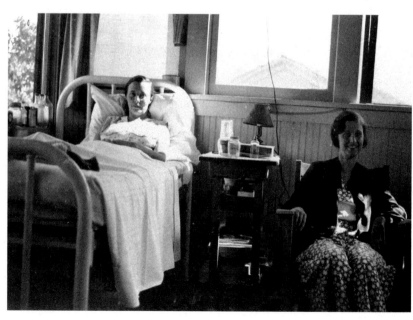

Toye, with unidentified woman (*seated*), convalescing, Mesa Vista Sanatorium, 2121 North Street, Boulder, Colo., 1931.

Dr. M. Scott Carpenter (*seated*), with son, Buddy, at Palmer Lake, Colo., 1933—the year of their first epic acorn battle.

Bud with his .22 rifle, Boulder, Colo., 1940. On the eve of World War II, National Guard marksmanship and riflery classes were well attended. Bud had additional instruction from Grandpa Noxon, himself a careful marksman and crack shot.

Bud with Lady Luck ("She's better than Seabiscuit!"), Seventh and Aurora, Boulder, Colo., 1938.

Scott Carpenter, age 19, U.S. Navy Apprentice Seaman, V-12, Colorado College, Colorado Springs, Colo., 1944.

U.S. Navy

Rene and Scott Carpenter, ensign (U.S.N.), young marrieds at the "cradle of U.S. naval aviation," N.A.S. Pensacola, Fla., Easter Sunday, 1950.

January 1958: Scotty, age 8, holding "The Red Menace"; Kris, 2½; Rene, 29; Jay, 5; Scott, 32 (*standing*); and Candy, 14 months. Scott's collection of bows and arrows, some of them handmade, are mounted on the wall. His prized "Hawaiian Sling," or spearfisher, is at the top.

CARPENTER FAMILY PHOTOGRAPH

Rene with children (*l to r*) Candace, age 3; Kristen, 4; Jay, 7; and Scott, 9, morning of the announcement, Project Mercury astronaut selection, April 9, 1959, Garden Grove, Calif.

LEONARD MCCOMBE, LIFE

Scott, in parachute silk,
July 1960. NASA had
determined possible
Project Mercury reentry
sites might include West
Africa. Desert-survival
training was therefore
mandated at the tough
U.S. Air Force survival
school, Stead A.F.B., and
in the nearby Nevada
desert.

NASA

Project Mercury astronauts (*l to r*) Gordo Cooper, Scott Carpenter, John Glenn, Al
Shepard (in deshabille), Gus Grissom, Wally Schirra, and Deke Slayton, desert-
survival training, Nevada desert, July 1960.

NASA

Scott, U.S. Navy centrifuge, Johnsville, Penn., August 1959. Note "CARP" in block
letters, signifying the Mercury astronaut's custom-made, fiberglass contour couch,
courtesy of NASA's high-end technicians at Langley Field, Va.

Scott Carpenter and John Glenn with Walter M. Schirra, Jr. (*background*), water-landing training for MA-7, Langley A.F.B. pool, Va., spring 1962.

Ralph Morse, LIFE

Scott, boarding U.S. Air Force F-106, Langley A.F.B., Va., 1961.

NASA

Scott, safely aboard the USS *Intrepid*, following his recovery at sea by helicopter on May 24, 1962. His spacecraft, *Aurora 7*, would be recovered by the "Fierce Pierce," as the *John R. Pierce* was affectionately known.

NASA

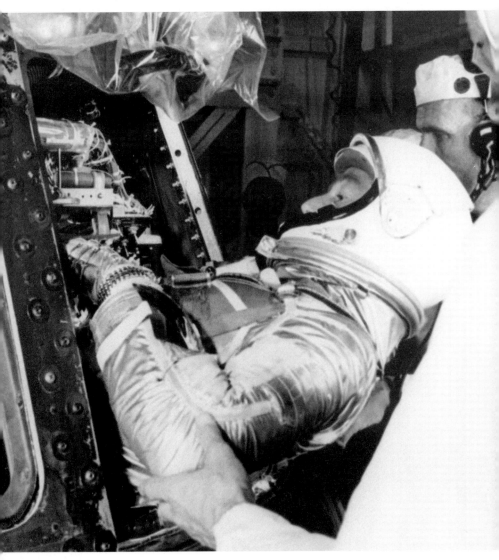

Scott's "insertion" into McDonnell capsule no. 18 (*Aurora 7*), Cape Canaveral, Fla.,
May 24, 1962. "You don't get in," John Glenn said, preparing for his own flight
aboard *Friendship 7* (MA-6). "You put it on."

NASA

Rene and Scott Carpenter, "Scott Carpenter Day," hometown parade, Boulder, Colo., May 29, 1962, the largest turnout of citizenry in Boulder history.

Scott, now working as an aquanaut, stands in front of Sealab II, July 23, 1965. He and Wilbur Eaton would live aboard Sealab, more than 200 feet below the surface off the coast of La Jolla, Calif., for one month.

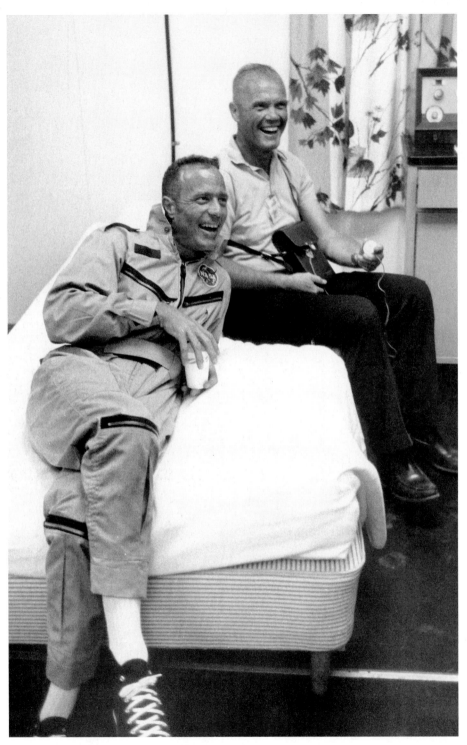

Scott Carpenter and John Glenn, postflight elation, May 24, 1962, Grand Turk Island.

thirty hours of testing *per* astronaut-candidate. Ruff later recalls being floored when the Space Task Group approved:

> Thirty hours of testing!…they were *never* going to allow 30 hours of psychiatric evaluation and psychological testing. But we put it in, and lo and behold they said OK, we'll do it. They told us that we could work at night. So after a day of stress testing, the pilots would come back and do the psychological tests with us. To our amazement, they did the whole program as we set it up.[37]

The decision sprang from the finest bottom-up traditions of the old Pilotless Aircraft Research Division and what some have called Gilruth's management by respect. With everyone in Project Mercury making it up as they went along—from engineers working on the hardware (rockets, capsules, propellants) to the aeromedical professionals busy with the flesh-and-blood part of the program (chimps, pigs, contour couches, humans)—the Space Task Group fell back on its NACA instincts: trust the workers.

Voas was the Navy's representative on the selection board. An industrial psychologist, with a doctorate from UCLA, he had been laboring at Pensacola's Naval Medical Research Laboratory on a number of stress and selection problems the Navy was encountering in the late 1950s, specifically its high rate of trainee DORs, or Dropped on Request. At 25 percent, the Navy's DORs were nothing new. But 25 percent of historically low recruitment levels meant the Navy wasn't meeting its military readiness levels. Someone thought the DORs were to blame, and the NMRL was asked to study the problem. Armed with the results of their aptitude and stress tests and surveys, Voas and his colleagues proffered their recommendations. Against their advice, the Navy relaxed its entrance requirements and performance-review standards. Sure enough, DORs dropped. But follow-up studies showed those scraping through under the revised standards were either dead or behind desks within a year. The Navy reinstated its original standards and lived with its high DORs.

What Voas and his colleagues found was that DOR rates are an immutable phenomenon—the problem being not stress, but a trainee's hard-wired response to it. The feeling that danger is nigh may in one trainee produce a pleasurable sensation, more like a fear-tinged thrill or a stimulating challenge. In another, the same situation might generate physical discomfort—sharp rises in adrenal corticosteroids, steep increases in pulse rate, respiration, perspiration, etc.—and then panic, followed in split seconds by the loss of judgment that leads to pilot error, death, or injury, and a wrecked million-dollar machine. It was best, really, considering the value of a life, the cost of training, and the price of an airplane, to let such candidates go. A DOR is not a failure, in other words, of the standard or of the individual—it is a flight candidate's way of saying he'd be a better landscape architect or engineer than a military pilot.

They were learning at the NMRL that performance standards saved lives and money. Flight surgeons, Air Force and Navy, do the same thing when they determine flight readiness—a pilot's mental and physical readiness to fly. The flight surgeon is like the friend who confiscates your car keys and hands you a blanket when he knows you shouldn't drive home. In a military setting, the car doesn't belong to you, the keys aren't yours, and your pal the flight surgeon has custodial power over the airplanes you crave. He also enters his observations in a file. Sprain your back? Feeling paranoid? Irritable? Drink too much? Having marriage problems? Tell the medics *zip*. This went for the wives, too. An indiscreet remark could ruin careers. The typical pilot, the one who lives for flying only, will plead, argue, lie, cheat, steal, pull rank, pull strings—whatever it takes to keep his flight status active. So medics occupy an ambiguous niche in the world of military aviation, playing cat-and-mouse with their robust, lying "patients."

NEWLY SPRUNG from the *Hornet* and dressed in slacks and a sports shirt, Scott landed at the Albuquerque airport on March 6, 1959, along with four or five other men in mufti. He was glad to see Solliday, his Marine buddy from Phase Two, along with two Air Force officers, Gus Grissom and Deke Slayton. John Glenn, who had left an earlier group midweek, showed up, too, and completed his own round of tests. Everyone was instructed to ask for "Tux" Turner when they landed. The Air

Force colonel kept track of arriving semifinalists and arranged for their rides to the Lovelace Clinic.

TOM WOLFE'S NOW-LEGENDARY account in his book, *The Right Stuff,* of the ordeals at Lovelace and Wright-Patterson in 1959 remains unsurpassed. The prostate-palpating exams, clipboard-toting medics, enema bags, beribboned stool samples, ice baths, anechoic chambers, panic boxes, peer reviews, jugs of urine. There were tests, more tests, and tests of tests of tests.

Wolfe chose to tell the story through the eyes of the late Pete Conrad, then a twenty-eight-year-old prankster and all-around wiseacre.[38] As smart as they come, funny, and confident (they all were), he griped rather too loudly while playing it all like an elaborate game. The griping won him some demerits, but although he was not selected for Mercury, Pete and his antics were recalled fondly by his more circumspect peers. In 1962 NASA selected him and eight other candidates as members of the second group of astronauts.

Although most of the guys appreciated the indignation Pete expressed so freely at Lovelace, they kept their heads down and their mouths shut. Scott, for one, acknowledged NASA's self-interest in determining his fitness. Later on, NASA had a term for the kind of reliability required of spaceflight: three nines, or 99.9 percent reliability—machines, systems, and men. Undetected health problems could result in catastrophic mission failure, including the death of the pilot. Of particular concern, he was finding out, were quirky psychological and physiological responses to environmental extremes—gravitational loads, noise, temperature, light, isolation, sensory overload and deprivation.[39]

One example of this psychophysiological nit-picking was a test for something called flicker vertigo, a rare but disabling condition. Navy flight surgeons had pondered it ever since an otherwise healthy aviator taxied off toward the hangar after an uneventful landing, heading west at sunset. While the control tower watched, his airplane simply stopped. Then nothing. There he and his airplane stayed, until a ground crew went out and found a mesmerized pilot in the cockpit, just sitting there like a hypnotized chicken. Navy doctors figured that

TABLE IV: SELECTION OF ASTRONAUTS
A. By Chronology

225	USAF personnel records screened
225	Navy personnel records screened
23	Marine Corps personnel records screened
35	Army personnel records screened
508	TOTAL records screened (Jan 1959)
110	TOTAL met minimum standards, in terms of test pilot school, jet hours, age, height, technical education, medical records (end Jan 1959)
69	Reported to briefing in Washington, two groups (Feb 2 and 9, 1959)
-5	Too tall
64	
-8	Declined
56	TOTAL given written tests, technical interviews, psychiatric interviews, medical history reviews
-1	Too tall
55	
-8	Declined
47	
-15	Eliminated (by NASA as undesirable)*
32	TOTAL sent through Lovelace Clinic
-1	Eliminated
31	TOTAL sent through WADC tests
0	Eliminated
31	TOTAL for final selection
-24	Passed over
7	TOTAL selected as Mercury Astronauts (Apr 1, 1959)

Source: Robert V. Voas, "Preliminary Draft of Astronaut Selection Section, Mercury Technical History," NASA Memorandum to Mercury Project Office, Mr. Robert T. Everline, MEO, August 28, 1963, table IV.

*Dr. Voas was quick to soften this term, in 2001, when the authors inquired. "That's the kind of language we used in 1959." It meant only that such candidates were considered unsuitable for a particular job or career.

the propeller blades had interrupted the sunlight at a frequency that temporarily undid the pilot's mind. NASA thought it wise to test for this peculiar sensitivity.

The relentless pace of testing also provided what Bob Voas later called a "mild test of stress tolerance and motivation." The semifinalists were seen first thing in the morning, all through the day, and late at night, after a full day of scrutinized indignities, when they were frustrated and tired. How did they respond, the researchers wanted to know? Could they keep their composure? Their sense of humor? NASA would be spending more than $1 million, in 1960 dollars, to train just a single astronaut; it wanted the investment to translate into useful, decade-long careers in space as the astronauts approached and passed their fortieth birthdays. With so much at stake, the evaluation committee decided that "any indication of a developing problem" would be disqualifying. Scott and Bob had meanwhile figured this out. They weren't going to let the bastards get 'em down.

As it turned out, the researchers disqualified only one of the thirty-two astronaut-candidates at Lovelace, after detecting a "minor and remediable" heart defect. Another semifinalist had a laryngeal polyp. An alert Captain Norman L. Barr (USN) ordered emergency surgery so this especially promising Navy candidate could be recommended to the selection board "without medical reservations."[40]

Like most of his rivals, Scott approached the weeks of testing as a kind of athletic competition with a distinct psychological component. The researchers, he figured, wanted in part to see him squirm. But squirmers lost. It was that simple. The science also piqued his curiosity. He also thought of his mother, Toye, enduring her own medical traumas with both strength and grace. God help him, Scott enjoyed the competition.

"He had us all psyched out," Solliday shakes his head at the memory. "He had the lowest body fat, the best treadmill test, cycled forever, held his breather longer, never lost his cool. We were afraid to armwrestle the guy!" When it was over, Scott had broken a couple of records. This on a pack a day of unfiltered Camels since 1943, when he joined the Navy. (He quit in 1985.) In 1959 he was just coasting, like most of his fellow pilots, on his unaccountably rude health and good habits from a youth spent hiking, camping, skiing, skating, sledding, wrestling, swimming, diving, riding, mowing, chopping, tumbling, and working: delivering ice, carrying hod, pushing cement-filled wheelbarrows, and lumberjacking at an elevation of 10,300 feet.

It was after the test on the bicycle ergometer that Scott knew he was doing well. In this test, the subject was to pedal "against increasing brake loads to measure how efficiently his body uses oxygen." The ergometer test measured not only oxygen uptake but also exhaled carbon dioxide, which the researchers captured in huge bags. Believing that susceptible hearts would cavitate at rates above 180, Scott was told the test would be stopped when his pulse rate reached that mark. He pedaled and pedaled but was finally told to stop. They had run out of bags for his CO_2. Besides which, his pulse rate never even approached 180.[41]

He also excelled at a test for the amount of blood oxygen during and after the exercise. This allowed doctors to detect the presence, if any, of tiny, defective openings in the heart chambers. With his nose clipped closed to prevent cheating, Scott was asked to blow into a rubber tube attached to a manometer—a U-shaped glass tube filled with mercury. The idea was to force the mercury column down on one side, with your breath, making it rise on the other side, where a ruler measured the height of the column.

The candidates were instructed to maintain the mercury column at a height of ninety millimeters for as long as they could. To judge from the protocol, this test appears to provide only three quantitative measures. One, obviously, is how long a subject can hold his breath. Breath-holding is not a requirement of spaceflight, but being able to endure personal discomfort to meet a goal you've set for yourself is. "It is possible," the candidates were told, "to hold your breath until you pass out." Although this would be a very *positive* measure of an individual's perseverance (the second measure provided by the test), it would be a very *negative* measure of a dangerous sensitivity to high CO_2 levels in one's lungs (the third measure). "Don't do that," everyone was served notice.

Their performances would be compared, so everyone tried to do his best, to excel—longer, stronger, higher, harder, better. The word was out, though, that the record on this test was ninety seconds. So Scott resolved to count slowly to one hundred, just to make certain he didn't get to ninety seconds too soon. But his count was slower than the second-hand, so that by the time he got to one hundred, Scott had held his breath for something like three minutes.[42]

The Lovelace Clinic trials spanned seven and a half days for each of the six groups, with some time set aside for recreation. Dr. and Mrs. Lovelace had some of the men over for dinner. The night Scott was invited, he saw Solliday was heading out at the same time, and they drove over together. With a rare chance to ski the southern Rockies, they asked their hosts about nearby slopes. Lovelace told them to ask one of the senior researchers, Dr. Ulrich Cameron Luft. Sure enough, there was a nearby slope called Cloud Croft. Luft said he was a skier and mountain climber himself and offered to take them—and to lend them some gear. At Luft's house, in the basement, Scott and Bob found enough heavy-woolen, prewar winter gear to outfit a small army—most of it sporting the unmistakable insignia of the Nazi SS. Dr. Luft was an "Operation Paperclip" asset, caught up in the U.S. Army's sweeping, preemptive raid on Nazi talent, before the Soviets arrived, in the waning days of World War II.

Scott and Bob found some inoffensive garb and skied all day under the bright New Mexico sun, never once asking their genial host what he had done during the war.[43]

Outgoing finalists gathered, at the end of each week, at a Mexican restaurant, inviting along, by tradition, the incoming group. At the feet of some of the outgoing candidates was a jug of urine, which they had been obliged to lug around all week in the interests of space medicine. Gus Grissom had yet to hand his over to the medics. Suddenly the most alarming expression transformed Gus's face. He glanced under the table, and soon guys downslope were shifting in their chairs and lifting their feet off the floor. Gus had knocked over his urine jug.

No matter. More beer, here! After another round or two, everyone took turns in the john with Gus's jug. They had it topped off before the check arrived.

AFTER LOVELACE, Scott and Bob and the rest of their group went straight to Wright-Patterson A.F.B., home of the Aeromedical Research Laboratory and the "premium man" studies. This was Phase Four of the selection process. The groups had been rotating through the facilities since February 16, 1959, when the first group arrived; the last group would finish on March 27.

Wright-Patterson was the site of the infamous thirty hours per candidate of psychiatric interviews, psychological tests, and observations of stress experiments.[44] The men were each rated on a ten-point scale. Psychiatrists assigned numerical scores in seventeen categories relating, for example, to "drive," "dependency," "reality testing," "somatization," or "social relationships." An "ideal" response garnered a score of ten. So, in category fourteen ("quality of motivation"), for example, a candidate could score a ten by evincing absolutely "no desire for narcissistic gratification" nor the slightest "self-destructive or adolescent fantasies of invulnerability." A score of five would represent an average response.[45] With these men, however, scores for each candidate consistently fell in the top third of the scale. None of the finalists had a "clinically significant" neurosis or personality disorder. These were test pilots and, it followed, obsessive-compulsives if anything, although their "defenses" weren't "overly exaggerated."[46]

In the cold-pressor test, the candidates were required to plunge their feet into a tub of ice water; the researchers measured pulse and blood pressure before and during the ordeal. Primarily a measure of physiological response to stress, it provided an incidental test of motivation. The tub was a simple galvanized pail, filled with ice cubes and water. Of course, the water was 32 degrees and everyone was instrumented, as always. They were told to put their feet in the ice water and leave them there as long as they could.

Again, you don't have to hold your feet in ice water in order to be a good spaceman or spacewoman, but you do have to have a measure of self-imposed discipline. With enough self-imposed discipline, you can, if you *want* to, hold your feet in a bucket of ice water all day long. The only things this test measured, as far as Scott could see, were perseverance and determination, important qualities to the medics screening you. In any event, he determined to show perseverance and determination and held his feet in those ice cubes for what seemed like a very long time. All he could think about was how much he wanted—no, *needed*—to be chosen. The examiners finally said, "That's long enough." He had broken another record.

RESEARCHERS FOUND that of the thirty-two finalists, only four men came from "nonintact" families. Of the seven ultimately chosen, Scott was the sole astronaut to have been reared by a single parent. In most other respects, however, he resembled his rivals, most of whom were only or eldest children. He had early expressed an interest in flying and had adjusted to adolescence and school in "comfortable fashion." Like many of the finalists, he had taken on leadership roles in school and had progressed since by taking on realistic challenges, achieving success, gaining confidence, and going on to the next life or career challenge.[47]

Motivation and personality were measured and evaluated with thirteen tests, from peer ratings to the Pensacola Z-scale. Twelve aptitude and intelligence tests were administered, including the Air Force officer qualification test, the Navy's aviation qualification test, and tests for mechanical and spatial skills. Peer ratings were unremarkable except for one testy remark: "If you have to fuck your way into space," one finalist wrote, "then————will be the first man there." The psychiatrists' observations were overwhelmingly favorable, with typical remarks including "extremely well integrated," "exceptionally mature," and "highly intelligent." The occasional unpleasant personality was noted: "'loud and obnoxious,' 'arrogant,' and 'seems to think very highly of himself and not so well of others.'" In the end, these less-than-pleasant character traits were not disqualifying.[48]

The psychiatric portion of the testing became very involved at Wright-Patterson. Scott was asked to comment on a series of paintings and illustrations, a commonly used "projective," or thematic apperception, test. One of the paintings showed a bedroom scene in which a despondent-looking man sat at the foot of a bed, chin in his cupped hand, his back to an equally gloomy woman, reclining among the bed-clothes. "The woman is pregnant," he told the psychiatrists, after deciding to tell them what he really thought. "She's just told the man."

Then, of course, there were the stress experiments, six of them "simulating conditions expected during the mission." These ranged from the pressure-suit test to isolation, centrifuge runs, and the Panic Box. Of all the stress experiments, the "Complex Behavior Simulator," which everyone called the Panic Box, was dreaded the most. A "panel with twelve signals, each requiring a different response, the device measured the ability to react reliably under confusing situations."[49]

Scott's recollection is that it had a *lot* more than twelve signals. However many signals the Panic Box had, it was pure sensory overload, featuring all kinds of different gauges and indicators and needles and lights and buzzers and control devices with which the subject could change those indicators. There were levers, there were wheels, toggle switches, push buttons, rings to pull, knobs to rotate. Every conceivable type of control was in this little box. The floor, the ceiling, and the walls in front and beside you were all you could see. And there you sat, surveying your pretend instruments, whose indicators you were to keep steady at zero. None was to be allowed out of its proper position: steady at zero.

If this machine got ahead of you—one gauge, for instance, could go out of the green and into the red area—and stayed there in the danger area for five seconds, then a big red light began to flash for perhaps five seconds. If that light flashed for five seconds and you still hadn't taken corrective action, then a siren went off—to let you know the machine had *really* gotten ahead of you. That's one indicator on one control panel display. Multiply this by twelve, with everything happening simultaneously. So while this entire contraption is going full-tilt, with maybe a red light flashing on one or two signals, you're busy on three or four others trying to keep their indicators centered at zero. Sensory overload.

Scott saw one of the finalists take a go at the Panic Box—all he could see was the back of his head—and his body looked like it was actually convulsing, all over, as he struggled to keep every indicator out of the danger areas. It was one of the funniest things Scott thought he'd ever seen—this man panicking before these various controls, trying to keep the instruments and the indicators centered. And that was just the first go-round. Each finalist had to endure one set of three successively faster Panic Box sessions, during which his physiological responses and performances were recorded for later analysis and comparison, for the Panic Box was also able to record how long each subject had allowed each of his twelve instruments, or control displays, to stay outside the range of proper indication.

Scott saw the original session, the first in a set of three, as an orientation. Each session was thirty minutes long, and you were instrumented—to measure heart rate, blood pressure, galvanic skin responses, and so forth. After a thirty-minute session, he found, you had learned where the control was for a certain indicator. The layout of the panel and the different controls became burned into your imagination and instinct. All the while, an observer was behind you, taking notes on your behavior, knowledge of which may have improved performance. As the half-hour proceeded, you could see improvements in technique and speed. You were allowed to rest after each thirty-minute session, because the Panic Box was very hard work.

After a rest period, the subject returned to the Panic Box, which the researchers ran at *twice* the original speed so that everything happened twice as fast. This was followed by another rest. Then they ran it double-speed again, making the final test four times faster than the first. Scott was interested to see how, with just a little practice, you could learn very quickly. It was very challenging to keep that red light from flashing. Scott was fascinated. The astronauts would encounter the Panic Box again, as the MPT, or the Mercury Procedures Trainer, at Langley Field, Virginia.

Doing absolutely *nothing*, in the isolation room, was a test of sensory deprivation—not a very good one, the researchers concede, for time constraints limited this stress test to only two hours. It elicited a range of responses. Deke Slayton got bored and went to sleep. John Glenn made lists of things to do. Like John, Scott viewed daytime sleep as a sign of moral turpitude. He worked on solving a pet physics mystery—the expanding universe.

Scott was happy at Wright-Patterson. He was told his performance on the Panic Box had broken the record. Then he broke another record on a treadmill test, conducted at 115 degrees Fahrenheit and 100 percent humidity; the treadmill elevated one degree every minute. Researchers had to stop this test, too, when his heart rate would not climb past 180. The medics had found an elite athlete, a genetic fluke, blessed with a strong heart and cardiorespiratory capacity, ideal combinations of fast-twitch and slow-twitch muscle fiber, plus hand-eye coordination, strength, and speed. Put this physical package together with high motivation, years of training, emotional maturity, and a 130-plus IQ, and records will fall. Then again, as Rene wrote Toye, Scott had been waiting "all his life for something like this."

Toward the end of Phase Four, Solliday declared in mock defiance, "They're gonna have to *kill* us if they want our DORs!" Scott agreed. Kill us—if you can. The candidates with the highest psychological scores, it turned out, had also pulled down the top scores on the stress experiments and garnered the highest numerical rankings.[50]

After Wright-Patterson, the working group scrutinized the data, tallied scores, discussed, compared, and quantified their subjective impressions. Then they numerically ranked the thirty-one candidates. In reviewing the records, Voas remembers being struck by John Glenn's consistently outstanding ratings, "even when examination of the numbers did not indicate *that* outstanding a physical condition." Voas concludes that the physicians were reacting as much to John's "very charismatic personality...as they were to their instruments."[51]

OVER THE YEARS a slightly contradictory picture has emerged about this historic selection process for the Project Mercury astronauts. On the one hand is NASA's official and largely unheralded account of its search for engineering test pilots with "superior technical abilities." NASA identified such men during Phases One and Two of the selection process, in Washington, D.C. The technical interview run by Charlie Donlan, Allen Gamble, and Warren North was by all reports decisive in this regard.[52] The more popular, and rival, view is Tom Wolfe's unforgettable account in *The Right Stuff* of Phases Three and Four, the ordeals at Lovelace and Wright-Patterson. It was there that the thirty-two finalists were winnowed and winnowed again in medical, psychiatric, and stress tests until, finally, the researchers had enough quantitative data to produce actual numerical rankings. This account, too, has an impeccable pedigree: *The Right Stuff,* early NASA press releases, and contemporaneous accounts by selection board members, speeches, scholarly articles, and interviews.

Both versions are true: NASA's less flashy account of its search for engineering test pilots, and the better-known tale popularized by books and movies. In the emerging culture of NACA-cum-NASA, the seven contest winners appear to have showcased their emotional maturity, engineering IQ, flight experience, and motivation. Finally, the other infallible indicator of likely future success: Had these men done well in the past? The working group members had all the personnel records of every candidate: "Team members therefore knew which candidates were ranked as superior by their military supervisors. . . . It made sense that a person who had done well in the past was most likely to do well in the future—a simple concept that has been regularly supported by the psychiatric literature."[53]

In the end it was as simple as that.

As FEBRUARY AND March 1959 passed, with their precious astronaut-candidates in the clutches of headshrinkers, STG honchos Charlie Donlan and Warren North may have gotten just a little antsy. *Do not make recommendations,* they told the selection board's working group members. Just give us the summaries and "we'll make up our own minds."[54]

But the working group had already assigned numerical rankings to each finalist. Worse, each was assigned to one of three categories: "Outstanding," "Recommended," and "Not Recommended."[55] They scrambled to reword their findings; it was the end of March 1959.

Someone hit on a solution: They'd recommend *everyone!* Eighteen finalists initially classified as either "outstanding" or "recommended" were grouped in a single category and recommended "without medical reservations"; the remaining thirteen candidates were recommended "with medical reservations." The selection board took the hint. The seven Mercury astronauts were drawn from the unreservedly recommended group of eighteen.

Almost everyone on the selection board convened for the decision: General Don Flickinger and Captain Norman Lee Barr; all the physicians and behavioral scientists from the working group (Augerson, White, Ruff, Levy, Gamble, Voas); and Charlie Donlan and Warren North from the Space Task Group. They chose seven men, but not, as it turns out, the *top* seven. Eschewing to some extent the numerical rankings, they chose the candidates ranked first, second, third, fifth, eighth, tenth, and fifteenth.[56] Medical confidentiality being what it is, there is no published account of who was ranked how. To this day, Ruff and Voas will not discuss the details of any individual records or data.

The final selection of three Air Force officers, three Navy officers, and one Marine colonel suggests some attempt to balance the services, but Voas insists this was "more accident than anything else—although NASA was relieved it came out that way."[57] One of them, of course, was Lieutenant M. Scott Carpenter (USN), just shy of his thirty-fourth birthday.

On April 3, 1959, T. Keith Glennan, NASA's new administrator, approved the recommendations and asked Donlan to make the calls. Charlie picked up the phone to dial the Carpenters' home number in California. Rene answered. No, Scott was aboard the *Hornet*. They were sailing that day, but she knew how to reach him.

On North Island, watching his air intelligence officer sprint down the gangway, Captain Marshall W. White got a bad feeling.

"Mr. Donlan? It's Scott Carpenter." He was speaking from a pay telephone on the wharf. "My wife said you—Yes, sir, thank you. I understand....I'll be the *hardest* worker you've got." Then he remembered Marsh White, and said, "We're sailing today. Someone'll have to square things with my skipper."

Back in Garden Grove, Rene was getting behind the wheel of the '50 Lincoln for a dash down the coast, where she imagined the *Hornet* weighing anchor. Donlan was working the phones in Washington, trying to reach the CNO. On the deck of the Fighting Lady, an incredulous Marsh White was bellowing, "You'll leave this ship over my dead *body!*" and other fine Navy invective. Consternation, a commander's fury, and excitement roiled the *Hornet* until the Chief of Naval Operations was once again brought to bear. Addressing a newly cordial captain, Admiral Arleigh A. Burke promised that the *Hornet* would get another air intelligence officer, but just now the country needed his.

Scott got his gear and headed down the gangway against the great tide of sailor traffic. Captain White asked him what he thought was in store for him, and Scott didn't hesitate.

"I'm going," he told the skipper with glee, "to ride the nosecone of a rocket around the world three times!"

"Bullshit!" is what the skipper said.

10
One Hundred Chimps

When NASA introduced its seven Mercury astronauts at a historic press conference on April 9, 1959, Dwight D. Eisenhower was president, the civilian space agency was nearly a year old, and Project Mercury was setting a breakneck pace to get into space. But as far as most Americans were concerned, the country had little to show for the $30 million just poured into NASA's coffers.

While the average American citizen was jittery about Soviet space achievements and unsure of NASA's accomplishments, American commentators were downright nasty. *Newsweek,* for one, wrote in a barbed piece how the new space agency might best lose the space race: "Start late, downgrade Russian feats, fragment authority, pinch pennies, think small, and shirk decisions." The high-minded *New York Times* refrained from sarcasm, but its reproach was evident: "It is not good enough to say that we have counted more free electrons in the ionosphere than the Russians have.... We must achieve the obvious and the spectacular, as well as the erudite and the obscure."[1]

Enter seven Mercury astronauts and the "obvious and spectacular." Enter seven military test pilots—husbands and fathers, sons and brothers—in their mid- to late thirties, confident and gritty. The country's ambitions for space now had human faces. They were, in alphabetical order: Lieutenant M. Scott Carpenter (USN), Captain Leroy G. ("Gordo") Cooper (USAF), Lieutenant Colonel John H. Glenn (USMC), Captain Virgil I. (Gus) Grissom (USAF), Lieutenant Commander Walter M. Schirra (USN), Lieutenant Commander Alan B. Shepard (USN), and Captain Donald K. (Deke) Slayton (USAF).

Dressed in civilian clothes, the men assembled as a group for the first time on April 9, 1959, at the Dolley Madison House, where two months earlier they had been hunched over IQ tests. They took their places at a long table facing the press, Scott at stage left—first in alphabetical order—Deke at stage right, last, their seven faces gleaming with perspiration and the joy of divulging a well-kept secret.

Longtime Washington correspondents, among them the self-described cynic Scotty Reston, admitted they were affected by the sight:

> Those gloomy students of the American character who think
> we've lost the hop on our fast ball should have been around
> here this week when seven young American men dropped in to
> Washington on their way to outer space.
>
> Somehow they had managed to survive the imagined
> terrors of our affluent society, our waist-high culture, our
> hidden persuaders, power elite and organization men, and here
> they were, aged 32 to 37 and all married, in the first stages of
> training for the first manned rocket flights into space. . . .
>
> What made them so exciting was not that they said
> anything new, but that they said all the old things with such
> fierce conviction.
>
> They talked of the heavens the way the old explorers talked
> of the unknown seas. They wanted to see what was "on the
> other side." They spoke of "duty" and "faith" and "country"
> like Walt Whitman's pioneers.[2]

The next day, newspaper headlines conveyed the spectacular news. The *New York Post* ran a banner headline: "7 Fliers Named as Spacemen: All Married, Wives Approve"—wifely approval was as astounding, apparently, as the announcement about their husbands. For nearly every American expected the seven men to die.

Thanks to home addresses provided in the NASA press kit, a few of the seven wives met with the press. Rene was as prepared for this important event as any Navy wife could be, a veteran of countless teas, arcane dress and behavior codes, funerals, officers' parties, elections, and other political and social functions. She had four attractive children, a newly acclaimed husband, and every expectation of encountering friendly reporters.

The first ones came calling before dawn.

In most of the photos from that day, Rene sits on a sofa slipcovered in a Paul Klee–inspired fabric. Scotty was sporting his father's Navy helmet, visor up; Jay sat, sometimes, between the sisters, who wore matching red dresses trimmed with gold and black rickrack. For four hours the children sat on the couch, taking turns sitting on their mother's lap, hanging from her neck, riding her back in a dorsal bear hug, or somersaulting backward off the sofa behind her. Rene had forbidden bragging, but she had said nothing about mugging for the cameras.

On April 8, the night before the Washington press conference, Rene had set her alarm for four forty-five, selected fresh clothes for the children, and laid them near their beds. On the kitchen counter she assembled the things she needed to make a "Sunday" breakfast— cinnamon toast (a family favorite) and a choice of dry cereal. The boys would stay home from school in the hope that the announcement would be broadcast on the radio. The night before, their father had told the boys simple things over the phone: "I'm going to ride a rocket."

A reporter or two might show up at the house, he told Rene, possibly someone from *Life* magazine, for talks were even then in the works for the astronauts' "personal stories." During dinner that night, Rene told her children in a serious voice: "Dad's new job is important and serious. People want to know about it." She expected them to be-have *well,* she emphasized.

For the seven women—Rene Carpenter, Trudy Cooper, Annie Glenn, Betty Grissom, Jo Schirra, Louise Shepard, and Marje Slay-ton—their lives became slightly more unusual than they already were. They adjusted as they always had to the public curiosity the space program provoked, the intense training periods, and, ultimately, its early-morning launches carried live on television while the whole country watched.

On that first morning, Rene dressed and started the coffee. The press conference in Washington was scheduled for ten A.M., Eastern Standard Time; news was embargoed until then. What this meant for California time, or for Colorado, Rene was unsure. Scott had briefed Toye by telephone, and she had taken a radio to her office at Boulder Community Hospital, hoping to hear a snippet on the noon news.

At five-fifteen, it was still dark outside. Astonished, Rene saw car headlights shining on still other parked cars. Who *were* they? How had they found this cul-de-sac? NASA had given her no guidelines or in-formation. Scott said there were "no secrets" in this program and he had "more faith" in what she'd say than in what he would. At dawn, Timmy Lane was lined with cars, out of which rumpled men emerged, holding notepads and thermoses. Technicians stretched and yawned, hauling equipment close to the house. The scene outside confirmed what Rene had known since that first ride to the airport in late Janu-ary. This was historic.

She answered the first knock on the door. A reporter greeted her.

"Mrs. Carpenter?" his voice boomed through the house.

"Yes?" she whispered, for the children were still asleep.

"We know you can't talk to us till seven A.M. But do you mind if we set up a few things in the yard?"

A Navy officer's wife has two personas: gracious is the first, and very gracious the second. Rene adopted persona number two: "Yes, *please* do," she managed before closing the door. Her voice had sounded strange. Plan B, not yet formulated, took shape as she wakened the children, toasted bread for the first stage of cinnamon toast, and steam-pressed the girls' dresses in hopes that Toye might see them in photographs taken that day. Promptly at seven, she opened the door and invited everyone in.

Although there were scores of reporters, it was not a mob scene. No one was in a hurry, and Rene sensed a self-organizing pecking order among the group. She offered them coffee, and some had brought rolls and doughnuts. They toured through the house, pondered books and family mementos on the shelves, and generally made themselves comfortable. The technicians and photographers evaluated the one big room. Not enough light.

"Do you mind if we move a few pieces of furniture?" they asked, hoisting a sofa. Soon the living-room arrangement occupied the dining room and clamp-on lights festooned the rafters. The aroma of percolating coffee wafted into the room. Someone had made a fresh pot. The reporters were fast and businesslike, unfailingly polite, funny, thinking of amusing things to do with the boys. One of them, wandering through the house, had found Scott's Navy flight helmet, complete with dark visor. Would Scotty like to wear it? He needed no encouragement, and donned it to the delight of the photographers. They arranged and rearranged the five family members on the sofa. The interviews began before eight.

The story, Rene saw, appraising the scene in her house, was every bit as amazing and mysterious to the reporters as it was to her. They were feature writers, she noticed, and not science reporters. The story about the selection process, conducted in secret, had affected them, too. At first their questions were animated, often tangled and long. They were obviously stunned that a wife would support such an endeavor. Standing and talking in groups, she heard them argue about it. "Jesus *Christ*!" Rene heard one of them say. "Would *you* do it?"

After all the secrecy of the tests and the domestic excitement surrounding her husband's breakout from the *Hornet,* Rene was bursting to narrate the family drama of the past eight weeks. She saw, though, that few could understand it without comprehending what it meant to be a naval aviator, his wife, a military family. The cross-country trips, the good-byes, the lonely deployments, the funerals, the Navy

hymn, the casseroles. They couldn't possibly understand how prepared she, each wife, was.

With an unflagging smile, she sounded themes that since Wednesday, January 27, had been crowding her imagination: Scott was born
for space. He lives for flying. Has worked so hard. Comes from a long
line of pioneers. Yes, yes, *yes,* Rene said, she was proud and pleased. No,
not afraid. "We all want to go with him," she insisted, "even the two
dogs!" Repeating the same to each new, but identical, question. Getting it better each time.

A CBS reporter showed up with a small crew. "I understand
you're a whiz at chess," the CBS reporter prompted Scotty, who
drawled a pleased account of his recent triumphs: "Well, yeah, I just
beat two sixth graders, who're two years ahead of me, and one fourth
grader."

They posed in their backyard, beside an orange tree heavy with
pale fruit. In her mind, Rene began to organize another packing day,
another cross-country trip, even as she listened to her own voice.
Scott would be *home,* she thought. Then she looked up and smiled
again for the photographer.

WITH THE ADVENT OF Project Mercury, a more cheerful mood swept
the country—sheer wonder a primary element, courtesy these seven
volunteers, whom Americans were already hailing as heroes in a pre-
funeral tribute. But once the heroics of the endeavor were well established, headline writers cast about for fresh angles on the spacemen, or
astronauts—the nomenclature was new and unsettled. A story about
a horse race attracts more readers than a story about a horse, so the
Washington Evening Star played up the rivalry: "7 VIE TO BE FIRST MAN IN
SPACE." Inspired by the chivalry of it all, the *Los Angeles Examiner* attempted, "7 'KNIGHTS OF SPACE' NAMED AFTER DAYS OF RIGOROUS TESTS."
The *New York Mirror* highlighted the family-man angle: "7 DADS CHO-
SEN FOR SPACE," while another paper sounded a reverent note: "SPACE
TEAM FACES THE FUTURE WITH FAITH," and the inevitable play on words:
"THOSE SEVEN SPACE CADETS NO IDIOTS."[3]

Congratulatory mail poured into Toye's mailbox from family and friends. "While listening to who had been chosen," one friend wrote, "my heart...swelled with pride along with yours, for it's such a satisfaction to have gallant sons. May he fly high and long."

THE "MILLION-DOLLAR" *Life* contract for the "personal" stories of the astronauts was a very big deal. Never before had military officers been paid for the story of their "routine" duties, and the arrangement created some unease and grumbling throughout the flying establishment. But "what Harry wants, Harry gets," everyone agreed. "Harry" being Henry Luce, who collected the Great and Famous, lionizing Hemingway, publishing the Duke of Windsor's memoirs, and excerpting President Eisenhower's book. If *Time* was his propaganda trumpet, *Life* became the peanuts and popcorn, and he reveled in the pictures. He would dote, too, on the American heroes he was to help create.

President Dwight D. Eisenhower had no intention of turning these military officers over to the public. He was instead inclining to house them, as the Soviets did their cosmonauts, in an isolated Star City. But his sometime tax attorney C. Leo DeOrsey, president of the Washington Redskins, began to talk him out of it. The seven families should be allowed to live lives that were as normal as possible, he argued, since they would in any event never be the same again.

DeOrsey brought in his friend and co-owner of the Kenilworth Hotel in Miami Beach, Arthur Godfrey, the popular and powerful CBS broadcaster, as well as aviation enthusiast, and a favorite of Ike's. Godfrey explained that space exploration was the story of the decade, and that the *Life* contract would protect the families. He stressed the need to protect their children, knowing that Eisenhower had been known to flare up over intrusions affecting his grandchildren.[4]

After DeOrsey and Godfrey got the president's ear, the precedent-breaking contract was signed. Each astronaut family eventually received about $70,000, before taxes. It was a shock for the Carpenters, after a decade in the Navy, to be in any tax bracket. They took Leo DeOrsey's advice and invested. They would have enough money on hand, two years later, to make a down payment on a three-bedroom house in Timber Cove, Texas, when home loans stood at 4 percent.

It's impossible to overstate Leo's influence on the seven astronauts, in those first two or three years. Like Luce, he collected celebrities, especially sports stars, but he took these men on as something larger than himself. He took no fee—ever. He counseled them; lectured them; took them to dinner; cautioned them on their personal lives ("don't diddle"); begged them to invest, not spend, their nest eggs; brought them investment opportunities. Through Lloyd's of London, Leo also tried to purchase million-dollar insurance policies for each of the seven. To no avail. The men were uninsurable. Leo persisted with private arrangements. On the eve of John's historic spaceflight, he wrote a personal check for $100,000, made out to Annie Glenn. She was to cash it should John fail to survive.[5] Leo motivated the seven much as a coach would—they were a team, he told them. He became obsessed with whether or not they would come out of this adventure alive.

Thanks to this intervention, in short, the astronauts could all report three weeks after the press conference, not to a guarded Star City compound, but to Langley Field, Virginia, where the Space Task Group was headquartered. Arriving on Monday morning, April 27, 1959, the seven began their professional lives together in a large office that held seven gray, government-issue desks, seven desk chairs, and seven matching gray-metal wastebaskets. After a briefing, they received their individual engineering assignments and immediately dived into the intense research and development already under way at NASA. They had a lot of catching up to do, both with the Soviets and with their new colleagues.[6]

They were keenly interested in Max Faget's design for the Mercury capsule. It was not, of course, the hypersonic beauty that Boeing designers had envisioned the year of the *Sputniks*. But it could be launched into space with the available technology, a definite design plus. An innovative, three-axis control stick would regulate pitch, roll, and yaw. In the rear of the craft were hydrogen peroxide–powered high and low thrusters, which could be activated by the pilot. Inelegant as it was, the Mercury capsule, or spacecraft, could be flown once launched into space.[7] Still, the pilot was riding inside what was essentially a bullet, facing backwards, on an unalterable flight path.

The space bullet could nevertheless be pointed in any direction. It could somersault, stand on its head, its haunches. It could execute yaw (a side-to-side movement), pitch (up and down), and roll. After the retrorockets jolted it into a blistering atmospheric embrace of earth, the capsule—with its ablative heat shield that cooled by boiling away the heat—became an ungainly if exceptionally heat-resistant pod and, upon splashdown, temporary watercraft. Was it seaworthy? Not very. But the astronaut could survive the splashdown, if the reentry trajectory were right and the parachutes deployed properly. Forget about toggling that switch for a backup manual release if you've lost consciousness while hurtling earthward.[8]

Reentry heating was perhaps the primary hazard the Mercury astronauts faced. But the water landing was a close second. For this latter event, it was agreed they needed training. Scott knew the Navy ran a tough water-survival school at Little Creek, Virginia, where the Underwater Demolition Team (UDT) was based—actually, UDT 21, considered the best of all the U.S. Navy teams. Bob Gilruth agreed; the Space Task Group director was the only boss the astronauts really had. Beginning in May 1959, the Navy's rugged UDT instructors, precursors to the Navy SEALs, took on the water-survival training of all seven Mercury astronauts. They began in the pool at Langley Field and graduated to the estuaries of Virginia's Eastern Shore; trying to keep up with the rugged divers of the Underwater Demolition Team on their obstacle course was probably the best physical conditioning the seven ever had as a group.

Deke Slayton had already begun his own personal water-survival course at home, in the kitchen sink. The Wisconsin native and Air Force officer did not know how to swim. So he filled the kitchen sink with water and, dunking his head in, rotated it for the swimmer's side breath, and then face down to exhale: side, *inhale,* down, *exhale.* The first nonswimmer to graduate from the Navy's tough water-survival program? Deke Slayton.

THE ASTRONAUTS' relationship with *Life* magazine began awkwardly. Privacy was a way of life in 1959, so the very thought of a reporter entering one's home to ask personal questions and use the bathroom was beyond the pale. NASA was more than a little uneasy—and specific: *Life* would have no access to the pilot on NASA property, that is, the Cape. Doctors and engineers would debrief them *first,* after a flight; a press conference would be held; only then could *Life* representatives interfere. But NASA made no rules for the wives, who set their own ground rules, in their own homes, about *Life* magazine's human interest stories.

Crunch time arrived when word came that Ralph Morse, *Life's* great photographer, would be in Langley Field to shoot a cover for the story on the wives. They were alternately stunned, terrified, and resistant, only two months into their public lives. It's hard to overstate how important a role *Life* played in the popular culture of 1959. Posing for this cover magnified the wives' cosmetic insecurities; it would also be the catalyst for creating a tight-knit band of sisters.

Hair was a source of special anxiety. Stuck in the Before Jackie era, women were sleeping in curlers or rags, setting their hair, pushing it into tight curls made crimpy from terrible perms. Next, clothes: Did this mean an extra, specific purchase of a particular garment? No, not to worry, the magazine people said; this would be a "head shot," revealing only a collar or neckline. In fact, no collars: please wear a scoop-neck top.

Head shots? This meant makeup and decisions about lipstick color. Rene's chickenpox scar would surely blaze up from the page. Marje Slayton feared her one endearing mole would rear up, volcano-like, from her chin. Betty Grissom stated, "I'm scrubbing my face, and that's it." They consulted each other on lipstick colors—each chose one shade or another of pink—and prayed the photo would be an unsmiling one. This was the Dark Age of cosmetics, when the semiotics of lipstick color spoke volumes about a woman's personality and character and would send her frequently to the powder room during social occasions, when lips needed recoloring.

On the appointed day, the seven women arrived nervous, self-conscious, talkative to the point of jabbering. Ralph had arranged choir risers, and now he experimented with their placement, up and down, up and down. He shot Polaroids in the first hour, adjusted lighting during the second, and arranged yet different groupings during the third. Mouths got dry and lips stuck to teeth as they reacted and reacted again to "Smile," "Smile," "Smile." The women reapplied their lipstick again and again and again. They climbed down, they climbed up. Marje needed several cigarette breaks. Their nerves sent them to the bathroom.

Ralph never stopped moving, thinking, changing positions. Less talkative now, the wives began to pay closer attention to their fellow sufferers, women they hardly knew but were beginning to like. Trudy Cooper, whose reserve was total; Betty Grissom, who sugar-coated nothing and said out loud what everyone else was only thinking; laconic Jo Schirra, observing, "Well, I'm glad I wore my seventy-dollar shoes." In the fourth or fifth hour, finally, "I think we've got it," from Ralph. Drained, grateful to be finished, relieved that they had conducted themselves well, a few groans but no complaining, the women hugged each other good-bye. They had done well together and sensed they were on the same wavelength.

Then came September 21, 1959, when *Life* hit the newsstands. Receiving no advance copies, Rene was scared to drive down to buy it, until Jo phoned her: "Get in your car!" she commanded. "See what they did to our lipstick!" "And there we were," Rene recalls, "seven broad, toothy smiles, sporting hideous lipstick in some never-before-glimpsed shade of red. "What happened?" went the calls to New York. "Well," said *Life,* "we changed the colors in the lab. You all came off better with the same color, and everyone agreed on that nice red."

As WIVES OF MILITARY pilots, the seven women knew the ropes. They had traveled from pillar to post with children and china, sorted out epidemics of irrational rumors that beset their small communities like chickenpox. They had a realistic view of their husbands, were proud of them but not starry-eyed. Shared laughter over male vanities was one thing among the wives, but discussion of anything more personal was *verboten*—the unwritten code they had absorbed a decade before, at the squadron level.

More than anything, the seven women were mothers, intent on

rearing "normal" children, which meant in large part protecting them from the public's growing adulation of their fathers. No one was better at this than Marjorie Slayton, who had the wit to ease the formality at a head table or the stuffiness of a receiving line. She was the first to identify the morbid curiosity many Americans experienced in their presence. Convinced their husbands would be dead within a year, strangers would take her hand, or Jo's, or Rene's, with the tenderest solicitude. "How *brave* you are," they would say. Marje responded with a laugh:

"Oh, don't worry! Wait till you meet my *next* husband!"

Unlike the other wives, Marje had a career in the civil service, marrying Deke when they were stationed in West Germany. The new NASA bureaucracy didn't have a clue, she saw, about how it might help the families manage their new public roles. Worse, she couldn't even get on base! Meanwhile the U.S. space program was trumpeting its openness around the world, and correspondents responded by flocking to Cape Canaveral; lobbyists, congressmen, and someone called the Duchess of Luxembourg were close on their heels. But not the wives.

They were never told why. They did not challenge the situation. Except Marje Slayton, who finally made her case to Deke: "Tell them I'm coming to wash your damn Ban-Lon shirts.... That I'm looking for a job.... That I'm your girlfriend. *That* ought to do it." Now Deke was gritty and profane, everybody's favorite tough-guy pilot, but when Marje got serious, he caved. He agreed to drive her aboard the base, but made her crouch on the floor of the back seat, covered by a quilt, as Deke whisked them through the gate with the obligatory salute. "It was awful," she confessed later, "I was having a nicotine fit and I had the urge to pop up and beg the guard for a cigarette."

FOR EVERYONE connected with Project Mercury, from the wives and their husbands to the engineers and technicians working on the spacecraft design and manufacture to the fellows setting up a ground control network from scratch, these were exhilarating times. Although the common perception was that these were grueling, even painful, months and years of unrelenting work, this simply was not the case. Everyone was working at the frontier of knowledge and experience, realizing things with minds, bodies, systems, and machines that had never before been accomplished. Yet no one was exhausted. The pace everyone set for themselves with Project Mercury—the excitement, resolve, and challenge—provided its own peace of mind and body.

Noting his background as a patrol plane pilot, NASA assigned Scott to tackle navigation ("the continual correction," as he likes to say, "of infinitesimal errors") and communications. But everyone took instruction in physiology, conducted at Langley Field by the NASA medics, and classes on astronomy and star recognition at Morehead Planetarium in North Carolina. The first capsule to be launched would have only a periscope, but the engineers were even then coming up with designs for a suitable window, hence the refresher courses in star recognition for navigational purposes.

At Langley, molds were made of the astronauts' seven individual backsides, which in turn were used to make custom contour couches for use on the Johnsville centrifuge and in the Mercury Procedures Trainer. There were many trips to the U.S. Navy centrifuge, in Johnsville, Pennsylvania. When astronauts weren't available for the grueling centrifuge work, other military pilots, many of them finalists from the 1959 selection process, including Bob Solliday and Pete Conrad, volunteered their bodies, time, and skill.

In September 1959, NASA sent the astronauts to San Diego for their first major group trip; Convair was to brief them on the Atlas missile they were building. Laid low by a virus at the last minute, Deke Slayton stayed behind. In September, Ralph Morse's group photo of the seven had just appeared on the cover of *Life*. The wives were on the cover the week the men were in San Diego. As it happened, however, one of the guys landed in a spot of trouble on that trip. So said a newspaper reporter when he called Colonel John A. "Shorty" Powers at two in the morning; he had photographs. Shorty called John Glenn. The story never ran.

Shorty had a ribald sense of humor: "Get this," he laughed. *Life* was publishing the "innermost *thoughts*" of the astronauts. "How about this instead?" he offered. "Their innermost *peckers*."

ONE AFTERNOON AT Langley Field, a tired Rene sat on the front steps of their family quarters, the picture of exhaustion. John Glenn came trotting down tree-shaded Eagan Street, stopping to chat. Rene brought him a glass of water and began to describe how she gathered steam for the evening chores.

"*Oxygen,*" John announced. "Oxygen to your brain." Or lack thereof. That was the key to her fatigue. Then in detail he described how this simple thing would change the biochemical something-or-other in her brain and contribute "more energy" and several more good hours to her day—as it did, John said, to his own. It kept his weight down, helped him to study at night *and* retain the information the next day. "I'll have Annie send you our book on the Royal Canadian Air Force Exercises," he offered, adding prophetically, "It will change your life."

John was a natural teacher. He spoke earnestly and straight to his listener without condescension. He addressed men, women, and children in the same manner. He did not flirt, nor get personal. Most surprising, the Marine could carry on a conversation with a woman well beyond the cultural limits of place (the U.S. military) and time (the mid-twentieth century), when men generally felt trapped after about forty-five seconds of conversation. The true John Glenn was more ambitious, more talented, funnier, and more charismatic than the humorless Calvinist of *The Right Stuff.*

He was not one of the boys, it is true. Where Al Shepard epitomized cool—the sixties-style "swinger" then coming into vogue—John was homespun. He was, at root, a Midwestern Presbyterian who took dead aim at his next goal and pursued it intensely, whatever it was. In 1959 he was already first among equals, the oldest of the seven, with the most military and combat experience, a television celebrity as a quiz-show winner, and holder of a transcontinental speed record. He wore old clothes, old cowboy hats, and lived next to his dearest friend, Tom Miller, his roommate and wing man from World War II.

John's marriage, his union with Annie, was downright mystical. When the sports-car craze hit, John bought instead a tiny Prinze automobile, big enough for one-and-a-half passengers. Sitting in the reserved parking space beside Al's brand-new Corvette, it was an eloquent visual joke. John and Annie liked to cook or barbecue for their friends, after which all gathered to sing. Annie played the organ, allowing John to harmonize in his strong, floating tenor that held high notes in perfect pitch. Annie, John, and Rene knew all five verses of every offertory hymn by heart and harmonized all the barbershop classics. In one of those mysteries of life, Annie's terrible stutter fell away when she sang.

THE SUMMER had passed, and with it the last gasp of Ike and Mamie Eisenhower's eight-year tenure at the White House. Project Mercury settled in quietly at Langley A.F.B. The Carpenters and Coopers located officers' quarters near each other on base. The Grissoms, Slaytons, and the Schirras found homes off-base. The Shepards and Glenns already had homes in Virginia. Al drove into Langley Field every day from nearby Virginia Beach. John moved into BOQs—Bachelor Officers Quarters—and drove home to Arlington on the weekends. Like the military gypsies they were, the Carpenters and Coopers blended into this Tidewater gem of an Air Force base, with its wide, tree-lined streets and sturdy brick rowhouses.

The air base was bracketed by two towns: Newport News, populated by white ship workers, and Hampton, where a prestigious black college, Hampton Institute, attracted the region's intelligentsia. In this still-segregated era, the three settlements might as well have been three separate planets: an off-limits air base, a historic community of black intellectuals and artists, and the white working class of hard hats worried about jobs in the up-and-down business of shipbuilding. As it happened, the boys, Scott and Jay, sometimes brought ethnic slurs home from school as impromptu and shocking language experiments. Rene tolerated none of it. Transgressions meant automatic trips to the kitchen sink, where she cooly supervised a mouth-washing with Dial soap, then laced with a foul-smelling antibacterial called Hexachlorophene. The humiliation was rendered even more pungent because Grandpa Carpenter was said to have invented the ingredient.

The Carpenter children entered a new decade, and a presidential election year, 1960, already pulsing with new sights and sounds of Cool. Astronauts were *not* cool in 1960. But Kid's Day on base was cool, with the silver F-106s lined up for inspection, the rapid-climb demonstrations, the model-plane competitions. Rene had located a kindergarten for Kris; Candy would follow her there the following fall. For the Carpenters, the contract with *Life* provided an undreamed-of material benefit. Scott could repay a thousand-dollar debt he had owed to his father for a few years. When ill health prevented Toye from paying the mortgage on her trailer home in Boulder, Scott and Rene paid it outright.

THE MEN HAD TRAINED and prepared for a water landing. But calculations about possible reentry sites for the orbital flights had the astronauts landing not in the Atlantic, as planned, but in West Africa. This called for survival training in the desert. For this they all reported on July 12, 1960, to the Air Force Survival School at Stead A.F.B., Nevada. The desert outside Reno was the classroom. NASA wanted the location of this exercise kept secret in order to conduct the seven-day trial in conditions as close to "real life" as possible. No one was to know the spot. "And that includes Ralph Morse," came the order. Understood. No one cracked.

Life magazine's editor, tough, caustic Ed Thompson, had assigned Morse to photograph the Mercury journey. Ralph was a natural hardware man with a knack for "seeing" a shape, a structure, a setting, and knowing how to shoot it. Most of the astronauts were camera nuts themselves, and so while Ralph was doing the first depictions of training, spacesuits, mock-up capsules, and so forth, his seven human subjects were full of questions about his exotic equipment. What setting was he using? Why? How could they get a Hasselblad?

Ralph worked very, very hard, over long hours, and he did not trick any of these men into a revealing shot—one of their first worries. Nor did he extend any reverence; Ralph wasn't impressed by anyone. He worked hard and they worked hard. As a hardware man, he assumed "this thing" (meaning spaceflight) "was going to work." His hustle and optimism and professionalism appealed to the astronauts.

He was clearly more fascinated by their machines than by their emerging status as gladiators. It was a relief: here was someone who hung on every detail about how to light something but had no interest in their personal psyches.

One incident during training solidified forever the astronauts' friendship with Ralph. He had learned about the desert-survival training, and learned, too, about NASA orders that he was not invited. So the ever-resourceful photographer discovered on his own where the desert-survival training was going to be held. He found out the flight plan and destination, and flew there first. He then chartered a small plane into which he loaded several bags of flour. Then Ralph and *his* pilot took off as the astronaut vans departed down a long, winding country road to the secret destination. Overhead in his airplane, Ralph tossed flour bombs to mark the circuitous route. Returning to the airport and his car, he then retraced his flour trail to their remote site, showing up before dinner. "Hi, guys," he said to the flabbergasted group. Ralph's story of this incident became their story, too, told and retold into legend to anyone who would listen.

SURVIVAL IN THE desert or at sea rested on surviving spaceflight itself. Enter the Mercury Procedures Trainer, the MPT, another type of survival training altogether. The astronauts had already encountered an earlier version of the MPT in the intentional and simultaneously cascading malfunctions of the Panic Box. The MPT differed in that it duplicated the cockpit of the Mercury capsule down to the smallest detail. With it, an entire mission profile could be simulated, pressure suit and all. But instead of the taped chaos used at Wright-Patterson with the Panic Box, the MPT used three system engineers who sat outside the trainer in front of control panels. Their job was to make it appear that one of the systems had failed. When this happened, sudden responses, the quicker the better, were required of the pilot.

As the astronauts became more familiar with the systems, the engineers began piling on, creating multiple, simultaneous system failures; the major difference was that the controls and instruments in the MPT represented reality, not the make-believe of the Panic Box.[9] The way

Scott saw it, the Panic Box determined proficiency; the MPT trained astronauts for specific mission profiles. So his approach to the MPT training sessions, particularly when preparing for flight, was just that, to treat them as training sessions—during which he placed a premium on learning. To his chagrin, though, he found his philosophy was not shared by all. Performance was being measured on *all* the training sessions. This in turn meant that six Mercury astronauts were competing (and not learning) for the highest performance scores, while a seventh, Scott, was aiming (and not competing) for the best possible learning experience. He was indignant, and personally disappointed, when he learned that performance on all the MPT sessions had been considered in determining who would get the first flight assignments, particularly since his performance on the Panic Box, at Wright-Patterson, was known to have been the best of the thirty-one finalists.

NASA's BREAKNECK PACE of training and engineering research and development continued through 1960. The country's first ballistic flight was just months away. But who would pilot it? While Americans were deciding on a new president the fall of 1960, Gilruth had determined that the first American in space would be one of three men: John Glenn, Gus Grissom, or Al Shepard. The backup team comprised Scott Carpenter, Gordo Cooper, Wally Schirra, and Deke Slayton. Wally in particular resented this gratuitous division of the group, sometimes referred to as Team Gold and Team Blue. Scott felt bad, too. But everyone pressed on with his work, with one eye always on the Soviets. They were utterly confident about the program.

Others were not so sure.

AFTER PRESIDENT JOHN F. Kennedy took office in January 1961, he appointed Dr. Jerome B. Wiesner, a well-known scientist and M.I.T. professor, to head the President's Science Advisory Committee, or the Wiesner Committee. President Eisenhower had presided over NASA's creation in 1958, but he was not especially keen about the civilian space agency. The new president was equally tepid, and the Wiesner Committee mirrored his views. Gilruth remembers one contemptuous committee member in particular, George B. Kistiakowsky, who said during one White House meeting that a manned space launch would "only be the most expensive funeral man has ever had."[10]

The committee's mood grew warier with the approach of the country's first manned flight—Al Shepard's. The closer it got, the warier and more risk-averse the committee became, until it finally informed Gilruth, flatly, that NASA was not to launch a man into space until ten more chimpanzee flights were first accomplished. To his stupefied reply, "Ten chimp flights?" the committee said yes, ten. These would provide a better "statistical sample."

Gilruth was adamant: NASA would make *one* chimp flight. If that succeeded, then they'd launch a man "in suborbital flight for six minutes of weightlessness." That first ballistic flight, he said, would provide everyone with "a pretty good idea of things."[11]

While the Wiesner committee dickered with NASA, naturally, the Soviets launched Yuri Gagarin into space—a "triumph of Lenin's ideas," claimed Khrushchev, "a confirmation of the correctness of Marxist-Leninist teachings."[12] A Japanese student agreed, telling *Life* magazine: "I knew Russia would do it first. Socialistic science is superior to that of the Western nation." It was April 12, 1961. Surveying the new damage to the country's international prestige, a newly thoughtful Wiesner Committee compromised: NASA wouldn't have to make those ten chimp flights, but it would have to "kill one hundred chimps" on the centrifuge "by stepping up the Gs until they died—a hundred times."[13] Paul E. Purser, still dumbfounded at the memory, remembers thinking: Apart from the ghoulishness of the request, NASA didn't have that many chimps to kill. Nor did it have the time for one hundred centrifuge runs.

NASA put its head down and plowed on, refusing to kill a hundred chimps and managing a flawless space launch of Commander Alan B. Shepard on May 5, 1961. Americans rejoiced. More to the point, American voters rejoiced. The reprieve gave the politically astute president an idea about the "the obvious and spectacular," which he now realized, with a kind of surprise, the overlooked space agency might be able to provide.

Much more was at work here than a young president's oppor-
tunism: President John F. Kennedy had a core conviction that a free society would prevail in any confrontation with tyranny. In June he
faced his own confrontation with a tyrant: his first summit meeting
with Soviet leader Nikita S. Khrushchev. With an East-West showdown
looming over the fate of West Berlin and a scrappy space agency at his
service, John F. Kennedy conceived of a brilliant geopolitical gambit:
bait the Soviet bear with a public, high-prestige contest, a race to the
moon.[14]

After Shepard's flight the president asked to meet with Gilruth, director of the Space Task Group and the wind beneath Faget's wings. Jim
Webb, NASA administrator, joined them. President Kennedy wanted to
know if it were *possible,* from a technological standpoint, to land a man
on the moon, say, by 1967. If so, could we beat the Soviets there?

As hypothetical questions go, this was child's play for Gilruth. The
research administrator entertained theoretical notions at all times.
Gilruth gathered his thoughts. Yes, he told the president, Americans
could land a man on the moon and bring him safely back. It would be
hard to do it in under ten years. But possible? Yes. And, yes, the United
States had a good shot at beating the Soviets. A lunar expedition would
call for new technology. Both countries, Gilruth explained, would
have to start from scratch. The Soviets' current advantage in space
would be meaningless.

A couple of weeks later, Gilruth and Webb were aboard one of
NASA's R4Ds when over the radio the president was addressing Congress, pledging NASA to a lunar expedition. Gilruth was "aghast." He
looked at Webb, who knew all about it.[15] In his special message to Congress, delivered on May 25, 1961, President Kennedy set out his vision
on a number of "urgent national needs," one of them the conquest of
space. In a resonant call to arms, the president asked the nation to
"commit itself to achieving the goal, before this decade is out, of landing a man on the moon and returning him safely to the earth." No
other space project, Kennedy declared, would be "more impressive
to mankind, or more important for the long-range exploration of
space."[16]

It was an electrifying national challenge and a great national address, which like many great speeches had several audiences: To the Soviet Union it threw down the gauntlet, challenging the giant to a race in which it appeared to have a lead. To the U.S. Congress and its constituents, President Kennedy was promising an unprecedented windfall of appropriations for facilities, jobs, manufacturing, services. But of everyone who heard the president speak, it was the World War II generation, his fellow veterans, who listened, haunted as Kennedy was by the fear that they had fought, trembled, bled, suffered, lost brothers and sisters, to win a world war for what—second place? Not on our watch, this great generation vowed, as they heard the president pledge: "While we cannot guarantee that we shall one day be first, we can guarantee that any failure to make this effort will make us last."

The Project Mercury missions of 1962 and 1963 were thus undertaken against this stunning national backdrop, with a determined young president and Americans back in the space race with a cheerful vengeance, their eyes fixed firmly on the stars—and on the foe beyond the iron curtain.

11

The Fibrillating Heart

Going to see a flight surgeon was a no-gain proposition; a pilot could only hold his own or lose in the doctor's office. To be grounded for a medical reason was no humiliation, looked at objectively. But it was a humiliation nonetheless!——for it meant you no longer had that indefinable, unutterable, integral stuff.

—Tom Wolfe

ALAN B. SHEPARD won a bet on the day of his historic flight. At the time, the term *space* was neither well understood nor well defined (the term *outer space* was in even worse shape). All the manned flights so far, with only two exceptions, have been in low earth orbit, or *cislunar* space—roughly between the earth and the moon. So as human beings began approaching the very outskirts of the earth's atmosphere, some tried arbitrarily to define the altitude at which space began, primarily for the purpose of awarding Astronaut Wings. That definition, plus the rivalry between the upstart Project Mercury gang and the X-15 team at Edwards A.F.B. (still trying to fly airplanes into space), inspired a bet between the two rival groups about who would be the first to reach an altitude of fifty miles. And on May 5, 1961, aboard *Freedom 7,* Al won that bet. The Mercury astronauts didn't beat the Soviet cosmonauts, but they trounced the X-15 pilots.

AT LANGLEY FIELD it was back to work. Al Shepard's fifteen minutes of suborbital flight in May 1961 had called for five hours on hold with no catheter or urine reservoir. Two months later, on July 21, 1961, Gus Grissom, the second American to be launched into space, had his spacesuit modified to include both. He had complaints, but his arrangement was still better than the diaper-wetting Shepard had to endure. The gloves on Al's spacesuit had made the astronaut's fingertips numb. Gus's were redesigned to increase mobility. Although an emergency prevented Gus from using it, his life raft weighed 45 percent less than Shepard's.

Early capsule designs had no means of emergency egress and were "nonstarters," everyone agreed, from the beginning. Only tiny side ports allowed Al to see outside.[1] But by the time Gus flew, McDonnell had in place an explosive side hatch, for quicker egress, a welcome trapezoidal window, and new rate-stabilization controls that worked "like power steering on an automobile." Al Shepard's flight plan had been "overloaded." Grissom's was changed so the astronaut had more time to make "exterior observations."[2]

Gus's wife, Betty, was an unpretentious woman from Indiana. Like Gus, she spoke in blunt, emphatic bursts: "I'm a Hoosier, if you want to know." Her husband detested the new moniker "astronaut," sensing the phony P.R. aspect, and announced one day to everyone's amusement, "I'm not 'ass' anything. I'm a *pilot.* Isn't that good enough, fer chrissake?"

Betty took a similar satisfaction from her accomplishments as wife, mother, and housekeeper. She was justly proud of the way she had supported Gus through his postwar college career and then maintained her home by the book, with the energy of three women, disciplining "my boys"—her two sons, Scott and Mark—who responded impressively. No eye-rolling or talking back from the Grissom boys.

It was after Gus's ballistic flight, when the Air Force pilot nearly drowned during a botched recovery operation, that Rene would finally get her trip on base at Cape Canaveral. "C'mon, Rene," Gus ordered her after he and Betty found her poolside at the Holiday Inn. "I want you to see something." NASA had given the networks heavily edited footage of his rescue, and Gus was angry. At the gates, he said to the guard, "They're with me," and drove on through. Up the gantry elevator the three of them went; Betty and Rene both stopped to touch the skin of a launch vehicle—"for Gemini," Gus explained. But the women were there to see, to witness, something else: the entire, awful, unedited tape of Gus's recovery.

ON A WEDNESDAY MORNING, October 4, 1961, Rene was sitting at her desk, writing in her journal. She was "looking out over the church-yard across the street to the Space Task Group buildings."

> Mr. Gilruth is... at the moment telling the men of his choices for orbital crews. I've straightened the house, played with the kids a while, tried mending the girls' nightgowns,... Trudy [Cooper] and I will know by noon—the other gals must wait till tonight, and even tonight will not be given to us for licking wounds or uttering a quiet Hurrah, for they must all leave on the five-thirty courier for the orbital simulations....

> *Wednesday afternoon*

> Scott dashed home mid-morning to tell me.... John will be first, Scott will stand by; Deke second flight, Wally standby— Al and Gus will troubleshoot respectively. Gordo was not named.... Walt Williams, the only other person besides the seven in attendance. Mr. Gilruth ran down the order of choices, followed by a silence broken when Gus said, "Well, I guess a handshake is in order for John." John was not visibly moved at the announcement. Then there was much handshaking and claps on the back after which the boys moved back to the office and Al passed around a drink for all.
>   Scott's disappointment is sharpened because he feels he has done far better than Deke in this program. But the hardware men cannot be expected to discount Deke's Edwards test experience. Just below the surface of Mercury boils this Hardware-vs-Medics feud.[3]

Although Rene had seen a "genuine and amused" smile on her husband's face, Scott would later write, in the same journal, that "the selection still smarts." He was philosophical, though, reasoning that he had never before "reckoned by anyone else's standards, and now would be a poor time to start."

Preparations for the country's first manned orbital, John's flight aboard MA-6, would eventually come to consume nineteen weeks of intense, exhausting work, mind and body. In the highly unlikely event John couldn't take the three-orbit mission (if he came down with a viral infection, for example, or had a serious injury), then it would be up to Scott to pilot the mission in his place. In 1962 machines, systems, and men, backup pilots among them, were expected to perform to a .999-percent degree of reliability, one chance in a thousand of failure. "I have resolved to train myself as thoroughly as John," Scott explained in a journal entry, just after the selection, "so the only thing I won't get out of this period is the actual flight"—which, he added, was "easily the quickest and simplest task of the lot."

The various Mercury capsules—test versions and the one John would fly—were being delivered to the Cape. Scott explained what he and John did with them in another journal entry, dated shortly after the selection, on October 16, 1961:

> John's capsule is next in line, and this is the one that I as backup
> pilot—sad words—am most interested in. No. 12 capsule is
> here, which is a sort of backup for No. 13, and 15 is here as a test
> capsule and is not scheduled for flight. What this whole business
> amounts to is this: The capsules are all put together in St. Louis
> and then shipped here, where they are partially torn down to
> make modifications (which result from new knowledge we
> have gained from recent flights) on equipment installed in the
> capsule many months ago. This is a terrible job because the
> capsules are so compact that to remove and change one item,
> you must first remove five other items before you can get to the
> one requiring modification.[4]

The Mercury astronauts had a lot of say in the design process. But their authority, sometimes described with some derision as "Astro Power," was never something they wrested from anyone at NASA. It was quite the reverse, for Gilruth gave it to them the day they arrived at Langley Field, when he promised them "they would be happy with the spacecraft before they flew." No one, he pledged, "would push them into anything." Glenn remembers Gilruth assuring them that "'if there was anything at any time in the program we didn't like, we had free access to him with our complaints.'"[5] They were chosen because they were "experienced engineers and test pilots," Gilruth said, and so he expected them to apply their skills "to the new area of testing spacecraft." Writing at the Cape, Scott explained their job in a journal entry: "We are here to observe, with a pilot's critical eye, that the various tests and results are being performed and plotted correctly. We are in a position to notice more discrepancies than anyone else, and it provides an excellent opportunity to become intimately acquainted with the machine which will carry you around the world in 90 minutes."

The Mercury astronauts may have been skilled engineers and test pilots, but to Gilruth they were much more than that. He was often heard calling them the country's "precious human cargo."

LIFE MAGAZINE HAD rented a secluded house on the Florida coast, to be used as an astronaut retreat. Scott repaired there when he could during this busy time leading up to John's flight, to "sit on the porch and watch the birds eating the bread I had left out, or watch the death's head spiders in their intricate but haphazard webs," noting, "These few quiet moments, alone with the setting sun, a scotch and ice, and complete quiet and isolation, were the most relaxing times I have spent since I was in the Australian outback."

Early one morning, starving as usual, Scott foraged without success for breakfast. There was nothing at the Holiday Inn at Cocoa Beach, and he was in a rush to report for work by eight. Making a beeline for the *Life* house, where he had a stash of Wheaties, he found it deserted, except for a pair of pumps under the couch in the living room—signs of an occupant. Looking through all the bedrooms, he found in one a sleeping girl "naked and spreadeagled," according to his journal entry. He left quickly, still ravenous, and fumed all the way to the Cape.

As John's flight approached, the launch date was set and postponed, set again, and again postponed. In six months NASA would relocate to Houston, Texas. Administrator James Webb had broken the bad news to Gilruth, who loved his boat and was extremely reluctant to leave his Tidewater haunts. "It did make more sense to stay in Virginia," he concedes in a long interview conducted in the late 1980s. But then he said Jim Webb had a question for him: "What did Harry Byrd ever do for you, Bob?" "Nothing," Gilruth admitted. Webb explained: "That's what I mean.... We've got to get the money, or we can't do this program." He appealed to the research administrator in Gilruth: "Texas is the center of the country." Then to the mariner: "You're on salt water there." Finally, the clincher: Houston was the home of Representative Albert Thomas (D-Texas), head of the House Appropriations Committee, the man who controlled the money.[6]

It is often claimed that a site-selection committee chose Texas over rival claimants like Boston and Washington, D.C. But it was simpler than that.

While Scott and John trained through the winter of 1961–62 for the country's first orbital flight, designated MA-6, their wives flew down to reconnoiter the public schools and the real estate of South Texas. Scott's only request was a backyard flat enough for a trampoline. John hoped to be on the water and to keep his ski boat tied up. NASA provided a Gulfstream for most of its employees taking these three-day trips, and two by two, the seven wives took turns babysitting each other's children and taking the trip down. Annie Glenn and Rene Carpenter flew down in January 1962.

One of the first misconceptions newcomers generally had about Annie Glenn, when confronted with her stutter, was that she was handicapped. Her huge brown eyes glowed out of an open, unguarded face as she struggled to form a difficult word filled with consonants. The effort left many listeners uneasy, anxious to help her out by providing the word. Early on, she made clear to Rene that she did not want help. "I learned to wait and listen," Rene says, "and with time her sentences came more easily."

Arriving on a very cold night in January at the Houston airport, where Annie had already reserved a rental car, Annie drove them to their motel, where she had already reserved two rooms. Utterly prepared, Annie had maps and had memorized the route, some forty miles south of Houston. Mile after mile, the Harris County landscape changed to scrub and became another place called Clear Creek. At the turnoff, the women stopped at a lone tavern and general store near the railroad tracks. Annie jumped out to get bottled drinks and returned with the news: "There's a lake ahead!" Rene was slumped in her seat, defeated by what passed for scenery.

To their right was Swan Lagoon, a subdivision built around a large sort of pond and a few newly constructed houses. But on their left was mile after mile of scrub, a huge parcel of land that Rice University owned and would soon donate to the space program—and where Brown & Root Construction Co., Lyndon B. Johnson's financial backers, would get the contract to build the structures. Annie drove on unerringly. They passed two signs that said "Lots for Sale." A large lake was on their right, Clear Lake, and a public boat ramp. "Let's go to Seabrook," she said, "and check out the town."

They had entered a world apart from Houston, boasting an independent school district and a proud population of oil workers, fishermen, and farmers who savored their rural life. They resented the wealth, pace, and boosterism of Houston to the north, and approved the huge billboards—"IMPEACH EARL WARREN"—dotting the roadways and mirroring their own very conservative lives. While not charming, Seabrook in 1962 was at least authentic. Rene and Annie cruised through and around the town. They found a large, interesting feed store and spotted Peggy Pounder's School of Dance, where the Carpenter girls and Susie Schirra were soon enrolled. There was a Methodist church, whose choir director, Miss Card, also taught in the elementary school. The Checker-driving Miss Card, with the soaring soprano, was the best choir director in twenty states.

Soon a flood of outsiders would mightily tax the good citizens of the region—their humor, their old ways, and their small public schools. Clear Creek High would soon be graduating bumper crops of college-bound students. Its class of 1967 boasted twenty-four National Merit Finalists. Twenty of them were NASA kids, Scotty Carpenter among them.

Annie and Rene both liked the feel of Seabrook, but they still had no idea where to live. "When in doubt, follow the FOR SALE signs," Annie said, as she turned the car around. "This is it," she declared at a sign that said TIMBER COVE, whipping into a right turn and driving down a long, pretty entrance road, flanked by open fields harboring stacked hay and herds of cattle. They cruised the streets of the new subdivision, feeling genuine excitement. Dotted here and there was the Texas version of the ubiquitous ranch house: soft, biscuit-colored brick, rarely a front window. The houses opened completely to the back, with patios and large backyards. And there was Taylor Lake.

The developer had built a canal that connected two blocks of houses directly to the lake. Several homes along the canal were already under construction. Scenting promise, the women got out of the car and walked through the large lot at the head of the canal, marked with a sign that said "Marsters' Construction Co." He was on their list of rec-ommended local builders. They drove to the builder's lakefront house, where Annie knocked on the door.

Mrs. Marsters appeared, welcoming the women with genuine warmth. She telephoned her husband and walked them through her own Marsters' Construction home. Then the three women drove over to the lot they liked, at the head of the canal. There they decided to di-vide it in half, Glenns on the right side, Carpenters on the left, and made appointments to work out the house plans. They drove back up the freeway congratulating each other.

By the end of that day Rene's admiration for Annie knew no bounds. Not only was she the best navigator the Navy wife had ever seen, the woman was prepared, organized, decisive, and knowledgeable about construction. She was fun. She made wise observations. She listened carefully. She made plans into family homes and lives. Scott and the kids had room for a trampoline. John could tie up his ski boat. Where Rene saw just scrub and Southern pine, Annie saw possibilities and in-teresting flora. And while her vision came into being, Annie Glenn made everyone feel better. There was no one like her in the world.

They built their houses there at the head of the canal, just as Annie envisioned. Later, the Grissoms and Schirras found homes just one block away. The Shepards chose a Houston apartment building, while the Slaytons built their home in Friendswood.

WHILE ANNIE WAS dazzling Rene on the trip to Texas, her husband, John, was setting a pace that astounded Scott: "John, I must say, is wearing me out," the Navy pilot confessed in the journal he shared with Rene. "Plug, plug, *plug*. It kills me. It amazes me. It makes me proud and a little sorry." After one dinner with the prime pilot for MA-6, Scott went back to his quarters, inspired, to perform "19 chins and 30 pushups on fingers." He wrote:

> I don't know if I can keep the pace (without alternately trotting and cantering) that John sets. He is a most dedicated person.... I feel a little like I did on the TPT tour—Patuxent—when after a week I was so tired of talking airplanes (my love) and aerodynamics that I couldn't bear the thought of another cocktail party where all I could hear was the same. I need some fresh pursuit occasionally—have a drink, listen to music, talk about a good book, play the uke, or just play a little—but not John. Anyway it is a pleasure to help John and I am proud that I am doing such a good job. I *am*. And leading him to decisions when it is necessary.

The men spent long hours in the simulator, fully suited up. Since the next flight was John's, the MPT was outfitted with John's custom contour couch:

> Spent eight hours in the suit and four hours in the capsule for my run—but John's couch doesn't fit me at all, and it was uncomfortable. Wrong angle and all, but I gave a good account of myself and came up with some good ideas. John had a long run—ten hours in the suit, and nine in the capsule. We ran into trouble, as we suspected, with the egress. All the additional equipment gets in the way so much that we can no longer get out the top. This will cause many repercussions up north unless we fix it quickly.[7]

John Glenn's historic flight, aboard *Friendship 7,* finally came on February 20, 1962. After holds, scratches, disappointments, and postponements, the country would have its first orbital mission. For Al's flight, the year before, Scott and Wally had flown F-106s, in solidarity with the Navy pilot his Redstone rocket streaked into the sky and beyond. For John's flight, Scott was also close by, but in the blockhouse not far from Pad 14.

Although piloting the sixth launch of the Mercury-Atlas (hence the designation MA-6), John would be the first human to be launched into space by the Atlas, fueled by 122 tons of kerosene and liquid oxygen—more than four times the fuel load of the Mercury-Redstone used to thrust Shepard and Grissom into space on their ballistic flights.

In the blockhouse at T minus 30 and counting, Scott was thinking about John and his need for speed. More than anything that morning, John needed speed. So as the powerful Atlas engines began to roar and the rocket slowly lifted off the launch pad, with anticipatory hoots and hollers of gladness rising with it, Scott patched into the voice communication loop: "Godspeed, John Glenn." It was a bon voyage to his good friend, and a plea to his Maker.

ALL SUPERLATIVES—greatest, most wonderful, most thrilling—fail to do justice to John Glenn's flight aboard *Friendship 7.* It was a stupendous success by anyone's standards, save perhaps John's. In fact, "a lot of things," he wrote in his flight report, "would be done differently" had he the flight to do over again. For example, there was his pilot error. No one noticed, but still, for future flights he thought to reveal that *upon reentry, he had left his face-plate open.* The mission, John conceded, was none the worse for the oversight. Had it been necessary, he wrote in his flight report, he could have closed his face-plate in time to prevent "decompression." Still, he had "not planned" a "face-plate-open reentry."[8]

The Marine's admission was only tactical, however, for John had in mind another, far more egregious error—one committed by Mercury Control. While pondering a suspected malfunction aboard *Friendship 7,* the flight controllers had elected to keep the pilot, John Glenn, out of the critical information loop. A warning light at Mercury Control

Center indicated—improperly, as it turned out—that the heat shield had become detached from the blunt end of the capsule. If, after retrofire, the automatic jettison of the retropack were to occur, then the straps that held it and (it was hoped) the heat shield in place would be gone. If the heat shield fell away prior to reentry, the pilot would lose all heat protection.

At 4,000 degrees Fahrenheit, such a reentry was a fatal proposition.

Forty million Americans, powerless to help, knew more about *Friendship 7*'s heat shield problems than its pilot did, knew about the something-or-other strap and a warning light. Chris Kraft, directing the flight from Cape Canaveral, later explains that John Glenn had "enough to do without worrying about" the heat shield. He decided not to tell the Marine pilot how, or why, he might soon be on the hot seat—make that *very* hot.[9]

Instead, Mercury Control instructed the pilot of *Friendship 7* to disable the automatic retropack jettison, allowing the straps to remain in place—a procedure that would also secure the heat shield. That was the plan, offered with no explanation.

"John's reply," Scott remembers, "still rings in my ears." It did not begin with "Roger."[10]

This is *Friendship 7.* What is the reason for this?

Information about my spacecraft is my lifeblood, Glenn argued in his flight report, submitted the week after the flight. *Knowledge,* not its absence, informs my decisions. You defraud pilots, steal what they need to fly and survive, when you withhold information. The angered Marine wrote, "I feel it *more* advisable" for Mercury Control to "keep the pilot updated" with information as it becomes available instead of submitting "a clear-cut recommendation" to him without facts.

During the exhaustive MA-6 postflight meetings and debriefings, everyone saw John's eyes narrow as he appraised Kraft across NASA conference tables; the flight director was on notice, and *everyone* knew it. Mercury Control responded to John's censure formalistically, loading future flight plans with multiple checks for face-plate position. But Operations, of which Mercury Control was a part, silently absorbed Glenn's central grievance—the advent of information-stingy, and thus dangerous, flight controllers—like a body blow it needed to conceal. Still the tension between ground control and pilot continued, as though foreordained. It would reach perhaps the breaking point during the follow-on flight, MA-7, only months away.

BY MARCH 1962, three Mercury astronauts, Shepard, Grissom, and Glenn, had flown in space and returned, alive and well, to President Kennedy's now-traditional shipboard call and two-day debriefings conducted by as many as thirty different people—medics, program managers, systems engineers, *Life* reporters, and public relations people fighting for face time. Test pilots are accustomed to these conventions, and after the exhilaration of spaceflight, they eagerly talked, talked, and talked, for hours on end in the debriefings that are integral to the problem-solving process called engineering. They knew the relentless questions would, maybe the next day or the next week or, hope-to-God, by the time the next guy flies, make it all a little safer or better.

Following John Glenn's historic orbital flight aboard *Friendship 7,* Project Mercury began transitioning into an operational groove. Orbital flight was possible. Capsule no. 18, which had arrived at Cape Canaveral late in 1961, was undergoing a number of modifications for the second orbital mission, to be piloted by Deke Slayton, Mr. Engineering Test Pilot himself. Fully aware of the mission's operational significance to the lunar flights to come, he named his capsule *Delta 7,* after the mathematical symbol for change, the sort of transcendental shift that occurs with the advance of knowledge gained through actual *flight.* This was the old pushing-the-envelope sort of thing Deke had done at Edwards all the time.

The man was sorely vexed, however, about the load of science experiments being planned for spaceflights that, in 1962, were themselves experimental. But NASA's mission planners had long planned for the follow-on flight to MA-6 to yield "as much scientific, as opposed to engineering, information as possible"—without endangering, of course, the well-being of the pilot or the success of the mission.[11]

But Deke wasn't so sure, and he pulled a lot of weight at Langley Field. If Mercury Control had a favorite son among the seven, it was Deke Slayton, who in the early days was still rough around the edges, diffident in social situations, inventively profane among his pals, and radiating the gruff Edwards mystique. He was stubborn, sometimes implacable, on design and engineering matters. While Scott championed the newfangled three-axis control stick engineers were devising for the Mercury spacecraft, Deke fought valiantly to keep the old stick-and-rudder controls, an artifact from airplanes. It was a lost cause.

At home, he was a respectful, if absentminded, husband, bemused by his new son, still in diapers. He had no hobbies, no time for reading, and no memory for women's names. Louise, Jo, Rene, Betty, Trudy, Annie—Deke called all of them "Doll," and they forgave him.

A bachelor for most of his career, he felt he had already accumulated his quota of women and offered up the philosophy that girlfriends "only screwed up the operation." He was indifferent to clothes. Marje, his wife, finally gave up on his wardrobe and bought him five short-sleeved Ban-Lon shirts, which he washed out at night in his bathroom sink at the Holiday Inn in Cocoa Beach. But Deke's taciturn habits ended when it came to the subject of airplanes. With airplanes, he forgot himself, became profligate with words. He talked, talked, and *talked* flying, more flying, maneuvers, close calls. Although lacking John's megawatt glow or the "oh-so-cool-number-one leader" shtick that Al had honed to perfection, Deke could nevertheless say "Cut the horseshit, Al" better than anyone in the world—a mightier contribution to group morale has never been made. Although he was a pilot among pilots, Deke was equally drawn to the important if less glamorous work being done over at Operations, under the direction of Chris Kraft, a thirty-five-year-old aeronautical engineer.

Gilruth had tapped Kraft to create Mission Control ex nihilo, and the Tidewater native responded brilliantly. He devised systems, trained men, installed equipment that hadn't been invented yet—and perhaps most difficult of all, undertook the entire, complicated trapeze act in full view of the Free World, an unruly press corps, and unhelpful oversight committees. At stake was nothing less than his single-minded goal—to launch "his" pilots into space and bring them back alive. Soon, in spite of these difficulties and frustrations, Mercury Control was a place, a system, *a state of mind.*[12]

Loudon Wainwright, the *Life* magazine reporter and Carpenter friend and confidant, watched with amusement as a cavalcade of headline-seeking congressmen, sycophants, and simple-minded, axe-grinding reporters descended on the Cape. The early press conferences, which Gilruth had asked Kraft to run, were boisterous affairs, at least the way the journalist described them to Rene. There, he said, a testy Kraft seemed undone, at times, by reporters posing their tricky questions, demanding to be fed information that, even when carefully explained to them, they were still not able to get right, and then, "Is that a 'C' in Kraft, sir?" Worst of all in Kraft's particular circle of professional hell, according to everything Rene saw and heard herself (or was told), were "the bureaucrats and know-nothing paper pushers, confronting Kraft, second-guessing him, ready to overrule him at any moment— who, given half a chance, would screw up a two-car funeral."[13]

As everyone at NASA raced against the clock, and the Soviets, to launch the first man into space, out from left-*fucking* field came this—what?—Presidential *Advisory* Committee whose aggregate contribution to the space race was the decree that NASA fly more chimps? Of course, as NASA passed up a March 24, 1961, launch date for Al Shepard, the Soviets leaped into the breach, rocketing the first man into space, and history, on April 12. *Sputnik* had been rebuke enough in October 1957. But now Gagarin in April 1961. It was enough to make grown men weep.[14]

Kraft also appeared to be uneasy about the increasing celebrity of the seven astronauts, which was surely being translated into power at the expense of his grunts in Operations. He could not have failed to note the Astro Power lesson from the year before, after Shorty Powers, the so-called Voice of Mercury Control, had appended "A-OK" to a readout of Al Shepard's voice transcript, something Al considered inelegant and foolish-sounding. Yet it screamed out of headlines and remains in the lexicon of the gung-ho to this day. Trivial? Perhaps. Still, Al was furious. Known for his rapier-sharp retorts and lacerating silences, the Naval aviator never forgave Shorty, who never spoke for Al again. A lesson to *all*.

AFTER GUS GRISSOM's suborbital flight, a botched recovery operation nearly ended in disaster and Gus's death. A helicopter winched to a sinking *Liberty Bell* was nearly pulled down into the ocean—and meanwhile Gus was twenty-five yards away, with no life raft, no pararescue men at his side, struggling for his life as his suit filled with water. Gus always thought he'd been left to twist in the wind after his own flight. Although he was exonerated after a formal inquiry (Gus had not panicked, the hatch had malfunctioned), the Air Force pilot figured that lingering questions suited Kraft's purposes fine. Made for more tractable astronauts all around.[15]

Not that any of the seven were willing to oblige. By his own account, Kraft's most vexing problems were with Glenn and Carpenter—hardly a tractable pair. Anyone could see that Glenn had the personal charm and heft at the new space agency to get pretty much whatever he wanted—and then be thanked for asking. And if John was NASA's cover boy, well, then, Scott was the agency's Shackleton—and, as some found odd for an astronaut, its resident, after-hours, folk singer.

Everyone at the Cape relaxed in different ways after the typical, brain-busting, eighteen-hour day. Of course, the bars on the strip were popular destinations for just about everyone. Still, Scott sometimes repaired to the beach, guitar in hand, where he played, sang in a melodious tenor, and watched the moonlight on the ocean—often alone, but sometimes with friends. This practice bemused and amused the less-musical types, who one suspects might have been equally flummoxed in Richard Feynman's company. The brilliant physicist was known for relaxing, passionately, with his beloved bongo drums.[16]

On top of this dissonance with the slide-rule set's prevailing custom, the guitar-toting Navy pilot didn't appear all that interested in ground control! Ground control was vital, though. So important, in fact, that Scott remembers "the seven of us insisting early on in the designing of the Mercury Control Network, that an astronaut in the control center would handle all the communications with the guy flying." In essence, the seven were designating a pilot's advocate at crucial capsule communicator (capcom) sites. Mercury Control agreed and early on incorporated the astronauts into the system and the procedures. But first the test pilots required training.

Where the hell have you been, Kraft remembers thinking when, according to his memoirs, Scott reported to Mercury Control for cap-com training. He writes that he'd never had "technical contact" with the Navy pilot "and his grasp of things was shallow." After a short familiarization, Kraft recalls leaving work that night "a worried man." The next day's training session, he said, confirmed his fears:

> The next day we did several sims [simulations], with Kyle and Kranz and others showing Carpenter what to do. His most complicated task was to activate a set of sequence switches on the console to make the Redstone trajectory look like an aborted Atlas. When the switches were set, we'd receive data from the Goddard Space Center. After a few runs, I decided to let Carpenter do it alone.
>
> The next sim was a disaster. A computer support technician at Goddard was immediately in my ear asking if we had noise on the line between the Cape and Goddard. We didn't. We ran the sim again and it was another disaster. . . .
>
> "He's not only throwing random switches," Kyle reported, "but he's so confused that he's still flipping switches after the Redstone aborts."[17]

Scott doesn't remember attending either of these training sessions. Gene Kranz *does* remember them, however, according to Michael Cassutt, the coauthor of Deke Slayton's 1994 biography, and of *We Have Capture*, with Tom Stafford. "In the first place," Kranz told Cassutt in 2001, "the astronaut capcom hadn't screwed up at all. He had been assigned an impossible task that turned out to be unneeded." What's more, Kranz added that "the astronaut capcom was *not* Scott Carpenter."[18]

Glenn and Carpenter, "the Gloryhound and Tonto," Rene called them. Whatever you called them, they were a powerful pair—and a burr in the side of Operations.

Yet the prickly Kraft had a softer side, for he adored Deke Slayton. But truth be told, everyone did. So after John's historic orbital flight, everyone's favorite tough-guy pilot got to the head of the line: first in line for all the training toys and the all-important MPT (Mercury Procedures Trainer), finally outfitted with his own goddamn contour couch.

Working on *his* own flight plan. Enough of this "Godspeed" crap! Enough with the goddamn Weather Bureau experiments! Deke couldn't wait to get into space and try a couple of yaw-roll maneuvers.[19]

One reason he couldn't wait was that, a month before John's flight in February 1962, NASA administrator James E. Webb told Deke his "case" was being reopened. Very bad news indeed. The "Slayton Case" in 1961 was a well-kept secret regarding a cardiac irregularity the Air Force officer had developed four months after a host of medics pronounced him and his six Project Mercury colleagues perfectly, heroically fit.[20]

It showed up for the first time in August 1959, at the U.S. Navy's centrifuge facility in Johnsville, Pennsylvania. The seven newly minted astronauts, and some of the finalists from the selection process earlier that year, were there to begin centrifuge training on what NASA was calling the "Atlas abort profiles." Faget expected that a *nominal* launch and entry could be expected to peak at about eight Gs (eight times the normal gravitational load) and to last a little more than five minutes. These were the launch and entry acceleration profiles for which the astronauts trained incessantly.

But Faget had come up with some troubling "launch-abort" profiles in which entry acceleration was pushed to more than twenty Gs, although the peak rate was relatively brief. Lieutenant C. Carter Collins and Dr. R. Flanagan Gray proved these profiles were survivable in 1958, but not without the temporary loss of consciousness. Although Scott set no records at Johnsville, he devised a breathing technique, sort of like explosive grunting, that allowed him to withstand 18 Gs with few ill effects. Other participants adopted the technique, which Bill Douglas, the astronauts' physician, called the "Carpenter grunt," with similar gains in performance.

Everyone knew the runs were stressful, at least temporarily, to even the healthiest heart. So when the medics picked up Deke's erratic heartbeat just prior to a high-G run, NASA was concerned. Deke continued with his centrifuge runs, carefully, but afterward Bill Douglas sent him to the Philadelphia Navy Hospital, where the Air Force major was pronounced perfectly fit—except for an irregular heartbeat, now confirmed and diagnosed as idiopathic atrial fibrillation. Although a fairly routine heart ailment among the elderly (where it usually signals underlying cardiac disease), the disorder occurs in only .004 percent of patients under the age forty—one of them, unfortunately, a Mercury astronaut.[21]

Years later, when asked if he had noticed the fibrillation before his April 1959 selection as an astronaut, Deke responded no. He said the medics were the ones who noticed his heart "skipped a beat now and then" in examinations before he began his centrifuge work in August 1959. After that, it began occurring with more frequency, especially after dinnertime. This caused him to think his diet was causing the problem, so he cut out tobacco and alcohol. This didn't help much, so he just lived with it. He would "run a mile or so," he told interviewers, and it would return to normal.[22]

Deke was an Air Force officer on loan to NASA, so Dr. Douglas (another Air Force officer on loan) had him examined at the Air Force School of Aviation Medicine, in San Antonio, where again Deke was told that, except for the fibrillation, he was fit. Afterward, however, one of the examining physicians, a "highly respected cardiologist," wrote a letter to Webb, the NASA administrator, recommending that Slayton *not* be given a flight.

In January 1962 Webb remembered the cardiologist's letter and re-opened the Slayton case. Deke and his medical file appeared before two medical groups: a special board convened by the Air Force Surgeon General and a panel of high-level NASA physicians. Bill Douglas, the entire NASA medical team, and his fellow Mercury astronauts stood united behind the embattled pilot. He should fly. Both medical groups reviewed the files, although they did not examine him, and approved him for spaceflight.

It was March 1962. The country's second manned orbital, MA-7, was scheduled for launch in about eleven weeks. Webb persisted. If anything happened to Deke during the flight, Webb may have imagined it would be *his* carcass hung out to dry—and properly so. He could make a popular decision, give Deke the nod, and bask in the agency's gratitude. But then the scenarios crowded in: In an Atlas "abort profile," gravitational loads can increase to as much as twenty-one Gs, the very reason the astronauts trained at the Johnsville centrifuge. What if a dehydrated Deke went into fibrillation during a high-G reentry? The man could die. How popular would Webb be then? And the mission? What was more important, the MA-7 mission, or the hurt pride of an Edwards test pilot? And what of the young agency? How would a fatality affect NASA's reputation? Or the president's pledge to put a man on the moon before the end of the decade?

Webb sent the case to three "nationally eminent" cardiac specialists in Washington, D.C.: Harvey Proctor, a professor of cardiology at Georgetown University; Thomas Mattingly, a heart specialist at the Washington Heart Center; and Eugene Braunwell, of the National Institutes of Health. "Their consensus," reports NASA's official history of Project Mercury, was that they were "unable to state conclusively whether Slayton's physiological performance would be jeopardized by his heart condition. Because of this unknown, they felt that if NASA had an available astronaut who did not 'fibrillate,' then he should be used rather than Slayton."[23] Finally, the NASA administrator had some medical logic he could live with: Deke was out. His decision was final. When the "word came down," the news shocked everyone, Gene Kranz recalls, "although not nearly as much as it did Deke." The well-liked Edwards pilot may have seen himself as invulnerable.[24]

For the seven, Deke's heart defect had been immaterial from the start—more than that, it was taboo. Pilots simply do not discuss embarrassing and potentially career-ending medical conditions. Everyone knew, including Deke, that had his heart hiccuped back at Lovelace or at Wright-Patterson he'd have been sent back to Edwards A.F.B. in a flash, with the Air Force none the wiser. The NASA selection board had promised all the astronaut-candidates that their files were sacrosanct. *Any* untoward, or less-than-optimal, finding unearthed in the grueling selection process—cognitive, marital, ocular, pulmonary, vestibular, legal, cardiovascular, aural, or psychological—would remain with NASA.

Three years later, however, the proud pilot's anonymity had evaporated. He and his heart defect were the subjects of a gloomy NASA press conference and a flurry of captious and second-guessing stories in the press. Dejection reigned in his hometown of Sparta, Wisconsin. Worst of all, as Wolfe relates in *The Right Stuff*: "The Air Force's Chief of Staff himself, General Curtis Le May, was taking the position that if he wasn't qualified to fly for NASA, how could be qualified to fly for the Air Force?"[25]

Deke was devastated. In *Moon Shot,* a book he wrote with Al Shepard, he recounts roaring at Bill Douglas, the team physician: "Goddamn it, Bill, those sons-a-bitches can't do this to me!" Then Deke was told to report to a press conference. "'This medical guy and I were to explain all of this,'" Deke writes, "and I was supposed to act like a fuckin' human being.... I could have killed everyone in the room."[26] So when Scott, perhaps his polar opposite among the seven, was chosen in his place—well, it didn't make things any easier. Adding insult to injury, the Colorado native had excelled in all the physical training. For his part, Scott admired and liked Deke, and appreciated his exemplary flight-test background, wishing the Navy had allowed him the same career freedom to pursue flying with the same focus. As for Deke, he betrayed his annoyance with Scott only once in an offhand comment that made the Navy pilot stew a bit. Deke had lobbied NASA for some decent jets to fly, so they could all keep up their flight proficiency. Thanks to his diligence, they ended up with some F-106s and a simulator.

There was Scott, in the simulator *again.*

"Why don't you fly the goddamn plane for a change!" Deke said. The unsubtle suggestion, of course, was that real pilots didn't stoop to simulator work—not an unusual stance among pilots, but it struck Scott as shortsighted. Simulators were the best, most time-effective way for pilots to familiarize themselves with new aircraft—a belief later borne out by NASA's extensive use of simulators for all aspects of the follow-on Gemini, Apollo, and Shuttle programs.

Deke was angry, hurt, and humiliated. The village elders had taken away his bride, *Delta 7,* and betrothed her to a younger, stronger rival. By way of redress, Deke was named coordinator of astronaut activities, where for more than a decade he helped to choose astronauts and control crew selection and flight assignments. The historic 1959 selection process came under particular scrutiny. How had Carpenter and Glenn, for example, advanced to Lovelace without their college degrees?[27] How come they had snagged the first two orbital missions? In Glenn's case, Dr. Allen Gamble, the NACA's old manpower director, had processed the records of the few Marine candidates. Gamble used his judgment and advanced the Marine colonel to Phase Two, where Glenn aced the interviews and exams, as Gamble suspected he would. Scott's IBM punch card had shown that he held an engineering degree. So he, too, advanced to Phase Two, after which the selection board found that Scott and thirty-one other finalists all looked, walked, talked, and tested like the first-rate military test pilots they were, having survived on their personal and intellectual merits alone.

Wally Schirra had his share of luck when a quick-thinking Navy flight surgeon secured his bid for selection by ordering emergency surgery (throat polyps were jeopardizing Schirra's medical status). Gus, too, was nearly disqualified (or in the kill-joy wording of the selection committee, "recommended with medical reservations") because of his hayfever—until he manfully argued to the board that he probably wouldn't encounter much pollen in space.

Atrial fibrillation. *Big deal.* Deke was in. He was an irreplaceable team member, everyone liked him, there was work to be done, and he had a lot to contribute just on the ground, where most of the important work was done anyway—the beauty of the selection process in the first place. So when Deke was assigned to the second orbital flight, no one had batted an eye, save Jim Webb, who remembered that back-channel letter from the Air Force cardiologist.

At the wakes that followed for the death of *Delta 7,* Space Task Group members came to commiserate and express their condolences. *Terrible,* everyone agreed. How could they do this, to *Deke,* of all the guys? Maybe the new space agency would have balked at grounding any of its Mercury astronauts; it's hard to say. It was easy to see, however, that the ruling was tantamount to a kind of death for Deke.

The seven were never the same.

12

DELTA BECOMES AURORA

S COTT WAS SUMMONED to see Bob Gilruth on March 16, 1962; Walt Williams, head of Space Task Group operations, was also in the director's office. Deke had been scratched, and they had decided Scott would take the flight. Gilruth's reasoning then and afterward was straightforward. As John's backup from October 1961 to February 1962, Scott had accrued nearly eighty hours of what NASA called "preflight checkout and training time." No one else, save John Glenn, was better prepared for the next spaceflight, and John had just flown. Scott absorbed the words. He was stunned. They congratulated him. Everyone shook hands.

Gilruth's arithmetic was accurate. As John's backup, Scott had accrued eighty hours toward a Mercury flight. Eighty hours amounted to a *lot* of training time—more than Wally had accrued as Deke's backup, and more even than Deke had logged while training in John's shadow for MA-7. Yet for all its first-time danger, MA-6 had been designed to answer the simple question: Could it be done? Now that the answer was a resounding yes, ambitions soared for follow-on missions. MA-7, now Scott's to plan and pilot, would have more of just about everything one could do, in space, in 1962: on-board science experiments, pilot activities, external observation, photographs, pilot control maneuvers. He had nine weeks before launch.

For Scott it was a moment both appalling and wondrous. Appalling because he had replaced Deke, a distinction no one would covet, and because in getting the nod, Scott had leapfrogged over Wally, Deke's backup. Worst of all, he had only two months to train. The wonder requires no explanation. So Scott's feelings ricocheted between wonder and dread, dread and excitement. Considering Deke, he was genuinely sad. With regard to Wally, there was chagrin at having snagged a mission at his friend's expense. But at home his four children were excited. In Boulder, Toye was proud. Rene had begun jotting down ideas for Loudon Wainwright, the *Life* reporter who would be writing the cover stories.

Add to these intense and conflicting emotions Scott's simple fatigue, body, mind, and spirit, following his training marathon as John's backup. Glenn was a machine, like no one Scott had ever competed against, roomed or argued with, flown or run miles with. It wasn't that the physical conditioning was especially intense, although it was. The truth was, Scott didn't need to train very hard. But John did, mostly to keep his weight down.

Glenn and Schirra (the group's other mesomorph) each carried about twenty more pounds than their wiry colleagues. Extra weight affected the mission payload because for every additional pound an astronaut weighed on launch day, an additional one thousand pounds of fuel was required to launch. The less you weighed, the more stuff NASA could cram into the capsule. So John ran. Determined to match every step the Marine took, Scott ran with him, and he *hated* running.

At the start of a typical training day leading up to MA-6, the two were up at five or five-thirty for a run, then breakfast and a briefing with flight controllers. A drive into Titusville for lunch, if they had the time, where too-avid attention invariably called for a rapid retreat, Scott at the wheel of a silver, government-issue Chevrolet. A grueling afternoon schedule invariably stretched on into evening, with a perfunctory break for dinner, usually soup or a can of Metrecal, and then—it never failed—two, three, four more hours of eye-glazing head work.

By March, proud of his part in the success of *Friendship 7,* Scott was content simply to be home. When he had thought about it, he had guessed he might get a long-duration Mercury mission, certainly one of the lunar missions even then being planned. But now they were saying the next launch would be in nine weeks, he'd been named the pilot, and it was back to the full-immersion baptism of spaceflight training.

The worst of it was that everyone seemed—well, so *angry.*

Wally had to learn of Scott's assignment during an impromptu gathering at the Carpenters' home, on base. He knew something was up—had heard rumors on a flight back to Langley Field—and stopped by the Carpenters' for a drink and the news. "Scott has the flight?" Wally said, stupefied. *Impossible.* He was backup. That's right, Gilruth said later, and now he was Carpenter's backup. "Truly," Wally admits forty years later, "I was very concerned, because the normal routine was to give the backup pilot the flight after the prime was dropped." In retrospect, though, he was glad to have snagged MA-8, "a much less complicated mission," he says. The worst part of being Scott's backup, for Wally, meant having to endure about two more months of listening to Scott sing "Yellow Bird"—with the inevitable guitar accompaniment.[1]

For Rene and Scott, the wakes for Deke and his flight became perfect ordeals after it was announced that he, and not Wally, would pilot MA-7. In addition to an angry Deke, there was an indignant Wally. John Glenn had meanwhile disappeared into the great American maw reserved for heroes of the first order and was unavailable for the moral support he provided so readily.[2] "I'm so *sorry,*" Scott found himself repeating at the parties, if you could call them that. Finally, he'd had enough. Returning home one night, he said to Rene: "Damn it! I'm tired of apologizing. This is *my* flight now." He would name his spacecraft *Aurora 7.*

In the meantime, the seven wives, solid as ever, adhered to

squadron code and continued to talk about "everything but nothing," hoping the furor would pass.

THE SCHIRRAS HAD brought a solid marriage to the astronaut squadron, with an absolutely equal balance between husband and wife. Beneath Wally's famous "Gotcha!" good humor was a perceptive and confident man. Well-read and opinionated, he was comfortable with serious conversation. He also was forever fighting weight gain and an addiction to cigarettes. With his voice always rumbling on the brink of a chuckle, he was one of the Navy's best storytellers, cheerfully obliging when friends or wife coaxed him to end an evening with one of his gems.

His wife, Jo, was tall and elegant, beautifully dressed and blessed with common sense. The daughter of a high-ranking naval officer, she kept one conscientious eye open, *always,* for her friends and the good of the group. No one appreciated her deadpan humor more than Wally, who guffawed with delight when he was her target. She spared few: "This *must* be a good party," she said, pondering her cocktail, "Al is laughing." At one raucous Cocoa Beach party, she and Rene watched with fascination the slow, giggling, drunken progression of one well-known groupie on her hands and knees, crawling toward her favorite astronaut—*underneath* the banquet tables. "Do you think her nylons will make it?" Jo wondered aloud.

SHORTLY AFTER THE announcement about Scott's flight, Rene took a long-planned trip. Her only sister, Peg, was marrying a young Marine helicopter pilot, John Cronin, shipping out any day for Vietnam. While she packed, she gave instructions to Scott about what was in the refrigerator, where the kids were supposed to be taken and when, and what he would need to get at the market. Her husband then told her about his schedule. "And, oh," he said, "Loudon will be here for a couple of days."

Loudon Wainwright was the writer from *Life* magazine. While Rene was away, he and Scott, already friends from their time together with John, spent additional hours poring over family scrapbooks, talking about their similar boyhoods, sharing notes. Loudon would write the first feature story on Scott. This river ran deep, he knew: sensitive boy, estranged parents, beloved grandfather. Lady Luck, the fastest pony. The 1934 Ford coupe. The near-fatal accident.

He'd sold his two-hundred-dollar boyhood clarinet for that roadster, Scott said, turning confessional. But it needed fancy new taillights—anyone could see that. So the teenaged, roadster-owning demigod who believed the whole earth his and all the car parts therein, walked into a Western Auto Parts store, furtively pocketed the tail lights, and walked out without paying for them. Scott Carpenter, Mercury astronaut, a juvie! Loudon went back to New York to finish writing. The first story went into galleys. The cover copy: "Comes a Quiet Man to Ride *Aurora 7*." A different kind of astronaut. A different kind of hero. More... Holden Caulfield than John Glenn!

Rene had returned home by the time the galleys arrived. She read through them expectantly and then screamed. Got on the phone, Loudon on the line:

"You've *betrayed* me, Loudon!" she declared.

"What!? What did I do?" Loudon answered, for he was truly hurt and clueless.

She reworked the small-town boyhood story as best she could— president of the ski club at Boulder High, cheerleader, best dancer, star gymnast, nearly voted "head boy"—the Rhodes Scholarship of Boulder High. One of Colorado's oldest families. Pioneer stock. Covered wagons. College-educated mother—all dignity and long-suffering heroism. Loudon promised, scout's honor, to take it all down a notch—"No, you're right, Rene," he corrected himself, "*two* notches." Rene *was* right, he admitted, once off the phone. He'd gotten carried away—Scott only *filched* those taillights.

Of course, once the genie is out of the bottle, it's hard to coax him back inside. The *Life* story ran pretty much as Loudon wrote it up the first time. If Rene was upset, NASA was hardly thrilled with its new antihero departing from the Boy Scout script. Yet another P.R. challenge, it thought, still blinking from the klieg lights turned on in 1959. The worst ribbing, of course, came from the other six. Scott didn't care; he liked Loudon's story. But Rene sure seemed bent out of shape.

His mother, Toye, was meanwhile enjoying her new celebrity. All mothers, she said, "love to talk about their children," and now she had "the freedom to talk about him all I want, and I enjoy that." Rene liked to talk about Toye's son, too. Although a natural, savvy story-teller, adept with journalists like Loudon, she was less sure-footed with the now-ravenous religious news services. Accustomed to John Glenn's open and pitch-perfect Presbyterian homilies, they turned expectantly to the next space couple. Would Mrs. Carpenter "pray," they asked her, for her husband's "safe return"?

Rene and Scott discussed the matter. Certainly they prayed. They prayed to do well, and for strength and courage. They prayed for their children. But what they prayed was private, and the space program was a public, civilian, scientific endeavor in which they had a different kind of faith. As for Scott, a cradle Episcopalian with perfect atten-dance at Sunday School and long service as an altar boy at St. John's, he would just as soon disclose the details of his prayer life as describe his bathroom habits.

For her part, Rene had struggled with her faith since Timmy's death eleven years before. They formulated their response: It would be "presumptuous" for them to pray for success. No PREFLIGHT PRAYER ran a headline in the *Denver Post* over a story that hastened to add that the Boulder native was a "devout Episcopalian." In the public drubbing that ensued over the doctrinal merits of their statement, the Carpen-ters figured they were learning, little by little, how to be Rene and Scott, from Boulder, Colorado, and not the inimitable John and Annie Glenn.

WHILE THE SWITCH to Carpenter brought little joy to some at NASA, for astronomer Jocelyn Gill the choice was cause for quiet celebra-tion. She got busy fast. As chairman of the Ad Hoc Committee on Sci-entific Tasks and Training for Man-in-Space, she had been working intensively with the two prime-alternate teams (Glenn-Carpenter for MA-6 and Slayton-Schirra for MA-7), preparing them for some of the "spatial observation" tasks required during their missions. She knew Carpenter to have an innate intellectual curiosity and an impressive background in navigational astronomy, thanks to his long hours aboard the P2V with Patrol Squadron Six. Once his assignment was announced, she called a meeting and asked the committee members to outline objectives for the next spaceflight.[3] Lunar-landing and Gemini mission specialists also had questions for the second U.S. manned orbital flight. The spacecraft itself was undergoing some modifications. Engineers had refined the two manual systems (fly-by-wire and manual) the pilot would use.

What about the Automatic Stabilization and Control System (ASCS)? The spacecraft's autopilot worked by comparing electronic sensory inputs with preset reference points furnished either by on-board navigational instruments, called gyroscopes, or by the horizon scanners. By controlling the small jets, or thrusters, the ASCS could automatically correct any deviations in attitude (pitch, roll, and yaw) and bring the capsule back into the proper alignment. How would the ASCS behave during MA-7, the second U.S. manned orbital flight? This was a pressing question because the thrusters had malfunctioned during the first orbit of MA-6, Glenn's flight, causing him to observe, with understatement, that "even where automatic systems are still necessary, mission *reliability* is tremendously increased by having the man as a backup."[4]

The mission planners wanted to test Glenn's proposition about mission reliability. Autopilot would be given a rest. But the manual system would be pushed to the limit. The pilot of MA-7 would be undertaking a number of radical spacecraft maneuvers—yaw-roll movements, long periods of inverted flight, whatever the three-axis control stick could produce. The purpose? To see what would happen—to the spacecraft systems and to the astronaut.

The Gill committee considered possible experiments; Kenneth Kleinknecht, head of the Mercury Projects Office, appointed Lewis R. Fisher to head up a newly created Mercury Scientific Experiments Panel. The Fisher panel, as it was known, would review the ad hoc committee's experiments "from an engineering feasibility standpoint" and on the basis of their "scientific value, relative priority, and suitability for orbital flight." On April 24 the panel agreed to propose five experiments to the astronaut training and activities group. The MA-7 flight plan was still in flux, and the panel hoped Carpenter would be able to work them into the three-orbit, nearly five-hour, mission.

NASA had made a good-faith pledge to the scientific community that MA-7 would be a science flight. Both temperament and training made Carpenter the perfect choice for the mission. He liked and admired scientists. As a Navy patrol plane pilot, he was a flying observer of the highest order. Scott also liked being a champion of embattled groups with high purpose. And in 1962 the scientists at NASA were already a beleaguered group.

As a matter of NASA policy, circa 1962, science missions were viewed with benign favor, at least at the upper echelons. Dr. Gilruth, for one, understood that Americans funded the space agency with their tax dollars. It was *their* Project Mercury, their National Defense Education Act, passed after *Sputnik* threatened their skies.[5] Pointing to the new heroes of a new age, American parents could tell their children, "You could go to the moon!" "You could go to Mars!" Their children imagined the possibilities with glee and hunkered down over science and trigonometry lessons. So, yes, experiment-performing Mercury astronauts were good value. Science missions on the way to the moon, or Mars, sounded good to them.

As a matter of emerging institutional culture at NASA, however, the science missions—which is to say, trained observation, measurement, and analysis of various phenomena—were viewed with a mixture of suspicion and ridicule, the butt of jokes when the reporters weren't around. As it happened, Scott found himself almost immediately at loggerheads with Project Mercury's flight director, Chris Kraft. Although never openly antagonistic, in the weeks leading up to launch the two men stubbornly resisted each other's ideas.[6]

A product of the NACA's Flight Research division, Kraft had done exemplary engineering work during the 1950s, solving tough, nuts-and-bolts airplane problems. Kraft made up for his lack of personal charm with sheer drive, bureaucratic savvy, and the will to dominate, all of which is described in his memoir, *Flight: My Life in Mission Control*. There Kraft writes affectingly of his hardscrabble childhood in Tidewater Virginia and his years as a disciplined engineering student at

VPI, when his father's crippling bouts of depression became something worse—paranoid schizophrenia that required institutionalization. He details his struggles and hard-won professional triumphs at the NACA and NASA. Yet threaded through a story of real achievement and generous praise for some are curt thumbnail sketches of notable space pioneers: A partial list is illuminating: Wernher Von Braun ("didn't know what he was talking about"), John Glenn ("damn upstart Marine"), Bob Voas ("allegedly an expert in flight training"). Even the American people, whose tax dollars and vision fueled an unparalleled national effort, are not spared. "A nation of quitters," he calls them, apparently for failing to support NASA in lockstep fashion after the lunar expeditions were eclipsed by other pressing national priorities.[7]

Kraft's view of the space agency's core mission, which as he saw it was machines, ran distinctly counter to Scott's more questing vision. It was a stark philosophical contrast. Both philosophies served valid, even complementary, interests, Scott realized. In time, he hoped the agency could accommodate them with ease. But in the meantime, the two factions were locked in a Hegelian battle for institutional supremacy. On the one hand the simple creed of Operations: "Get 'em up. Bring 'em down. No fancy stuff. Everybody gets out alive." On the other that of science and exploration, championed by John and Scott. Add to this Scott's genuine confidence about spaceflight and his intense curiosity about space at the dawn of a new age of exploration and you have exactly what the MA-7 mission planners had hoped for: a scientist-astronaut.

John had proved a man could handle the machine under difficult circumstances. To Scott it was obvious that the next astronaut in space had the freedom, amounting to a responsibility, to observe, measure, and study events *outside* the capsule.[8] He remembers thinking that if Kraft had been in charge of the first expedition to the South Pole, his one question would have been "how's the sled working?" A valuable man, to be sure, but strangely blinkered.

THE FISHER PANEL ultimately recommended that the pilot of MA-7 incorporate five experiments into his flight plan. The astronaut would be asked to observe, measure, analyze, and photograph:

1. a tethered multicolored balloon
2. the behavior of liquid (in a weightless state) inside a closed flask
3. different visual phenomena, celestial and terrestrial, using the Voasmeter, a special type of photometer named after its inventor, Bob Voas
4. weather patterns and land masses
5. the airglow layer.[9]

The balloon experiment used a two-pound, thirty-inch inflatable Mylar sphere, divided into five equal lunes painted an "uncolored aluminum, Day-Glo yellow, Day-Glo orange, white, and a phosphorescent coating that appeared white by day and blue by night." Carpenter was to observe and photograph the effects of space and the angle of the sun on the differently colored surfaces. Which color was more visible in space? At what times?

The answers would help in the design of spacecraft NASA needed for future docking missions, preparatory for the lunar expeditions. Because of questions about atmospheric density at orbital altitude, the scientists designed a tensiometer, or strain gauge, to measure the tension on the balloon tether. The astronaut would be trained to determine the amount of atmospheric drag and turbulence in the slipstream by observing the oscillations and general behavior of the balloon as it trailed the capsule.[10]

The experiment involving liquids was to build on theoretical and experimental work being done at the Lewis Research Center, where researchers had already learned that liquids behave differently in a zero-G environment. But this raised questions about how, exactly, the agency was going to transfer fuel from one tank to another for the longer-duration flights to come. What sort of pumping action would work best in space? The Lewis researchers surmised that surface tension could be used to pump fuel—using capillary action—from one tank to another. So they designed a little glass flask with a small capillary, or meniscus, tube. By observing the behavior of the liquid in the flask, NASA could measure how effectively a given amount of surface tension translated into pumping action simply by measuring how far the fluid was drawn up into the tiny glass tube.

Were constellations more, or less, visible in the blackness of space? Could a pilot use them for navigational purposes? What about the airglow layer first observed by Glenn?[11] John A. O'Keefe, working out of the Goddard Spaceflight Center, defined the airglow phenomenon as "a faint general illumination of the sky visible from the ground on a clear moonless night." But it required further study, in space. Carpenter could be trained to observe three of the phenomenon's physical characteristics: its wavelengths, brightness, and height. Bob Voas, head of astronaut training activities, devised a photometer for just this purpose. Its formal name, "extinctospectrophotopolariscopeoculogyrogravokinetometer,"[12] had more then twenty syllables, each one describing an "observable."

The team from M.I.T. proposed that Carpenter take photographs of the daylight horizon from space, a contribution considered "particularly valuable" for the design of Apollo spacecraft navigation systems.[13] So the institute equipped the astronaut with a German-made 35mm SLR camera, called a "Robot Recorder." It had a wind-up, spring-powered motor with a 250-frame magazine, and it exposed more than two frames per second. Quite a camera for its day. In keeping with the mantra *keep it light,* NASA technicians drilled out all the unnecessary structural aluminum in the camera body, reducing its weight by perhaps half a pound. The camera and its dual red-blue filter would get lots of use during the flight: Eastman provided NASA with thirty feet of color negative film for the pilot's general color photography of land masses, cloud formations, the booster rocket, and tethered balloon, the "flattened sun" effect, and the luminous particles, or "fireflies," first observed by Glenn.[14] The Weather Bureau's Meteorological Satellite Laboratory also wanted special photographs, for which Carpenter, with rubberized aluminum gloves, would have to load "Tri-X and infra-red sensitive" film and then shoot photos through a "five-filter unit."

Glenn's flight had finally established that G-loads and weightlessness were hardly the performance killers and health hazards feared ever since spaceflight became feasible.[15] But a sample of three flights (one, if you're counting orbital missions) is not what scientists consider meaningful, and the NASA medics, particularly the psychiatrists, were collecting performance and validation data for a long-term stress study: They wanted to analyze the output of stress hormones (adrenal and corticosteroids) in the blood and urine. They ordered on-board exercises at specified intervals, to be followed by blood pressure readings. They pressed for immediate postflight examinations and debriefings aboard the aircraft carrier, insofar as the U.S. Navy's recovery operations allowed.

By 1962, NASA medics were anticipating the longer-duration two- and three-man flights. These missions raised innumerable psychological and biomedical questions about possible adaptive behaviors. They were thus studying nontechnical, nonengineering behavioral issues such as the astronauts' moods, pre- and postflight performance levels, and the sensitive vestibular workings of the human body in a zero-G environment. MA-6 hadn't really pushed the envelope on "perceptual reorientation." By calling for inverted flight, MA-7 might yield data on how the pilot perceives "up" and "down." How does the pilot know the difference?

While in flight, the astronauts were instrumented to a fare-thee-well. Breaths per minute were measured with a device mounted on the microphone in the helmet. Rectal thermometers, built into the suit, provided automatic readouts of body temperature. Semiautomated blood-pressure, pulse-rate, and ECG measurements were pilot-activated with devices built into the silver spacesuit. Although manufactured with great care by the bespoke tailors at Goodyear, the first-generation spacesuits were uniquely uncomfortable, mostly because of materials technology, circa 1962. The suits underwent continual design refinements—requiring "more alterations," Wally told *Life* magazine, "than a bridal gown"—ultimately resulting in a nearly comfortable version, worn by Gordon Cooper for his 1963 mission aboard *Faith 7.*[16]

The pressure suits were both uncomfortable and ungainly because, like a balloon, when inflated, they took on only one shape. Like pinching a balloon, any change in shape reduced the volume of the suit and required its occupant to work to overcome the increased internal pressure. Moreover, the suits had to be designed to fit the sitting posture in the contoured couches of the Mercury spacecraft. If an astronaut attempted to walk in a pressurized suit, he would be bent over and soon out of breath from the exertion. In order to avoid such exertion, it was necessary to invent "constant volume" joints, which allowed the arms and legs to move without changing the pressure of the suit. These were not available until the lunar flights, and even then were primitive.[17]

Then there were the famous fireflies, already the subject of several rather excited scientific symposia since Glenn's flight. NASA's Dr. John O'Keefe was studying the phenomenon, reasoning that the luminous particles were some sort of flash-frozen vapor created by the spacecraft itself—their luminosity coincident with extraneous light sources. Whether or not NASA liked it, the fireflies were now a celebrity space phenomenon with lives of their own. A few scientists recklessly offered that they might be some form of alien life form—perhaps living, beryllium-devouring space bugs attracted by the orbital commotion around our normally tranquil planet. (*The Day of the Triffids* was released in 1962). No one knew for certain, and the burden of discovery was on the next pilot out there.

SCOTT'S FIRST FORMAL meeting as the pilot for MA-7 was held on March 16 and, naturally, concerned the flight plan. In the weeks that followed, technical briefings and systems reviews would dominate his time, along with the all-important training sessions on the air-lubricated free attitude (ALFA) trainer and Mercury Procedures Trainer (MPT). From mid-March to the third week of May, Scott had eight sessions on the Langley MPT and fourteen on the one at the Cape. The flight plan was discussed for a second time in a formal meeting on April 24, when the Fisher panel submitted its recommendations. Then, along with more ALFA training, Scott took a trip to the Morehead Planetarium in North Carolina, followed by a briefing with M.I.T. scientists for the photography experiment.

As John's backup, Scott had accrued many hours' practice on egress procedures. But Gus suggested he work in more; the preflight schedule shows two days spent in this fashion in early May. He spent three full days at Mercury Control Center—on May 9, 10, and 18—in "BDA simulation," practicing for the first tracking station, Bermuda ("BDA" on the control center's plotboard). Two days before launch, on May 22, Scott had one last go in the MPT.

Mercury Control was also making preparations for the next manned orbital flight. For the past three years, doggedly and without fanfare, Kraft had overseen the development of a truly amazing worldwide spacecraft-control system. It virtually ensured that the Mercury capsule could be flown *from the ground* no matter where it was positioned overhead. By stationing capcoms at consoles around the world, the flight director and NASA would have nearly constant voice contact with the astronaut orbiting overhead. Going east, in geographical order, the capcoms for MA-7 were stationed at Cape Canaveral (or Mercury Control); Bermuda; the Canaries; Kano, Nigeria; Zanzibar (now part of Tanzania); the Indian Ocean; Muchea, Australia; Woomera, Australia; Canton Island; Hawaii; Guaymas, Mexico; and California.

Critical to the success of this system, however, were, first, the proper operation of preprogrammed automatic systems aboard the spacecraft, and, second, the constant, timely flow of information to Kraft, the flight director—especially in the event of an automatic system failure. Directing all the early spaceflights from the Cape, he was like an earthbound copilot for the astronaut orbiting overhead. And in the early days, as the kinks were being worked out, some tensions developed between the two pilots—one occupying a chair at Mercury Control, the other orbiting in space, lying in a custom-made, $25,000 contour couch. These tensions, already high during Glenn's flight, reached the breaking point during the flight piloted by Carpenter.

WHEN RENE MADE UP her mind to take the children to the Cape to witness the launch of their father's rocket, she obediently phoned the chief of NASA public relations, Shorty Powers, "The Voice of Mercury

Control." Shorty couldn't believe it. "You're going to the Cape?" None of the previous astronaut families had gone to Florida for the launch. But Rene and Scott had discussed it: their sons Scotty and Jay, then twelve and ten years old, should witness the liftoff. The decision bucked what Shorty already viewed as hoary tradition. Louise Shepard, Betty Grissom, and Annie Glenn had all remained in their homes, with their children and perhaps a close friend, for the long hours leading up to the countdown and liftoff, the flight itself, and safe recoveries at sea. Now, a renegade wife!

But Rene told Shorty she'd decided, and would make the arrangements herself, asking only that the information be kept between the two of them for now. "No problem," he answered. Forty minutes later, she picked up the phone to hear Peter Hackes, an NBC correspondent, wanting to know the details of the trip.

"So when will you go? Where will you stay? Will the kids see their dad?"

She talked the fine line between charm and noncooperation, refusing information.

"I'll find you, Rene," Hackes signed off, laughing.

Rene was shocked, *shocked* by Shorty's betrayal. Actually, she knew the man was just doing his job. A small, tough-talking Air Force officer, he was initially assigned to the pilots as a kind of minder during press conferences and group goodwill trips. But his habit of rephrasing their sometimes rambling, banal comments into terse "flyerese" could grate on their sensibilities—most famously when he attributed the gung-ho "A-OK" to Al during his suborbital flight.

Hackes may have tried, but he never found Rene and the four children. A Langley Field neighbor, U.S. Navy captain John Strane, arranged for the CNO's airplane, an A3D, to be available for their trip, taken a few days before the launch. A nondescript car was provided at the air base. Sporting huge sunglasses, her conspicuous blonde coif under a kerchief, Rene took the wheel. Everyone would be looking for a blonde mother of four, so she ordered her daughters beneath blankets on the floor in the back, where Scotty rode herd. Jay sat next to his mother in the front passenger seat. She was now a well-disguised mother of two.

The *Life* house, as it was called, stood at the end of a long, tree-shrouded driveway, about ten miles down the coast from Pad 14. Surrounded by an acre of shaded lawn, it was the perfect hideaway. North on a spit of land stood Carpenter's Mercury-Atlas. Perched atop was the tiny, dark Mercury capsule, waiting.

National curiosity had meant that the astronaut families were required to relinquish a few chunks of their privacy to *Life* magazine, which on launch days meant access to the family proceedings. Depending on family arrangements, which varied, this required the presence of Ralph Morse and sometimes Loudon Wainwright. Beyond the stories *Life* magazine showed the world, however, the seven families enjoyed a nearly complete news blackout. One woman's club in North Carolina suspected "government brainwashing," and complained to the president about it. Rene tells the rest of the story, which was later read into the *Congressional Record:*

> Dear ladies, The President has forwarded your letter to me and asked me to give you the very best answer I can. First, let me tell you that NASA has never instructed us in any way. In fact, in our lives as servicewomen, many times have been more difficult for us than this one on flight day.
>
> It is unfortunate that the only glimpse you get of a wife is that brief appearance before a collection of microphones and bobbing cameras. You mention that it is humanly impossible to have "no feeling, no emotion," and you are right. I'm sorry you miss the hugs and kisses, the hand clappings, the hard and grateful smiles—for it *is* emotional. But then the joy sometimes turns into frozen faces when we step outside to have that emotion recorded by a blur of peoples' faces.
>
> On the morning of the flight, the good people of this country turn on their radios and TV sets to keep track of the countdown. For the first time, the man's name and face begin to meld together and form a person. And these good people say to each other in their homes and on the street, "How can they stand lying up there on that thing—don't you know their wives are a wreck?"

I would remind them of the length of time that has already
ticked off, from the beginning of our military service in the
1940s until now, the space program. That's a lot of lonely
bedtimes. So at T minus 10 and counting, while you are holding
your breath, they wait, expectantly and confidently—man in
the capsule, woman on the ground. She is glad he is there and
that the weather is good.

ORIGINALLY SCHEDULED for an April launch, MA-7 was postponed first
because of naval exercises in the Atlantic, and then once more for bad
weather. Scott welcomed the delays. If John had needed speed for his
historic mission, then what Scott needed for his own flight was more
of just about everything—time, practice, confidence. The delays gave
him a chance to practice more with the flight equipment and to study
up on a few things he was worried about. With more practice his confidence returned. He ate and slept well. As the launch approached, he
kept waiting for the anxiety to return, but it never did. He remembers
reaching the crest of a hill while driving and becoming "part of the
machine.[18] He was amazed at his calm.

While waiting for launch date, he got a letter from his father, who
had recently retired to Palmer Lake, Colorado:

Dear Son,
Just a few words on the eve of your great adventure for which
you have trained yourself and anticipated for so long—to let
you know that we all share it with you, vicariously.

As I think I remarked to you at the outset of the space
program, you are privileged to share in a pioneering project on
a grand scale—in fact, the grandest scale yet known to man.
And I venture to predict that after all the huzzahs have been
uttered and the public acclaim is but a memory, you will derive
the greatest satisfaction from the serene knowledge that you
have discovered new truths. You can say to yourself: this I saw,
this I experienced, this I know to be the truth. This experience is
a precious thing; it is known to all researchers, in whatever field

of endeavour, who have ventured into the unknown and have discovered new truths.

You are probably aware that I am not a particularly religious person, at least in the sense of embracing any of the numerous formal doctrines. Yet I cannot conceive of a man endowed with intellect, perceiving the ordered universe about him, the glory of the mountain top, the plumage of a tropical bird, the intricate complexity of a protein molecule, the utter and unchanging perfection of a salt crystal, who can deny the existence of some higher power. Whether he chooses to call it God or Mohammed or the Turquoise Woman or the Law of Probability matters little. I find myself in my writings frequently calling upon Mother Nature to explain things and citing Her as responsible for the order of the universe. She is a very satisfactory divinity for me. And so I shall call upon Her to watch over you and guard you and, if she so desires, share with you some of her secrets which she is usually so ready to share with those who have high purpose.

With all my love,
Dad

THE DAY BEFORE a launch is always deliberately low-key. Scott attended the prelaunch pilot briefing. That night, he studied a bit and retired at approximately ten minutes after ten o'clock (requiring "no sedative," according to the notes of Bill Douglas, the Mercury team physician). A few hours later, at one-fifteen A.M. on May 24, he was awakened. For breakfast he had steak, eggs, toast, and strained orange juice. Launch time was set for seven A.M. A small but smoky fire moved slowly through the Florida scrub not too far from Pad 14. Might be some visibility problems. They'd have to wait until morning.

Ten miles down the sandy coast, Rene waited and watched through three fifteen-minute holds. She and Scott had decided that a last-minute call from the launch pad might be too difficult. But with the several holds and time stretching out a bit, Scott arranged to be patched through to the phones at the *Life* house, where everyone took turns with the receiver of the black rotary wall phone. Accustomed like her siblings to the many tests her father had taken up to this moment, Kris assumed this was yet another one. The six-year-old asked her father how his latest test was going. Alert to the word's larger meaning, Scott teared up for a moment. "The test," he assured her, was going fine.

Finally, at a little after seven forty-five, the great Atlas engines were fired, sending out billows of steam, flames, dust, smoke, fumes, and heat. At this signal, all four Carpenter children abandoned their posts in front of the television, where all three networks were covering the launch live, and dashed out to the beach. Already the pale morning sky was streaked with contrails, and in the distance they could see the Atlas lifting off. Against the low slant of the sun, Rene saw the Atlas streak into the sky and then disappear.

Just before liftoff, Scott had been thinking about his grandfather, Vic Noxon. "At last I'll know the great secret," the old man had told Dr. Gilbert on a golden Sunday morning on the Front Range. He was dying. He knew he was dying. He wasn't afraid. Scott was confident that May morning, like his Grandpa Noxon, that everything was going to be all right—that this experience so long anticipated had finally arrived. As the rocket engines began to rumble and vibrate beneath him, he became preternaturally alert to the many sounds and sensations of liftoff.

There was surprisingly little vibration, although the engines made a big racket and he felt the rocket swaying as it rose. The ride was gentler than he expected. He looked out his window, placed directly overhead, to see the escape tower streaking away like a scalded cat. One especially odd thing, for one accustomed to level flight after the required climb, was to see the altimeter reach seventy, eighty, then ninety thousand feet and yet know that he was still going straight up.

No one noticed at the time—there was no dial to measure its functioning—but the capsule's pitch horizon scanner had already started malfunctioning. The Mercury capsule was chockfull of automatic navigational instruments, among them the PHS, which does just what the name implies: It scans the horizon for the purposes of maintaining, automatically, the pitch attitude of the capsule. For MA-7, however, the PHS immediately began feeding erroneous data into the Automatic Stabilization and Control System (ASCS), or autopilot. When this erroneous data was fed into the ASCS, the autopilot responded, as designed, to fire the pitch thruster to correct the perceived error. This in turn caused the spacecraft to spew precious fuel from the automatic tanks. Fuel was a finite commodity.

Forty seconds after tower separation, the pitch horizon scanner was already 18 degrees in error. It was indicating a nose-up attitude, or angle, of plus-17 degrees while the gyro on the Atlas showed pitch to have been minus 0.5. By the time of spacecraft separation, the pitch gyro aboard the capsule had "slaved" to the malfunctioning pitch-scanner output and was in error by about 20 degrees. NASA later found that the error would persist, intermittently, to greater and lesser degrees, throughout the three-orbit flight, with near-calamitous effect as MA-7 readied for reentry less than five hours later.[19]

At the moment, Scott was focused on the gravitational forces, which peaked at a relatively gentle 8 Gs. He marveled at the intense silence, but then experienced an even greater sensation of weightlessness. At five minutes, nine seconds into the flight, he reported to Gus, listening as capcom at Cape Canaveral:

00 05 09   P   I am *weightless!*—and starting the fly-by-wire turnaround...

The sensation was so exhilarating, his report to the ground was more of a spontaneous and joyful exclamation than the routine report he had expected to make. The fly-by-wire manual controls were exquisitely responsive and quickly placed the Mercury capsule into a backward-flying position for the beginning of Scott's first circumnavigation of the earth. John had accomplished this maneuver on autopilot, as specified by his flight plan, causing the system to expend more than four pounds of fuel in the process. In the fly-by-wire control mode, it could be done using only 1.6 pounds.

The three-axis control stick (or hand controller) designed for Mercury was a nifty device that allowed the pilot to fly the capsule using either the "manual proportional" or "fly-by-wire" ("wire" here meaning electrical) systems. The manual proportional system required only minute adjustments of the control stick—of perhaps 2 or 3 degrees—to activate the one-pound thrusters. Fore and aft movements controlled pitch, which is the up or down angle of the spacecraft, while side-to-side movements controlled roll. The pilot could control yaw, or change the direction left or right, by *twisting* the control stick—a hand control that replaced the old rudder pedals used in airplanes. The MA-7 flight plan specified only limited use of the ASCS.

Gus Grissom (capcom is CC in the transcript) headquartered. He gave Scott (P) the good news:

| 00 05 32 | CC | We have a Go, with a seven-orbit capability. |
| 00 05 36 | P | Roger. Sweet words. |

The pilot of *Aurora 7* explains in his own words:

Sweet words indeed. With the completion of the turnaround maneuver, I pitched the capsule nose down, 34 degrees, to retroattitude, and reported what to me was an astounding sight. From earth-orbit altitude I had the moon in the center of my window, a spent booster tumbling slowly away, and looming beneath me the African continent. But the flight plan was lurking, so from underneath the instrument panel I pulled out my crib sheets for the flight plan, written out on three 3 X 5 index cards, and Velcroed for easy viewing. I could just slap them up on a nearby surface, in this case the hatch, covered with corresponding swaths of Velcro.[20] Each card provided a crucial minute-by-minute schedule of inflight activities for each orbit. They gave times over ground stations and continents, when and how long to use what type of control systems, when to begin and end spacecraft maneuvers, what observations and reports to make on which experiments. In short, they told me, and the capcoms, who had copies, what I was supposed to be doing every second of the flight—every detail of which had been worked out, timed, and approved before liftoff. A brief investigation of these cards is enough to suggest constant pilot activity. But to get the best appreciation of just how busy we all were during those early flights, read the voice communication reports between the capcoms and the astronaut.

It was time to open the ditty bag. Stowed on my right, it contained the equipment and the space food for the flight. First out was the camera, for I needed to catch the sunlight on the slowly tumbling booster still following the capsule. The camera had a large patch of Velcro on its side. I could slap it on the capsule wall when it wasn't in use. Velcro was the great zero-gravity tamer. Without it, the equipment would have been a welter of tether lines—my idea, incidentally, and not a very good one, for John's flight. He had ended up in a virtual spaghetti bowl full of tether lines and equipment floating through his small cabin.

Also in the ditty bag were the air-glow filter, for measuring the frequency of light emitted by the air-glow layer, star navigation cards, the world orbital and weather charts—adjuncts to the earth path indicator (EPI) globe mounted on the instrument panel. The EPI was mechanically driven at the orbital rate so that it always showed the approximate spacecraft position over the earth. There were also bags of solid food I was to eat (a space first), and the densitometer.

But the most important items at this point in the flight were probably the flight plan cards. I had been tracking the booster since separation, maneuvering the capsule with the very good fly-by-wire system: "I have the booster in the center of the window now," I reported, "tumbling very slowly." It was still visible ten minutes later, when I acquired voice contact with Canary capcom.

00 16 19   P   I have, west of your station, many whirls and vortices of cloud patterns. [Taking] pictures at this time— 2, 3, 4, 5. Control mode is automatic. I have the booster directly beneath me.

The brilliance of the horizon to the west made the stars too dim to see in the black sky. But I could see the moon and, below me, beautiful weather patterns. But something was wrong. The spacecraft had a scribe line etched on the window, showing where the horizon should be in retroattitude. But it was now above the actual horizon. I checked my gyros and told Canary capcom my pitch attitude was faulty.

00 16 19   P   I think my attitude is not in agreement with the
                 instruments.

Then I added an explanation—it was "probably because of that gyro-free period"—and dismissed it. There were too many other things to do.

John had also had problems with his gyro reference system. Kraft described it in an MA-6 postflight paper, where he wrote that the astronaut "had no trouble in maintaining the proper [pitch] attitude" when he so desired "by using the visual reference." All pilots do this—revert to what their eyes tell them when their on-board tools fail. But future flights, he said, would be free of such "spurious attitude outputs" because astronauts would be able to "disconnect the horizon scanner slaving system," called "caging the gyros" in these future flights.[21] Because my flight plan for the follow-on mission called for so many large deviations from normal orbital attitude (minus-34-degree pitch, 0-degree roll, 0-degree yaw), I was often caging the gyros when they weren't needed for attitude control.

The Canary capcom picked up on my report, and asked me to "confirm orientation." Were my autopilot (ASCS) and fly-by-wire operating normally?

00 17 53   P   Roger, Canary. The manual and automatic control
                 systems are satisfactory, all axes....

The procedure for voice reports on the attitude control system did not call for determining agreement in pitch attitude as shown by (a) the instrument and (b) the pilot's visual reference out the window. The reporting procedure also assumed a properly functioning pitch horizon scanner, in the case of MA-7 a false assumption. Because of the scanner's wild variations—careening from readings of plus-50 degrees at one place over the horizon and then lurching back to minus-20 over another, without any discernible pattern— I might have gotten a close-to-nominal, or normal, reading at any given moment in the flight.

A thorough ASCS check, early in the flight, could have identified the malfunction. Ground control could have insisted on it, when the first anomalous readings were reported. Such a check would have required anywhere from two to six minutes of intense and continuous attention on the part of the pilot. A simple enough matter, but a prodigious block of time in a science flight—and in fact the very reason ASCS checks weren't included in the flight plan. On the contrary, large spacecraft maneuvers, accomplished off ASCS, were specified, in addition to how many minutes the MA-7 pilot would spend in each of the three control modes—fly-by-wire, manual proportional, and ASCS.[22] Because of this, I would not report another problem with the ASCS until the second orbit. I had photographs to take and the balky camera to load.

When I spoke with Kano capcom, over Nigeria, on that first pass, I was able to relay a lot of valuable orbital information as well as data on the control and capsule systems. I also checked out the radios and, as ordered by the flight surgeon, telemetered my blood pressure reading. While preparing to take the M.I.T. pictures of the "flattened sun" halfway through that pass, I saw I was getting behind in the flight plan and reported that I wouldn't be able to complete the pictures on that pass. Just as I was making that report, I figured out the problem, managed to install the film, and was able to take the pictures after all.

Before I lost voice contact with Kano capcom, I was able to get horizon pictures with the M.I.T film. The first picture was at f8 and $1/125$ taken to the south directly into the sun. The second picture was taken directly down my flight path, and the third was 15 degrees north of west at "capsule elapsed time" (elapsed time since launch) of 00 30 17. I was very busy.

Tom Wolfe wrote in *The Right Stuff* that I was having "a picnic" during my flight and "had a grand time" with the capsule maneuvers and experiments. He kindly noted that my pulse rate, which before liftoff, during the launch and in orbit, was even lower than Glenn's admirably calm readings. The second part, about my pulse rate, may be true, perhaps because nature wired me that way (and Wally, too, for that matter, if you look at his telemetered readouts). But Wally and I were also following in John's historic steps, had been fully briefed, and knew pretty much what to expect. Knowledge and training create confidence.

MA-7 was no picnic. I had trained a long time, first as John's backup, and then for my own surprise assignment to the follow-on flight. To the extent that training creates certain comfort levels with high-performance duties like spaceflight, then, yes, I was prepared for, and at times may even have enjoyed, some of my duties aboard *Aurora 7*. But I was deadly earnest about the success of the mission, intent on observing as much as humanly possible, and committed to conducting all the experiments entrusted to me. I made strenuous efforts to adhere to a very crowded flight plan.

The cabin became noticeably hot during the first orbit, when I was over the Mozambique channel, forty-five minutes into the flight. I wasn't the first astronaut to be bothered by a hot cabin, and all of us were prepared for varying degrees of discomfort, and even pain, while we trained for and went through actual spaceflight. During the selection process, we ran the treadmill at 100 percent humidity and 115 degrees Fahrenheit—and gladly—just to be chosen.

So the term "tolerable temperature," something the NASA medics determined was endurable with little loss in performance, is relative. You need to know how long the discomfort will likely last, how hard you have to work during that time, and how badly you need to withstand it. It also helps to have an idea of when you believe relief will come. So after giving the Indian Ocean capcom all the normal voice reports, I explained for the record what I was doing inside to bring the high cabin temperatures down.

During all this time, I was also getting some readings with O'Keefe's airglow filter. All of a sudden my periscope went dark. It really surprised me:

00 43 25   P   What in the world happened to the periscope? Oh.
                   It's dark. That's what happened. It's facing a dark
                   earth.

A simple, and elegant, explanation: Day had become night. I was still getting accustomed to moving 17,500 miles per hour.

My flight plan at this point consisted mostly of photography. I had crossed the terminator, which is the dividing line between the dark and sunlit sides of the earth, which caused the light levels to change very rapidly. It was exceedingly important that I photograph the changing light levels. To myself, I read off a lot of camera F-stop and exposure values and was thinking aloud about my next capcom:

00 44 12   P   It's getting darker. Let me see. Muchea contact
                   sometime. Oh, look at that sun! F11.

No one was listening, so I reported to the tape,

> It's quite dark. I didn't begin to get time to dark
> adapt.... cabin lights are going to red at this time.
> Oh, man, a beautiful, *beautiful* red, like in John's
> pictures. Going to fly by wire.

A mysterious red light had cascaded through the window just as I went into a new control mode, as specified in the flight plan. It reminded me of the pictures John had taken through his red filter. But mine was only the reflection of the red cabin lights. "That's too bad." I was disappointed.

But then I was visited by Venus.

00 46 10   P   I have Venus now approaching the horizon.
00 46 37   P   It's about 30 degrees up. It's just coming into view.
                   Bright and unblinking. I can see some other stars
                   down below Venus. Going back to ASCS at this
                   time.
00 47 05   P   Bright, bright blue horizon band as the sun gets
                   lower and lower—the horizon band still glows. It
                   looks like five times the diameter of the sun.

The sun completely disappeared at this point in my flight, and I reported the exact time—00 47 34 elapsed—and my total incredulity.

00 47 46.5   P   It's now nearly dark and I can't *believe* where I am.

My wonder gave way to surprise just a minute later, when I saw how much fuel I had already used.

00 48 08   P   Oh, dear, I've used too much fuel.

"Oh, dear"—a Noxon expression. Over Australia, I would have voice contact with two different capcoms—the first with Deke

Slayton at Muchea, the second at Woomera. Over Muchea, Deke and I talked about our Australian friends, John Whettler in particular, who had been a Spitfire pilot during World War II. Then I said "Break, Break," which is voice communication procedure meaning "change of subject." We talked about cloud cover, too heavy for me to see the lights in Perth turned on for my encouragement. Deke consulted the flight plan and saw it was time to send some teleme- tered blood pressure readings. Then some arcane navigational mat- ters—how to determine attitudes, yaw, pitch, and roll—on the dark side:

| 00 53 31 | P | You'll be interested to know that I have no moon, now. The horizon is clearly visible from my present position; that's at 00 54 44 [capsule] elapsed. I believe the horizon on the dark side with no moon is very good for pitch and roll. The stars are adequate for yaw in, maybe, two minutes of tracking. Over. |
| 00 54 01 | CC | Roger, understand. Sounds very good. |

In 1962 we didn't know what was visible on the horizon, on the dark side without moonlight. So Deke and I were discussing how one might establish attitude control under such unfavorable condi- tions. I relayed what reliable visual references I had out the window or periscope. In the absence of valid attitude instrument readings during retrofire, the pilot can use such external visual references, manually establishing proper retroattitude control with the control stick. Pitch attitude can be established and controlled easily, with reference to the scribe mark etched in the capsule window. Accom- plishing the proper yaw attitude, however, is neither easy nor quick.

Attitude changes are also hard to see in the absence of a good daytime horizon. At night, when geographic features are less visible, you can establish a zero yaw attitude by using the star navigation charts, a simplified form of a slide rule. The charts show exactly what star should be in the center of the window at any point in the orbit—by keeping that star at the very center of your window you know you're maintaining zero yaw. But there are troubles even here, for the pilot requires good "dark adaption" (or a dark-adapted eye) to see the stars, and dark adaption was difficult during the early flights because of the many light leaks in the cabin. The backup measures ("backup" here meaning human) were absolutely critical to have in place at retrofire—in the event of attitude instrument failure.

Deke and I discussed suit temperature, which like the cabin was hotter than I liked. He suggested a different setting, which I tried. Then Woomera capcom hailed me, and I replied: "Hello, Woomera capcom, *Aurora 7*. Do you read?" while still in voice contact with Deke, at Muchea. "Roger, this is Woomera," came the capcom's voice. "Reading you loud and clear. How me?" Deke was confused. He couldn't hear Woomera and thought to correct me:

00 55 00	CC	This is Muchea capcom. They will not be contacting you for another three minutes.
00 55 08	P	Roger. Go ahead, Deke. Just trying to get a word on the flare.

Between Muchea and Woomera, I was trying to see the ground flares, a check for visibility. Deke gave me the attitudes to view the first flare, which involved a whopping, plus-80 degrees yaw maneuver and a pitch attitude of minus-80 degrees. But the cloud cover was too dense. "No joy on your flares," I told Woomera and then went to drifting flight, where I found that just by rocking my arms back and forth, like attempting a full twist on the trampoline, I could get the capsule to respond in all three axes, pitch, roll, and yaw.

The Cape advised me to keep the suit setting where it was, because the temperature was coming down. I continued in drifting flight, and at capsule elapsed 01 02 41.5, over Canton, we checked attitude readings with telemetry. The Canton capcom told me my body temperature was registering 102 degrees Fahrenheit, clearly a false reading:

01 13 13.5	P	No. I don't believe that's correct. My visor was open; it is now closed. I can't imagine I'm that hot. I'm quite comfortable, but sweating some.

A food experiment had left crumbs floating in the cabin. I remarked on them, and reported the dutiful downing of "four swallows" of water. At his prompting, however, I could not confirm that the flight plan was on schedule. But I reported what I could:

| 01 14 16.5 | P | At sunset I was unable to see a separate haze layer—the same height above the horizon that John reported. I'll watch closely at sunrise and see if I can pick it up. |

Canton capcom wished me "good luck," and then LOS—loss of signal.

Everyone on the ground had had an eye on the fuel levels since the end of the first orbit. Gordo Cooper, capcom at Guaymas, had told me to conserve fuel, which was then at 69-percent capacity for the manual supplies, and 69 percent for the automatic. By the time I returned for my second pass over Kano, they had dropped to 51 and 69, respectively.

| 01 55 08.5 | P | The only thing of— to report is that fuel levels are lower than expected. My control mode now is ASCS. |

I explained to the Kano capcom:

| 01 55 08.5 | P | I expended my extra fuel in trying to orient after the night side. I think this is due to conflicting requirements of the flight plan. |

Live and learn. I spoke to the flight recorder, although Kano capcom still had voice contact:

| 01 55 08.5 | P | I should have taken time to orient and then work with other items. I think that by remaining in automatic I can keep— stop this excessive fuel consumption. |

When I went to fly-by-wire aboard *Aurora 7*, very slight movements of the control stick in any axis activated one-pound thrusters and changed the attitude very slowly. Larger stick movements would activate the twenty-four-pound thrusters, which would change the attitude much more quickly but use twenty-four times as much fuel. If the manual proportional control mode were chosen, the change in capsule attitude would be proportional to stick movement, just as in an airplane. (Move the stick a little, get a little bit of thrust; move it halfway, get half thrust; move it all the way, get full thrust.) Each increment of movement had attendant increases in fuel expenditure. If, however, both control modes were chosen concurrently—and this happened twice during MA-7 as a result of pilot error—then control authority is excessive and fuel expenditure exorbitant.

For my flight the twenty-four-pound thrusters came on with just a wrist flick, that I then corrected with a wrist flick in the other direction. This countermovement often activated the twenty-four-pound thrusters yet again, all for maneuvering power not required during orbital flight. The high thrusters weren't needed, really, until retrofire, when the powerful retrorockets might jockey the capsule out of alignment. The design problem with the three-axis control stick as of May 1962 meant the pilot had no way of disabling, or locking out, these high-power thrusters. Because of my difficulties and consequent postflight recommendations, follow-on Mercury flights had an on-off switch that would do just that, allowing Wally Schirra and Gordo Cooper to disable the twenty-four-pound thrusters.[23] Gemini astronauts had a totally different reaction control system.

But I understood the problem and resolved to limit my use of fuel. Consulting my index cards, I saw that I still had voice reports to make on the several experiments—the behavior of the balloon, still tethered to the spacecraft; a night-adaption experiment; and the ingestion of some more solid food. Holding the bag, however, I could feel the crumbled food. If I opened it, food bits would be floating through my work space. I made a mental note: "Future flights will have transparent food bags." See-through bags would make crumb strategy easier during these zero-G food deployments. I was beginning to regret my lack of training time.[24]

Before loss of signal, Kano capcom asked me to repeat my fuel-consumption critique.

| 01 59 59 | CC | Roger. Would you repeat in a few words why you thought the fuel usage was great? Over. |
| 02 00 06 | P | I expended it on— by manual and fly-by-wire thruster operation on the dark side, and just approaching sunrise. I think that I can cut down on fuel consumption considerably during the second and third orbits. Over. |

The Zanzibar capcom took over ground communication. Consulting the same flight plan I had, he reminded me I was supposed to be on fly-by-wire. I thought better of it and said so:

02 06 25.5   P   That is negative. I think that the fact that I'm low on
                   fuel dictates that I stay on auto as long as the fuel
                   consumption on automatic is not excessive. Over.

The irony is that even the ASCS control mode, ostensibly thrifty with fuel, was now guzzling fuel because of the malfunctioning pitch horizon scanner. "Roger, *Aurora 7*," replied Zanzibar capcom and then congratulated me on my trip so far. "I'm glad everything has gone—" but the rest of his message dropped out. "Thank you very much," I said, hoping he could still hear me.

After Zanzibar was the Indian Ocean capcom, stationed aboard a United States picket ship called *Coastal Centry,* permanently anchored at the mouth of the Mozambique channel. After the usual preliminaries ("How do you read? "Loud and clear. How me?"), he reminded me to conserve fuel and then inquired: "Do you have any comments for the Indian Ocean?" I replied, but not with a greeting. I was having that old ASCS difficulty:

02 08 46.5   P   That is Roger. I believe we may have some automatic
                   mode difficulty. Let me check fly-by-wire a minute.

Going to fly-by-wire is the best way to diagnose any problem with the thrusters, the small hydrogen peroxide–spewing jets that control spacecraft attitudes. I checked them again. The thrusters were fine. We didn't know it at the time, but the thrusters were receiving faulty information, through the autopilot, from the pitch horizon scanner. Worse, the error from the automated navigational tool was intermittent and thus hard to identify. I reported that the gyros, my on-board navigational tools, were not "indicating properly." This sort of problem requires patient investigation. I told the Indian Ocean capcom to wait:

02 09 11   CC   Roger.
02 09 27   P   The gyros are…okay, but on ASCS standby [the off
                  position]. It may be an orientation problem. I'll
                  orient visually and see if that will help out the
                  ASCS problem.

I went off autopilot to fly-by-wire, oriented the capsule visually, and then returned to ASCS, autopilot, to see what would happen. My hope was to catch the autopilot misbehaving. It was an angel. Imagine that you own a high-performance car that develops a quirky habit, when on autopilot, of veering off the interstate as you're speeding along at 80 miles per hour. You take it to the dealer, describe the trouble, and the mechanics can't duplicate the malfunction when they take it out to the freeway the next day. Imagine this happening in space, with your space car, and you have only two circumnavigations left on the orbital highway. Imagine further that your precisely timed exit off the orbital highway will be performed using this intermittently malfunctioning autopilot. This is what I was facing, but didn't know it. No one did.

Technicians, pilots among them, often make erroneous assumptions when troubleshooting a problem. An erroneous assumption early on can invalidate all subsequent efforts to find a solution. Nobody realized that the problem lay in the pitch attitude indicator. From the pilot's viewpoint, the problem with the ASCS was an anomaly, and the intermittent failure meant little. When your navigational tools disagree with the view out your window and this persists in any great disparity, the instruments are malfunctioning. When the instruments are malfunctioning, you have no recourse but to navigate visually with reliable reference points—the horizon, the position of a known star, geographical landmarks. This is what I did.

The Indian Ocean capcom waited patiently. Nearly a minute passed while I tried diagnosing the problem. We were working off a tight flight plan, so he reminded me I was "supposed to, if possible, give a blood pressure." This was a simple matter of pressing a semiautomatic device on my suit, which I did, and felt the blood pressure cuff inflate. "Roger," I said, "I've put blood pressure up on the air already. Over."

Mercury Control had in the meantime picked up on my *earlier* transmission about the thrusters. During MA-6, a thruster malfunction had forced John to assume manual control for his final two orbits. Rightly concerned about a repeat of the old problem, Mercury Control pressed the capcom to get me to submit a complete report on the thrusters.

02 11 07.5   CC   Report to Cape you have checked fly-by-wire, and
                    all thrusters are okay. Is there anything else?

"Negative," I said. Mercury Control was working on an erroneous assumption about the thrusters malfunctioning and needed to be sure I had checked them thoroughly. Having satisfied my own questions about the thrusters, and done the best I could with the ASCS, I had moved on to grappling with my spacesuit's coolant and steam-vent settings and said so: "Except for this problem with steam-vent temperature." It wasn't the heat now, but the humidity, in this case inside my suit: I knew that the cabin temperatures were high, at about 103 degrees. The dry air would at least provide some evaporative relief from the sweat now pouring down my forehead, plowing through my eyebrows, and stinging my eyes with salt.

02 11 13   P   I'm going— I'll open the visor a minute, that'll
                 cool— it seems cooler with the visor open.

The capcom persisted. Mercury Control needed me to reconfirm that I had used the fly-by-wire control system to check out all the thrusters.

02 11 45   CC   *Aurora 7,* confirm you've checked fly-by-wire, and
                  all thrusters are okay.
02 11 51 5   P   Roger. Fly-by-wire is checked, all thrusters are
                   okay.

But the information coming from the horizon scanner was faulty. During the orbital phase of spaceflight, a malfunctioning automated navigational system is tolerable—for my flight this was especially so because the ASCS was so rarely used. But during an ASCS-controlled *retrofire*—that critical exit off the orbital highway—an accurate horizon scanner is crucial. For retrofire, the spacecraft must be aligned exactly in two axes—pitch and yaw. Pitch attitude, or angle, must be 34 degrees, nose down. Yaw, the left-right attitude, must be steady at 0 degrees, or pointing *directly back along flight path*. The ASCS performs this maneuver automatically, and better than any pilot, when the on-board navigational instruments are working properly.

If the gyros are broken, not all is lost: A pilot can do two things to bring yaw attitude to zero. The first is to point the nose in a direction he *thinks* is a zero-degree yaw angle and then watch the terrain pass beneath the vehicle. This is nearly impossible to do over featureless ocean or terrain. Far better to have a certain geographical feature or cloud pattern to watch. Because the pilot is traveling backward, the geographical features he is trying to track must begin at the bottom of the window and flow in a straight line from there to the top. When this happens, the pilot knows he is in a zero-degree attitude. This can be done through the periscope too, but it takes a little longer and is less accurate.

My travails with a hot cabin and a humid spacesuit continued over Australia. Deke, the Muchea capcom, assumed ground communications. It was his unhappy job to tell me that my cabin temperatures had climbed to 107 degrees Fahrenheit (they would peak, during the third orbit, at 108 degrees). Dehydration under such conditions is a worry, and for these and other reasons NASA medics had lobbied for some of the capcom posts, to no avail.[25] By the time I had completed another solid-food experiment, by eating some Pillsbury-made morsels, I was within voice range of the next Australian capcom, at Woomera, and still fussing with my suit temperature controls. The capcom there asked me for suit temperature and humidity readings. They were at 74 degrees Fahrenheit, with the "steam exhaust" registering a miserable 71 degrees of humidity inside my suit. Still, the numbers had come down since Australia, so the Woomera capcom asked rather hopefully:

02 33 58.5   CC   ...Are you feeling more comfortable at this time?

A noncommittal "I don't know" was the best I could manage. I was frustrated with the suit controls and realized with exasperation that for all the exhaustive testing of the suits prior to this and other early launches, no one thought to test its cooling capacity with the faceplate open! And so many in-flight activities required me to keep my visor up.

02 34 02.5   P   I'm still warm and still perspiring. I would like to— I would like to nail this temperature problem down. It— for all practical purposes, it's uncontrollable as far as I can see.

He consulted the flight plan and asked:

    02 35 20   CC   ...How about water?

That would be a no.

    02 35 22.5   P   I had taken four swallows at approximately this
                                  time last orbit. As soon as I get the suit temperature
                                  pegged a little bit, I'll open the visor and have some
                                  more water. Over.

At this point in the flight, over Canton, I was scheduled to take a xylose pill (which is a biomedically traceable sugar pill for later analysis in my collected urine). I could feel the melted Pillsbury mess in the plastic bag and said "I hate to do this," more to myself than to the Canton capcom. Then, surprise, when I opened it: "It didn't melt!" I found the xylose pill, but all my cookies had crumbled. Chocolate morsels escaped their confines to float, weightless, around my tiny workspace. The rest of the stuff in the bag was a mess. The Nestlé concoction, more fruit and nougat than heat-sensitive chocolate, held up far better.

I was approaching Hawaii, and my second sunrise in space. Referring to the flight plan, the Canton capcom prompted me, before LOS, for an update on the balloon experiment: Which of the five colors was most visible?

    02 47 36.5   P   Roger. I would say that the day-glow orange is best.
    02 47 41   CC   Roger. For your information, the second sunrise
                                    should be expected in approximately 3 to 4 minutes.

"The Surgeon is after me here," he added, for another blood pressure check. "Is this convenient?" My in-flight duties at sunrise called for vigorous physical activity, so I waved him off:

    02 48 47.5   P   Negative. I won't be able to hold still for it now.
                                    I've got the sunrise to worry about.

He let me alone.

    02 48 52.5   CC   Okay. Roger. We have no further queries. If you
                                    have any comments we'll be listening down here.

Sunrises and sunsets were extremely busy time-blocks during Mercury flights. There were important measurements to make of the airglow and other celestial phenomena and innumerable photographs to take. John O'Keefe had some solid hypotheses about the "fireflies" John had seen during his flight. But they remained unexplained. Whatever the critters were, they were particularly active, or at least visible, at dawn, adding to the scientist-pilot's burden. At 02 49 00 I reported the arrival of a beautiful dawn in space: "I'll record it," I told the Canton capcom, "so you can see it." As a patrol plane pilot, I had trained to serve as the U.S. Navy's eyes and ears— a militarily indispensable role. In space, as a Mercury astronaut, I was now the eyes and ears for an entire nation. I felt an obligation to record what few would ever have a chance to see.

I was just beginning to go through my crowded schedule of sunrise-related work when Hawaii took over from Canton, announcing, "Hawaii Com Tech. How do you read me?" prompting me for a short report. The Navy has a one-through-five scale for grading the volume and clarity of voice transmissions. An old Navy quip came to mind, "I read you two by two"—a voice-report shorthand for "too loud and too often." But I reserved the smart answer and said only, "Stand by one. My status is good. My capsule status is good. I want to get some pictures of the sunrise. Over."

| 02 49 37.5 | CC | Roger. Give me the short report first. |
| 02 49 40 | P | Roger. Fuel is 45-62. Over. |

The 45-62 figures were the percentages of *Aurora 7*'s fuel supply. I had less than half my manual fuel supply left; my automatic fuel supplies stood at 62 percent. Not alarmingly low yet, but low enough. Still Kraft, directing the flight from the Cape, later reported that he wasn't worried: "except for some overexpenditure of hydrogen peroxide fuel," he wrote in his own postflight analysis of MA-7, "everything had gone perfectly." I still had 40 percent of my manual fuel, which, "according to the mission rules," Kraft figured, "ought to be quite enough hydrogen peroxide... to thrust the capsule into the retrofire attitude, hold it, and then to reenter the atmosphere using either the automatic or the manual control system."[26]

But I myself was running low on water—hadn't drunk any even after the prompting over Woomera. This was a mistake. I was in good physical condition and could tolerate dehydration, but I still should have been drinking copious amounts of water to compensate for what I was losing through sweat and respiration. Someone, probably the flight surgeon, directed the Hawaii capcom to inquire about my water intake:

| 02 50 31 | CC | *Aurora 7.* Did you drink over Canton? Did you drink any water over Canton? |
| 02 50 44.5 | P | That is negative. I will do, shortly. |

The water would have to wait. But Hawaii capcom persisted: "Roger. Surgeon feels this is advisable." More cabin and suit temperature readings were asked for and given. It was at this time that Mercury Control, alert to potential problems, had pondered one of my earlier voice reports (at capsule elapsed 02 08 46) about the difficulty I was having *not* with the thrusters, but with the ASCS. It directed Hawaii capcom to have me conduct an ASCS check:

| 02 52 20.5 | CC | *Aurora 7.* This is Cap Com. Would like for you to return gyros to normal and see what kind of indication we have; whether or not your window view agrees with your gyros. |

Sixteen seconds passed. I was feverishly working through the sunrise-related scientific work, too busy to drink water, too busy to send a telemetered blood pressure reading, and ground control had just asked me to perform an attitude check. "Roger. Wait one," I replied.

Mercury Control had chosen an awkward moment to troubleshoot the (intermittently) malfunctioning ASCS. They wanted an attitude check, at dawn, over a featureless ocean while I was busily engaged with the dawn-related work specified in my flight plan. Again, adequate checks for attitude, particularly in yaw, are difficult enough in full daylight over recognizable land terrain, requiring precious minutes of continuous attention to the view of the ground out your periscope and the window.[27] In my postflight report I explained the difficulty:

Manual control of the spacecraft yaw attitude using external references has proven to be more difficult and time-consuming than pitch and roll alignment, particularly as external lighting diminishes.... Ground terrain drift provided the best daylight reference in yaw. However, a terrestrial reference at night was useful in controlling yaw attitudes only when sufficiently illuminated by moonlight. In the absence of moonlight, the pilot reported that the only satisfactory yaw reference was a known star complex nearer the orbital plane.[28]

But Mercury Control had requested an attitude check, and I complied, first reporting that I had to get back within "scanner limits," that is, to an attitude in which the horizon was visible to the pitch horizon scanner. That required more maneuvering, which required more fuel. I was still trying to cram in more observations.

02 54 33.5   CC   Can we get a blood pressure from you, Scott?

I sent the blood pressure, reported on the transmission, and continued voice reports on the experiments: the behavior of the "fireflies"; the balloon, still shadowing *Aurora 7* like a stray animal, was oscillating some. Just before LOS, I reported I was going to "gyros normal. Gyros normal *now*." Hawaii capcom replied: "Roger, TM [telemetry] indicates your—zero pitch." And then "LOS, Scott, we've had LOS."

Loss of signal. I was moving on to voice contact with Al Shepard, California capcom, and approaching the start of my final, most perilous circumnavigation of the planet.

13

COMMANDER CARPENTER
AND HIS FLYING MACHINE!

THE PILOT OF *AURORA 7* speeded toward California, where Al Shepard was capcom, in charge of ground communications. Scott first gave Al his short report on fuel, cabin-air temperature, and control mode ("manual, gyros normal, maneuver off"). But then the *important* issue: the suit steam-exhaust temperatures. They were "still reading," he told Al dispiritedly, "70 degrees."

But Al had good news:

02 59 55   CC   Understand you're GO for orbit three.

While the GO business was nice to hear, it was really hot in the cabin, and Scott still had lots of work to do. As it happened, more than the MA-7 cabin temperatures were hot. From all reports, Kraft was full-out fuming as Scott approached the continental United States.[1] The flight director appears to have concluded, erroneously, that the pilot of MA-7 had deliberately ignored his request for an attitude check over Hawaii. Now, in addition to his anxieties about fuel use, Kraft was nursing a grudge about a snub that never took place.

In his memoir, he writes that as Carpenter approached California, he directed Al Shepard, the California capcom, to set things right. Al's new job, Kraft told the famously self-possessed Navy commander, was "to find what the hell was going on up there," adding that he left the California capcom with "no doubt" about his "frustration" with Carpenter. Kraft was in fact bellowing through the earpieces of Al's headset.[2]

The flight director told Al he needed two things from Scott: an attitude check and a tight curb on fuel use. In an exercise of judgment as California capcom, Shepard relayed just one of Kraft's two requests. Note the trademark acid delivery:

03 00 15   CC   General Kraft is still somewhat concerned about
                  your auto fuel. Use as little auto— use no auto fuel
                  unless you have to prior to retrosequence time.[3]

Shepard then turned to the matter at hand, which was the heat in the cabin and an apparently malfunctioning heat exchanger in Scott's suit. He suggested another, more comfortable setting. He omitted Kraft's request for an attitude check. Al then did unto Scott as he hoped others might one day do unto him, offered the pilot a little time, a little quiet, and some encouragement.

03 00 49.5   CC   Roger. You're sounding good here. Give you a
                  period of quiet while I send Z and R cal.

The two men carried out these quiet space chores over the next three and a half minutes. Then Al gathered information. Either he knew enough to ask, or he was prompted by the flight surgeon:

03 02 12   CC   Do you—have you—... have you stopped
                  perspiring at the moment?

No, Scott told him, he was "still perspiring." A good sign. No impending heat stroke. Catching the drift of the conversation, Scott reported he might open his visor "and take a drink of water."

03 02 27   CC   Roger. Sounds like a good idea.

He let Scott drink. Sixteen quiet seconds passed. Then Al asked a question. Note the man's impeccable manners:

| 03 02 42 | CC | Seven, would you give us a blood pressure, please, in between swallows. |

It was a remarkable moment of earth-to-space human solicitude. A minute later, a refreshed Scott reported:

| 03 03 27 | P | Okay, there's your blood pressure. I took about twenty swallows of water. Tasted pretty good. |
| 03 03 38 | CC | Roger, Seven, we're sure of that.... |

In a final, reassuring exchange before LOS, the California capcom would send *Aurora 7* on her way:

03 04 45	CC	Seven, this is California. Do you still read?
03 04 47	P	Roger, loud and clear.
03 04 50	CC	Roger, we have no further inquiries. See you next time.

The "next time" would bring the two men, Shepard and Carpenter, together again in an even more life-saving conspiracy of astronauts.

After four hours in orbit and a long period of drifting flight, *Aurora 7*'s cabin temperature had dropped to 101 degrees Fahrenheit; the vexing problems with the suit temperature were being resolved. The balky camera was now a memory. Scott had succeeded in shooting all the M.I.T. film for the "flattened sun" photographs. The experiment on the behavior of liquids in zero-G was a success. Capillary action *can* pump liquids in space. Over Woomera, Scott described and analyzed various successful valve settings for his suit—in-flight observations that would assist with a later redesign of the Mercury suit; he also took photometry readings and measurements on Phecda, a star in the Big Dipper, then sinking into the haze layer of the horizon. His short report had good news:

| 04 06 35.5 | P | I'm quite comfortable. Cabin temperature is 101 ... fuel reads 46 and 40 percent. I am in drifting flight. I have had plenty of water to drink. |

For the next eleven minutes of spaceflight Scott transmitted an uninterrupted flow of observations. The partially inflated balloon, which had failed to jettison, as planned, over the Canaries, still bumped along behind the capsule. It kept "a constant bearing," Scott reported, "at all times." Still transmitting to Woomera:

04 09 52   P   I have 22 minutes and 20 seconds left for retrofire. I
                                think I will try to get some of this equipment
                                stowed at this time.

Coming up on sunrise, rich with "observables," the pilot of *Aurora 7* prepared for one final observation of the airglow phenomenon, reporting for the tape recorder:

04 15 04   P   There is the horizon band again; this time from the
                                moonlit side.

Scott complained once more about the light leak:

04 15 04   P   Visor coming open now. It's impossible to get dark-
                                adapted in here.

NASA had molded an eye patch for John Glenn so he could keep one eye covered through daytime on one orbit and emerge on the night side with a dark-adapted eye. But the small cabin was so dusty that the sticky tape (designed to keep the patch secured over his eye socket) became covered with dust and would not stick to his skin. NASA did not reattempt this dark-adaption patch with MA-7. Managing to get a good view through the filter, Scott continued: "Haze layer is very bright through the air glow filter. Very bright." He then concentrated on the photometer measurements, reporting with some puzzlement that the width of the airglow layer was exactly equal to the width of the X inscribed on the lens. "I can't explain it—I'll have to—to—"

And then the sunrise, at 04 19 22. Scott would remember the sunrises and sunsets as the most beautiful and spectacular events of his flight aboard *Aurora 7.* "Stretching away for hundreds of miles to the north and the south," they presented "a glittering, iridescent arc" of colors that, he later wrote, resolved into a "magnificent purplish-blue" blending, finally, with the total blackness of space.[4] Thinking the camera might help with the air-glow measurement, he quickly grabbed for it, and in doing so inadvertently rapped the spacecraft hatch.

A cloud of tiny, luminous particles swarmed past the window.

"Ahhhhhhhh!" He exclaimed, to the tape recorder, "Beautiful lighted fireflies that time," explaining,"it was luminous that time." Banging repeatedly on the hatch, he was rewarded with explosions of cloud after cloud of luminous particles from the spacecraft.

"If anybody reads," Scott explained excitedly, "I *have* the fireflies. They are very bright. They are"—he announced with triumph— "capsule emanating!" He quickly explained the cause and effect that proved his finding: "I can rap the hatch and stir off *hundreds* of them. Rap the side of the capsule: Huge streams come out."

He would yaw around the other way to get a better view, he reported. With his photometer handy, Scott estimated that the fireflies might register at a nine on the device and proposed to find out. "I'll rap," he told Woomera, now out of range. "Let's see."

The official NASA history of Project Mercury notes that:

> Until *Aurora 7* reached the communication range of the Hawaiian
> station on the third pass, Christopher Kraft, directing the flight
> from the Florida control center, considered this mission the most
> successful to date; everything had gone perfectly except for some
> overexpenditure of hydrogen peroxide fuel.[5]

This overexpenditure was traced to a spacecraft system malfunction that went undiagnosed until after the flight.

At 04 22 07, Hawaii capcom established ground communications. Scott responded:

04 22 10   P   Hello, Hawaii, loud and clear. How me?

But the signal from *Aurora 7* was weak, so for half a minute pilot and Hawaii capcom struggled with communication frequencies:

04 22 35   P   Roger, do you read me or do you not, James?
04 22 39.5   CC   Gee, you are weak, but I read you. You are readable.
                  Are you on UHF-Hi?
04 22 44.5   P   Roger, UHF-Hi.

Reading off the flight plan, the capcom immediately told Scott to reorient the capsule and go to autopilot—the old ASCS. Scott replied six seconds later: "Roger, will do," and, complying, at 04 22 59, repeated:

"Roger, copied. Going into orbit attitude at this time." Retrosequence, as both Scott and capcom were aware, was fast approaching. With retrorockets to be fired at 04 32 30—ten minutes away—the flight plan called for equipment stowage and retrosequence checklists to begin at 4 24 00, allotting two minutes for these tasks, and then one more minute until LOS. Hawaii capcom's sense of urgency was evident:

| 04 24 20 | CC | Roger, are you ready to start you pre-retrosequence checklist? |
| 04 24 23 | P | Roger, one moment. |

The Navy adage, "Aviate, Navigate, Communicate," always in that order, was never more apt—now for the first time in space. In the grip of this instinct, Scott was properly engrossed with a critical retrosequence maneuver. He finally explained to Hawaii capcom:

| 04 24 36 | P | I am aligning my attitudes. Everything is fine. |

Anticipating the capcom's request, he said:

> I have part of the stowage checklist taken care of at this time.

Stowage is important. You can't have equipment flying around the cramped compartment during entry. More important still, however, is aligning the spacecraft. Twice more, at 04 25 11 and 04 25 55, the Hawaii capcom prompted Scott to begin the pre-retrosequence list.

| 04 25 55 | CC | *Aurora 7,* can we get on with the checklist? We have approximately three minutes left of contact. |
| 04 26 00 | P | Roger, go ahead with the checklist. I'm coming to retroattitude now, and my control mode is automatic, and my attitudes [are] standby. Wait a minute. I have a problem in— |

Thirty-three seconds passed. Scott confirmed the "problem."

| 04 26 33.5 | P | I have an ASCS problem here. I think ASCS is not operating properly. Let me— Emergency retrosequence is armed and retro manual is armed. I've got to evaluate this retro— this ASCS problem, Jim, before we go any further. |

Thirty seconds of silence ensued, for good reason. The automatic pilot was not holding the capsule steady for retrosequence. Again, at retrofire (an event that determines your landing point three thousand miles away) the capsule's pitch attitude must remain steady at *34 degrees,* nose down. Yaw angle, too, steady at *zero degrees.* These two attitudes, in conjunction with a precisely timed retrofire, precisely determine the capsule's landing point. At retrofire, two-thirds of the impulse, or thrust, delivered to the capsule at 34 degrees, nose down, tends to slow the capsule down; the remaining third tends to alter the capsule's flight path downward. If yaw and pitch attitudes, together with the timing of retrofire, are correct, then both events—the reductions in speed *and* altitude—would send *Aurora 7* homeward along the predetermined reentry path, somewhere in the waters southeast of Florida.

Mindful of these contingencies, the Hawaii capcom, Jim, replied: "Roger," told Scott he was standing by, and squeezed in two critical retrosequence items—the pilot was to switch off the emergency drogue-deploy and emergency main fuses. Scott replied:

04 27 13.5   P   Roger, they are. Okay, I'm going to fly-by-wire, to
                   Aux Damp, and now— attitudes do not agree. Five
                   minutes to retrograde, light is on. I have a rate of
                   descent, too, of about 10, 12 feet per second.

Hawaii capcom did not hear, and transmitted: "Say again? Say again?" He had a rate of descent, Scott repeated, "of about twelve feet per second." The capcom asked: "What light is on?" Things were happening quickly. Scott replied only, "Yes, I am back on fly-by-wire. Trying to orient." With only a minute until LOS, the Hawaii capcom finally proposed a run through the checklist. Scott finally said: "Okay. Go through it, Jim," and then, prompting, once more:

04 28 26.5   P   Roger, Jim. Go through the checklist for me.

Approaching the most critical moment of the flight, Hawaii capcom and the pilot of *Aurora 7* used the remaining minute of voice contact to report back and forth on the arming of various squib switches, the periscope levers, up or down? Manual fuel handles (as backup for the ASCS)—were they in or out? Finally:

| 04 28 42 5 | P | Roll, yaw, and pitch handles are in. |
| 04 28 46.5 | CC | Transmitting in the blind....We have LOS. Transmitting in the blind to *Aurora 7.* Make sure all your tone switches are on, your warning lights are bright....Check your face-plate is closed. |

With *Aurora 7* nearing reentry, Kraft learned with as much dismay as the pilot himself that the spacecraft's ASCS was not, in the best traditions of astronaut understatement, "operating properly."

Scott had in fact noticed the symptoms, now and then, of a malfunctioning pitch horizon scanner, and was puzzled, at times, by some instrument readings. He reported them as the anomalies they were. But the intermittent nature of these instrument failures made repeated checking of little value. The view out the window was a very good backup, and it was impervious to failure.

It was clear at Mercury Control that day that Kraft's indignation, simmering since the second-orbit incident over Hawaii, was now compounded by the man's genuine anxiety. Speaking of MA-7, Kranz explains: "A major component of the ground team's responsibility is to provide a check on the crew." And the ground, Kranz says, "waited too long in addressing the fuel status and should have been more forceful in getting on with the checklists."[6] A thoroughgoing attitude check, during the first orbit, would probably have helped to diagnose the persistent, intermittent, and constantly varying malfunction of the pitch horizon scanner. By the third orbit it was all too late. MA-7's fuel problems dictated drifting flight. A third-orbit attitude check, particularly in yaw, would have used prodigious amounts of fuel—at reentry, an astronaut's lifeblood.

Scott, meanwhile, was busy aviating and navigating. The California capcom, Al Shepard, took over voice communications for the retrofire sequence, one minute away:

04 31 50	CC	Seven, this is Cap Com. Are you in retroattitude?
04 31 53	P	Yes. I don't have agreement with ASCS in the window, Al. I think I'm going to have to go fly-by-wire and use the window and the [peri]scope. ASCS is bad. I'm on fly-by-wire and manual.
04 32 06	CC	Roger. We concur.

But in going to fly-by-wire, Scott forgot to shut off the manual system that he'd activated during the pre-retro checklist over Hawaii as backup for the automatic system. So his efforts to control attitude during retrofire were accomplished on both fly-by-wire and manual control modes, spewing out fuel from both tanks. Halfway through his fifteen-minute flight the year before, Al himself had committed the identical error.[7] Retrosequence was coming up.

| 04 32 21 | CC | About ten seconds on my mark....6, 5, 4, 3, 2, 1. |
| 04 32 36 | P | Retrosequence is green. |

Green is good. Green means that everything is set right for automatic retrofire. But not in this case, because the automatic system was locked out and the gyros were caged. Scott would have to fire the retros manually, throwing switches upon Al's count, coming up fast. Suddenly a critical intervention from Al. If Scott's gyros were caged, Al reported, he would have to "use attitude bypass." His gyros were off, Scott answered, and Al repeated his remark:

| 04 32 54.5 | CC | But you'll have to use attitude bypass and manual override. |
| 04 32 58.5 | P | Roger. |

Then two seconds. Al counted down, "4, 3, 2, 1, 0."

Before, during, and after the retrofire firing, Al offered Scott two crucial observations. Because of the instrument failures, the cockpit was in a configuration never before envisioned, and Al perceived the effect it would have on the required cockpit procedure. His contribution to Scott's safe reentry was a resounding endorsement of the decision made a few years before to place astronauts in the communication loop, as knowledgeable buffers between the ground-control people and the man doing the flying. Al's insight at a crucial moment probably kept Scott's landing from being even farther off target than it was.

The last thirty minutes of my flight, in retrospect, were a dicey time. At the time I didn't see it that way. First, I was trained to avoid any active intellectual comprehension of disaster—dwelling on a

potential danger, or imagining what *might* happen. I was also too busy with the tasks at hand. Men and women who enter high-risk professions are trained to suppress, or set aside, their emotions while carrying out their duties. After the job, and after the danger has passed, is the time for emotions.

Without the ability to detach oneself from the peril in a situation, one has no chance of surviving it. What perils did I face? They were the same perils faced by Al, Gus, and John—and later by Wally and Gordo. The retros might not fire. They might explode or not burn properly. The heat shield might not work. The drogue or the main chute might not deploy or reef properly. Thinking about all the things that could go wrong, no one would ever climb into a spacecraft. A pilot counts on all those things going right, not because he needs to believe in a fairy tale, but because he has confidence in the hardware, in the systems, in the men and women on the ground. In himself.

Still, I do remember being surprised by the power of my detachment. It felt as though I were watching myself, with fascination and curiosity, to see how my great adventure might turn out. The rockets were supposed to fire automatically. I watched the second-hand pass the mark, and when they didn't, punched the retrobutton myself a second later. An agonizing three seconds passed until the reassuring sound and vibration of firing retrorockets filled the cabin. I was prepared for a big boot, which never came. Deceleration was just a very gentle nudge, not at all the terrific push back toward Hawaii that John had reported feeling from his own retrofire.

Al was still in voice range and we continued to transmit information about retrosequence. I noticed smoke in the cabin and the smell of metal. Two fuses had overheated. I was worried about the delayed firing of the retrorockets. At that speed, a lapse of three seconds would make me at least fifteen miles long in the recovery area. Al asked me if my attitudes held, and I said, "I think they were good," but I wasn't sure, adding that "the gyros are not quite right."

My visual reference was divided between the periscope, the window, and the attitude indicators. My views out the window and the periscope helped me attain the desired pitch of 34 degrees, nose down, although the attitude indicator read minus-ten. I tried to hold it there, at minus-ten degrees, a false but at least steady reading, throughout retrofire, continually cross-checking with the window and the scope. The long hours on the Mercury Procedures Trainer were paying off.

I had commented, many times, that on the MPT you cannot divide your attention between one attitude reference system and another and still do a good job in retrofire, although it appears I pretty much nailed the pitch attitude. But the nose of *Aurora 7,* while pitched close to the desirable negative 34 degrees, was canted about 25 degrees off to the right, in yaw, at the moment of retrofire. By the end of the retrofire event I had essentially corrected the error in yaw, which limited the overshoot. But the damage was already done.

In the end I was 250 miles long. The yaw misalignment alone caused the spacecraft to overshoot the planned impact point by about 175 miles. The three-second delay in firing the retrorockets added another fifteen miles to the error in trajectory. Under-thrusting retrorockets piled an additional sixty miles onto the overshoot.

"But retrojettison...," I said to Al, changing the subject. It was a question. "Roger," he told me, "ten seconds until retrojettison." Right on time. I heard barely audible ignition sounds from the retrojettison rocket. I reported on my fuel supplies, now at 20 percent for manual control, 5 for automatic. My next job was to damp out any oscillations the spacecraft might develop during the next stage of reentry. But in a little more than a minute, the manual control system would be out of fuel and thus worthless. I still had the fly-by-wire system:

04 35 27.5   P   I am out of manual fuel, Al.

As always, Al was cool. I had merely reported the depletion of manual fuel.

AS IT HAPPENS, Max Faget had foreseen the reentry dangers posed by an aerodynamically unstable craft. He prepared for this theoretical possibility of attitude-control failure by designing a near-perfect reentry body. The vehicle was designed, Max explains, "so that in the event the attitude control system failed, we would still make reentry."[8]

Fuel starvation had rendered my attitude control system ineffective. Still, during the final stages of reentry, I remember thinking the capsule's oscillations were being damped, or suppressed, without any control inputs I was attempting. I remember thinking Faget's design was working: the Mercury capsule had positive aerodynamic stability—as advertised back in 1959, when we were invited to volunteer for this grand adventure. My safe reentry was virtually guaranteed.

Aerodynamic stability is a good thing, but there were still things I could do to improve my situation. At 04 35 13.5, the capsule was oscillating between ± 30 degrees in pitch and yaw, but I was able to use my fly-by-wire controls to further damp the oscillations. A postflight report noted that "by manually controlling the spacecraft during retrofire," I had "demonstrated an ability to orient the vehicle so as to effect a successful reentry, thereby providing evidence" that human beings can "serve as a backup to malfunctioning automatic systems of the spacecraft."[9]

About three seconds after reporting to Al the depletion of my manual fuel, I inquired about the next key event during reentry, called ".05g." That's when you feel that first gentle deceleration signaling the loss of weightlessness.

04 35 34.5	P	.05 should be when?
04 35 37.5	CC	Oh, you have plenty of time. Take your time on fly-by-wire to get into reentry attitude.
04 36 05	CC	I was just looking over your reentry checklist. Looks like you're in pretty good shape. You'll have to manually retract the scope.

No, the scope had come in during a retrosequence check over Hawaii.

04 36 18.5	CC	Roger. I didn't get that. Very good.
04 36 54	P	Going to be tight on fuel.
04 37 02.5	CC	Roger. You have plenty of time. You have about 7 minutes before .05 g so take—

Now I was literally dropping out of the sky and had a beautiful view of the earth below. On his own way down, aboard *Freedom 7* Al had strained for a similar view through the tiny portholes of *Freedom 7*. He hadn't been able to see anything on his way down, so I treated him to a vicarious thrill—my newer version of the Mercury capsule offered a panoramic view of the earth below:

04 37 28	P	Okay. I can make out very small— farmland, pastureland below. I see individual fields, rivers, lakes, roads, I think. I'll get back to reentry attitude.

"ROGER," AL CONCURRED. "Recommend you get close to reentry attitude...." Listening to Scott, Al may have recalled that his own
attempts at reentry sightseeing had left him behind in his work.[10]
Coming up on LOS, he reminded Scott for the last time to use "as little
fuel as possible and stand by on fly-by-wire until rates develop. Over."

04 38 08.5   P   Roger, will do.

With Scott now in range over Cape Canaveral, Gus read off the
final stowage checklist items—reminders in case the pilot had been
busy with other things. Was the glove compartment "latched and
closed"? Roger, "it is," Scott replied. He read off the face-plate check.
"Negative. It is now. Thank you." Everything else was done. Gus transmitted a weather report for the expected impact point:

04 42 28.5   CC   The weather in the recovery point is good— you've
                       got overcast cloud, 3 foot waves, 8 knots of wind, 10
                       miles visibility, and the cloud bases are at 1,000 feet.

Scott reported matter-of-factly on "the orange glow," using the definite article because the glow, in that particular blazing color, had been
reported by his predecessors in these fiery precincts. He also saw burning
particles from the heat shield form an immense orange wake behind him
and struggled against increasing G loads to switch on the auxiliary damping mode. G forces would peak in a few minutes at eleven times the normal gravitational load. The capsule steadied. Auxiliary damping worked!
    "I assume we're in blackout now," Scott transmitted to Gus, refer-
ring to the expected loss of voice contact that sets in at about 75,000 feet.
    "Give me a try." *Nothing.* "There goes something tearing away,"
Scott said, now for the voice recorder. Atmospheric drag was creating
temperatures outside of close to 4,000 degrees Fahrenheit—incinerat-
ing trivial bits of the spacecraft, as expected.

SCOTT CONTINUED talking, for the voice recorder, using the old Carpenter grunt perfected at Johnsville to force the words out. It took all
his strength. *Aurora 7* was reaching peak deceleration rates. Telemetered cardiac readings coming in at Mercury Control registered the

physical effort required to produce words, observations, status reports. He never stopped, every three to five seconds bringing a new, concise transmission. The capsule was now oscillating badly.

Faget recalls that back in 1958 they decided that 60 degrees of oscillation was "good enough" when they worked on prototypes in the wind tunnels. But he laughed rather sadistically at the memory—oscillations of 60 degrees would have produced a wild ride.[11] By 1962, more circumspect human-factors engineers had settled on the oscillations of a mere 10 degrees. And Scott was right at the edge of "tolerable." He tried to find reassurance in the evenness of the oscillations, which signaled good aerodynamic stability.

But then, something new: The orange glow gave way to green flashes, and then to a distinctly greenish gleam, unreported by his predecessors. Must be the ionizing beryllium shingles, Scott thought. Again at fifty thousand feet, the oscillations returned.

The Cape should be able to hear him by now, he thought. His transmissions became more expectant:

04 49 18.5   P   And I'm standing by for altimeter off the peg. Cape, do you read yet?

Scott's rate of descent was slowing to only one hundred feet per second. Cabin pressure was "holding okay." He was at forty-five thousand feet, already arming the drogue parachute, the first of two chutes designed to steady and slow the capsule on its descent toward splashdown. Then he heard a voice, maybe Gus, and replied, "Roger, *Aurora 7* reading okay."

04 50. 29.5   P   . . . Getting some pretty good oscillations now and we're out of fuel.

His "pretty good" oscillations were actually pretty bad—registering now outside the "tolerable range" of 10 percent, the worst so far. Not yet. *Not yet.* He was waiting for twenty-five thousand feet, the upper limit for a drogue-chute release, performed entirely at the astronaut's discretion. His heart rate, which had averaged about seventy beats per minute throughout the flight, hit a peak of 104. Not unexpected. Then:

04 50 51   P   ...Drogue out manually at 25. It's holding and it
                     was just in time....

The drogue chute did its job steadying the capsule. "Just in time"
was a reference to its welcome effect on the oscillations. Still falling. Still
reporting at thirteen thousand feet. Scott was "standing by" for the
main chute at "mark 10"—the altimeter mark of ten thousand feet:

04 51 33.5   P   ...Mark 10. I see the main is out and reefed and it
                     looks good to me. The main chute is out. Landing
                     bag is auto now. The drogue has fallen away. I see a
                     perfect chute. Visor open. Cabin temperature is
                     only 110 at this point. Helmet hose is off.
04 52 39.5   P   Does anybody read? Does anybody read *Aurora 7*?
                     Over.

Then Cape capcom, and Gus Grissom:

04 53 13   CC   *Aurora 7, Aurora 7,* Cape Cap Com. Over.
04 53 16   P   Roger, I'm reading you. I'm on the main chute at
                     5,000, status is good....

Some back and forth. *Aurora 7* was beneath the clouds now:
"Hello." "How do you read?" "Loud and clear, Gus. How me?" But Gus
heard not a single transmission from Scott. Transmitting blind, Gus
announced:

04 54 56.5   CC   *Aurora 7*...your landing point is 200 miles long.
                     We will jump the Air Rescue people to you.
04 55 06   P   Roger. Understand. I'm reading.

Gus repeated: "Be advised your landing point is long. We will jump Air
Rescue people to you in about one hour."

04 55 36   P   Roger. Understand 1 hour.

Scott could see the water now and prepared for the landing. The
impact was not at all hard, but the capsule went completely underwater, only to pop back up and list sharply to one side. He was dis-
mayed to see a good bit of water splash down on to the voice recorder.

———

ALL THINGS CONSIDERED—the unexpected amount of water, the sharp listing of the capsule (sixty degrees, although it would soon recover to a more reasonable forty-five degrees as the landing bag filled with water and began to act like a sea anchor), and the growing heat in the cabin—Scott thought it sensible to get out quickly. With a pararescue team an hour away, this meant egress through the nose of the capsule, a procedure practiced many times in preparation for just such situations. Al and John had orderly side-hatch exits, John's aboard a destroyer, the USS Noa. An appalling side-hatch explosion had sent Gus scrambling out, against an incoming tide of seawater, into the ocean where he nearly drowned—recovery helicopters focused on the task of keeping his waterlogged capsule from sinking sixteen thousand feet to the ocean floor. Scott's top-hatch egress would be Project Mercury's first and, as it turned out, only one. It took him four minutes.

First, he removed the instrument panel from the bulkhead, exposing the narrow egress up through the nose of the capsule, where until recently two parachutes had been neatly stowed. It was a tight fit, but with some scooting and muscling upward, he made his way to the small hatch opening. Egress procedures mandated Scott deploy his neck dam. But he was *very* hot. Surveying the gently swelling seas and all his flotation gear, he decided not to.

Perched in the neck of the capsule, Scott rested for a moment. It was 80 degrees. Egress procedure called next for deploying the life raft. He placed his camera on a small ledge near the opening and dropped the raft into the water, where it quickly inflated. The SARAH (Search and Rescue and Homing) beacon came on automatically, allowing aircraft to home in on his position, somewhere southeast of the Virgin Islands. After grabbing the camera, Scott ventured down the side of the capsule and climbed into the raft. It was upside down. There was nothing to do but to turn it over, so back in the ocean he went and flipped the raft over with one arm, holding the camera aloft with the other. He tied the raft to the capsule, and only then did he deploy the neck dam. Finally in the raft, with his water and food rations and the camera dry at his side, he said a brief prayer of thanks and relaxed for the wait. He had never felt better in his life.

As Scott was getting into his raft, Walter Cronkite was presiding over CBS's news coverage from a van in Florida. Known as "old iron butt," Cronkite could, and would, monopolize an anchor desk all day and through the night to broadcast a breaking story. Here he was, reporting a space mission, with something unexpected and unscripted: a missing astronaut and an unknown landing site, if the astronaut had landed at all. He reported that a "worried" Mission Control had repeatedly tried contacting the astronaut: *"Aurora 7" "Aurora 7" "Aurora 7."* Repeatedly the call went out, Cronkite announced. *Aurora 7's* SARAH beacon was in fact then beaming Carpenter's exact coordinates, and his telemetered heartbeat, steady and strong, had been heard throughout the reentry period. All these reassuring data Mercury Control could easily have provided to the waiting world but for some reason did not.[12] Why?

Aboard the recovery ship *USS Intrepid,* somber-faced reporters, among them CBS's Joe Campbell, were shown on a live feed dismantling their tripods and packing up their gear. Campbell reported on the disconsolate scene and the "concern" being expressed for the astronaut. A now morose Cronkite recapped what he knew. Astronaut Carpenter, he said, had experienced "half a ton" of pressure, 8 Gs, during his reentry ride (it had in fact been 6.7 Gs), and Mercury Control was now "standing by" after having lost voice contact. Astronaut Carpenter's expected landing site was "two hundred miles downrange."

Cronkite let this news sink in. After compressing his lips in somber fashion, he added: "That's the announcement," another head bob downward, "and that is a serious one to hear."

Yet Carpenter was almost exactly where the IBM computers at Goddard had calculated he would be after factoring in radar-tracking data, plus the capsule's error in yaw at retrofire: two hundred and fifty miles downrange from his predicted landing site. Still in the dark, Cronkite continued to report mournfully: "While thousands watch and pray.... Certainly here at Cape Canaveral the silence is almost intolerable."

While networks and wire services speculated on worst-case scenarios, the crew of the *USS John R. Pierce* was giddy with knowledge about the location of the Navy lieutenant commander. The signal from the

SARAH beacon was strong and unmistakable. CBS newsman Bill Evenson, reporting from the destroyer *Pierce*, was the picture of news-gathering glee: "Believe you me," he reported, "this bucket of bolts is really rolling now, and what a happy crew we've got." Evenson was ex-hilarated. He had glad news, and he had it first, reporting with a trilling, rat-a-tat-tat delivery from another era:

> Of course, there's no gambling in the Navy, but believe you me, everybody's gonna be collecting bets tonight! Headed out at *flank* speed, thirty-two knots—with a wake a mile long behind us, water breaking over the bow, and *we're on our way*! Of course, we hear some rumored reports that the Air Force may, possibly, get there before us. Maybe so. But there isn't a man-jack aboard who will go along with this.
>
> Reporting from the *John R. Pierce*, on its way to pick up Commander Scott Carpenter and his flying machine!

Cronkite, at the anchor desk, absorbed Evenson's report with something like chagrined interest, then wondered out loud why he "couldn't seem to get an answer out of Mercury Control." Indeed.

Carpenter, meanwhile, proud and happy in his life raft, surveyed the empty sky and sea. Gus had told him he would land long, so he settled in for a wait. Stretching out his legs the length of the raft, Scott crossed them at the ankles, clasped his hands behind his head, elbows out—a favorite resting posture. For five hours of spaceflight, he had been piloting, working, observing, taking photographs, navigating, making voice reports, pacifying flight controllers, mollifying flight surgeons, and planning the next three seconds without letup. He had endured anomalous instrument readings, a tyrannical flight plan, un-pleasant cabin temperatures, multiple and contradictory demands from the ground. After nine months of training for five hours of space-flight, he had delivered the goods. His capsule, although listing, was not sinking. He was safe on a gentle sea with water and rations. He felt satis-fied, grateful, and relieved. He even had a companion, a curious, eighteen-inch-long black fish who wanted nothing more than to visit.

Shortly, he heard the sound of an aircraft, then recognized the welcome silhouette of a Lockheed P2V, the great patrol plane that he had flown during the Korean war. He signaled with a hand mirror to the pilot, who responded in customary fashion by circling his position. The pilot immediately radioed his visual sighting to Mercury Control. Shorty Powers confirmed the sighting in an official NASA announcement, saying "a gentleman by the name of Carpenter was seen seated comfortably in his life raft."

Now aircraft were filling the skies over Scott's head. Twenty minutes later two frogmen jumped from an SC-54 transport. First into the water, an hour and seven minutes after the splashdown, was Airman First Class John F. Heitsch, soon joined by Sergeant Ray McClure, later in his long rescue career the recipient of the Air Medal. They swam to Scott, opened their own rafts, and tethered them together. The astronaut broke open his space-food rations. Want some? No, thanks. But they enjoyed some space water, they told debriefers, and described their astronaut as "smiling, happy, and not at all tired." They were still out of radio contact.

Recovery supplies began dropping nearby—first, the spacecraft flotation collar, landing with a loud bang, the sound of one of its compressed-air bottles breaking. The frogmen went about attaching the flotation collar to the capsule. The official NASA history of Project Mercury explains what happened next.

> Shortly a parachute with a box at the end came floating lazily
> down some distance from the spacecraft. The men on the rafts
> supposed this was the needed radio, and one of the frogmen
> swam a considerable distance to get it. He returned with the
> container, opened it, and found that there was no radio inside.[13]

Only a battery. At the postbriefing, all three men, Carpenter, Heitsch, and McClure, declined to repeat the expletives the discovery inspired.

Carpenter watched in amazement as a confusing aerial ballet continued overhead against all patrol-plane protocol—some aircraft flying clockwise, others counterclockwise. Then an enterprising Air Force seaplane arrived on the scene. The sea conditions, calm enough for a landing, prompted the Air Force pilot to radio for permission to land and recover the astronaut. Mercury Control said no. Heroic frogmen, air-dropped recovery supplies, and Carpenter were all still in the water. An inter-service rivalry appeared to spell another ninety minutes in the water for all three men. The U.S. Navy, with its helicopters and aircraft carriers, would recover the astronaut. Not an Air Force seaplane. Mercury Control would later be asked to justify the decision in testimony before Congress.[14] More grief it didn't need.

Scott was eventually retrieved by an HSS-2 helicopter that flew him to the deck of the *Intrepid,* which had been steaming toward his location since it picked up the SARAH beacon signal. The *John R. Pierce,* rewarded for its hustle, would recover the capsule. When the recovery helicopter lowered the horseshoe collar down to the astronaut, Scott fit it under his arms and gave the sign. A rotor-disturbing gust—or a malfunctioning winch—plunged him into the sea. The recovery crew saw Carpenter's upraised arm, struggling to keep his historic film dry, disappearing beneath the waves.

Half of the film was lost to water damage.

14

THE COLOR OF FIRE

Looking up at the stars, I know quite well
That, for all they care, I can go to hell,
But on earth indifference is the least
We have to dread from man or beast.

How should we like it were stars to burn
With a passion for us we could not return?
If equal affection cannot be,
Let the more loving one be me.

—W. H. AUDEN

NOTED FOR THE COOL understatement of their voice reports, military pilots are the masters of a remarkable spoken craft. The most alarming transmissions—"I've been hit and my number-two engine is on fire" or "Looks like we'll have to ditch"—are delivered with a crisp nonchalance that inspires confidence, brings focused solutions from the ground, and saves lives. But this craftsmanship involves more than cool delivery. The language itself is different, drawing on a rich, epigrammatic lexicon designed to give pilots optimal amounts of time to carry out their most important duties: thinking and flying—or: *Aviate, Navigate, Communicate.*

After the U.S. Navy reeled in the country's latest astronaut, like a silvery catch of the sea, NASA's Dr. Richard Rink was there to observe the proceedings—and to offer medical assistance, if such was needed: "How do you feel?" he asked his celebrated patient. "Fine," the sopping wet astronaut responded. Scott's one-word reply was immediately relayed to the Cape, according to voice-reporting procedure. The Cape then disseminated the news to a waiting press corps, which passed the news on to an expectant world.

It was thus with a kind of pain, after his hours of laborious and sometimes emotional reporting, that CBS newsman Walter Cronkite told his television audience that the country's newly recovered astronaut felt "fine." *Fine.* Fine was what he got from the man, after having to endure what he confessed on air was one of "the worst moments in my thirty years of reporting." Following a commercial break, Cronkite said there would be a "CBS Evening Special," recapped the day's dramatic events, and then primed his audience with another kind of voice reporting, this one with feelings:

> Well, it started out like Buck Rogers and wound up like Robinson Crusoe—our most ambitious challenge yet to the alien environment called space. It required the pilot to do things we hadn't *dared* ask of his predecessors: a large degree of control in maneuvering his space capsule, more tests to help measure the way things move in space, and how they appear to the man observing them.

Fine was Carpenter's voice report, military-pilot style. But he felt much, much more than that. Rene said as much during her own post-flight press conference, dressed in red, white, and blue and flanked by her four children. The two pararescue divers saw the man's joy, when they arrived, raftside. So did Dr. Rink. But Scott also felt hot and wet. So, once aboard the helicopter, the first thing he did—after submitting his one-word voice report on his health status—was to pull the rubber neck dam from around his neck and let the ocean air whooshing through the helicopter cabin cool him off.

Despite the neck dam, Scott had shipped in some water, so after taking off his flight boots, he borrowed someone's pocketknife and cut a hole in the left sock in his pressure suit. Then he let his sweat and seawater drain out the toe hole he'd created. (Medics were nonplussed. Someone should have measured the salty liquid.) Scott didn't want to get the cabin floor wet, so he stuck his leg out of the chopper.

He was "eager," Dr. Rink observed, "to talk and to discuss his

experiences, and was cooperative and well controlled." Too exhila-
rated to sit, apparently, he moved forward to speak with the pilot,
"paced about a bit," Rink observed, "and finally relaxed as one normally would after an extended physical and mental exercise."

A brief medical exam aboard the *Intrepid* found him in good
health, if "moderately dehydrated." The *Intrepid*'s scales said the five-
eleven Navy pilot weighed 148 pounds. Although he had drunk 1,250
cc's of water during his flight and while in his raft, Carpenter had lost
seven pounds through sweat and exhalation.

The next day, on Grand Turk Island, another physician reported
that Scott "entered the dispensary with the air and greeting of a man
who had been away from his friends for a long time." The Mercury astronaut had been gone for perhaps half a day, yet he had journeyed
eighty thousand miles. "He was alert, desiring to tell of his adventure,"
the medical team reported, "and seemed very fit.... His appearance
and movements suggested strength and excellent neuromuscular coordination."[1]

NASA medics, circa 1962, were rigorous about their data collection: the three specialists—in aviation medicine, internal medicine,
and neuropsychiatry—present for Carpenter's preflight exam on May
17 also conducted the comprehensive postflight examinations, held on
May 25. The workups were in part comparative. How did his preflight
exams differ from the postflight workups? How did these compare
with those of his colleagues? The NASA medics knew each flight was
different, with different stresses, and each man was different, with a
different assortment of strengths.

But the researchers were also collecting "performance" data on
the astronauts, part of a validation study on the original astronaut-
selection criteria established in 1958, when NASA was in its pioneering
research and development mode. The idea at the time, as one researcher explains it, was that the "performance data would then feed
back to validate the original selection criteria or justify changing the
criteria." NASA agreed.[2] So by the fourth manned spaceflight, to their
great satisfaction, and not much surprise, the researchers were finding

that the astronauts' postflight exams produced scores up there in the optimal ranges they had predicted back in 1959, when the original seven astronauts were selected.

Gratifying news: The astronaut-selection criteria, established before any human being had journeyed into space, had been right on the spot. The performance data were also feeding into a long-term stress study. Spaceflight was stressful, no doubt about it. Soon it would be stressful, long, and crowded—with two- and three-man crews in very close quarters. What could NASA learn in the meantime about the adaptive techniques astronauts were developing to help them during these later lunar missions?

As it happened, Scott's postflight performance scores—in the upper ranges, like those of his predecessors—were unusual for two reasons. First, many of them went *up* from his preflight scores across a range of performance criteria. Common sense dictates performance dips following strenuous physical and mental exertions. Shepard, Grissom, and Glenn each bore this out by relaxing slightly for their own postflight exams. They had trained and trained. They had run the race, flown the mission, done well.[3] No need to be super-optimal after the fact. So why not—on the balance beam with your eyes closed, feet feeling forward for the next step—teeter just a little bit sooner?

Not Scott. The medics noted the anomaly and said only that "the significance of the findings" was unknown.

The other unusual thing about Scott's postflight data? They were the last ever collected for what was to have been NASA's pioneering, long-term stress study on astronauts and spaceflight. Dr. Ruff was fired on the eve of the next Mercury mission, and then all the medical files disappeared into what one account describes as "a black hole." About the termination of the stress study, Ruff confessed he was mystified: "All we ever saw in our flights," meaning the four Mercury flights for which there were data, "was very positive.... We psychiatrists sat in on all the debriefings, long and short," he added, dismissing as nonsense talk of "Carpenter using a lot of fuel for his flight and not having the 'Right Stuff'."[4]

On May 26, 1962, two days after his spaceflight, Scott spent three hours skindiving in the blue waters off Grand Turk. It felt good to be weightless once more.

He would never fly in space again.

WITH CARPENTER and *Aurora 7* safely recovered, the hardworking crew at Mercury Control rejoiced along with other Americans about the country's latest space achievement. As Kraft noted in his postflight report, NASA's backup systems, redundancies, flight controllers, and skilled astronauts all worked, even when automatic systems failed.

Kraft writes that he grew "so angry," during one postflight debriefing, at the astronaut's "cavalier dismissal of a life-threatening problem"—i.e., the failure of his on-board navigational instruments—that he "swore an oath that Scott Carpenter would never again fly in space." In *The Right Stuff,* Wolfe has Kraft delivering this oath with more spontaneous gusto, yelling, during reentry, "That son-of-a-bitch will never fly for me again!!"[5] In his book, Kraft suggests, but provides no evidence, that he made good on the threat. For years, the flight director's animus toward Scott circulated as lore at NASA, under the official radar. Unopposed there, it hardened into something like myth. Forty years after the flight of *Aurora 7,* Kraft's private view has taken on all the weight and gloss of legend. Completing this information cycle, Kraft wrote a book, devoting a chapter to Carpenter. "The Man Malfunctioned" is the title of this chapter, as though astronauts are machines. They are not.

As for Scott these many years, his response was, why dwell on "the unpleasantness" when his flight spoke for itself?

DID KRAFT *really* threaten to end an astronaut's career? He hasn't denied it, when asked, and in fact Carpenter never flew another mission. One is tempted to assume a cause and effect. In the end, however, one needs to ask: Beyond the rancor Kraft admits harboring about the pilot of *Aurora 7,* beyond the angry words and the whisper campaign described in *The Right Stuff,* could the flight director have blacklisted Scott? Ask the surviving Mercury astronauts. Their answer is no. In

1962 or 1963 or 1964 Kraft may have wanted this kind of institutional clout but his actually having it is quite another thing.[6]

Tom Wolfe captures this baleful spirit of vendetta and ambition in *The Right Stuff*. Carpenter, the new apparatchiks at NASA maintained, had:

> nearly skipped off into eternity because he panicked! There! We've said it! That was the worst charge that could be brought against a pilot on the great ziggurat of flying. It said that a man had lost whatever stuff he had in the most awful manner. He had funked it. It was a sin for which there was no redemption. Damned eternally! Once such a verdict had been pronounced, no judgment was too vile.

Then Wolfe weighs in:

> One might argue that Carpenter had mishandled the reentry, but to accuse him of *panic* made no sense in light of the telemetered data concerning his heart rate and his respiratory rate. Therefore, the objective data would be ignored. Once it had begun, the denigration of Carpenter had to proceed at any cost.[7]

One other thing: Did Kraft think the astronauts were flying for him, as his spontaneous utterance ("that so-and-so will never fly for me again!") suggests? That these tough, talented men risked their lives, spent months of training so they could report to someone whose "greatest danger on launch day," Wally notes, "involved falling out of his chair"? The answer is yes, he may have. He was the flight director. "There's only *one* flight director," he explained to the Associated Press while on a publicity tour for his memoirs:

> From the moment the mission starts until the crew is safe on board a recovery ship, I'm in charge. No one can overrule me. Not my immediate boss...Not his boss...Not even Jack Kennedy, the president of the United States. They can fire me after it's over. But while the mission is under way, I'm Flight. And Flight is God.[8]

"In a way," says Paul E. Purser, forty years after Project Mercury, "Chris was right. The flight director was *omnipotent*. No one could overrule him during the operation." Gilruth's assistant points out, though, that his old colleague "apparently forgot...that he was not *omniscient*, and his ego would not let him back down from his early misconception that [the overshoot] was all Scott's fault."[9]

Bob Voas explains: "Kraft, along with everyone else on May 24, 1962, failed to perceive that *Aurora 7*'s onboard navigational tools were malfunctioning." As the flight progressed and the anomalies with the fuel? the thrusters? the onboard navigational tools?—whatever they were—grew more ominous, Voas writes that Kraft "grew angrier and more frustrated as the astronaut, busy with a science-heavy flight plan that he had deplored from the beginning, was insufficiently responsive." At reentry, Voas believes the flight director saw "the magnitude of the danger, felt the tension as Carpenter assumed manual control of the capsule, and worried during the critical reentry period that Scott might not survive."[10] He may even have feared that someone might blame him.

Chris Kraft and Walt Williams "both came up," Purser explains, "through the NACA Flight Research Division under Gilruth. He taught them a lot, technically," concedes Purser, Gilruth's special assistant of thirty years, "but he never taught them to control their egos." But then, Purser hailed from the more altruistic work culture of PARD. Over at Flight Research, Kraft and Williams "were more interested in doing a good job in order to get promotions and higher rank than in the foolish attitude I had, " Purser adds ruefully, "which was, 'do the best job you can and take a genuine interest in helping your boss get the overall job done.'"[11]

Bob Voas, another old hand at NASA, says that the truth about this Mercury flight was that, without Scott, *Aurora 7* was not coming home. He explains:

> *Aurora 7* was the first flight in which the success of the mission
> depended on the performance of the astronaut. In the two
> suborbital flights, the flight path was fixed: Al and Gus were

coming home anyway. In John's flight, aboard *Friendship 7,* he took over the spacecraft attitude control because the small thruster controls were malfunctioning. But Glenn's capsule would have reentered safely in any case because the ASCS, the basic automatic control system, remained operational. The concern with the air bag separation was a false alarm.

But with *Aurora 7,* the gyro problem went undetected on the ground and the attitude control system was malfunctioning. The astronaut's eye on the horizon was the only adequate check of the automated gyro system. With its malfunctioning gyros, the spacecraft could not have maintained adequate control during retrofire. Mercury Control may have viewed the manually controlled reentry as sloppy, but the spacecraft came back in one piece and the world accepted the flight for what it was: another success.

Aurora 7 provided proof of why it was important for man to fly in space. It was proof of what the members of the Space Task Group had told the skeptics at Edwards back in 1959: *the Mercury astronaut would be a pilot.* Many in the test pilot profession were still deriding the program as a "man in a can" stunt, with a guinea-pig astronaut along for the ride. The irony, of course, is that as Kraft's anger over MA-7 seeped through the ranks of NASA, subsequent missions came as close to the "man in a can" flights that everyone was deriding in the first place.

With the increasing complexity of the Gemini and Apollo flights this early, intense conflict between control from the ground and control from the cockpit faded. But NASA missed an important opportunity to help the nation understand how putting man in space was not simply a stunt but a significant step toward conquering space.[12]

FOLLOWING THE FLIGHT, with its two days of debriefings and press conferences, the Carpenter family flew to Colorado, where they would spend Memorial Day weekend. (The White House, incredibly, offered Air Force One to the astronauts and their families for these postflight goodwill trips home.) In Denver a crowd of three hundred thousand cheering Coloradans lined the streets for a ticker-tape parade. Boulder went Denver one better, declaring May 29 "Scott Carpenter Day" and sponsoring the largest parade in Boulder history for its hometown hero.

Toye was honored, too. Jim Williford was on hand that day to serve as her escort. The strapping, six-foot-two helicopter pilot was stunned as eager Boulderites literally knocked him off balance just to reach past him to touch his frail charge, now sixty-two years old and entering the final year of her life. She was delighted by the fuss. She had a place on the dais during a university ceremony honoring her one child. At Folsom Stadium she beamed as the chancellor said, in essence, all is forgiven; here, finally, is your undergraduate degree in engineering. Scott's heat-transfer experience in space, the engineering department decided, translated into some impressive work credits—three of them—applicable toward his degree. Then, of course, there was that fifty-six-hour course in thermodynamics (or heat transfer) at Patuxent, in which he earned a perfect 100.

Scott's father was also present for the ceremonies that day. Dr. Marion Scott Carpenter finally made his peace with the son he didn't raise and never understood—a son with flying in his heart. Once C.U.'s most accomplished graduate, at least in the sciences, in 1962 he watched his son lay claim to that distinction.

AFTER MEMORIAL DAY weekend, Scott returned to Langley Field for more technical debriefings, followed by the now traditional postflight visit to the White House, where the president thanked the Carpenters, and the family of Walter C. Williams, for service to the country. This was followed by a trip to New York, where at City Hall Scott was awarded the city's Medal of Honor in a ceremony attended by former presidents Herbert Hoover and Harry Truman.

For these events, the children had been primed and pumped and instructed in good manners. In the pictures with President John F. Kennedy, the boys appear alert enough, but then there are two unhappy, tired girls. What the photos don't show is that the Carpenter girls had turned to the president in the middle of the Oval Office pomp and small talk, stopping him cold with two loud questions. "*Where* is Macaroni?" from one. "And Caroline?" the other asked, accusingly.

Girls this young could be forgiven for believing that something as marvelous as a pony, named Macaroni, lived at the White House, or that a president's daughter might be free for playtime. President Kennedy bent down to their faces: Macaroni, America's most famous pony, needed pasture and lived in the country, he explained. The girls stood their ground, unsmiling.

Two or three weeks later, a formal invitation arrived at the Carpenters' home in Langley Field. Jacqueline Kennedy was inviting Rene and the two girls, "Kristen and Candace," it said, to tea at the White House at two P.M. on the appointed day. Rene assumed it augured a social gathering of mothers and daughters who had been in the news— a small-scale Easter Egg Roll. So the three flew from Langley Field and arrived at the gate, a bit uneasy because no one else was there. Then they were driven to the south entrance, where an aide escorted them to an anteroom. There Jackie was speaking her grateful thanks and good-byes to a small group of people, who, she later explained, had undertaken the restoration of the White House library.

Her public voice, as she spoke to her departing guests, was exactly as Rene had heard it on television, during her famous "Tour of the White House" with Charles Collingwood. But when she walked toward Rene, beaming and brisk, her entire demeanor changed. Here was a straightforward, down-to-earth, entirely natural woman. Her voice went a tone lower and the trademark breathiness vanished. Shaking hands with each of her new guests, the first lady fastened on the Carpenter girls, touching the tops of their heads and spelling their names aloud, to get them right. "Let's find my children," she said, "and I'll change out of my finery."

Rene was struck by the first lady's size, for she had a large, bony frame, a large head carrying a mound of back-combed hair. Her skin was carefully made up, and her two incisors crossed over, creating a piquant, closed-mouth effect, especially since her lips were so full and defined. At five-foot-three, Rene felt small beside the nearly five-foot-ten Jackie.

The first lady changed quickly, leaving the door open and calling out to her guest, alone for a moment in this comfortable room. She emerged in a cotton shift and sandals. They continued talking as refreshments arrived—huge, tall iced glasses with strong spiced tea. "The very best this house has to offer you," she said. Talking about children is a traditional icebreaker among women. Jackie and Rene were no different. The first lady was articulate and fierce about her motherhood, and Rene detected no hint of noblesse oblige in her manner.

Rene responded with accounts of her own brood—how she tried to give each child a niche, even though at certain times the four individuals needed to operate as "a team." It was Rene's turn to explain, as it began to dawn on her that this unusual invitation had grown out of her daughters' unvarnished disappointment expressed in the Oval Office—and after that, whatever communication had passed between president and first lady.

"I want to show you the garden and the swing," Jackie said. They carried their glasses, pausing at the door, where she placed her hand on Rene's arm. A finger rose to her lips for a long second before they exited toward the elevator. Shielded by shrubbery from the long South Lawn and the tourists at the fence, the women put their legs up and talked. Jackie tested her guest with the oldest sort of social opening: she'd been told Rene had "the most beautiful skin ever," and now she could see it was true. Rene demurred, providing her clinical formula: the Edna Wallace Hopper white clay mask, Nivea cream, and a Swedish mother. Relieved of conversational spade work, Jackie clapped her hands and released her first real flash of humor: "You mean 'you all have lied'? Carbolic acid won't work for me?" She said it well and Rene recognized the line, from a poem in Edna St. Vincent Millay's *Renascence*: "Time does not bring relief; you all have lied." She responded from the *Second Fig*—"Safe upon the solid rock the ugly houses stand." After a pause the first lady shot back: "Come and see my shining palace built upon the sand!"

They talked about *Life* magazine and the Luces, especially gossip about Clare. Envious of the unfailingly positive *Life* coverage the astronauts enjoyed, Jackie admitted she didn't know what the magazine was after when it came to her personally. Referring ruefully to *Life*'s account, the year before, of the astronauts' first White House visit, she said, "You couldn't have missed that rear-end shot of me and my bow legs, walking with Mrs. Shepard."

She relished stories of the well-known—and their foibles. So Rene dished the Luces' twenty-fifth anniversary party. Jackie responded with an account of the Shah of Iran and Empress Farah, who was "*loaded* with jewels, so huge, we had to check the photos to see what they were." They talked books. Both were puzzled by *Life*'s infatuation with Hemingway and entranced by Durrell's *Alexandria Quartet*. As the conversation went on, Rene determined that her own reading habits may have been broader, but the first lady had an extraordinary background in art history. A mention of bequests by the French painter Odilon Redon brought her upright. "I am dying to get into an old storage closet. Let's go upstairs. I think there are prints there I can use. Are you game?" She added, "We need the bathroom!"

Certainly this was the point, Rene thought, for the Carpenters to take their leave. She said so. But her host wouldn't hear of it: "I don't want you to go. The children are playing," she said. "Stay for supper." The president would be busy "on a budget all-nighter," so they were dining alone that night. "It would be gay," she insisted, "having you for company. We'll make all the arrangements to get you to your friends' house snug and safe." She was sincere. Rene gave the only acceptable answer.

"*Good!*" she replied. "Let's explore that closet I was telling you about." And for half an hour they searched for a floral still-life that would remotely resemble a Redon. Nothing. The first lady finally gave up, chose two prints that might be useful, and left them by the door to be retrieved. "Everything by the book," she explained.

Working their way back, the mothers were joined by the three girls, who gave accounts of their playtime. Preparing for supper, they washed their hands. "You've got a lot of lipsticks," Candy, five and a half, noted. "That's true," the first lady replied, "but I don't have real color for my lips anymore, and you do." The small, formal family dining room was wallpapered with a glorious panoramic scene. Jackie lit candles. "I *hope* I'll like this," Kris offered, with characteristic dubiety.

When the rolls and butter arrived, Candy asked, loudly: "WHAT is this?" The butter had come on separate plates; at each place there now sat a large yellow golf ball, stamped with an early-American hexagonal design—unrecognizable by everyday standards, and to children who ate in the kitchen. The first lady rose with knife in hand and circled the table, cutting the balls in half to aid in spreading them on the bread, apologizing about her "ambitious kitchen."

"Let's visit Daddy," she said to Caroline after dinner. "Let's surprise him." Down the elevator one last time, to the Oval Office, where indeed, at seven P.M., the president and his assistants remained at work. How to describe the delight, Rene thought, the president expressed when his wife and daughter entered the room. He beamed at Jackie; Caroline he simply devoured. He explained the phones to the Carpenter girls and how the drawers to his desk worked. "What did you have for supper?" he asked. They told him. Then, teasingly, to the girls who at their previous meeting had told him how sorry they were to have come: "Did you manage to have a good time today?"

"Yes, very much, thank you," the elder girl replied. "My dad says when we move to Texas, I'll have my own horse, and not a pony." Skewered, the president laughed out loud, and reached toward his wife: "Did you hear that?"

THE CARPENTERS arrived in Houston during the July Fourth weekend in 1962 along with the other six Project Mercury families. Home at first for most of the families were suites of rooms at the grand old Shamrock Hilton, with its Olympic-sized pool and a ten-meter diving platform. More camping out, after that, at the cabañas of the Lakewood Yacht Club, a landmark near Clear Lake and closer to the public schools in Seabrook. A new school year had started.

Finally, in October, their house complete, the Carpenters moved into 202 Sleepy Hollow Court. It was a three-bedroom brick ranch house, with a small study and a two-car garage. Out the back of the house, which was faced mostly with glass, one could see oak trees, tall southern pines, expanses of the greenest grass, and knots of children traveling to and fro. There was a pretty view down the canal to Taylor Lake and the community pool, for which Rene and other mothers raised funds that first fall. Built in time for the summer of 1963, the pool was in the shape of a Mercury capsule. In the nose of the capsule, the deep end, the pool had one- and three-meter diving boards and a competitive diving team, called the Timber Cove Dolphins, which Scott coached for a few seasons. The shallow end fanned out in Faget's famed blunt-end reentry shape. The pair of steps leading up and out of the shallow end, and where toddlers splashed, were shaped like retrorockets.

School buses for the Independent School District of Clear Creek came all the way to Timber Cove. Up and down its streets the school bus plied its child-collection trade. Day after day the same children and their faces, wonderful in their familiarity, boarded the bus, which by the time it lumbered left on to Old Kirby Road was packed to the rafters. Along Old Kirby, the occasional child in overalls stood, usually at the head of a long dirt road leading back behind the trees to a farmstead. Here too the bus slowed and stopped, and the child clambered aboard quietly. His life too had changed.

Only weeks after moving in, Scott was attacking the black Texas clay of the side yard with pick and shovel. He dug down about six feet into what locals called gumbo and then carved out a nine-by-five hole. It was for the trampoline, which he would set flush to the ground. Blue, weatherproof pads covered the metal frame. Soon too a thick cable of rope, twenty feet long, was hanging from a towering oak in the yard. One could scramble up the sloping trunk to a comfortable crook about ten feet off the ground, and, rope in hand, launch himself into space.

And the children came. On some summer nights, after a swim-team victory or other community vindication, older children gathered on the trampoline for no other purpose than to enjoy their youth, their freedom that humid night, the perfection of the day, their critical generational mass, while overhead bats swooped for insects and lightning bugs gleamed, it seemed, just for them.

During the days there were games of "Add One" on the trampoline, and feats of skill. With some early instruction from "Mr. Carpenter," the more athletic children were soon executing flawless twisting somersaults, double back flips, and more. Some bad injuries were avoided with the flush-to-the-earth installation—no concussions or broken bones. Trampoline conditioning at NASA was less successful. Scott invited George Nissen, his gymnastics coach from St. Mary's Pre-flight, to set up a program for the space agency. Walt Cunningham, an Apollo astronaut, gamely signed up—and broke his neck.

AT NASA, FOR the rest of that year, John and Scott traveled a great deal, mostly for purposes of lionization and space agency diplomacy. Scott was Guaymas capcom for Wally Schirra's six-orbit mission in October 1962. He and others were involved in the design reviews and construction of the Gemini capsule. In 1963 Scott worked on Gordon Cooper's launch simulations and flight team; he was Hawaii capcom for Gordo's twenty-two-orbit flight aboard *Faith 7,* the final Mercury mission. Afterward a host of Project Mercury and Capitol Hill notables were invited to a large and festive White House ceremony to see President Kennedy award Gordo the NASA Distinguished Service Medal. It was May 1963.

Touring Japan as goodwill ambassadors, the Glenns were the only Mercury couple not present for the ceremony. White House photographs of the ceremony show Rene standing at the back of the large crowd, beneath the portico, and at her side, Jackie Kennedy. The first lady and a White House usher had just located a pair of gilt hallway chairs for the two Grissom boys to stand on so they could have a better view of the proceedings. "All of you should come back tonight," Jackie told Rene. "We've got nothing on." That night six Mercury astronauts and their wives returned to the White House for a gathering that was mostly social, and partly political. It was not an unusual overture. The president liked these men. He enjoyed asking them about spaceflight, liked hearing their answers, asked their opinions about things.

The president and his wife were in high spirits when their guests arrived. Jackie, four or five months pregnant, had started to show. She would lose this baby, a son they named Patrick, only two days after his full-term birth in August. In November she had sufficiently recovered to join the president in Dallas. But these unspeakable devastations, personal and national, were yet to be, and on that May evening in 1963 President and Mrs. Kennedy were in a high, merry mood. While drinks were served the first lady made everyone comfortable, grouping occasional chairs with the sofas.

"Is it true you're all Republicans?" the president asked the assembled astronauts. "I don't know *what* the hell we are," Gus replied, to guffaws. Later that night over dinner with his wife, an amused president would repeat the story to Ben and Toni Bradlee.

Then the president decided to put Gordo in his rocking chair. "Take a swing in *this* capsule," he said to Cooper, who cheerfully complied. Jackie arranged for photographs of everyone gathered around Gordo in the president's famous rocking chair. Finally, she wanted group pictures taken in front of the fireplace, by which time the mood in the room was just short of rollicking.

Afterward, back in Texas, it was learned that the astronauts were in hot water—again. Their White House invitation, word was, should have been cleared with NASA officialdom.

THE STORIED INDEPENDENCE of the original astronauts, from Carpenter to Slayton, singly and collectively, had been a thorn in Jim Webb's side from the beginning. It couldn't be helped. The Gilruth system, called "management by respect" in one NASA history, was in place before Webb's appointment. This system meant that the original seven astronauts enjoyed princely design and decision powers over the experimental launch systems and space vehicles they had volunteered to test. It was the only way Gilruth could conceive of managing the initial, pioneering phases of space flight.

Although their authority pleased astronaut and Gilruth alike during the course of Project Mercury, for Jim Webb, who held a political post, it meant notable confrontations, some of which he lost badly. For example, NASA had insisted after John Glenn's historic flight in February 1962 that only the Glenns be present for the gala parades and celebrations in New York City. "They don't go," said John, meaning his fellow astronauts and their wives, "I don't go." All seven went.

In a recently declassified recording of a November 1962 meeting, President Kennedy tells Webb, the NASA administrator, that getting to the moon is NASA's "top priority." Odd to hear Webb reply, "not exactly," to the president's obvious annoyance. The previous month the administrator could be seen applauding on the dais at Rice University while the president gave a bracing address, spelling out a central national vision. Part of what the president wanted was space exploration, and he sounded the usual resonant themes: progress, science, freedom, peace. But what Kennedy really wanted was to beat the pants off the Soviets in a race to the moon—a pure, naked, international, interplanetary thrashing of a dangerous foe.

At Rice he explained why, and in one of his most stirring national summons declared:

> We choose to go to the moon. We choose to go to the moon in
> this decade and do the other things, not because they are easy,
> but because they are hard, because that goal will serve to
> organize and measure the best of our energies and skills, because
> that challenge is one that we are willing to accept, one we are
> unwilling to postpone, and one which we intend to win, and
> the others, too.

But that was September 1962—in a public address with public faces. In November, Webb was in the Oval Office telling the president that the lunar program was one of "a couple" of NASA priorities. No, the president repeated, *the lunar program* was the country's priority. He was adamant on that point and then said "put your arguments in writing," before leaving the meeting.[13] "Not because it is easy," Kennedy may have been muttering as he left the room, "but because it's *really* hard to get some cooperation around here."

Back at the White House six months later, another Astro Power headache: unleashed astronauts loose on the White House lawn, accepting a first lady's impromptu social invitation so the president could schmooze space policy over drinks and gather unvarnished astronaut opinion (probably pushing that lunar program again).

IN A TRIBUTE TO Bob Gilruth's R&D philosophy, the country had lost not a single man through all of Project Mercury. A Yorkshire pig, alas, had expired in its contour couch at the Johnsville centrifuge. A well-liked Rhesus monkey, Able, died on an operating table while under anesthesia. But not a single man. The Soviets had an abominable safety record. To this day it's not clear how many cosmonauts, researchers, and technicians died in space-related work. With the success of Mercury, soon the Gemini and Apollo programs were taking shape, this time in new buildings in a new state with new organizational headquarters—and a bunch of new fellows along to help.

When the nine new astronauts were selected in September 1962, the expanded corps of astronauts became a team of sixteen all doing the same things. In the fall of 1963 another, larger group of new astronauts arrived. They all went through the jungle- and desert-survival training together. Everyone spent a lot of classroom time on geology and computers. Apollo-related study and training were also being conducted. Everyone reported to N.A.S. Pensacola to log the required twenty-five hours of helicopter flight training—a precursor to lunar landing simulations and LEM training. Astronauts spent time laying out the instrument panels of the Gemini capsule and the Apollo command module. Scott worked specifically with Buzz Aldrin on a number of different ideas for the Apollo reentry instrumentation. He flew with Neil Armstrong, later on, to get a better handle on window placement. During this period, for however long it was, Scott was just another member of the team devoted to getting Gemini and Apollo off the ground. For a while, no one had flight assignments.

Some time after the conclusion of Project Mercury, perhaps early in 1964, Deke Slayton, now coordinator of astronaut activities, sent a questionnaire around asking who wanted a Gemini flight, the two-person training missions to prepare for the lunar expeditions. Scott said no, he wasn't interested. For one thing, he'd just met his longtime hero, Jacques-Yves Cousteau.

DURING HIS FIRST squadron duty (1951–54), in Hawaii, Scott and his crew of eight were conducting water-survival training exercises in the deep water off N.A.S. Barber's Point in Oahu. He and his crew had jumped off a small Navy boat with their survival gear and begun setting up the raft and their equipment. While thus engaged, their corner reflector fell overboard. *Not* a good thing. If you're in a raft on open ocean, and you want to be found by a search plane with radar, a corner reflector is a critically important piece of gear. Scott's gunner's mate, alert to the potential catastrophe, knew this and immediately dived into the waters. He was gone for a long time, but up he came, the reflector in hand.

Scott was relieved—and chastened. His fear of the deep ocean had compromised his performance. He, the commanding officer, had hesitated when his gunner's mate had acted. He resolved to conquer his fear in an effort that would take him again and again into the water. Oddly enough, his first substantial opportunity to train underwater came with Project Mercury in May 1959, with the water-survival training the seven endured at the hands of the U.S. Navy Underwater Demolition Team in Little Creek, Virginia.

After his Mercury flight, without a flight assignment and bored by the public-relations appearances, Scott heard that the charismatic French oceanographer Jacques-Yves Cousteau was scheduled to address an audience at M.I.T. He knew the man's work through *The Silent World,* an immensely popular book and film. Surely, he thought, the technology required to keep humans alive underwater might draw on the technology NASA was developing to keep humans alive in space. Perhaps Cousteau might offer him a place on his diving team. Cousteau's underwater programs were not well funded, and the Mercury astronaut knew he could bring free and directly applicable technology.

He approached Bob Gilruth, who gave him leave to pose the idea to Cousteau after his address. Cousteau's talk at M.I.T. was eloquent and moving—he discussed the beauty of the underwater world, what he hoped to accomplish there *and* on dry land, by explaining the crucial importance of a healthy ocean to life on this planet. Lack of interest meant lack of funds and talent, which, he said, was holding up important research in saturation diving and underwater exploration. After the lecture the two men talked. Scott met Cousteau's divers. It was fine with them, Cousteau said, if he joined the team. But the oceanographer said he couldn't pay much, and Scott spoke little French. Maybe, Cousteau offered, the best place for him to begin was with his own U.S. Navy. They had a program called Sealab. This was how Scott met Captain George A. Bond (USN, M.C.) and began an adventure underwater that in many ways eclipsed his adventure in space.

Here in one fell swoop was a chance to satisfy four compelling needs Scott had at that time: to conquer his unreasoned fear of the ocean, to satisfy his curiosity about an environment every bit as mysterious and unexplored as space, to meet the personal challenge it represented, and to share richly funded space science with poorly funded ocean science. All four were fulfilled.

Deep-water divers, except snorkelers and breath-holding skin divers, must have a high-pressure gas mixture to breathe, equal in pressure to that of the ambient water. In shallow water, divers can breathe regular air—a mixture of oxygen and the inert gas nitrogen—with no problems. But nitrogen becomes poisonous at higher pressures, so breathing mixtures for diving at greater depths contain helium instead, an inert and nonpoisonous gas. The rub, however, is that the inert gas in a breathing mixture has been forced into the body tissues by the higher pressures created by the deeper diving depths and must be given some time to be released through respiration—a process called decompression. Were it not for the fact that pure oxygen itself is poisonous at depths below about thirty feet, inert gas in the breathing mixture would not be needed, and decompression, the cross borne by all deep divers, would never be required.

Time spent in decompression is a function of the depth and the duration of the dive; but beyond twenty-four hours at any depth the body becomes saturated with the inert gas and is unable to absorb more, and the duration of the dive no longer affects the decompression time. Give divers a high-pressure place to live, something the U.S. Navy was preparing to achieve with Sealab, and their working time compared with decompression time is dramatically increased. This, in short, is the world of the saturation diver, and in 1963 Captain George Bond, known as "Papa Topside," was the Navy's preeminent figure in this elite and dangerous field. Bond himself stood on the shoulders of giants, most notably those of Admiral Charles B. "Swede" Momsen, who in 1939 rescued thirty-three men from the USS Squalus with his invention, the diving bell, in what remains the single greatest submarine rescue in history.[14]

After many discussions with Captain Bond in Washington, D.C., followed by talks with Gilruth in Houston, Scott was lent back to the

U.S. Navy. It was the spring of 1964. He reported to Bond in Panama City, Florida, where he was introduced to the four Navy divers for Sealab I, an experiment in underwater habitation, work, and science. The crew included two chief petty officers, Bob Barth and Tiger Manning; Lester Anderson, an enlisted man; and Bob Thompson, who was a diving medical officer. Bond gave them the news: these four vastly experienced Navy divers had to teach an upstart spaceman how to be a saturation diver. To their credit, they never protested the ignominy within Scott's earshot.

In July 1964 the entire Sealab contingent went to Bermuda for more training exercises. Near the Plantagenet Bank, a formation off the Bermuda coast, the Sealab divers could dive in two-hundred-foot waters close to a Navy tower called Argus Island. On the first visit, teams of two were sent to the bottom with specific assignments. Wilbur Eaton and Scott Carpenter, who would later dive together to the Sealab II habitat, were told to go to the bottom, find one of the big cables radiating from the tower, and follow it for what they thought was one hundred yards, turn around, swim back to the tower, and begin their ascent to the surface. They got to the bottom and found a cable. But visibility was bad and the cable was buried in places.

Scott ended up spending too much time trying to find both the cable and his buddy diver, Wilbur. He started to consider heading for the surface, without his buddy diver, when he spied the errant cable in the sand. He chose to follow it to the right and with his left hand tried to lift it clear until, suddenly, it *moved*. He had laid hands on the *huge* tail of a stingray—schools of stingrays collected around the base of the tower. To say Scott was startled is an understatement of the first order. Wilbur and Scott finally found each other and made it back to the tower and the surface. Then the next team started down. Scott warned them to watch out for stingray tails.

While everyone was waiting for all the pieces of the Navy operation to come together, two U.S. Air Force planes suffered a catastrophic midair collision. The wreckage was on the ocean bottom nearby, in more than 230 feet of water. Although the Navy forbids its divers to work at such depths, the Sealab operation was exempt. So down they swam to the wreck to recover the bodies—an exhausting and horrible task. Scott was struck in particular by the bravery of Charlie Aquadro, one of the Navy's consulting physicians to Sealab I—the only diver not totally undone by the depth, the cold, the narcosis, and the horror of recovering dead bodies, hauling them to the surface, hoping they held together until they could be stuffed into body bags.

Not long after this gruesome recovery operation, Scott suffered a collision of his own, crashing his Bermuda motorbike into a coral wall and sustaining a compound fracture of the ulna, in his left forearm. The distal joint of his left great toe, in addition, was pulverized. Doctors at Kindley A.F.B. hospital cleaned him up for Medevac stateside.

One look at Scott in the dispensary, Captain Bond recalls in a journal entry, and he "realized that his terribly painful injuries were nothing to him in view of the anguish of missing Sealab I. But after examining the X-rays, I had to tell him he was on the scratch list....I promised him a permanent billet with our next mission."[15] An emergency conference involving NASA principals and Rene soon resolved that surgeons at M. D. Anderson, in Houston, would perform the needed bone-setting. The next day Rene and the four Carpenter children met husband and father at Ellington A.F.B., where Scott hobbled down the airplane stairs, his left arm in a sling and his left leg in a makeshift cast up to the knee. He would go straight to M. D. Anderson.

THE YEAR 1964 was beset with particular woes for the Glenns and Carpenters of Sleepy Hollow Court. Life there had begun happily enough in the fall of 1962, with everyone settling into new homes and schools and friendships. The Glenns had a hand-cranked contraption for making vanilla ice cream after barbecued suppers. John inaugurated the felicitous tradition, when Scott was out of town, of mowing both lawns with his John Deere tractor-mower, a Christmas gift from Annie. Then the president was assassinated.

The murder of President John F. Kennedy, in November 1963, was felt deeply among NASA personnel.[16] Rene moved about in a pall of grief for what seemed like months. But the president's death probably affected the Glenns more than any other space agency family.

Before the assassination and before the war escalated in Vietnam, a two-term Kennedy administration was a safe political assumption. It was logical to assume that NASA would get the country to the moon and back and even that John might get a shot at going. These hopes and assumptions presented among other things a comfortable family timetable for the Glenns. John could take part in the lunar expeditions and then turn to politics, a natural move for the Ohio-born Democrat—one, moreover, urged on him by two Kennedys, John and Robert. The man was, after all, the most popular and recognized man on the planet—a priceless asset for the Democratic administration struggling on the one hand to get civil rights legislation passed while juggling, on the other, a profoundly conservative bloc of Southern Democrats—Democrats who might give a little on crucial votes if the new senator from Ohio paid their districts a campaign visit.

The assassination changed everything. For the Glenns, it changed their near-term priorities. Personal ambition about a lunar mission suddenly seemed selfish. John and Annie soon resolved that he would run for the U.S. Senate; a seat was opening up in 1964. Three months later he resigned from NASA, and soon the Glenns were throwing themselves into the Ohio Democratic primary. They had a good shot at winning.

But then John slipped. It happened in the bathroom of the Glenns' new apartment in Columbus, Ohio. Annie had bought some throw rugs, and John, atop a new one, reached for something and took a flier, walloping his head hard on the way down—specifically, the bone behind his right ear. The very serious concussion, plus damage to his semicircular canals, meant incapacitating, nauseating balance problems. Although he recovered by the end of the year, and even regained his active flight status (John was still in the Marine Corps), it was not in time to save his bid for office.

Scott's underwater projects and Rene's political activity on behalf of the Glenns did not escape the notice of NASA administrator James Webb. In a memorandum written at this time, he sounds displeased. He also appears not to know that Gilruth had approved Scott's leave. Why is the man *not* on active-duty astronaut status, he wanted to know:

March 29, 1964

MEMORANDUM for Admiral Boone

The enclosed correspondence relates to Scott Carpenter and the long conversation I had with him on the West Coast to the effect that he believes there are areas in the program where he believes he could contribute more than as a full-time working astronaut. The reports are not encouraging, and I must confess some concerns over the activities of Mrs. Carpenter in Ohio. While I know a wife is completely free to engage in activities not encouraged or sponsored by her husband, the circumstances are such that some people have doubts about the complete independence of her actions. My own concern as Administrator is more along the line of a failure to understand how a wife of a man in the program would not at least consult with the officials of the Agency about the effects her actions may have on the program. Either she is oblivious to these or not concerned about them. If she had consulted NASA officials and then proceeded, I would feel better about it; but to take these actions without even informing us seems to indicate a failure to appreciate the effects of such action on the Agency to which her husband is attached.

After discussion with Dr. Dryden and Dr. Seamans and a canvassing of possibilities, we are wondering if we should not suggest to the Navy that Carpenter is available for return to duty with his home organization. If he is not to participate actively as an astronaut and if there is not a place where we believe he can make other contributions, then I do not believe we are justified in continuing his detachment. It may well be that the Navy could use him to excellent advantage in its own program.

Would you wish to discuss this informally with the Navy?

James E. Webb
Administrator

John and Annie Glenn solved one of Webb's Carpenter problems the next day by pulling out of the Senate race and focusing on John's rehabilitation. Over the next several months the Carpenter girls, on horseback miles from Timber Cove, often encountered an unusually stern John Glenn pounding the hot country lanes, raising his arms up and out over and over again in a series of choreographed rehabilitative movements. "Hi, Uncle John!" they yelled, cantering past him. He hardly noticed.[17]

Following Scott's accident in Bermuda that summer, the surgeons at M. D. Anderson had chosen a "closed-reduction" procedure to set the fractured bone in his left arm. The other option was a more invasive, open-reduction surgery that ran the risk of introducing a limb-threatening infection. While he was under anesthesia, the doctors also opened up his big toe, removed the pulverized bone, and inserted a pin so the toe could function.

SOMETIMES YOU CAN be too strong. As Scott's left arm healed, blood and bone all rallied to the injury site with the body's unthinking resolve to become even stronger. The result was a bony formation on the ulna that bumped into the radius as Scott tried to rotate his forearm. He could pronate some, to make his palm face down, but he had lost his ability to supinate, or rotate his left hand in the palm-up position. The loss of mobility, Scott was told by NASA medics, was a grounding injury. Surgery was an option, but no orthopedic surgeon consulted was terribly optimistic. They could go back in, but with the calcification, they feared causing more harm than good.

Scott absorbed the news about his arm with something like equanimity, except it was darker than that. He began refocusing on what he could do, which involved preparing for Sealab II, where he would be commanding officer. It was to be conducted off the coast of California the following summer, in 1965.

The Sealab I habitat for the Bermuda dive was a reconditioned float originally used for mine defense projects in Panama City, Florida, but the Sealab II habitat was fabricated by the Navy in San Francisco specifically for this experiment. Its purpose was to support, in two hundred feet of water, three teams of ten men each for a total of forty-five days. In addition to the Navy's most experienced divers, the group included six fine divers from Scripps Institute. Chief Petty Officer Bob Barth was the only Sealab I diver present. Another Sealab I alumnus reported for duty, but when he refused to undertake the physical conditioning program his commanding officer had established for the tough crew of mostly Navy UDT divers, Scott dismissed him.

Everyone reported to the Hunter's Point Naval Shipyard in 1965, where they began to assemble, equip, supply, and become thoroughly familiar with the habitat. In July of 1965, the "Lab" was moved to Long Beach for final fitting out and testing. A month later she was lowered to the bottom at 205 feet, off the Scripps Pier in La Jolla. Wilbur Eaton and Scott Carpenter entered the Lab on August 28 to set up housekeeping. In space on the last day of their eight-day Gemini mission, Gordo Cooper and Pete Conrad arranged to speak with Scott on his first day in his new underwater habitat, conversations notable in part for the Mickey Mouse vocal quality of helium speech.

President Lyndon B. Johnson, too, wanted to speak with Scott, a conversation that was finally arranged four weeks later, when Scott and his fellow Sealab crew members were in the decompression chamber. Jack Valenti and a White House operator patiently waited on the president's end. A local operator, meanwhile, worked the Sealab line and made the mistake of confusing Scott with Gordo, asking, "Commander Gordon Cooper, astronaut, would you speak a few test phrases to check our circuit?" Captain Bond, on hand for these historic phone calls, tells the rest of the story: "The reply, typical of Scott's intellectually fastidious approach, went about as follows: 'Negative, this is Scott Carpenter, aquanaut. Astronaut Cooper was last heard in Tanganyika; would a test phrase in Swahili do as well?' "[18] The rest of his remarks were "conveyed in pure helium speech," Bond writes, the perfect vocal foil for President Johnson, possessor of the warmest baritone speaking voice of the century. "The conversation went superbly," Bond concluded—the president understood not a word of what Scott was saying.

Upon the successful completion of Sealab II, Bond mused in a journal entry on October 12, 1965:

> The job is all but done. Four hundred and fifty man-days of
> life and work on the ocean bottom have been accomplished
> without serious accident. More than a half million items
> of specific information have been punched on to cards or
> processed through the undersea multiplexer for direct
> computer analysis. Correlation and cross correlation of these
> data will be in process for months to come. From these data will
> come our guidelines for extension of human exploration of the
> continental shelves or beyond, perhaps even to the abyssal
> plains.

Great plans from one of the Navy's great visionaries and pioneers. Yet today the U.S. Navy, once at the world's forefront of saturation diving, no longer maintains this fleet capability.[19]

As it happened that fall, Scott and three Sealab II colleagues were summoned for a Pentagon "nooner"—to be held on Thursday, October 21, 1965. Walt Mazzone and George Bond had the required blue uniforms. Bob Sheats, who along with Scott was to receive the Legion of Merit that day from the hand of the Secretary of the Navy, had to fly to Seattle, Washington, for his uniform. "At the Pentagon," says Bond, "the ceremony and news conference were dignified and well managed. Scott, unfortunately, could not appear, being grounded by fog in Hartford, Connecticut."

During the debriefing sessions that followed the flight of *Aurora 7,* Scott had compared the weightless state "to that of being submerged in water." However, the notion that water immersion would be a useful technique for training astronauts to conduct extravehicular activity or "space walks" evoked mixed emotions at the Manned Spacecraft Center. Gene Cernan checked out the method at MSC Director Bob Gilruth's request. Cernan, only the second American to conduct EVA, had encountered tremendous difficulty as he attempted to execute the overly ambitious flight plan that NASA managers had devised for him. In the giant water immersion tank at

MSFC, Cernan found that moving about underwater in a pressure suit closely matched his EVA experiences aboard *Gemini IX-A*. Soon, the method would become the principal technique for preparing astronauts to work outside their spacecraft.

Scott, back at NASA after Sealab II, established himself as a proponent of this training; with his aquanaut background, he played a key role in turning the concept into reality. For part of that time he served as assistant to Bob Gilruth, although he really reported to Paul Purser. In the meantime, the Navy was so encouraged by the results of Sealab II that plans were under way for a repeat project in a year or two. It would be run out of the Navy's Deep Submergence Systems Program, headquartered in Bethesda, Maryland.

The year 1966 passed and still the Glenns and Carpenters lived side by side. Dave Glenn and then Lyn went away to college. Soon Scotty Carpenter, too, would graduate. John Glenn had left NASA early in 1964; it seemed inevitable that Scott would follow. Until then there was always yard work, or things to fix around the house, for Scott Carpenter, in his prime, was one of the twentieth century's great putterers—with the utter and mad devotion to the principle that every mechanical, electrical, and technical item in the house-universe should work perfectly at all times.

Although yard work was not as compelling to Scott as the grave engineering problems posed by the family plant, it had its charms, particularly during hurricane season, when whole tree limbs could crash down on what had been a rational expanse of lawn. These tree limbs were soon dispatched with the services of a double-headed axe, kept in a high state of sharp readiness.

Scott was thus engaged during one particular hurricane season. Along for company was a rake-toting daughter. Burning on the adjoining, empty lot was a small fire, fueled with yard debris. Overhead, clouds scudded into formation for what soon became a bad storm. The wind kicked up. It began to rain—and thunder. *Kkrrrreee-KAK!* followed by a terrible, spitting sound and the unusual sight of a live, spasming power cable. A lightning strike had severed a high-voltage power line not twenty yards from Scott and his daughter, who that day understood, in part, that bravery is not caring whether you live: You care that others will. For closer still to the flailing cable were three small children, huddled in fright, within reach of the flailing cable.

At the back door of that house, a mother emerged to scream don't move. The children did not move, frozen like the woman screaming. But Scott moved. He moved with long steps, the kind that do not run yet are full of speed. In one hand was his axe. Then more steps full of speed. For an instant he stood judging his foe and then, quickly, swung the axe, pinning cable against telephone pole. He then twirled the handle in his hands for the better bite of the other blade and again, twice or three times more, severed the power line high up against the telephone pole (his height plus the reach of his axe blade, maybe eight feet). The twenty-two thousand volts usually lived and coursed safely through tame-looking cables that brought sweet domestic services, like light and power and cool air, without once, that anyone can remember, threatening to kill.

THE GEMINI LAUNCHES continued, which for the Mercury wives meant meeting to watch and to celebrate these still thrilling national events. In Timber Cove, where the Grissoms made their new home next door to the Schirras and a block from the Carpenters and Glenns, Betty presided over her house proudly. On the day of their rare get-togethers—lunch, coffee, swimming, a launch—the seven women generally arrived at the designated home early, bringing along food, new snapshots, knitting, a bathing suit. With the kids in school, they were eager to drop their public faces in the security of a friend's living room.

Betty was always the last to arrive on launch days, after her pals had subjected her to a ritual series of entreaties. Jo would make the initial overture, starting with a cajoling reminder and culminating in a gentle threat: "I'm coming over to unplug that vacuum!" Betty gave her standard demurrals. At seven minutes and holding, their designated saint and diplomat, Louise Shepard, was pressed into telephone duty: "Darling *girl*! We are not *whole* without you." And sure enough, in minutes, Betty slipped through the back patio doors. The band was complete.

Late one morning, with four women all packed into Jo's car—

Annie Glenn, Betty Grissom, Jo Schirra, and Rene Carpenter—they headed for the Shepard apartment in Houston, where Louise was holding a tea for the nine new astronaut wives. It was early 1963. Marje Slayton drove in from Friendswood. They had mixed feelings about the meeting, a foreboding that the newcomers might bring even greater social responsibilities when the women were already drowning in a sea of fund-raising events and visits with lobbyists, congressmen, and journalists. Privacy was harder than ever to maintain, when here before them was an instant group of eager, terrific women with plans to organize and compose a monthly newsletter—in short, Get Together. It was quiet in Jo's car on the drive back to Seabrook as everyone pondered the changes afoot in their lives. Betty finally spoke. "Well," she summed up, "they're a hippy bunch." At that the four women—Jo and Annie up front, Rene and Betty in the back—fell apart laughing.

Jo, in her droll way, focused them on the possibilities of her newsletter entry: "Today, dear reader, I wrote two hundred and twenty-five thank-you notes, watered the plants, drove the ballet car pool, and woke up with the curse." She continued, "Which means, dear reader, that I am, once again, Not Pregnant." Laughter erupted, and they were suddenly back in fighting trim, shouting, laughing, interrupting each other with one loony item after another for this imagined space-wives' newsletter. The miles zipped by and they rolled back to their private caves in Timber Cove.

The inimitable Gus Grissom had his own perspective on NASA and flight assignments. "Look, Rene," he explained to her in exasperation one day, "I just close my eyes and kiss his ass," referring to flight director Chris Kraft. Sitting poolside at a Schirra party, a year before he was immolated in the Apollo 1 fire, Rene and Gus had their last heart-to-heart. He had heard about her newspaper column and sounded a combative note. "So. You gonna write about *me*?" No, Rene explained, but she needed the job. She might need to support herself soon—a reference to the difficulties she and Scott were having.

Gus softened. "He tried to get me, too—" He always spoke in vivid image fragments. "Tried to hang me with the 'hatch' *crap*.... All that investigation *bullshit*....I didn't give a good god*damn* about the White

House," he said. "But my *boys* did. *Betty* did...." He chuckled, "Look at her. She's *still* mad." In a protocol foul-up, the Grissom family did not go to the White House after Gus's flight, and years later it still rankled.

His good humor restored, they reminisced about the recovery film he had shown her at the Cape, the tape that showed him floundering and drowning as *Liberty Bell* sank beneath the waves, nearly pulling a chopper down with it. They stepped carefully around the subject of Deke's lingering, hard-edged resentment about his lost flight.

"Scotty's so goddamn *SEN - si - tive*," Gus said, drawing the word out in three distinct syllables. "First off—wasn't all Deke," meaning the bad-mouthing, in some quarters, Scott had endured since his flight. "Kraft pissed in his ear all the way to Houston....Deke was *always* his meal ticket....Al wouldn't play his game." Al Shepard, too, had been grounded since early 1964, succumbing to crippling bouts of vertigo and nausea brought on by Menière's disease. Reverting to that impish look signaling the disclosure of secret information, Gus then said: "Kraft crapped his pants worrying Kennedy'd hand NASA to John," meaning Glenn, then adding, "John was bigger than *Jesus!*" Pausing for effect, he looked at Rene, "And maybe better than Webb— for *us,* anyway."[20]

ON THE JANUARY DAY that Gus Grissom, Ed White, and Roger Chaffee died on the pad in Apollo 1, Rene heard the news on the television and immediately ran to Betty's house—dashing through the backyard of the Glenns, skirting past the Hammacks and the Hoylers, across the street, and through the front door, standing ajar, where others were already gathering. Betty was stone-faced and composed. No one was able to speak of the horror, or the cataclysmic folly, where a cockpit became a locked-in firestorm with no way out.

At the NACA, in the old days, Gilruth's exhortation was always the same to his workers stuck on a problem: "Use your *head!*" he implored them. "Think!" he'd say. Imagine his concern with Project Mercury, with seven men he described as "precious human cargo"— men he knew were risking their lives to promote great national goals. The research administrator and civil servant never shrank from asking the hard questions. Max Faget recalls that "shortly after we decided to go with the Bare Atlas, Gilruth came around and said, 'Max, what are you going to do when the Atlas blows up?'"

In 1958 it wasn't clear how an astronaut perched atop a rocket might survive such an explosion, with all that fuel beneath him. Gilruth had assumed the Atlas would blow. What was Max, he wanted to know, going to do about it? "I don't know!" Faget responded, to which Gilruth said, "Well, you'd better figure something out!" In the oral history, there is laughter at the memory—not, it appears, because anyone thought explosions and death were particularly humorous, but because Gilruth knew, and so did Faget, that there were worse things than dying. One of them was living with the knowledge that you were responsible for death-dealing engineering stupidity. So Max figured something out—the launch escape tower.

Ten years and tens of millions of dollars later—long after Gilruth's Pilotless Aircraft Research Division at the NACA had given way to the manned space program—NASA placed three men into a locked, flammable, pure-oxygen environment with no egress, no fire retardants, and no escape except death. Key NASA personnel, holdovers from Gilruth's team at PARD, were still asking the simple, hard Gilruth questions: "What are you gonna do *when* there's a fire?" But in 1967 the right people weren't listening.

So Gus Grissom, Ed White, and Roger Chaffee died.

"They didn't feel anything," Betty intoned. Someone told her that. "It happened in ten seconds. They didn't feel anything....They didn't feel anything." Over and over. Food was arriving, and the old ritual had begun again. Later, to get him out of the house, Rene took Mark Grissom down to the Seabrook feed store, where he helped her put twenty-five-pound sacks of sweet feed into the back of the station wagon. They had a popsicle and drove slowly back to Timber Cove and his home, where the tragedy's aftermath was being organized.

Betty became their leader then, for the funeral: "I'm in the *first* limousine this time," she said pointedly. "Catch up to me." At Arlington they followed her walking up the hill. She was easy to see in her orange bouclé suit. The color of fire. The same tired dignitaries shuffled into prominent spots for the inevitable graveside photographs. Their public faces were on now. They had been drunk the night before, paying their respects at the bar at the Georgetown Inn. Rene sat with Jo. They were numb. Their husbands were angry. The government inquiry had already begun before their charred remains were lowered into that hallowed ground.

Later that spring, the findings were published. Some at NASA resigned. Others lost their jobs. Financial settlements with manufacturers were quietly arranged for the survivors. Two years later, in July of 1969, NASA fulfilled President Kennedy's pledge to land a man on the moon before the decade was out, in a national effort that at its peak drew on the strength and ingenuity of more than one million Americans.

That summer of 1967 Scott sat in the NASA public affairs office; there he and Doug Ward drafted the press release on his resignation from the Astronaut corps. Outside, the winds picked up, followed by a walloping subtropical downpour. From time to time the two men looked up from their work to consider the rain. Finally the resigning Mercury astronaut got up to leave, declaring to no one in particular with no particular emotion: "I left the top down on the Cobra," meaning his spectacular 427 Shelby Cobra, blue metal flake. He shook Doug's hand and walked out.

He was forty-two years old.

AT THE END OF THE summer, the Carpenters left Texas on an August morning so early and so damp the light wasn't light at all but a pearlescent sort of gray. Some milling about ensued as Scott and Rene waited for someone to arrive with a check: the girls' horses had been sold. The Glenns, in their bathrobes, emerged from their home for the somber send-off, and out of neighborly respect, the Carpenters quit their driveway and joined the Glenns on theirs until, check for the horses in hand, the six family members plus one Samoyed dog climbed into yet another car for yet another cross-country trip to yet another new home—this one in Bethesda, Maryland.

It would be their last journey together as a family.

Epilogue

That fall of 1967, Rene and Scott sent their eldest child off to college, settled the remaining three into a large rented house in Bethesda, Maryland, and separated in de facto fashion. Rene, then thirty-nine years old, plunged headlong into Sen. Robert F. Kennedy's presidential campaign. Scott was soon busy with Sealab III, flying back and forth between the Bethesda headquarters of the Navy's Deep Submergence Systems Program and San Francisco, where the underwater habitat was being prepared for its new home under six hundred feet of water. Busy parents were nothing new for the Carpenter children, except now they inhabited the Washington suburbs and when their father was home, their mother was gone—and vice versa. No one asked for explanations. Nor were any ever offered.

Off Hunter's Point Navy Shipyard, San Francisco, Sealab III crew members were struggling more than ever with bone-chilling waters and mail-order parts. With his men sleep-deprived and fearful about equipment failures (and the project underfunded at $15 million), Captain George F. Bond noted with dismay that "almost every error of design and fabrication that could be made had in fact emerged in the Sealab III habitat."[1] Then more bad news: X-rays of Scott Carpenter and Joe MacInnis showed that both men had developed bone necrosis.[2] More saturation diving, particularly for Scott, would bring crippling injuries.

But Bob Barth, still with the strength of three men and the courage to match, reported once more for duty. When the habitat developed a bad leak, he and another Sealab II alumnus, electronics engineer Berry L. Cannon, dived down for the repairs. Film footage shows Cannon and Barth at work, then Cannon in evident distress. Barth is seen motioning toward his diving buddy's mouthpiece. But in seconds Cannon's jaws are locked in a rictus of death—horrible, spasmodic jerking throws up clouds of silt, obscuring an already murky scene. Before the picture is entirely shrouded, Cannon can be seen dying convulsively in Barth's powerful embrace.

Investigation found that Cannon, an experienced diver with the U.S. Navy Mine Defense Laboratory, had dived to a depth of six hundred feet without a CO_2 scrubber, an operational lapse soon traced to an overworked Navy technician. As the board of inquiry on Cannon's death wound down, so did the U.S. Navy's experimental programs in underwater exploration and habitation.

After twenty-five years of distinguished service in the U.S. Navy, Scott resigned his officer's commission. He had served in the skies as a naval aviator, in space as a Mercury astronaut, and underwater as a U.S. Navy aquanaut. But his many exertions, and some reckless driving, had brought grounding injuries. He could no longer fly high-performance jets. Bone necrosis limited his usefulness as a saturation diver.

Accounts are sketchy, and no one talks about it much, but Rene may have asked for her husband's resignation across the board—from his old life in the Navy, from marriage, and from his now mostly episodic role as father to their four children. Candy was twelve, Kris, thirteen, Jay, sixteen. Scotty was nineteen and showing the first symptoms of chronic schizophrenia, symptoms which began as vague complaints about the weather.

Rene wrote a syndicated column, called "A Woman Still"—a verse from an Edna St. Vincent Millay poem. The lifelong Democrat campaigned energetically for RFK in all the primary-election states in 1967 and 1968; she attended all the victory parties—except for the final one, in California, where Bobby was murdered in a hotel kitchen. She went on to have a career in television, even covering an Apollo mission for NBC with Chet Huntley and David Brinkley. Mostly she hosted two local television shows in Washington, D.C. She remarried in 1977.

Scott remarried in 1973, a union that produced two sons, Matt and Nick. Divorced in 1986, he returned to Colorado in 1987, remarried in 1988, and had another son, Zachary. After a third divorce, in 1999 he married one more time. By this time Rene and her husband had also returned to Colorado. Kris and Candy followed in 1994 and 1996.

The journeys of Noxons and Carpenters took them far from their safe and substantial farms in seventeenth- and eighteenth-century Massachusetts and New York, where a gunshot fired in the air brought uncles, cousins, and brothers running, and where cozy hearths beckoned at nightfall with lamplight and shelves were filled with Scripture and commentary. Within a few generations descendants had ventured west to wilder and more dangerous places, with few books, scant lamplight, and sparse settlement on the frontier—from northeastern Connecticut, to Franklin County, Ohio; Gallatin, Missouri; Winterset, Iowa; and finally Idaho Springs, Colorado.

Traveling about this vast country today is a good bit easier than it was in the seventeenth century. Then, journeys were the most perilous undertakings one could imagine, beset by evil weather and evil men—blinding rainstorms, lamed horses, broken axles, unscrupulous highwaymen, downed bridges. Journeys so perilous that farewells were in fact small prayers. "Good-bye" is itself an invocation that God attend every step, as with "adieu" and "Godspeed," for that matter—for speedy journeys bring travelers home sooner rather than later. And home soon is always good.

The space race is over. Men have walked on the moon. Old friends and pioneers are gone. Still, a frontier's cardinal rules remain unchanged: Be ready in trouble, endeavor to be a jolly companion, remember and tell good and true stories around lonely campfires.

They say the nights on Mars are cold and long.

On February 1, 2003, the *Columbia* readied for reentry in what had become, in the twenty-first century, a commonplace event. Not that anything had ever really changed about reentry temperatures.

As in the early 1960s, temperatures for reentry vehicles were still a whopping 3000 degrees Fahrenheit. But gone was the hardy, meteor-shaped Mercury spacecraft, impervious to just about anything untoward. In its place was the shuttle, with vulnerable leading edges—equal to reentry stresses, certainly, given the proper care.

Gone, too, apparently, were NASA technicians, managers, and engineers who in the 1960s would have moved heaven and earth to bring astronauts safely home to their families. Their country. The CAIB (*Columbia* Accident Investigation Board) report describes a broken safety culture at NASA.

In an Op-Ed piece for *The New York Times* on February 9, 2003, Kris Stoever describes children who wait for parents to return from dangerous missions in perilous places, trusting that those who sent them away have the wisdom and the courage to bring them safely home.

WAITING FOR DAD

FOR MORE THAN FORTY YEARS Americans have waited on tarmacs and beaches. They have filled the stands at Cape Canaveral, Florida, waiting for astronauts to return, safely, to earth. There, too, dressed in their best warm-weather clothes, some with shiny new shoes, the children of astronauts wait on the edge of joy for their fathers and mothers to return.

It is 1961. It is 1967 or 1987. It is Feb. 1, 2003.

Waiting thus, children know their father or mother has survived the hazardous launching. But reentry, even more perilous, remains.

The danger of reentry, in fact, was a central obsession of NASA's early and most brilliant engineer, Maxime A. Faget. While Wernher von Braun designed rockets to take men into space, it was Max Faget who concerned himself with the trip home—one in which astronauts would scrape against the atmosphere at 17,000 miles per hour in craft that would reach temperatures of close to 4,000 degrees Fahrenheit. He came up with the perfect reentry vehicle—the Mercury capsule.

It could survive reentry simply by slowing down as it met atmospheric drag. And the best way to slow down? By entering the earth's atmosphere blunt end first, as meteors do. Add an ablative, or heat-sink, shield for the blunt end, an aerodynamically stabilizing conical afterbody, and some pilot controls, and Max Faget virtually guaranteed an astronaut's safe reentry.

This was the theory anyway.

In the spring of 1962, when I was nearly seven years old, my younger sister, Candy, and I ran, shoeless, out of our rented house at Cocoa Beach, across the sandy yard and finally to the beach to see our father's tiny Mercury spacecraft launched into space from Cape Canaveral. As it climbed out of sight, we settled back in the house for the five long hours of waiting. My brothers wrestled each other. Candy and I drew in new coloring books with a new box of Crayolas. Then my mother's voice commanded our presence in front of the television for the final phase of the flight.

We waited and waited. It seemed a long time. While I was sharpening my favorite color, periwinkle, in the crayon box's built-in sharpener, my father, Scott Carpenter, was being treated to a pyrotechynic show known to few—a blazing orange wake of fire that eventually gave way to greenish gleams of ionizing beryllium—while manually piloting his capsule safely home. This after finding to his surprise that his automatic attitude controls had failed with retrofire only minutes away.

My father was lucky to have survived. Lucky in that sure way that comes with uncoincidental combinations of skill, national determination, long months of training, and some truly brilliant engineering.

We all welcomed him back at Patrick Air Force Base. Candy and I were dressed nicely and well behaved, our hair tamed by huge barrettes. My brothers wore jackets and ties and assumed their most composed public faces. Amid the hugging, Candy held up her elbow for inspection and pointed. "I have a bruise," she said, and was rewarded with intense fatherly concern. After that, my grandmother wept.

Last week, again in Florida, astronaut children were waiting for a father, a mother. Again spacecraft encountered the orange glow signifying 4,000 degrees Fahrenheit. Children, some with new shoes, sat in the stands waiting for the final glide path. For seven minutes they sat, as the NASA clock ticked past the time for touchdown. None would get to say: "Welcome back. Hello, Daddy."

NOTES

2: A FROZEN SEA

1. At the time, E. B. White, a contemporary of Carpenter, was publishing his first poems in both the *New Yorker* and "The Conning Tower," a poetry column that appeared in the *New York World*. Carpenter subscribed to both, typing up "A Prayer at Bedtime" on his own letterhead in 1928—appending only "E. B. W." at the bottom of the page. The stationery bears the unmistakable intaglio of a thumbtack.

7: LOVE, WAR, AND QUONSET HUTS

1. Guy Howard was TPT Class 2. The Naval Institute Press published a fine book (1985) on Patrol Wing Ten's heroic service during World War II, by Dwight R. Messimer, *In the Hands of Fate: The Story of Patrol Wing Ten, 8 December 1941–11 May 1942*. Guy Howard's daughter, Madeline H. Smith, kindly lent her copy to the authors.

8: FOR SPACIOUS SKIES

1. Paul E. Purser, who was Scott Carpenter's boss at NASA in the mid-1960s, sent courtesy copies of these oral histories of Max Faget, Paul E. Purser, and

Joseph Guy ("Tibby") Thibodaux, Jr., to Scott soon after they were compiled in mid-September 1996 (hereinafter "Space Stories"). Professor Robbie Davis-Floyd, an anthropologist at the University of Texas at Austin, and Dr. Kenneth J. Cox, historian at the Johnson Space Center, directed the project. The interviews, numbered 1 and 2, may be found online on the website maintained by the Institute for Advanced Interdisciplinary Research at space.systems.org/oh/thibodaux/part_1.htm and space.systems.org/oh/faget/part_2.htm. Page cites refer to the authors' printout.

Davis-Floyd and Cox also excerpted a *New Yorker* article by Henry S. F. Cooper (which they "sometimes adapted and amplified"), called "Annals of Space: Max Faget and Caldwell Johnson," *New Yorker,* September 2, 1991, pp. 41–69. Portions of these interviews also appear in a forthcoming book edited by Robbie Davis-Floyd and Kenneth J. Cox, *Space Stories: Oral Histories from the Pioneers of the American Space Program* (New York: Routledge). In addition, NASA historian Summer Chick Bergen conducted an extensive interview with Paul E. Purser, on February 3, 1999, in a separate oral history project sponsored by the Johnson Spacecraft Center (hereinafter "Oral History Transcript.")

2. See Thibodaux, in "Space Stories," interview no. 1, p. 43. Elsewhere, Purser notes with glee, " 'Louisiana State University and A&M College' " is where *we* came from." Thibodaux chimes in: "We are Aggies, Louisiana Aggies!" [*laughter*] Professor Davis-Floyd adds: "In other words, they are products of one of the universities intentionally set up by the federal government to make sure America kept up with Europe's agricultural, technological, and military progress." In "Space Stories," interview no. 2, p. 102.

3. James Oberg, "Max Faget: Master Builder," *OMNI,* April 1995, p. 62; also posted at astronautix.com.

4. "Space Stories," interview no. 1, pp. 2–4.

5. See the six-part interviews of Dr. Robert Rowe Gilruth (hereinafter "Gilruth Transcript") on the website maintained by the National Air and Space Museum (NASM) as part of its Oral History Project (nasm.si.edu/nasm/dsh/TRANSCPT/GILRUTH1.HTM). Dr. Gilruth's remarks about Faget and Thibodaux appear in interview no. 5.

6. Thibodaux explains:

Because I was lazy, I became, I think, an outstanding supervisor because I didn't mind letting other people do the work. I didn't have to do the work, or try to be smarter than the sum of the guys in my division. But I knew enough to guide them. And because I had no ambition, I was never a threat to any boss I had. I never walked over any of them. I walked *around* quite a few of them, but I never walked over any of them. And I never worried who got credit for the work. I think I parlayed those two things other people think are not too hot into a pretty good career. And I had an awful lot of fun doing it. I don't think anybody could have worked in anything more exciting than Max and I and Paul did. We were right in the forefront of everything. We always had the best tools. We had tremendous support in everything we did. You just couldn't ask for a better deal.

See "Space Stories," interview no. 1, p. 9.

7. Purser, in Bergen, "Oral History Transcript," p. 6.

8. Faget, in "Space Stories," interview no. 2, p. 67.

9. Purser, in "Space Stories," interview no. 2, p. 57.

10. Building on the insights of Lynn White, the great medieval historian, Frances and Joseph Gies describe these cascading technological innovations in their *Cathedral, Forge, and Waterwheel: Technology and Invention in the Middle Ages* (New York: HarperCollins, 1994), p. 56.

11. Quoted in Gies, *Cathedral, Forge, and Waterwheel,* p. 57.

12. Faget, in "Space Stories," interview no. 2, pp. 60–61.

13. Thibodaux, in "Space Stories," interview no. 1, p. 15.

14. Faget, in "Space Stories" interview no. 2, p. 61.

15. Faget, in "Space Stories," interview no. 2, p. 64. Another history notes that the Ames theoretician Harvey Allen "conceived of the blunt nose principle for reentry vehicles" on June 18, 1952. "This principle was first used on the intercontinental ballistic missile nose cone and was later incorporated into the configuration of the Mercury spacecraft." *Project Mercury: A Chronology,* prepared by James M. Grimwood (Washington, D.C.: NASA, 1963), p. 4.

16. Faget, in "Space Stories," interview no. 1, p. 50.

17. David Hackett Fisher, *Albion's Seed: Four British Folkways in America* (New York: Oxford University Press, 1989), p. 878.

18. In the 1950s, as the newest branch of the United States military services, the U.S. Air Force lacked the institutional clout of the other branches. This may account for its unorthodox civilian-industrial alliances that army general Eisenhower considered so unholy. Faget, Purser, and Tibby all discuss Eisenhower and Dryden and the birth of the civilian space agency throughout "Space Stories," interview no. 2.

19. See "Space Stories," interview no. 2.

20. Loyd S. Swenson, Jr., James Grimwood, and Charles C. Alexander, *This New Ocean: A History of Project Mercury* (Washington, D.C.: NASA, 1998), p. 75.

21. A chronology of Project Mercury milestones shows Faget making his first presentation on manned orbital flight on November 1, 1957—three weeks after *Sputnik I!* "The concept included the use of existing ballistic missiles for propulsion, solid-fuel retrorockets for reentry initiation, and a nonlifting ballistic shape for the reentering capsule. This concept was considered to be the quickest and safest approach for initial manned flights into orbit." See astronautix.com, "Mercury."

22. Faget, in "Space Stories," interview no. 2, p. 71.

23. Members of this space committee (fondly called "space cadets") shifted over the eight-month period, but the original members were, according to a document Thibodaux provided, "Bruce Lunden, from Lewis, Walter Olsen, from Lewis, W. J. O'Sullivan, Jr., Paul E. Purser, Joe A. Shortal, Guy Thibodaux, Floyd L. ("Tommy") Thompson, J. W. Crowley from NACA headquarters, Ray L. Zavasky, secretary, Clinton E. Brown, Edward C. Buckley, Robert Crane, Ames, Max Faget, and R. L. Krieger." As members dropped out for various reasons, they were replaced by "Clotaire Wood, Adelbert Tischler, Edgar Cortwright, and Mort Stoller." See Thibodaux, in "Space Stories," interview no. 1, p. 20.

24. Zimmerman was an engineer of note at the NACA. His invention, the "Captain Keds Rocket Belt" (fanciful versions of which may be seen in early James Bond movies), was made by the Bell Laboratories. Thibodaux explains: "if you had a controllable thrust vector passing through your center of gravity and it exceeded your weight, you could just take off and fly anywhere you wanted." See Thibodaux, in "Space Stories," interview no. 1, p. 21.

25. Faget, in "Space Stories," interview no. 2, p. 75.

26. These were the theoretical weights with which Faget was working in 1958. John Glenn points out, however, that by 1962 and the first manned Mercury-Atlas mission (MA-6), his spacecraft, *Friendship 7,* weighed a hefty 4,265 pounds at launch (including the launch escape system that was jettisoned shortly thereafter), dropping to only 2,987 pounds by insertion. John Glenn—Kris Stoever, June 13, 2002.

27. Commentary (n.a.), in "Space Stories," interview no. 2, p. 62.

28. The Air Force was being territorial, and thus purposely obtuse, about both Faget's human factors assumptions and his radical launch theories (i.e., the "Bare Atlas"): It knew, for example, that "German centrifuge experiments during the Second World War had proved that pilots could withstand as much as 17 Gs for as long as 2 minutes without losing consciousness." Swenson, Grimwood, and Alexander, *This New Ocean,* p. 80. These are the studies Faget consulted.

29. Commentary, in "Space Stories," interview no. 2, p. 65; Swenson, Grimwood, and Alexander, *This New Ocean,* p. 132.

30. Faget, in "Space Stories," interview no. 2, p. 81.

31. R. Flanagan Gray, a Navy physician at the Johnsville laboratory and inventor of the Iron Maiden, an aluminum centrifuge capsule, also sustained twenty Gs at Johnsville at this time, supplying the all-important confirmation Faget required. Swenson, Grimwood, and Alexander, *This New Ocean,* pp. 43 and 46.

32. Faget, in "Space Stories," interview no. 2, p. 82.

33. *Project Mercury: A Chronology,* prepared by James M. Grimwood, Historical Branch, Manned Spacecraft Center (Washington, D.C.: National Aeronautics and Space Administration, 1963), p. 58.

34. Neil Simon, *Rewrites: A Memoir* (New York: Simon and Schuster, 1996), p. 239.

35. Although not thinking, perhaps, of twentieth-century naval aviators and their wives, John Demos captures the absorbing self-abnegation of such marriages in his social history of Plymouth Colony, quoting Milton's famous line in *Paradise Lost,* "He for God only, she for God in him." The aviation parallel, of course, is "He for flying only, she for the flying in him." *A Little Commonwealth: Family Life in Plymouth Colony.* New edition, thirtieth anniversary (New York: Oxford University Press, 2000), p. 82.

9: You Are Hereby Ordered

Dr. Barr, the great U.S. Navy flight surgeon and pilot with 12,500 hours of flight time, predicted the effects of spaceflight on the human body in an eloquent address to his colleagues at the 1959 annual meeting of the American Academy of General Practice in San Francisco.

1. Rene Carpenter to Florence N. Carpenter, n.d.

2. Dr. Allen O. Gamble, "Personal Recollections of the Selection of the First Seven Astronauts," p. 3. Paper presented to the Men's Club of the Bethesda United Methodist Church, Bethesda, Maryland, March 10, 1971; emphasis added. The authors are grateful to Mrs. Edith Gamble, Dr. Gamble's widow, for her help in locating this invaluable paper, available online at geocities.com/mingomae/index.html.

3. Gamble, "Personal Recollections," p. 3.

4. Loyd S. Swenson, Jr., James Grimwood, and Charles C. Alexander, *This New Ocean: A History of Project Mercury* (Washington, D.C.: NASA, 1998), p. 130.

5. Swenson, Grimwood, and Alexander, *This New Ocean,* pp. 130–31; Dr. Robert B. Voas to Kris Stoever, e-mail, January 16, 2001, p. 2. A member of the historic 1959 working group, Dr. Voas generously agreed to read early drafts of the chapters on NASA's astronaut selection and training.

6. Quoted in "Space and the Atom," *Newsweek,* April 20, 1959, p. 64.

7. These seven job qualifications were the official NASA criteria, see Swenson, Grimwood, and Alexander, *This New Ocean,* p. 131. In establishing these criteria and in other respects, the STG was adapting the U2 pilot-selection process earlier devised by the U.S. Air Force. Robert B. Voas–Kris Stoever, e-mail, January 16, 2001, p. 2. But Dr. Gamble explains that in the original draft announcement, "we had no phrase 'or equivalent,' because we needed an easy 'in-or-out' due to the hundreds of personnel records to be scanned," in "Personal Recollections," p. 6.

8. George E. Ruff and Edwin Z. Levy, "Psychiatric Evaluation of Candidates for Space Flight," *American Journal of Psychiatry* 116, no. 5 (1959): 385–91. This paper was read at the 115th annual meeting of the American Psychiatric Association, Philadelphia, Pennsylvania, April 27–May 1, 1959.

9. Robert B. Voas, interview with Kris Stoever, June 1999, Vienna, Virginia.

10. Voas, e-mail, January 16, 2001, p. 2. Also, Dr. Gamble recalls:

    Incidentally, it was my good fortune to be the one to review the Marine
    Corps records. One man's record was exceptionally outstanding. This
    pilot had won the Distinguished Flying Cross five times and an Air Medal
    with 18 clusters for service in World War II and Korea. He had made a
    transcontinental speed record, and had flown some tricky experimental
    planes. He was such a good aeronautical engineer that he was serving on
    an NACA technical advisory subcommittee, and was teaching graduate
    courses at the University of Maryland. The only problem was he did not
    have the required college degree. His college education, in his second
    year, had been interrupted by World War II. (He did, however, finish his
    degree later.) Despite the lack of a degree, I believed his qualifications
    justified my decision not to automatically eliminate him. The other team
    members agreed that he should be kept in the running. His name was
    John Glenn. Gamble, "Personal Recollections," p. 7.

11. Voas interview, June 1999, and Robert B. Voas, "Preliminary Draft of Astro-
    naut Selection Section, Mercury Technical History," NASA memorandum,
    August 28, 1963. There he writes that a "total of 508 service jackets were pro-
    vided; 225 Air Force, 225 Navy, 23 Marine Corps, and 35 Army." p. 13. Cap-
    tain Charles A. ("Chuck") Yeager (USAF), who had never attended college,
    was a casualty of this rather arbitrary education criterion devised by the
    working group (as Gamble explains, "an easy 'in-or-out'") to create more
    manageable numbers of potential candidates.

12. Voas, "Preliminary Draft," p. 13.

13. Voas, "Preliminary Draft," observes on p. 14 that

    The committee was greatly assisted by information concerning the
    achievement of the candidates in test pilot schools. Both the Navy Test
    Pilot School at Patuxent, Maryland, and the Air Force School at Edwards
    Air Force Base, California, provided the grades and class standings of the
    candidates. Further, one of the senior instructors from each school went
    through the list of candidates and rated them in terms of his knowledge
    of their performance, both in test pilot school and since graduation from
    the school.

    The NASA history of Project Mercury describes the three groupings for Phase
    Two as "arbitrary"; see Swenson, Grimwood, and Alexander, *This New
    Ocean,* p. 161. But Gamble, in "Personal Recollections,"confirms Voas's ver-
    sion that the three groups were in fact ranked, with the first group of candi-
    dates considered more highly qualified, at least on paper, than the second,
    and the second more highly ranked than the third group of test pilots, many
    of whom, the working group decided, had far too many children to orphan.

14. Voas, "Preliminary Draft," p. 17.

ner Committee during the Kennedy administration (see chapter 10, "One Hundred Chimps") to play a vexing and risk-averse role—one that allowed the Soviets to be the first to launch a man into space.

37. Santy, quoting Ruff, *Choosing the Right Stuff,* p. 17.

38. "Wolfe's description of these events is accurate," Ruff says. "I talked with him when he was writing the book and was amazed by how much research he had done." Dr. George E. Ruff, note to author, January 2001.

39. Dr. W. Randolph Lovelace II was a pioneer himself in "near-space flight studies." In 1943 he "investigated the effects of an extremely high-altitude parachute jump by personally bailing out at 36,000 feet. He speculated that the fall into denser atmosphere might create severe shocks on the human system. It did—and almost killed him—but the special equipment he had designed saved his life." In Henry C. Dethloff, *Suddenly Tomorrow Came: A History of the Johnson Space Center* (Houston, Texas: NASA, 1993), p. 119.

40. Voas–Stoever e-mail, January 16, 2001, p. 4. One of the seven original Mercury astronauts, Deke Slayton, was grounded by an unforeseen cardiac condition, which NASA medics identified only four months after this historic selection process. But he was cleared to fly in the mid-1970s, when G forces at takeoff were only about 4 Gs. Al Shepard was grounded a few years after his historic suborbital flight—another unforeseeable medical condition at the time of selection. He, too, regained his flight status and flew an Apollo mission. Two others, Scott Carpenter and John Glenn, had accidents (motorbike and bathroom fall, respectively). John regained his active flight status and went on to become the oldest human, at the age of seventy-seven, to go into space. Prior to his selection, Wally Schirra was diagnosed with a laryngeal polyp. Inter-service rivalry being what it was, Dr. Norman Lee Barr (USN) arranged emergency surgery for this very promising Navy candidate so he could be recommended to the selection board "without medical reservations." Gus was also nearly recommended "with medical reservations" because of his hayfever, although he argued successfully that he would not likely encounter much pollen in space.

41. Scott's nearly contemporaneous account in *We Seven* (p. 48) has him exhausting the seventeen-bag supply on hand for exhaled CO_2.

42. For the Valsalva Maneuver, as this test with the mercury column is known, Scott held his breath for 177 seconds—three seconds shy of the three-minute mark and a new record in 1959, no doubt broken many times since then by nonsmokers. John Glenn, a nonsmoker, also broke the record, keeping the mercury column at 90 mm for about 150 seconds. See *We Seven,* p. 49.

43. The authors are indebted to Bob Solliday for his remarkable memory of events at Lovelace and Wright-Patterson. Dr. Luft had conducted high-altitude aeromedical research in Berlin throughout World War II, perhaps as

an adjunct to Nazi advances in aviation design. For example, the Luftwaffe had developed the first jet fighter, ME262, which went so high so quickly (without the proper cabin pressurization) that its test pilots ruptured their eardrums; regular pilots therefore had their eardrums punctured as a pre-emptive measure.

Before the war, Luft wrote his doctoral thesis on "the physiological effects of oxygen deprivation." He then joined the 1937 and 1938 German expeditions to Nanga Parbat in the western Himalayas. (One team member, Heinrich Harrer, went on to Tibet and fame for having tutored the teen-aged Dalai Lama for seven years.) As research physiologist and team physician, Luft realized that the team's Sherpa guides showed astonishing "adaptive mechanisms" to altitude that could be studied. "He collected data on the climbers, noting that tolerance to altitude increased over time and that this acquired tolerance persisted after descent. This effect was important in the unpressurized aircraft of the time and would become of vital importance during World War II." The research physician's papers can be found at the archives of the University of California at San Diego. See the UCSD archival notes online at orpheus.ucsd.edu/speccoll/testing/html/mss0475a.html.

Stories also persist that Joachim "Jack" Kuettner, another Operation Paperclip asset, and the famous female test pilot Hannah Reich, both "flew" the V-1, an early rocket, in test flights during the war. A colleague of von Braun's, Kuettner worked closely with all the Mercury astronauts at the Cape.

44. Ruff and Levy, "Psychiatric Evaluation," p. 386.

45. The psychiatrists explain their method: "Categories 1, 2, 4, and 10 are largely economic constructs; 3, 5, 6, and 7 are ego functions; while the rest are specific characteristics considered important for space flight." In Ruff and Levy, "Psychiatric Evaluation," pp. 386–87.

46. Santy, quoting Ruff and Levy, in *Choosing the Right Stuff,* p. 21.

47. Santy, *Choosing the Right Stuff,* p. 18

48. Santy, *Choosing the Right Stuff,* p. 17.

49. NASA press release, April 9, 1959.

50. The stress tolerance levels of the thirty-one Project Mercury finalists "were among the highest of the hundreds of men subjected to these procedures in the past." Drs. Ruff and Levy noted with approval that "uncomplaining acceptance of the discomforts and inconveniences of this phase of the program appeared to reflect not only their strong motivation, but also their general maturity and capacity to withstand frustration," in their "Psychiatric Evaluation," p. 391.

51. Voas–Stoever e-mail, January 16, 2001, p. 4.

52. "This was the official story," writes Dr. George E. Ruff, "but the selection

matched our rankings more than the technical qualifications. Pete Conrad, for example, had more of an engineering background than Scott," although accounts have Scott distinguishing himself in the decisive Phase Two technical interview at the Pentagon. See also Swenson, Grimwood, and Alexander, *This New Ocean,* especially n. 80. p. 547, quoting Dr. Stanley C. White (USAF).

53. Santy, *Choosing the Right Stuff,* p. 22.

54. Dr. George E. Ruff, note to Kris Stoever, January 2001.

55. Ruff and Levy, "Psychiatric Evaluation," pp. 385–91.

56. Ruff adds that the Space Task Group was "originally looking for twelve, but cut it to seven. The rumor was that there wasn't enough room for twelve in the office NASA was going to put them in." Note to Kris Stoever, January 2001, msp. 440, first draft. Also Voas, e-mail, January 16, 2001, p. 5. When queried on this matter, Paul E. Purser, Gilruth's assistant, recalls no difficulty about office space. See also Santy, *Choosing the Right Stuff,* p. 22. She cites Carlos J. G. Perry, "Psychiatric Support for Man in Space," *International Psychiatry Clinics* 4 (1967): 197–221.

57. Voas–Stoever e-mail, January 16, 2001, p. 5

10: One Hundred Chimps

1. Parts of this account of press reaction circa 1960 are drawn from Loyd S. Swenson, Jr., James Grimwood, and Charles C. Alexander, *This New Ocean: A History of Project Mercury* (Washington, D.C.: NASA, 1998), pp. 281–83.

2. *New York Times,* probably April 10, 1959; Carpenter family scrapbook.

3. Carpenter family scrapbook.

4. Rene Carpenter, draft manuscript, March 2002. Rene interviewed Godfrey for her local television show, on WTOP, Washington, D.C., in the 1970s. See also Henry C. Dethloff, *Suddenly Tomorrow Came: A History of the Johnson Space Center* (Houston, Texas: NASA, 1993), the NASA History Series, p. 123. There John Glenn is said to have argued persuasively at the time that "if the astronauts were to permit people to come into their homes and interview families and children and be part of their life, there should be some compensation for their loss of privacy." Members of the press may have criticized the *Life* contract, Dethloff adds, "but the end result was that the astronauts' privacy was protected more than it might have been by precluding 'free' access to the astronauts." Most important, the *Life* contract meant the astronauts "were not thrown in to competition with each other (as modern athletes might be) for media contracts and profits."

5. Dethloff, *Suddenly Tomorrow Came,* p. 123.

6. This intensive training and R & D period is covered rather exhaustively in Swenson, Grimwood, and Alexander, *This New Ocean,* pp. 235–48.

7. Usage regarding *capsule* and *spacecraft* highlights the engineering sensibilities of the era. Max Faget and his fellow designers normally referred to their invention as a *capsule* because that's what it was, a ballistic pod that could be mated to the nosecone of a rocket, inserted into space as efficiently as possible, and then reenter earth's atmosphere, blunt-end first, so as to create as much drag (and thus to slow down) as quickly as possible. But pilots don't fly capsules, they fly aircraft, just as admirals command battleships or aircraft carriers, not inflatable dinghies. Max Faget, Guy Thibodaux, and Paul Purser dramatize this difficulty by recalling, with some laughter, that the successor organization to the Space Task Group (STG) had to be called the Manned Spacecraft Center (MSC). Somehow "Manned Capsule Center" didn't sound quite right.

8. Gilruth ordained that the capsule had to address seven "elements of design" before NASA could launch a man in space: a "blunt body with the ablative or heat-sink shield, the pressurized cabin, the supine couch for G-loads, the need for a correct atmosphere in the cabin, retrieval by parachute, and an available launch system." See "Gilruth Transcript," interview no. 4, at nasm.si.edu/nasm/dsh/TRANSCPT/GILRUTH4.HTM.

9. The Procedures Trainer dates back to the Link Trainer of World War II, when Edward Link developed a machine (that eventually took his name) for training aviators to fly in bad weather. Bryce Hartmann adapted this machine at Wright-Patterson, where it gained fame as the Panic Box. The Link Trainer became the granddaddy of the many, incredibly sophisticated trainers used during the Gemini and Apollo programs to simulate orbital rendezvous and docking and lunar approach and landing tasks. Landing on the moon was made much easier and safer because of these grown-up Link Trainers. The same types of complex trainers, incidentally, are used to train airline pilots and captains of large cruise ships and oil tankers.

10. In "Gilruth Transcript," interview no. 4, at nasm.si.edu/nasm/dsh/TRANSCPT/GILRUTH4.HTM.

11. See n.l, chap.8. Max Faget, in Robbie Davis-Floyd and Kenneth J. Cox, eds., "Space Stories: Oral Histories from the Pioneers of America's Space Program"(hereinafter "Space Stories"), interview no. 2, p. 80. These oral histories may be found online on the website maintained by the Institute for Advanced Interdisciplinary Research at http://space.systems.org/oh/thibodaux/part_1.htm and http://space.systems.org/oh/faget/part_2.htm. Page numbers refer to the authors' printout.

12. *Life,* April 26, 1961, p. 37.

13. Paul E. Purser, in "Space Stories," interview no. 2, p. 80.

14. Foreign correspondent Flora Lewis covered this tense two-day summit, held in Vienna, for the *Washington Post,* and recalled in a 1996 interview that the meeting shook the young president to his core: "This was just after the Bay

of Pigs and Khrushchev obviously considered Kennedy a weak, callow young man that he could intimidate, and [Khrushchev] went out of his way, very far, to intimidate him. And Kennedy was deeply shaken."

Upon his return to Washington, D.C., Kennedy requested a security assessment of fatalities in the event of a nuclear war. He was told that 70 million people would die. "Then, you know," Lewis adds, "it really turned [Kennedy] around, and then he realized he had to resist." These cold war–related interviews are now accessible only through subscription to National Security Archive, through proquest.com.

15. Gilruth admits he "just couldn't believe" President Kennedy "was going to go through with it"—meaning the race to the moon. See "Gilruth Transcript,"interview no. 5, at nasm.si.edu/nasm/dsh/TRANSCPT/ GILRUTH5.HTM:

> He was very nice, very good to talk with, easy to talk to, and very quickly understood. I thought he was great. That's what a lot of people thought. I saw him quite often. After we got into our temporary buildings down at Houston, he came down there a couple of times, and we showed him some of the things we were doing. This was early in the program.

Regarding the president's lunar ambitions, he admits, "Yes. I knew it," but added:

> I still was aghast that he was saying it, and that we were going to try to do it. I was on an airplane flying with Mr. Webb. We were the only two people in the airplane when we turned on the radio, and there was the President talking to Congress. Now, I don't know whether we got the thing live or whether we got a replay, but that's what was on the radio at that time. That's the first time I heard.

See Gilruth interview no. 4, at nasm.si.edu/nasm/dsh/TRANSCPT/ GILRUTH4.HTM, for an even more fascinating account of his earliest discussions with President Kennedy regarding a possible lunar landing.

16. Swenson, Grimwood, and Alexander, *This New Ocean,* p. 362.

11: The Fibrillating Heart

The chapter epigraph is taken from Tom Wolfe, *The Right Stuff* (New York: Farrar, Straus, and Giroux, 1979), p. 356.

1. "Postlaunch Memorandum Report for Mercury-Redstone No. 4 (MR-4)," National Aeronautics and Space Administration, Space Task Group, Cape Canaveral, Fla., August 6, 1961, 5–10.
2. Loyd S. Swenson, Jr., James M. Grimwood, and Charles C. Alexander, *This New Ocean: A History of Project Mercury* (Washington, D.C.: NASA, 1998), p. 369.
3. Rene Carpenter and Scott Carpenter, "Journal," vol. 4 of a nine-volume set. In pencil on the cover, she has written "Rene IV—Scott's comments on

MA-6." In researching *The Right Stuff,* Tom Wolfe had access to this mother-lode of incisively written, contemporaneous, first-hand accounts of the early days of the space program. Today only volume 4 survives.

4. Carpenter, "Journal," vol. 4.

5. Henry C. Dethloff, *Suddenly Tomorrow Came: A History of the Johnson Space Center* (Houston: NASA, 1993), p. 125.

6. "Gilruth Transcript," interview no. 6, at <u>nasm.si.edu/nasm/dsh/TRANSCPT/ GILRUTH6.HTM</u>. He also relates there how NASA invited the former NACA research centers, Ames, Lewis, and Langley, to send their space-related personnel to join the space agency in South Texas. All the Ames personnel, in beautiful Mountain View, California, declined the offer.

7. Carpenter, "Journal," vol. 4.

8. John Glenn, "Pilot's Flight Report," in *Results of the First United States Manned Orbital Space Flight: February 20, 1962* (Washington, D.C.: NASA, 1962), p. 136.

9. Chris Kraft, *Flight: My Life in Mission Control* (New York: Dutton, 2001), p. 158.

10. The pilot's omission, in this exchange, of the customary "Roger" (meaning, "I hear you") is noteworthy. John Glenn was *steamed.* John Glenn–Kris Stoever, phone conversation, June 13, 2002. See, for the flight transcript, *Results of the First United States Manned Orbital Space Flight,* p. 189.

11. Regarding Deke's oft-voiced objections to the science experiments, one of which he called "the goddamn balloon experiment," see Deke Slayton and Michael Cassutt, *Deke!* (New York: Forge, 1994), pp. 110, 114. See also Gene Kranz, *Failure Is Not an Option: Mission Control from Mercury to Apollo 13 and Beyond* (New York: Berkley, 2001), pp. 78–79; Swenson, Grimwood, and Alexander describe the science goals of mission planners for MA-7 in *This New Ocean,* p. 443.

12. As Project Mercury took shape, Chris Kraft recounts his incredulity and frustration with a wide range of colleagues, institutions, medics, and, bureaucrats in *Flight.* "Is this guy stupid?" he writes about one engineer on p. 94. In another milder confrontation, Kraft claims with relish that he could prove to be "as obtuse and stubborn as the most seasoned bureaucrat." See, for example, pp. 82, 84–85, 94, 106–112, 127.

13. Rene Carpenter, draft manuscript, March 2001.

14. "At the time," recalls Max Faget, "we were in a big argument with the medical people and the National Academy of Sciences on how many chimpanzee flights we ought to make." This was the risk-averse Wiesner Committee, which prior to the Bay of Pigs debacle, and prior to the Vienna summit, was notably lukewarm about the country's space program. Its influence withered to nothing after Gagarin's historic flight. "We had 'em by the short hairs," writes Al Shepard, "and we gave it away." See Shepard et al., *Moon Shot: The Insider Story of America's Race to the Moon* (Atlanta: Turner, 1994), p. 90.

15. Gus's bitterness about the inquiry, and about what he always viewed as his

being scapegoated for the malfunctioning hatch, is well-known and documented in the standard histories. He shared his views with, among others, Rene Carpenter. See chapter 14, "The Color of Fire."

16. Scott's folk singing was the object of much fun. An early account appears in a 1971 *Esquire* story on the early astronauts. The same anecdote is recycled in Kranz, *Failure Is Not an Option,* p. 87.

17. Kraft, *Flight,* p. 130.

18. Michael Cassutt–Kris Stoever, e-mail, September 10, 2002. "In the spring of 2001, I met Gene Kranz at a function at the San Diego Aerospace Museum. Among other subjects, we spoke about Chris Kraft's book, *Flight,* which had just been published. I asked Kranz what he thought about it.... He specifically noted the story about Carpenter's 'foul-up' as a trainee capcom as one which did not match his recollection...."

19. Slayton's objections to the science-heavy flight plan then being planned for MA-7 were well known to the principals. Kranz, for one, describes it in *Failure Is Not an Option,* pp. 78–79.

20. See "The Slayton Case," in chapter 13, Swenson, Grimwood, and Alexander, *This New* Ocean: "The fact was," the authors write, "Slayton had been under close medical surveillance for over two years," p. 441. "Shortly after the beginning of the new year [1962] NASA Administrator Webb, remembering the one dissenting vote he had received from an Air Force physician, and, mindful of the fact that Slayton was an Air Force officer on loan, directed a complete reevaluation of the case." See, more generally, pp. 440–42.

21. These younger, well-conditioned patients, like Deke, researchers find, have an "adrenergic" (adrenal hormone–linked) fibrillation, meaning the attacks tend to be preceded by exercise or emotional stress. Other causes may be linked to food allergies or nutritional deficiencies, which Deke himself suspected and self-treated. As for the effect on performance capabilities, trainers and doctors have learned that well-conditioned individuals with atrial fibrillation, like Deke (who was a varsity boxer in college) "can tolerate" the high "ventricular rates" associated with atrial fibrillation, both at rest and during exercise. "The need for maximal cardiac output" during competition, however, "makes persistent AF incompatible with optimal performance." Optimal means the vaunted "three nines," or 99.9 percent reliability. Deke was no longer three nines. See Robert A. Reiss, M.D., "Managing Atrial Fibrillation in Active Patients and Athletes," Internal Medicine Series Editor, Donald M. Christie, M.D., *Physician and Sportsmedicine,* vol. 27, no. 3 (March 1999); emphasis supplied. See online articles at physssportsmed.com.

22. See Swenson, Grimwood, and Alexander, *This New Ocean,* p. 442, quoting Deke: "'I was terribly concerned over what in my diet might be causing it, but every hypothesis turned up wrong.'" See also Kraft, who writes that

Deke "was experimenting with different foods to see if something he ate caused the problem," in *Flight,* p. 163.

23. Swenson, Grimwood, and Alexander, *This New Ocean,* p. 442.

24. Interestingly, Kranz assumed at the time that Deke was dropped "because he had raised hell about all the added experiments." He learned the real reason, the astronaut's cardiac irregularity, only later. See Kranz, *Failure Is Not an Option,* pp. 78.

25. Tom Wolfe, *The Right Stuff* (New York: Farrar, Straus, and Giroux, 1979), 367. Wolfe's treatment of this and other key incidents during Project Mercury gets it more right in a single typeset page of pure storytelling, without footnotes, than do most of the first-person, ghostwritten memoirs by the principals using three times the ink.

26. "I was devastated," Deke writes in his memoir, about his reaction to the news of his grounding. See Deke Slayton and Michael Cassutt, *Deke!,* p. 112. Deke says he also concluded that his grounding was "politically motivated." NASA administrator Webb wanted to "send the astronauts a message" that Webb, and not the Mercury astronauts, controlled the space program (p. 112). Deke's vivid, and violent, reaction to the news of his grounding is recounted in Shepard, Slayton, et al., *Moon Shot: The Insider Story of America's Race to the Moon* (Atlanta: Turner, 1994), pp. 153–54.

27. Regarding this rather petty issue of who did and did not possess undergraduate degrees, it's interesting to note that the NACA was historically and famously heedless of academic credentials. Just after *Sputnik,* when the Eisenhower administration realized it needed to create a civilian space agency, the National Academy of Sciences was charged with canvassing the talent pools at different organizations; the NACA, it concluded with disapproval, had "only two professionals" on its staff. Although correct in a formal way—the agency had only two staff scientists with doctorates—the Academy's credentials-conscious approach was incapable of gauging the deep pool of talent there; many of the agency's most gifted scientists, among them the brilliant Caldwell Johnson, possessed not even undergraduate degrees. Faget, Purser and Thibodaux never tire of making this point in their oral histories.

12: *DELTA BECOMES AURORA*

1. Wally Schirra to Kris Stoever, March 2, 2002.

2. Wally admits to being thoroughly provoked by the decision. Deke, too, fought for Wally, his backup, to be named to MA-7. But Gilruth was immovable. See Alan Shepard et al., *Moon Shot: The Insider Story of America's Race to the Moon* (Atlanta: Turner, 1994), p. 154. As for his indignation at the time, Wally was plain in a recent e-mail: "I was mad as hell about being

named Scott's backup. What kind of competitive astronaut would think differently?" Wally Schirra to Kris Stoever, August 16, 2002.

3. Loyd S. Swenson, Jr., James M. Grimwood, and Charles C. Alexander, *This New Ocean: A History of Project Mercury* (Washington, D.C.: NASA, 1998), p. 443.

4. John Glenn, "Pilot's Flight Report," in *Results of the First United States Manned Orbital Space Flight: February 20, 1962* (Washington, D.C.: NASA, 1962), p. 136; emphasis in the original.

5. "Gilruth Transcript," interview no. 6, p. 54, at nasm.si.edu/nasm/dsh/TRANSCPT/GILRUTH6.HTM.

6. Chris Kraft's later and more open antagonism toward Carpenter reaches its fullest expression in his memoir, *Flight: My Life in Mission Control* (New York: Dutton, 2001). There, he devotes a chapter to the successful MA-7 flight, entitled "The Man Malfunctioned."

7. Kraft, *Flight,* pp. 103 (von Braun); 54 (Glenn); 84 (Voas); and 340 (the American people).

8. This language is borrowed throughout this chapter and the next from a teletyped transcript sent to the Chicago editorial offices of *Life* magazine, May 31, 1962. *Life* arranged for almost instantaneous access to the astronauts' accounts of their flights, its editors and writers hammering out gripping and beautifully written stories for their many avid readers. The May 31 transcript of Carpenter's oral report formed the body of the astronaut's "first-person" account of his spaceflight aboard *Aurora 7.* See Scott Carpenter, "The Great Secret," *Life,* June 8, 1962, p. 30.

9. Swenson, Grimwood, and Alexander, *This New Ocean,* p. 444.

10. Swenson, Grimwood, and Alexander, *This New Ocean,* p. 444.

11. Airglow in particular was of intense interest to NASA and other scientists. Project Mercury experiments eventually allowed astronomer John O'Keefe to describe the phenomenon as follows:

> Around the horizon, all the astronauts report that they saw a band of light, which appeared to them to be centered at a height of some 6 to 10 degrees above the visible horizon.... The nature of this band was made clear by Astronaut Scott Carpenter, who employed a filter that passed on the 5577 Angstrom line of the neutral oxygen atom.... Through the filter, the band continued to be visible, although all other details of the horizon vanished. It was thus clear that the band resulted from the phenomenon of nightglow; that is, the emission of light by gases of the high atmosphere.

In *Mercury Project Summary, May 15 and 16, 1963,* NASA publication SP-45, p. 343. See also John A. O'Keefe and Winifred Sawtell Cameron, "Space Science Report," in *Results of the Second United States Manned Orbital Space Flight, May 24, 1962* (Washington, D.C.: NASA, 1962), p. 35.

12. Jack Hereford, who worked on the light meter back in 1962, was kind enough to break the word down in an e-mail to the authors:

extincto- (the extinction-photometric method); *spectro-* (use of tristimulus colorimetry filters); *photo-* (the base instrument, a photometer); *polari-* (ability to measure polarization); *scope-* (a visual instrument); *oculo-* (of, or pertaining to, the eye); *gyro-* (the bright-line orientation test); *gravo-* (the zero-G aspect of the latter); *kineto-* (the dynamic aspect of the same); *meter* (a measuring device). The light meter, Hereford explains, or "extinctospectrophotopolariscopeoculogyrogravokinetometer," was designed "to measure the brightness of objects in white light, by polarity, and by color. The same variety of tests," he adds, "could measure the sensitivity of the eye." Because gravity and motion affect the eye's ability to determine the relative alignment of the body and an external object (a phenomenon known as the oculogyric effect), "the bright line on a dark field facilitated testing for the effect without the influence of [unintelligible]."

13. Swenson, Grimwood, and Alexander, *This New Ocean,* 444.

14. See *Postlaunch Memorandum Report for Mercury Atlas No. 7 (MA-7),* Part I: Mission Analysis (Cape Canaveral, Fla.: National Aeronautics and Space Administration, Manned Spacecraft Center, June 15, 1962), pp. 5-29–5-30. The title page lists the following editors: E. M. Fields (senior editor); J. H. Boynton (asst. to senior editor); R. D. Harrington; R. G. Arbic; E. A. Horton; S. C. White, M.D.; C. A. Berry, M.D.; V. I. Grissom; R. B. Voas, Ph.D.; and W. J. North.

15. Russian speculation, quite sensibly, never ran amok about the dangers of weightlessness or high G-forces. Consternation tended, instead, to focus on space radiation, to the point that samples of human skin were launched into earth orbit for later study.

16. Those who have seen *The Right Stuff,* Philip Kaufmann's 1984 movie adaptation of Tom Wolfe's book, will recall the spectacular shot of the seven striding—space-age phalanx style, in their silver spacesuits, helmets on, visors shut—down the corridors of what is presumably Hanger S at the Cape. They could never have pulled a stunt like that. The suits were too uncomfortable. (Imagine, as a corollary, Navy SEALs in full underwater regalia, including wetsuits, face masks, SCUBA gear, and flippers, striding in like fashion around the Naval Amphibious Base at Coronado, California.)

17. Dr. Robert B. Voas, comments on draft chapter, November 2001.

18. Carpenter, "The Great Secret," *Life,* June 8, 1962, p. 30.

19. NASA's postlaunch report on the malfunction explains: A nominal gyro "slaving rate" is about eight degrees per minute. By comparing "known astronaut reference positions" during the orbital phase of *Aurora 7* with the "pitch horizon scanner output," a postflight analysis found that the pitch horizon scanner was off throughout the flight anywhere from plus-50 degrees to minus-20. Three orbits later, during retrofire, a trajectory computation based on radar-tracking data yielded a mean pitch attitude of

minus-36.5 degrees, whereas the maximum horizon scanner was minus-16 degrees. This comparison, NASA said, and the one made at the beginning of the flight, during the launch phase, are "the only independent sources that verify the scanner bias, and these are in excellent agreement."

Twice during the flight the gyros did not "cage to zero." Each time, however, Carpenter recycled the gyro switch. They "immediately caged properly." *Postlaunch Memorandum Report for Mercury Atlas No. 7*, p. 5-2.

20. A postlaunch report explains:

> Equipment stowage: All equipment had female velcro applied to strategic points, whereas male velcro was applied to the stowage areas. Four equipment areas were provided within the MA-7 spacecraft. During the launch, retrofire, and reentry phases, the equipment was stowed in three locations. First, the equipment container located to the pilot's right, below the hatch, contained the: 35mm hand held camera and associated accessories; photometer, binoculars, and extinction photometer. Second, the "glove compartment," located in the left central section of the center instrument panel console, contained the: exercise device, film, filter mosaics, airglow filter, and the night adaption eye cover. Third, the chart holder, located below the periscope, contained the: map booklet, star navigation device and inserts, and the flight plan cards. During the orbital phase, the equipment was stowed either in these locations or on the velcro applied to the hatch for this purpose. The pilot reported no difficulties with the stowage of any of the equipment.

See *Postlaunch Memorandum Report for Mercury Atlas No. 7*, pp. 7-17.

21. Christopher C. Kraft et al., "Flight Control and Flight Plan, in *Results of the First United States Manned Orbital Space Flight: February 20, 1962* (Washington, D.C.: NASA, 1962), p. 74.

22. NASA engineers say that the "brief periods of [ASCS] operation involved may have prevented the pilot from recognizing improper attitude reference." See *Postlaunch Memorandum Report for Mercury-Atlas No. 7 (MA-7)*, p. 5-3.

23. "Working under his crowded experiment schedule and the heavy manual maneuver program, on six occasions Carpenter accidentally actuated the sensitive-to-the-touch, high thrust attitude control jets, which brought about 'double-authority control', or the redundant operation of both the automatic and the manual systems." These six occasions came to a total of approximately seventeen minutes of "double-authority control"—seventeen minutes during which two fuel tanks (one for fly-by-wire and the other for manual proportional control) were used to power a single movement of the control stick. See Swenson, Grimwood, and Alexander, *This New Ocean*, p. 450.

Wally Schirra took special pains to avoid double-authority control while piloting *Sigma 7* on October 3, 1962. Still he, too, engaged an improved system all too easily, reporting with frustration on his fifth pass:

P   In manual proportional, with manual lever pulled out, and having selected rate command I'm slowly but surely coming into retroattitude. All axes are working very well. Setting up in roll. Getting yaw rates, pow, pow. And I want this to count—I'm going to go back to fly by wire low.

P   That was stupid. Now we go to fly-by-wire low. I had a case of double authority and really flotched it. But better conserve our fuel. It's much too easy to get into double authority, even with the tremendous logic you have working on all these systems. The pitch is in; yaw is in; selecting reentry attitude; roll is in; going to ASCS, reentry now. And she's in.

24. Wally Schirra and Gordo Cooper would also benefit, in their follow-on Mercury flights, from another one of Scott's recommendations: A sixty-day training period prior to spaceflight. *This New Ocean* observes that "Carpenter had received his MA-7 document late, and major revisions had been inserted almost until launch day." Swenson, Grimwood, and Alexander, *This New Ocean,* p. 459.

25. The terms "medic" and "NASA medic" sound quaint in the twenty-first century, but they have their roots in the battlefield cry for help: "Medic!"

26. Swenson, Grimwood, and Alexander, cite Kraft's postflight memorandum on MA-7, dated June 12, 1962, in *This New Ocean,* p. 453.

27. John Glenn agrees, reporting after his own mission that, with a brightly lit horizon, pitch and roll attitudes can "easily be controlled.... Yaw...however, is not so good." After a "learning period" aboard MA-6, Glenn devised a way to determine yaw. He needed three paragraphs and about two hundred words to describe a task only a highly skilled pilot could understand—much less accomplish in space with a three-axis control stick. See John Glenn, "Pilot's Flight Report," in *Results of the First United States Manned Orbital Space Flight,* p. 122.

28. Helmut Kuehnel et al., "Pilot Performance," in *Results of the Second United States Manned Orbital Space Flight,* pp. 65–66.

13: COMMANDER CARPENTER AND HIS FLYING MACHINE!

1. Carpenter "was completely ignoring our request to check his instruments," Chris Kraft states in *Flight: My Life in Mission Control* (New York: Dutton, 2001), p. 165. "Kraft was furious," Wolfe writes in *The Right Stuff* (New York: Farrar, Straus, Giroux, 1979), p. 374.

2. The flight director's "controlled fury" during MA-7 is also described in Gene Kranz, *Failure Is Not an Option* (New York: Berkley Books, 2001), p. 89. Deke

Slayton reports, for his part, that "Meanwhile, from what I heard later, things were pretty intense at MCC. Chris Kraft was pretty incensed about the way Scott had handled things, and announced for everybody to hear, 'That son of a bitch is never going to fly for me again.' I was in Australia at the Muchea tracking site. It was a good place to be, all things considered." See Deke Slayton and Michael Cassutt, *Deke!* (New York: Forge, 1994), p. 114.

3. "Shepard tried to stress my feelings," Kraft writes, "by resorting to military terms." But "somehow," Kraft opines, "Shepard missed that we'd been asking Carpenter questions about his ASCS problems," in *Flight*, p. 166. When, the authors wonder, did Al Shepard, the Icy Commander, miss anything related to his aviation, engineering, or ground control duties?

4. Scott Carpenter, "The Great Secret," *Life*, June 8, 1962, p. 33.

5. Loyd S. Swenson, Jr., James M. Grimwood, and Charles C. Alexander, *This New Ocean: A History of Project Mercury* (Washington, D.C.: NASA, 1962), p. 453.

6. *Failure Is Not an Option*, p. 91.

7. Loyd S. Swenson, Jr., James M. Grimwood, and Charles C. Alexander, *This New Ocean: A History of Project Mercury* (Washington, D.C.: NASA, 1998), pp. 359–60.

8. A couple of months after *Sputnik I* was launched, before NASA was even formed, Faget was busy with an eight-inch model of the Mercury capsule, in the NACA wind tunnels (he calls them "spin tunnels" in the oral histories), intent on proving the Ames theory about blunt-end reentry. He recounts how he and his colleagues kept adding:

> various conical afterbodies, making them longer and longer and longer to reduce the dynamic instability as more and more surface became exposed to the oncoming air. Finally the oscillation was decreased to about plus or minus sixty degrees without tumbling. And we said, "That's good enough!" [*laughter*] That's how the length of the nose cone got established. We knew that it would always have to get to some angle of attack before the cone would get enough aerodynamic force on it to limit the oscillation.

Max Faget, in "Space Stories," interview no. 2, p. 66. These oral histories (see n.1, chap. 8) were compiled by Robbie Davis-Floyd and Kenneth J. Cox, eds., *Space Stories: Oral Histories from the Pioneers of the American Space Program* (New York: Routledge, forthcoming), and can be found online at space.systems.org/oh/thibodaux/part 1.htm and space.systems.org/oh/faget/part 2.htm. Page cites refer to the authors' printout.

9. See Helmut A. Kuehnel et al., "Pilot Performance," *Results of the Second United States Manned Orbital Space Flight, May 24, 1962*, p. 67; emphasis supplied.

10. Swenson, Grimwood, and Alexander, *This New Ocean*, p. 356.

11. Faget, in "Space Stories," interview no. 2, p. 66.

12. In his memoirs, Kraft says, "We knew exactly where he was and had even told him that the frogmen would be there in an hour." Still, Kraft writes that seeing a photo in the morning paper "of Carpenter floating casually in his raft," made him "furious all over again." See *Flight*, p. 169. Why?

13. Swenson, Grimwood, and Alexander, *This New Ocean*, p. 457.

14. Who should be monitoring this momentous military recovery operation, out of patriotic, professional, and service-branch interest, but Florida resident Thomas J. Dubose, former commander of the U.S. Air Force's Air Rescue Service. He complained to Spessard L. Holland (D-Fla.), his representative in the the U.S. Senate, "that Carpenter floated in the raft an hour and twenty minutes longer than was necessary." D. Brainerd Holmes, a NASA official, testified in hearings before Congress that "Admiral John L. Chew, commander of the Project Mercury recovery forces, feared the seaplane might break apart if it landed on the choppy waters. Because of this, according to Holmes, the decision had been made to proceed with helicopter and ship pickup as originally planned." Admiral Chew and Brainerd Holmes additionally testified that not "a particle" of interservice rivalry marred the recovery operation. Swenson, Grimwood, and Alexander, *This New Ocean*, p. 457.

14: THE COLOR OF FIRE

1. *Postlaunch Memorandum Report for Mercury Atlas No. 7 (MA-7)*, Part I: Mission Analysis (Cape Canaveral, Fla.: National Aeronautics and Space Administration, Manned Spacecraft Center, June 15, 1962), p. 7–29. The title page lists the following editors: E. M. Fields (senior editor); J. H. Boynton (asst. to senior editor); R. D. Harrington; R. G. Arbic; E. A. Horton; S. C. White, M.D.; C. A. Berry, M.D.; V. I. Grissom; R. B. Voas, Ph.D.; and W. J. North.

2. Patricia A. Santy, *Choosing the Right Stuff: The Psychological Selection of Astronauts and Cosmonauts* (Westport, Conn.: Praeger, 1994), p. 9. The goals of this original study "were to (1) determine whether significant psychophysiological changes are produced by suborbital or orbital flight, (2) assess the degree of stress imposed on the astronauts, (3) investigate mechanisms employed for maintaining adaptive behavior under stress, and (4) provide data for application to future selection and training programs," p. 26.

3. Gus Grissom narrowly escaped death by drowning, as readers will recall, during recovery operations for MR-4 in July 1961. "Narrowly escaped," however, does not fully capture the risk the man faced. Gus had at most ten seconds to exit his flooding spacecraft, once the hatch blew, against a powerful incoming tide of seawater. That he survived this effort—never mind the botched recovery efforts that followed—is a tribute to no one but Gus. He was, as a consequence, observed to be both angry and dejected during his

postflight exams. Everyone assembled, particularly the medics, viewed these emotions, if you can call them that, as wholly in keeping with his harrowing, near-death experiences in service to country.

4. Dr. George E. Ruff, with service dating back to the "premium man" studies at Wright-Patterson, was a stalwart of the 1959 Mercury astronaut selection process. This early clash of cultures, or mindsets, at NASA—between the Shackletonian scientists, who wondered what was out there, and Operations, who wondered how the sled was working, is covered in Santy, *Choosing the Right Stuff.* This under-reported but important institutional contest would eventually lead, after Scott Carpenter's flight in May 1962, to the ouster of the behavioral sciences, and its advocates, from the space program.

See also Santy, *Choosing the Right Stuff,* p. xvi. There she describes an agitated Kraft interrupting her presentation, in the fall of 1988, on the history of NASA's astronaut-selection methods: "Young lady, you are a dangerous person and are out to destroy NASA! I will not permit that to happen." Santy responded only that she had been unable to unearth any of the performance data, which she explained she needed to validate the psychological selection criteria. She had been "unable to find it," she told Kraft, who replied:

> You never will, because it's [the data] in here [pointing to his head] and it's going to stay there so people like you can't use it against NASA. (p. xvi, editorial interpolations in the original)

The former NASA psychiatrist adds that also present that day was Professor Robert L. Helmreich, a human factors researcher at the University of Texas, Austin, who can confirm the incident. Dr. Patricia A. Santy to Kris Stoever, e-mail, April 15, 2002.

5. Chris Kraft, *Flight: My Life in Mission Control* (New York: Dutton, 2001), p. 170.

6. As late as 1964, NASA administrator Jim Webb, for one, appears *not* to know that Kraft had arranged, as he claims, to have Scott's wings clipped. See Webb's March 29, 1964, memorandum to an Admiral Boone, cited later in this chapter.

7. Wolfe spends five pages on this issue of baseless whisper campaign against NASA's "forces of experimental science" (including, as it happened, one of their chief advocates, Scott Carpenter). See *The Right Stuff,* pp. 374–379.

8. "All Systems Weren't Go at NASA," *Longmont (Colo.) Daily Times,* April 2, 2001, B-1, B-5. See also *Flight,* p. 2.

9. Paul E. Purser to Kris Stoever, May 14, 2002.

10. By the time of reentry, according to Gene Kranz, MA-7 "had been close to perfect...and now everything went to hell." Kranz was assistant flight director for Scott's flight. He offers an explanation for the difficulties—part flight plan, part busy pilot, part ground control: "A major component of the ground team's responsibility," he explains, "is to provide a check on the

crew. The ground had waited too long in addressing the fuel status and should have been more forceful in getting on with the checklists." See *Failure Is Not an Option* (New York: Berkley Books, 2001), pp. 89, 91. Kranz would eventually eclipse his mentor, Kraft, as flight director. "Gene was a pilot as well as an engineer," Paul E. Purser observes, and "was, to my mind, a far better flight controller than Chris." Purser to Stoever, May 28, 2002.

11. Paul E. Purser to Kris Stoever, May 14, 2002.

12. Dr. Robert B. Voas to Kristen C. Stoever. After Carpenter, Voas probably knows more about the flight of *Aurora 7* than anyone alive.

13. Recordings of this November 21, 1962, White House meeting were recently declassified by the John F. Kennedy Presidential Library. In the tape one can hear "a spirited exchange of views" between Administrator Webb and President Kennedy. Webb, on the tape, using a tone of voice that can only be described as patronizing, is telling the president that NASA had "priorities," among them the lunar program, that would create "an overall program of U.S. preeminence in space." No, the president responded. NASA had one "top" priority, which was to beat the Soviets to the moon.

14. See Peter Maas, *The Terrible Hours: The Man Behind the Greatest Submarine Rescue in History* (New York: HarperCollins, 1999).

15. George F. Bond, *Papa Topside: The Sealab Chronicles of Capt. George F. Bond, USN,* ed. Helen A. Sitieri (Annapolis, Md.: Naval Institute Press, 1993), p. 54. This is an invaluable book for anyone interested in the history of saturation diving, Bond's account of his argument with Carpenter, during Sealab II, about the accuracy of pneumofathometers vs. depth gauges is particularly entertaining.

16. "He came into Houston," Bob Gilruth recounted, "and then he went up to Dallas the day he was shot. That was a bad day, I'll tell you. We cried. A lot of us stood in front of the television there and cried." See Gilruth interview no. 5 online, nasm.si.edu/nasm/dsh/TRANSCPT/GILRUTH5.HTM.

17. It was rumored that President Kennedy, or his successor President Lyndon B. Johnson, had dictated that the sunny-faced Marine pilot was too valuable a national asset to risk again in spaceflight. The story was bruited about with renewed vigor as Glenn took his Shuttle flight in 1998. There was no such directive. The story probably began a facetious comment at lower levels, along the lines of "Yeah, Glenn's too precious to fly again." Yet Glenn resigned from NASA in January 1964, fourteen months before the first Gemini flight was made, and well before crews were even assigned.

18. Bond, *Papa Topside,* p. 133.

19. James Vorosmarti, Jr., M.D., "A Very Short History of Saturation Diving," *Historical Diving Times* 20 (Winter 1997). See online article posted at www.thehds.com/hdt/saturate.htm.

20. This is one of the many anecdotes Rene Carpenter drafted, in her customary longhand on foolscap, for inclusion in this book; draft manuscript, March 2002.

EPILOGUE

1. "Helium is an elusive and pervasive gas," Bond explains, "that will leak into and out of any enclosed cavity. Currently the best containment theory calls for metal-to-metal seals with a minimum of gaskets. Predictably, the helium skipped blithely past the metal interfaces in our [Sealab III] equipment at all points tested. As a rare, costly, and highly unpredictable gas, whether found in the human body or a piece of functional hardware, helium deserves a respect rarely accorded." Bond hoped that the latest manufacturing error he and his fatigued crew had found would "instill a new humility on the part of our designers and hardware merchants, and gaskets will be put only where they belong." It was not to be. See George F. Bond, *Papa Topside: The Sealab Chronicles,* ed. Helen A. Sitieri (Annapolis, Md.: Naval Institute Press, 1993), p. 156.

2. "In Scott," writes Bond, "the films showed clear-cut lesions a few inches above the knees, both port and starboard, corresponding all too well to the areas about which he had complained during decompression almost three years ago—and which I had dismissed as inconsequential muscle disorders." Bond, *Papa Topside,* p. 154.

ACKNOWLEDGMENTS

THE DEBTS TEND TO PILE UP in writing a book like this one—equal parts adventure, history, psychotherapy, eulogy, memoir, science writing, lamentation, and biography. This seems particularly true when family members collaborate (and conspire) in the writing. Although these debts can never be paid, they can be named: Cassandra Volpe, archivist at the University of Colorado, for years pursued a huge cache of Kodachrome slides—ten thousand images—taken over the decades by my grandfather, amateur photographer Dr. M. S. Carpenter, who left them to his one son, my father, upon his death in 1973. Could the university have them? Cassandra asked, in her persistent, pleasant, and ultimately successful phone calls to my father.

It fell to me to organize the slides, the index, the appraisal, and, at Cassandra's request, to assemble a genealogy of five generations of allied Colorado families. "It would be interesting," she explained. The book began to take shape with that request. I am grateful to Cassandra since then for her unflagging interest in the book and its progress, and, at the end, for her help, together with that of the inimitable Kellie Masterson, on the selection of photographs during one marathon day on campus. At C.U., David Hayes and Alvie Sellmer, also at the Archives, were paragons of industry and virtue.

I thank Mike Gentry, at the NASA History Office, and the great Jody Russell, keeper of photographs at NASA's Johnson Space Center, the Media Resources Center.

Dr. Patricia A. Santy, former NASA psychiatrist, read and commented on the selection chapter. Dr. Herbert Rothenberg, venerable Denver internist (and former U.S. Air force flight surgeon), helped me on several notable occasions with my medical questions. He educated me about the difficult pre-antibiotic therapies for T.B., which my grandmother, Toye, endured for decades. He read Dr. Bartholomew's medical charts from 1946 (Boulder Community Hospital) and described how one generally dies from the traumatic injuries my father sustained in his earliest, and most spectacular, car accident. He explained that, yes, the forearm's ulna and radius might fuse irreparably following the compound fracture my father sustained—in his most fateful crash—in 1964.

The online newsgroup devoted to space history (sci.space.history) is a raucous, high-octane, and often obnoxious consortium of know-it-alls. I love them all, but some more than others. They gave me a free, if bracing, education in space lore and legend; and their debates gave me insights I could have gained in no other way. Speaking of technical help, Roger Linkenhoker, stalwart friend and gracious know-it-all, made sure I (and my father) had the best wireless technology, research tools, laptops, and intranets available. He recovered and reconstituted lost book files after one spectacular crash of the harddrive variety. I thank him—and his colleagues at Arnold & Porter (Denver): Jim Scarboro, Zeke Williams, Sherry Ford, Tona Salazar, and Pat Dinkel.

My sister Candace read, organized, and indexed thirty years of family correspondence that ultimately formed the backbone of the early chapters. My brothers Scotty and Jay helped, too, especially with the recollections of Langley Field, Virginia, and Timber Cove, Texas. Matthew, Nicholas, and Zachary provided moral support. Caroline, my daughter, was my earliest reader—of drafts I shared with no one else. When I saw her eyes track across first one line and then another and another, it was enough. The story had kept her attention for more than ten seconds and all would be well. Steve Kennedy, peerless friend and editor, was on hand with incomparable editorial judgment and assistance as the book neared completion.

In a kinder world, Rene and Scott Carpenter, like John and Annie Glenn, might have cowritten a wonderful memoir after fifty or so years of marriage, which their daughter, an editor, might have researched, polished, and refined. The world is not kind, however, and it is the rare marriage that lumbers along happily for fifty years. As it happened, therefore, a father-daughter team was pressed into service—bereft, they soon found, without Rene's wit, courage, and memory. Without her tenacious dedication to the women in this story—tough women devoted to children, to country, to men who risk their lives for a living, to each other—For Spacious Skies could never have been written.

The book is chock-a-block with heroes. This author has one hero, and he is my husband, Tom, who in his wisdom read not a single draft page I wrote but always wished for the best. I hope he likes the book he now promises to read.

—K.C.S.
Denver, Colorado

I AM GRATEFUL TO SO MANY PEOPLE—old friends and colleagues, and new friends I made as the idea for this book, and finally the book itself, took shape. Among my oldest friends are Dot Beeson, Jim and Pat Williford, Frank Franco, Liz and Dick Scott, all of whom volunteered fifty-year-old memories of fateful early morning drives home, and of young-married, U.S. Navy adventures, in war and peace, from Pensacola, to Corpus, to Barber's Point, Patuxent, and Monterey. I am profoundly grateful.

Our research and the writing on hardware matters—Mercury capsule design, solid fuels, ballistics, Yorkshire pigs—were aided by the late Paul E. Purser principally, but also by Guy "Tibby" Thibodaux and Max Faget, whose oral histories of a remarkable time, the birth of Project Mercury, and the race to the moon, greatly enriched the authors' understanding of the era. Paul read drafts, offered technical and historical insights; and his friendship and continued involvement with the writing for more than a year often gave us the confidence to go on.

John Glenn and Wally Schirra were stouthearted readers of the draft NASA chapters. John in particular caught gross errors of fact seen by no one else. As usual, Wally volunteered the best lines with his trademark irascibility. Jim Oberg, spaceflight operations veteran and author, was always there in a pinch, for which we thank him. At the end, Professor David G. Michelson of the University of British Columbia provided an enormously helpful, and humbling, external review of the manuscript, for which the authors are deeply grateful. I also thank Colin Burgess, of Sydney, Australia, for his many helpful notes regarding matters of fact as we readied the paperback edition for publication. Doug Grad, at New American Library, has been intrepid and cheerful. I thank him.

My friend Bob Solliday offered up an astounding supply of anecdotes about the historic selection process of January through March 1959, which he and I endured side by side. If the account herein is at all a contribution to the literature, it is because of Bob, who, had he been selected, would have been a *truly* great Mercury astronaut. He is a truly great friend.

I am also grateful to Mrs. Edith Gamble, widow of Dr. Allen O. Gamble, who helped Kris locate her husband's paper on the events of 1959. Dr. George E. Ruff read early drafts of the selection chapter and made valuable contributions.

Dr. Robert B. Voas—who like Ruff was a member of the historic 1959 working group that selected first the one hundred and ten, then the thirty-two, and finally the seven original Mercury astronauts—was also a vital member of the working group that helped to produce this book. Bob's work at NASA did not end with the selection of seven men. He promptly moved into astronaut training and activities, which means he worked on, among other things, flight plans. It is impossible to calculate the ways in which he contributed to our account of the flight of *Aurora 7.*

At Harcourt, Jane Isay and her assistant, Jenna Johnson, have worked long hours turning an idea into a draft manuscript into a hardcover book. Kris and I thank them, as we thank the elegant, unflappable Wendy Weil, a source of strength throughout.

It has been Tom Mallon's particular burden, since the idea of *For Spacious Skies* first flickered to life, to be the authors' unfailingly optimistic, encouraging, uncritical friend and trusted counselor. Although he was amply justified on innumerable occasions, having to slog through the early drafts, not once did the word *incoherent* slip from his pen or lips. He is the book's principal champion, and the authors thank him most profoundly.

My wife, Patty Carpenter, has been a constant source of encouragement and understanding over the long stretches of thinking about, and writing, this book.

I am grateful to my daughter Kris—historian, researcher, and senior writing partner—for her tireless devotion to this story. I knew at the outset the general outlines of my tale. My beloved Grandpa Noxon, who so indelibly marked my boyhood—and my life. My flying experiences in the U.S. Navy airplanes of the mid-twentieth century. My unparalleled good fortune to be part of an extraordinary flying fraternity, the Project Mercury astronauts, and then, later, more good fortune: training and serving with the courageous deep divers of Sealabs I, II, and III. I did not know, however, that another, more retiring hero might emerge in the telling of our family tale. Kris found her. She was my mother, champion and letter-writer of the very first order. Everyone called her Toye. I call her hero.

—M.S.C.
New York, New York

Index

PHOTO BY JON HATCH, *BOULDER DAILY CAMERA*

Scott Carpenter is one of the seven original "Right Stuff" astronauts. The fourth American in space and the second to orbit the Earth, Carpenter went on after Project Mercury to participate in the U.S. Navy's pioneering "Man in the Sea" program (Sealabs I, II, and III) as an underwater explorer and researcher. He lives with his wife in New York City and in Vail, Colorado.

Kris Stoever was six years old on May 24, 1962, when her father rocketed into space. Since her graduation from Georgetown University with a degree in history, she has worked as an editor and writer. She lives with her husband and daughter in Denver.